CATO
SUPREME COURT
REVIEW

2013 — 2014

CATO SUPREME COURT REVIEW

2013—2014

ROGER PILON
Publisher

ILYA SHAPIRO
Editor in Chief

TREVOR BURRUS
Associate Editor

ROBERT A. LEVY
Associate Editor

TIMOTHY LYNCH
Associate Editor

WALTER OLSON
Associate Editor

CENTER FOR CONSTITUTIONAL STUDIES

Washington, D.C.

THE CATO SUPREME COURT REVIEW (ISBN 978-1-939709-56-1) is published annually at the close of each Supreme Court term by the Cato Institute, 1000 Massachusetts Ave., N.W., Washington, D.C. 20001-5403.

CORRESPONDENCE. Correspondence regarding subscriptions, changes of address, procurement of back issues, advertising and marketing matters, and so forth, should be addressed to:

Publications Department
The Cato Institute
1000 Massachusetts Ave., N.W.
Washington, D.C. 20001

All other correspondence, including requests to quote or reproduce material, should be addressed to the editor.

CITATIONS: Citation to this volume of the Review should conform to the following style: 2013-2014 Cato Sup. Ct. Rev. (2014).

DISCLAIMER. The views expressed by the authors of the articles are their own and are not attributable to the editor, the editorial board, or the Cato Institute.

INTERNET ADDRESS. Articles from past editions are available to the general public, free of charge, at www.cato.org/pubs/scr.

ISBN 978-1-939709-56-1 (Paperback)
ISBN 978-1-939709-57-8 (Digital)

Printed in the United States of America.

Cato Institute
1000 Massachusetts Ave., N.W.
Washington, D.C. 20001
www.cato.org

Contents

CONTENTS

FOREWORD

The "Long View": Toward Restoring the Constitution?

Roger Pilon*

The Cato Institute's Center for Constitutional Studies is pleased to publish this 13th volume of the *Cato Supreme Court Review*, an annual critique of the Court's most important decisions from the term just ended, plus a look at the term ahead—all from a classical Madisonian perspective, grounded in the nation's first principles, liberty through limited government. We release this volume each year at Cato's annual Constitution Day conference. And each year in this space I discuss briefly a theme that seemed to emerge from the Court's term or from the larger setting in which the term unfolded.

The most striking fact about this term, perhaps, is that nearly two-thirds of the Court's decisions were unanimous, the highest percentage in over six decades, even if that was achieved in several cases through narrow rulings, or if the rulings camouflaged very different rationales. Complementing the Court's high unanimity rate, only 10 cases were decided 5-4, another low in recent years. On the surface, therefore, it looks like Chief Justice John Roberts is maneuvering the Court to speak as much as possible with one voice, as he had hoped to do, even if the often narrow or fractured opinions that result give less than clear guidance to the 13 federal appellate courts below where some 60,000 cases a year are terminated.

It appears also, or at least it is said, that the 59-year-old Roberts is taking the "long view," even if it isn't entirely clear what that means. About to begin its tenth term, and its fifth under the current cast of justices, the Roberts Court seems to be following the course

* Vice president for legal affairs at the Cato Institute, founder and director of Cato's Center for Constitutional Studies, B. Kenneth Simon Chair in Constitutional Studies, and publisher of the *Cato Supreme Court Review*.

foreshadowed by its namesake during his confirmation hearings. "A certain humility should characterize the judicial role," the soon to be confirmed chief justice told the Senate Judiciary Committee. Likening his role to that of an umpire—neither ignoring nor making the rules of our political life but simply applying them—Roberts made it clear that he stood not for politics but for law, for the idea that judges "are servants of the law, not the other way around." It was a fitting image for the nonpolitical branch, especially after nearly eight decades, by fits and starts, of seemingly rudderless judicial deference to the political branches on one hand or judicial usurpation on the other, yielding anything but modest demands upon a Court increasingly required to adjudicate our ever expanding public life.

Not all would call the Roberts Court modest or restrained, of course, much less solicitous of the liberty that many of the Roberts majorities believe to be embedded in the constitutional text and structure. Critics on the Left, especially, point to its decisions concerning business, unions, campaign finance, voting, abortion, religion, affirmative action, and more—sometimes reversing established precedent, more often laying a foundation for possible future reversals—and they cry "judicial activism"—as if a change in legal direction were the touchstone of that charge. Yet their complaint, too often reducing law to politics, is not entirely groundless: In fact, in those very confirmation hearings, Roberts himself said that "judges have to have the humility to recognize that they operate within a system of precedent, shaped by other judges equally striving to live up to the judicial oath."

First Principles v. Precedent

Regardless of whether that line was meant to calm committee members apprehensive about change, it brings us to a very old question: Should constitutional cases be decided by constitutional principles—first principles embedded in the document itself—or by established precedents? When the two are one, there is no problem, of course. It requires but a casual acquaintance with our constitutional history, however, to appreciate that many of today's constitutional precedents are derived from the Constitution by only the most strained reasoning. To illustrate that point most broadly and generically, if James Madison was correct when he wrote in *Federalist* No. 45 that the powers of the new government were "few and defined"—surely, we must presume that he understood the document for which he, more than any other, was responsible—then there must have been many judicial mistakes over the next two centuries, many unmoored precedents, to have given us today's Leviathan. And of course there were. No one can read Madison's discussions in *Federalist* Nos. 41, 42, and 44 regarding, respectively, the Taxing (General Welfare), Commerce, and Necessary and Proper Clauses and come away thinking that the expansive readings the New Deal Court gave those clauses are correct.

But what is the Court to do now, after nearly eight decades of cascading decisions that have left us a body of "constitutional law" only occasionally derived from the Constitution itself? For practical reasons at least the Court can hardly overrule the Social Security Act, for example. Yet few were more surprised when the Court upheld that act than many of its supporters. As Massachusetts Rep. Allen T. Treadway had said two years earlier, in 1935, "The Federal Government has no express or inherent power under the Constitution to set up such a scheme." And in the Senate that same year, here is Louisiana's Huey Long, shortly before his untimely death: "Everyone doubts the constitutionality of the bill. Even the proponents of the bill doubt it." The Court's subsequent pronouncements notwithstanding, the same can be said for countless other schemes Congress has created over the years, including some pre-dating the constitutional revolution that followed Franklin Roosevelt's infamous 1937 Court-packing threat. Based on constitutional principles authorizing only a limited federal government, and later amendments aimed at limiting state power as well, those schemes are all *ultra vires*.

To be sure, on occasion the Court can check power and even reverse course with only limited repercussions. In 1995, for example, the Court held the 1990 Gun-Free Schools Act unconstitutional, as it did five years later with the Violence Against Women Act—finding in both cases that Congress had exceeded its authority under its commerce power. But in both cases also the actions addressed by the acts were already prohibited under the police power of the states, so there was little change on the ground. One could make a similar point about the Court's 2012 ruling that Congress's power to regulate interstate commerce did not enable it, pursuant to the Affordable Care Act, to mandate that individuals buy insurance so that they might then be regulated under the Commerce Clause. Never had the commerce power—with or without the Necessary and

Proper Clause—been used to *compel* commerce, so again the decision never really changed things on the ground. In each of those cases it was the modern, boundless reading of the commerce power that was reversed. Rejecting 58 years of Commerce Clause precedent, Chief Justice William Rehnquist said in the 1995 decision, "We start with first principles. The Constitution creates a Federal Government of enumerated powers."

On the rights side, reversals grounded in first principles—both liberty and equality—are more common and often more clearly reversals of precedents. Most famously, of course, and notwithstanding the possibility of repercussions, when the Court decided *Brown v. Board of Education* in 1954 it reversed the separate-but-equal precedent and the practical course it had sanctioned in 1896 in *Plessy v. Ferguson*. *Brown*'s unfortunate "psychological" opinion aside, one can safely say that as a matter of law the equal protection *principle* trumped *Plessy*'s 58-year-old *precedent*. Similarly, in 1965 the Court reversed what amounted to precedent—its fairly well-established deference to state police power—when it ruled that Connecticut's prohibition on the sale and use of contraceptives was unconstitutional. And in 2003 the Court reversed a clear precedent—its own ruling barely 17 years earlier—when it found a Texas statute criminalizing same-sex sodomy to be unconstitutional.

But looming between the arguably mistaken precedents that, as a practical matter, are impossible to reverse except through legislation—like *Helvering v. Davis*, upholding the Social Security Act—and those that the Court alone can more easily fix, we find a wide variety of cases where principle and precedent part company and it is not always clear, both tactically and strategically, what the Court should do, much less what the "long view" calls for. In fact, what exactly *is* the object of this long view?

The Long View?

Let's note first that although Chief Justice Roberts may indeed be taking the long view, the talk about it does not come from him but from those of us who follow the Court's business. Thus, many on the Left have answered the question just posed in narrow political terms, expressing their fear that the Roberts Court will continue to undermine campaign finance limits, economic and environmental regulations, civil and consumer rights, and more. They discern a clear *political* agenda in the Roberts Court's decisions. No one can doubt, of course, that in a particular case a justice's legal analysis might be influenced by his political views—and opinions occasionally give evidence of that. But in the main, I submit, a justice's opinion on any given case is driven far more by his understanding of the Constitution, the laws enacted under it, and the decisions rendered pursuant to that law. Still, that is more likely true of dissents and concurrences than of opinions for the Court, for the simple reason that it takes at least five justices to speak for the Court, and those five (or more) may have different views on those three sources of law. In such cases, the final opinion must be acceptable enough to all, even if not fully acceptable to any, which means that the Court's opinion may not accurately reflect "the law."

Let's assume, however, that we can speak meaningfully of the Roberts Court's having an "agenda" and take up the question of what that agenda might be, what its "long view" is. Unless we are prepared to say that Roberts's confirmation statements were disingenuous or, at best, naive aspirations, then the narrow political objectives that some attribute to him must be dismissed. Consistent with that, and taking Roberts at his word as outlined above, securing the Court's reputation as the nonpolitical branch in an increasingly politicized and polarized nation must surely rank high on his list of objectives, as evidenced by his press for unanimity, even if, given that polarization, not all will agree with given decisions. For unanimity signals to a deeply divided people that despite the polarization beyond the Court, at least one branch of government, the nonpolitical branch, can agree about what the law is—shades of the Marshall Court, seeking to cement the new federal government against the political storms of its day.

But that "institutional" objective, that effort to assure a skeptical public that law can be discerned and applied in a nonpartisan way, is itself, of course, a *political* goal, albeit a broad nonpartisan one. Still, there are critics who contend that Chief Justice Roberts is employing unanimity more cunningly, in service of narrower political ends. Several have pointed, for example, to his 2009 narrowly written unanimous opinion in *Northwest Austin v. Holder*, upholding (while raising questions about) a key section of the Voting Rights Act of 1965, which served four years later, in *Shelby County v. Holder*, as a precedent for undermining that provision—a 5-4 decision with Roberts again writing for the Court. I'll reserve judgment on whether that was all part of a grand plan. It needs to be said, however, that this larger effort to encourage unanimity should surely not count as the Court's *main* objective. For the Court needs to say not simply what the law is; it needs also to get it right when it so says. Its main job, that is, should be to state the *correct*, not just the agreed upon, reading and application of the law, even if that means that not all of the justices may agree with a decision doing that.

To see this dilemma played out, let's look first at one of the more important unanimous decisions the Court decided this term, *NLRB v. Noel Canning*.

NLRB v. Noel Canning

In a ringing unanimous decision below in *Noel Canning*, Judge David Sentelle went to the heart of the matter, writing an opinion for the U.S. Court of Appeals for the D.C. Circuit on the question of whether President Obama's three "recess" appointments to the National Labor Relations Board—which he made on January 4, 2012, when the Senate was in pro forma session—were constitutional. They were not, Sentelle ruled, doubtless influencing the two other circuit courts that later reached the same result. Not only was the Senate in session when the appointments were made, but the vacancies the president filled did not "happen" when the Senate was not in session. Thus, the president violated both the background separation of powers principle implicit in the requirement that upper-level executive branch appointments be made "by and with the Advice and Consent of the Senate," and the exception afforded by the Recess Appointments Clause: "The President shall have Power to fill up all Vacancies that may happen during the Recess of the Senate, by granting Commissions which shall expire at the end of the next Session."

Noel Canning should have been an easy case for the Supreme Court to affirm—in fact, with an opinion pretty much along the lines of Sentelle's. After all, the constitutional text concerning how appointments are *normally* to be made is clear: "by and with of the Advice and Consent of the Senate." And the text of the exception, the Recess Appointments Clause, presents little if any ambiguity as well. It concerns only "Vacancies that may *happen* during the Recess of the Senate," when the Senate is not there to advise and consent, not those that happen when the Senate *is* in session; and it refers not to *a* recess of the Senate—to the several "intra-session" recesses that may occur *within* either of the one-year sessions that take place between congressional elections—but to *the* recess of the Senate, the single "intersession" break that occurs between those two one-year sessions. And all this as determined not by the president, as President Obama purported to do, but by the chambers themselves, as the Constitution provides. Finally, since the Court had never been called upon to rule on the question, it found before it a straightforward constitutional question unencumbered by any judicial precedent.

But there were *historical* precedents—mostly recent departures from the constitutional text, culminating finally in Obama's going a step too far—and those precedents served to keep the Court's majority from reaching a principled decision. True, the Court held unanimously that Obama's appointments to the board were unconstitutional because here the Senate was in pro forma session—it falls to Congress to say when it is in session, not to the president. But Justice Stephen Breyer, writing for himself and Justices Anthony Kennedy, Ruth Bader Ginsburg, Sonia Sotomayor, and Elena Kagan, gave everything else to the administration. All but ignoring the purpose of the Senate's advice and consent role—to serve as a check on executive power—Breyer focused instead on the purpose of the recess appointments power—to fill offices when the Senate is out and thus unable to advise and consent—reading out of the clause the requirement that the vacancy "happen" during the recess. If a vacancy is still open when the Senate goes out of session, even if it arose when the Senate was *in* session and could have given its consent, that's good enough. And Breyer temporized in spades when it came to the definition of "*the* recess." It doesn't matter, he ruled, whether a recess is between or within sessions as long as it's long enough to be a "recess." And how long is long enough? Looking to history again, three days is too short, but ten days is "normally" enough to constitute a recess, he concluded.

That was all too much for Justice Antonin Scalia, who read from the bench, no less, his "furious concurrence," as Adam Liptak of the *New York Times* put it. Joined by the chief justice and Justices Clarence Thomas and Samuel Alito, Scalia took the gloves off. Like Judge Sentelle in the court below, he would have held the recess appointments power to its structural and textual moorings, limiting its exercise to filling vacancies that *happen* during *the* recess of the Senate—"that is, the intermission between two formal legislative sessions." Sounding uncharacteristically like a judicial "activist," in truth he issued a clarion call not for rudderless activism but for judicial engagement with principle, text, structure, and precedent. "The majority's insistence on deferring to the Executive's untenably broad interpretation of the [recess appointments] power," he charged, "is in clear conflict with our precedent and forebodes a diminution of this Court's role in controversies involving the separation of powers and the structure of government." And with the errant Justice Kennedy repeatedly in his "cites," Scalia added, "[s]o convinced were the Framers that liberty of the person adheres in structure that at first they did not consider a Bill of Rights necessary."

That quote is from Kennedy's 1998 concurrence in *Clinton v. City of New York*, where he also wrote, responding there to Justice Breyer, that "[l]iberty is always at stake when one or more of the branches seek to transgress the separation of powers"—precisely the principle at stake here. And Kennedy added: "Separation of powers was designed to implement a fundamental insight: concentration of power in the hands of a single branch is a threat to liberty." By contrast, Breyer's main rationale for so limited a ruling in *Noel Canning* had the clear ring of restraint and deference: "We have not previously interpreted the [Recess Appointments] Clause, and, when doing so for the first time in more than 200 years, we must hesitate to upset the compromise and working arrangements that the elected branches of Government themselves have reached." But as Justice Scalia showed, far from "working arrangements," those ambiguous "late-arising" historical practices, which President Obama stretched to the breaking point, spoke of anything but "compromise." Yet here, Kennedy joined Breyer's deference, the same Kennedy who in *Clinton* had written that "our role is in no way 'lessened' because it might be said that 'the two political branches are adjusting their own powers between themselves.'"

So why did Kennedy not see the parallels here, where his vote would likely have made the difference between a constitutionally principled resolution of the case, protecting liberty, and a resolution that leaves a muddy prospect, difficult to police, while compromising the Senate's advice and consent role? Or, more likely, is it that he did see the parallels, but thought it more important, perhaps, for the Court to speak with one voice on this question? If so, does that rationale help to explain why he, as the senior most justice among the majority, assigned the opinion on this politically charged case to Breyer, perhaps to make the loss more palatable to supporters of the president? We can only speculate here, of course. But if it was a concern for unanimity that animated either Kennedy or Roberts (or both), then this admittedly broad *political* objective, as noted above, trumped the unambiguous text of the Constitution—leaving us to wonder in what way or sense this decision serves the "long view." Assume that it was Kennedy's vote that was in the balance: Had he joined Scalia's opinion, making it the opinion of the Court, and had the Court's four liberals then dissented, the separation of powers principle and the liberty it secures—a connection Kennedy has frequently recognized—would have been protected in this context, far better than under the decision the Court rendered, where both remain essentially unprotected. If the long view entails preserving or, better, restoring constitutional principles, as surely it must for both Kennedy and Roberts, would not the Scalia opinion have better served that end than this dubiously grounded unanimous decision? Apart from the limited holding the Court reached—that it falls to Congress to say when it is in session—it is hard to see what unanimity gained here, but easy to see what the Constitution lost, and to see also the opportunity missed.

Burwell v. Hobby Lobby

The Constitution fared somewhat better in another decision that drew much attention this term—more attention, perhaps, than any other—*Burwell v. Hobby Lobby*. Although not a constitutional but an as-applied challenge to a Department of Health and Human Services (HHS) regulation issued pursuant to the Affordable Care Act (ACA), *Hobby Lobby* was immersed in and replete with constitutional issues and implications. Yet here too the decision left us asking why the Court could not have done a better job of restoring constitutional principles.

Without doubt, the answer rests in substantial part with the question before the Court, which emerges from the tall grasses of modern "constitutional law." It was whether the Religious Freedom Restoration Act (RFRA) protected Hobby Lobby, a closely held for-profit corporation founded and owned by a deeply religious family, from having to provide its female employees, pursuant to an HHS mandate, with health insurance that included coverage for 20 contraceptive services, the four at issue being arguably abortifacients, at no cost to the employees. Writing for the Court, Justice Alito, joined by the chief justice and Justices Scalia, Kennedy, and Thomas, held that the HHS contraceptive mandate violated RFRA. Thus, the Court upheld the religious liberty of Hobby Lobby's owners.

Let's begin with first principles. In a free society of the kind implicit in the Constitution following the Civil War Amendments, employers, regardless of their organizational form, would be at liberty to offer group health insurance of whatever kind to their employees. But as detailed in Professor Richard Epstein's extensive discussion of *Hobby Lobby* later in this volume, a vast body of law of various kinds has accumulated over the years, covering everything from markets to employment, insurance, health care, drug policy, and more, much of it inconsistent with that original free-market vision. Of particular relevance here, in 1990, in *Employment Division v. Smith*, Justice Scalia ruled for the Court that the Free Exercise Clause of the First Amendment did not prohibit the state of Oregon from denying unemployment benefits to plaintiff Smith, a Native American, after he was fired by a private drug rehabilitation organization because he ingested peyote, a controlled substance, for sacramental purposes at a ceremony of his Native American Church. Thus, a person's religious beliefs and practices, Scalia held, will not excuse him from compliance with an otherwise "valid and neutral law of general applicability"—here, the federal Controlled Substances Act.

The principle Scalia articulated would pose only a small range of problems in a world in which such laws were limited to policing common law matters like torts, crimes, contracts, and remedies, and to providing a limited range of public goods, properly defined. But today, when government regulates vast areas of life—not only to protect such common law rights but in pursuit of manifold public and political ends—it's another matter. Thus, recognizing the implications for religious liberty of the *Smith* decision, religious organizations of every stripe rushed to Congress for relief, which they got in 1993 in the form of RFRA, a broad statute that carves out a religious exception from the *Smith* ruling. It was under RFRA that Hobby Lobby's owners sought relief: Not only did the ACA require them to offer health insurance to their employees, but the HHS mandate, at issue in the litigation, specified coverage that violated the owners' deeply held religious beliefs.

It was fairly easy for Alito to dismiss the government's first objection—that a for-profit corporation could not come under RFRA's protection. Nothing in the statute precluded corporate "persons" from coverage. Besides, the rights of the corporation, at bottom, are simply the rights of the owners who pursue their interests through the corporate form. And Alito noted also that HHS's concession "that a nonprofit corporation can be a 'person' within the meaning of RFRA effectively dispatches any argument that the term 'person' as used in RFRA does not reach the closely held corporations" here.

With the question of coverage settled, Alito turned to RFRA's three requirements. First, did the contraceptive mandate substantially burden the owners' exercise of religion? Here too there was little difficulty demonstrating that it did. By facilitating the performance by their employees of acts the employers considered immoral according to their religious tenets, the HHS mandate clearly burdened the employers' exercise of religion, leaving them unable to conduct their business consistent with their religious beliefs. Moreover, if the company refused to comply with the mandate or to provide health insurance altogether, it would face huge, continuing fines, thus putting the owners to a choice of either following their faith or likely going out of business.

It was on RFRA's next two requirements, however, that the Court fell short. In drafting RFRA, Congress had incorporated the judicial methodology that the New Deal Court invented in 1938 in (in)famous Footnote Four of its *Carolene Products* decision. In that case the Court had asked not what long had been the first question, whether the statute at issue was authorized under the doctrine of enumerated powers: congressional authority was simply assumed since that bedrock constitutional principle had died a year earlier. Rather, the Court asked whether the statute implicated a "fundamental" or a "nonfundamental" right. If the former, the statute would survive "strict scrutiny" only if the "interest" of the government was "compelling" and the means the government employed were "narrowly tailored" to serve it. If the latter, a "rational basis" for the statute was sufficient for its survival. Needless to say, the potential for all manner of judicial value judgments and mischief was unleashed, and it ensued.

In 1993, therefore, determining religious liberty to be a "fundamental right," Congress imported that methodology into RFRA, requiring that if government were to burden religious liberty it must have a "compelling interest" for doing so, and it must do it by the "least restrictive means." For his part, Alito, having determined that the contraceptive mandate substantially burdened the religious liberty of Hobby Lobby's owners, did not of course ask the fundamental *constitutional* question—whether the ACA, pursuant to which the HHS contraceptive mandate was promulgated, was constitutionally authorized—for that was partly "settled" two years earlier when the Court rewrote the ACA's individual mandate to uphold it under Congress's taxing power. But neither did he ask the basic *statutory* question—whether the government had a compelling interest "in guaranteeing cost-free access to the four challenged contraceptive methods." Instead, he simply assumed *arguendo* that the government's interest was compelling and then proceeded straight to the final RFRA step, concluding that the mandate failed the statutory test because there were other, less restrictive means by which the government could accomplish its interest, such as itself taking on the costs of contraceptive services, or by extending the accommodation that HHS had already established for *nonprofit* organizations with religious objections.

There are several problems with the Court's having elided the compelling interest test, as Epstein discusses in his essay in this volume. But the core of the matter is that the government's "interest" must be defined with particularity regarding the person whose religious liberty is at stake such that that interest outweighs the individual's interest in religious liberty. And the government did not do that— nor did Alito, in the end, require it to. This is not a case in which the employer is *preventing* the employee from obtaining contraceptive services, which are readily available in the market or, for indigent employees (if any), from various social services. Given that ready availability, why is the government's interest in providing women with free contraceptive services so compelling that it must force employers with religious objections to provide and pay for the services?

Had Alito pressed that issue, he would not have had to go to the final step, of course. But having assumed that the government had a compelling interest that justified restricting religious liberty, his finding that the contraceptive mandate violated RFRA because there were less restrictive means available put the Court in something of a dilemma only a few days later. It arose when Wheaton College, a nonprofit organization with religious objections, came before the Court seeking an interim order allowing it to refuse to offer contraceptive coverage without filling out a required form that also gave notice of its position to its health insurer or third party administrator, which the college believed would implicate it in facilitating the provision of such coverage. The Court granted the order, holding that one of the less restrictive means it had found available only days earlier was *not* a less restrictive means here. That apparent back-tracking could have been avoided if the Court, in *Hobby Lobby*, had weighed in on RFRA's compelling-interest requirement. (This "accommodation" had never been offered to Hobby Lobby and the other for-profit enterprises challenging the contraceptive mandate, so it is unknown whether some or all of these plaintiffs share Wheaton College's objection to the form-filing.)

Here too, then, it is unclear what this decision says about our larger theme—what it says about the "long view." Although religious liberty was protected in *these* circumstances—a limit that Kennedy's concurrence seemed to emphasize—the Court could certainly have put its decision on firmer ground. To be sure, the decision advances liberty marginally by employing *part* of RFRA's response to the unfortunate *Smith* decision. (And it might have gone the other way.) But look how far into the tall grasses of modern "constitutional law" this case was from the start, as noted earlier. *Smith*, for its part, began uncritically with the Controlled Substances Act, which had been "law" for decades, notwithstanding that the commerce power that "authorized" the act was originally written not to interfere with but to facilitate interstate commerce, even in substances disapproved of by some, and notwithstanding that the Fourteenth Amendment empowers Congress and the courts to block states from exercising their police powers in ways that interfere with private transactions that injure no one. Yet when Congress sought to check *Smith*'s deference to "valid and neutral law[s] of general applicability," it did so simply by carving out a single "exception"—for religious liberty—an exception to the general idea that government may rule as it will.

Think about that: government first, liberty second, as an "exception" to the general rule—an "accommodation," as the *Hobby Lobby* Court styled it. Where did such an idea come from? It came, obviously, from the Progressive Era, which slowly reversed our Founding first principles, then instituted that reversal during the constitutional revolution of 1937-1938. The reversal began years before, with property rights and economic liberty: the right to use property as one wished unless someone had a demonstrably valid objection was replaced by permit regimes, zoning and the like; so too, economic liberty came increasingly under regulatory restraints and licensing regimes. After *Carolene Products'* Footnote Four reduced the protection of such "nonfundamental rights" through the toothless rational basis test, a surfeit of legislation poured forth—federal, state, and local. And then, with the demise of the nondelegation doctrine in 1943, the modern administrative state blossomed—today's executive state—resulting in ever-widening incursions on individual liberty—and selective efforts by the Court to "accommodate" such liberties when they concerned "fundamental" rights. But with our increasing dependence on the "entitlements" provided by the executive state—free contraceptives, for example—those seeking relief from the ever-expanding social obligations entailed by that state, such as religious objectors, have had to plead for "accommodations"—at least if they were still free to do so. What could be next, an accommodation for speech?

McCutcheon v. FEC

Well yes. Although the Court has held that political speech is "the primary object of First Amendment protection" and "the lifeblood of a self-governing people," Congress, aided over the years by numerous uneven judicial decisions, has imposed a vast array of restrictions on the campaign contributions and expenditures that for most Americans are the essence of political speech. Beginning with the Federal Election Campaign Act of 1971 (FECA) and running through the Bipartisan Campaign Reform Act of 2002 (BCRA), this amazingly complex body of law—mimicked also in many state laws—has become so far-reaching that the most innocent of acts, like joining with one's neighbors to put up yard signs, can put one on the wrong side of the *criminal* law, no less, if one fails to register with officials before doing so.

And so we come to one of this term's more important free speech decisions, *McCutcheon v. FEC*. Here it was not restrictions on yard sign activity but on campaign contributions in the ordinary sense that led Shaun McCutcheon to sue the Federal Election Commission. Under FECA as amended by BCRA, *base* limits restrict how much money a donor may contribute to any particular candidate or committee while *aggregate* limits restrict how much he may give in total to all candidates or committees. In the 2011–2012 election cycle Mc-Cutcheon contributed $1,776 to each of 16 different federal candidates—well within the base limits applicable for each; and he contributed also to several noncandidate political committees, again in compliance with the base limits applicable for each. But since those contributions brought him up against the aggregate limits in the two categories, he was unable to contribute to *additional* candidates or committees—as he wished to do, and do in future as well—even though each of his contributions was within the base limits. Thus, the effect of the aggregate limits was to restrict how *many* candidates and committees he could support.

However complex this body of law is in its entirety, the issues at the core of this case were quite simple. Holding the aggregate limits unconstitutional under the First Amendment, Chief Justice Roberts wrote for himself and Justices Scalia, Kennedy, and Alito. Justice Thomas concurred in the judgment, but wrote separately. Writing for the plurality, Roberts began with the seminal 1976 case of *Buckley v. Valeo*, a challenge to FECA as amended in 1974. There the Court distinguished expenditure and contribution limits, "based on the degree to which each encroaches upon protected First Amendment interests." Applying "exacting scrutiny," the *Buckley* Court found FECA's expenditure limits unconstitutional because they reduced the quantity of expression. But under a lesser but still "rigorous standard of review," contribution limits were upheld because they impose a lesser restraint on political speech. They "permit[ ] the symbolic expression of support evidenced by a contribution but do[ ] not in any way infringe the contributor's freedom to discuss candidates and issues," the *Buckley* Court said. And as *Buckley* and later Courts have held, the sole legitimate purpose of any such limits is to limit quid pro quo corruption and its appearance—political contributions for political favors.

As for the constitutionality of aggregate limits, the *Buckley* Court noted that the parties had not separately addressed that issue at length, and Roberts added here that, in its 139-page opinion, the Court had devoted only one paragraph of three sentences to the question, finding that, although the aggregate limits do limit the *number* of candidates and committees an individual may support, this "quite modest restraint" serves to prevent evasion of the base contribution limitation.

For his part, Roberts then set about showing how arguments for the aggregate limits, rooted in the corruption prevention rationale for the base limits, do not in fact prevent corruption, but do invade First Amendment speech rights. Not only are the circumvention arguments even less persuasive today than they were in 1976—because statutory and regulatory safeguards have been considerably strengthened since then—but the circumvention scenarios the government and the dissent imagine are both speculative and highly improbable. Circumvention aside, however, the argument for aggregate limits based on corruption prevention is not credible on its face, Roberts argued. Under the current base limits, an individual may give the maximum allowed under those limits to each of up to nine candidates before he reaches the aggregate limit. If there is no corruption in that, because he has kept to the base limits for each candidate, how would giving the same base limit contribution to the tenth candidate constitute corruption? Or as Roberts put it succinctly: "The Government may no more restrict how many candidates or causes a donor may support than it may tell a newspaper how many candidates it may endorse."

McCutcheon was thus an important if modest advance for individual liberty—modest, because here too the Court stopped short, despite requests to do more. As Roberts wrote, "[t]he parties and *amici curiae* spend significant energy debating whether the line that *Buckley* drew between contributions and expenditures should remain the law." Notwithstanding that debate, he saw no need here to revisit that distinction "and the corollary distinction in the applicable standards of review." Why? Because, though the *Buckley* Court had found the corruption prevention rationale "sufficiently important" to justify contribution limits, later Courts have found it satisfied a higher "compelling" standard, so "the interest would satisfy even strict scrutiny." Moreover, because here "we find a substantial mismatch between the Government's stated objective and the means selected to achieve it, the aggregate limits fail even under the [less demanding] 'closely drawn' test. We therefore need not parse the differences between the two standards in this case."

For Thomas, however, "[c]ontributions and expenditures are simply 'two sides of the same First Amendment coin,' and our efforts to distinguish the two have produced mere 'word games' rather than any cognizable principle of constitutional law." The original "proxy speech" argument, for example—contributions deserve a lesser standard of review because they involve speech by someone other than the contributor—has been rejected by the Court itself, like other "discarded rationales" Thomas listed but the Court ignored. Indeed, he pointed to "*Buckley's* last remaining reason for devaluing political contributions relative to expenditures"—that a contribution limit involves "little direct restraint" on an individual's political communication since it permits the "symbolic expression of support evidenced by the contribution but does not in any way infringe the contributor's freedom to discuss candidates and issues."

As Thomas then demonstrated, that proposition cannot be squared with a key premise in the plurality's opinion. For the government here has made essentially the same argument that the *Buckley* Court made for limiting contributions—an individual facing the aggregate limits can still contribute less money to more people. That is no answer, said the plurality: "[t]o require one person to contribute at lower levels than others because he wants to support more candidates or causes is to impose a special burden on broader participation in the democratic process." But that "same logic also defeats the reasoning from *Buckley* on which the plurality purports to rely," Thomas wrote. "Under the plurality's analysis, limiting the amount of money a person may give to a candidate *does* impose a direct restraint on his political communication; if it did not, the aggregate limits at issue here would not create 'a special burden on broader participation in the democratic process.'"

We are left, then, with the same question that arose earlier. Here too we have a marginal gain, but, as Thomas concluded, a missed opportunity as well. Did the continuing emotional reaction to *Citizens United* play any part in the course Roberts chose? Perhaps, but more likely, I expect, it was Roberts's "modesty" and his preference for deciding only what is absolutely necessary that informed his approach to a case like this, and to others too.

There are, however, at least two problems with that approach. First, as a practical matter, the Court does not always or even often get an opportunity to correct later what it missed correcting in the case before it. To paraphrase John Maynard Keynes, in the long run the Court changes—which is to say that missed opportunities can become lost opportunities. And second, to the extent that the Court puts forth a better but still not accurate reading of the law, and of the Constitution in particular, the rule of law still suffers. It is no answer to say, "I'll seize the day, tomorrow."

Introduction

Ilya Shapiro*

This is the 13th volume of the *Cato Supreme Court Review*, the nation's first in-depth critique of the Supreme Court term just ended. We release this journal every year in conjunction with our annual Constitution Day symposium, about two-and-a-half months after the previous term ends and two weeks before the next one begins. We are proud of the speed with which we publish this tome—authors of articles about the last-decided cases have no more than a month to provide us full drafts—and of its accessibility, at least insofar as the Court's opinions allow. This is not a typical law review, after all, whose prolix submissions use more space for pedantic and abstruse footnotes than for article text. Instead, this is a book of articles about law intended for everyone from lawyers and judges to educated laymen and interested citizens.

And we are happy to confess our biases: We approach our subject matter from a classical Madisonian perspective, with a focus on individual liberty, property rights, and federalism, and a vision of a government of delegated, enumerated, and thus limited powers. We also try to maintain a strict separation of law and politics; just because something is good policy doesn't mean it's constitutional, and vice versa. Similarly, certain decisions must necessarily be left to the political process: We aim to be governed by laws, not lawyers, so just as a good lawyer will present all plausibly legal options to his client, a good public official will recognize that the ultimate buck stops with him.

*　*　*

* Senior fellow in constitutional studies, Cato Institute, and editor-in-chief, *Cato Supreme Court Review*.

Despite the predictable ideological divisions over certain cases, the 2013–2014 term recorded a level of unanimity not seen since the 1940s. To wit, all the justices agreed on the final judgment in about two-thirds of cases decided on the merits: 48 of 73, or 66 percent.[1] (The previous five terms registered 36, 44, 46, 45, and, last year, 49 percent.) This development logically resulted in dramatically fewer dissenting opinions than any term in modern history (31, whereas last term there were 52 and the average going back to 2000–2001 is 56.8). Not surprisingly, the total number of all opinions (majority, concurring, and dissenting) was also historically low (145, down from 169 last term)—and the average of 1.99 opinions per case was down from an average of 2.33 over the preceding decade. And due to the scarce 8-1 or 7-1 decisions (just two), only Justices Ruth Bader Ginsburg and Sonia Sotomayor wrote solo dissents. Notably, neither Chief Justice John Roberts nor Justice Elena Kagan has ever written one of those during their entire tenures on the Court (nine and four terms, respectively).

Some commentators called the above level of agreement a "faux-nanimity" given that some of these rulings were either quite narrow or had strident concurrences that were dissents in all but name—especially in high-profile cases like *McCullen v. Coakley*, *NLRB v. Noel Canning*, and *Bond v. United States* (all analyzed in these pages), which also share the distinction of having Justice Antonin Scalia write the lead "concurrence." But even if you count only cases where every justice joined some part of the majority opinion—not just the judgment—you get unanimity in more than half the docket (38 cases, or 52 percent). That's significantly higher than the previous five terms—which came in at 27, 29, 33, 36, and 41 percent, respectively—but continues that increasing trend. And if you further narrow the unanimity count to cases where every justice joined the majority opinion in full, you're still left with a large chunk (28 cases, or 38 percent),

---

[1] These figures include two 8-0 cases and six summary (without oral argument) reversals. All statistics taken from Kedar Bhatia, Final Stat Pack for October Term 2013 and Key Takeaways, SCOTUSblog, June 30, 2014 (updated July 3, 2014), http://www.scotusblog.com/2014/06/final-stat-pack-for-october-term-2013-and-key-takeaways-2. See also Kedar Bhatia, A Few Notes on Unanimity, SCOTUSblog, July 10, 2014, http://www.scotusblog.com/2014/07/a-few-notes-on-unanimity. For more detailed data from previous terms, see Stat Pack Archive, SCOTUSblog, http://www.scotusblog.com/reference/stat-pack (last visited Aug. 28, 2014).

which, except for 2002–2003's 39 percent, is the highest for any term going back at least two decades

Part of this dynamic can be attributed to the Court's considerable control of its docket, such that it can decide not to hear what would otherwise be divisive cases. About 10 percent of this term's docket consisted of non-ideological patent cases, for example, and the Court has stayed away from the Second Amendment since 2010—to its shame, in my view, because lower courts have been willfully confused (to put it charitably) in protecting the individual right to keep and bear arms in states that have engaged in massive resistance to the Court's rulings in that regard.[2] Irrespective of the reason and any way you slice it, the Court definitely spoke more often with one voice this term than it has in the past—which accords with Chief Justice Roberts's stated wishes.

At the same time, only 10 cases went 5-4 (14 percent, the lowest rate since at least 1995–1996 except for 2005–2006's 13 percent)—but those included contentious rulings on campaign finance (*McCutcheon v. FEC*), legislative prayer (*Town of Greece v. Galloway*), workers' rights (*Harris v. Quinn*), and Obamacare's contraceptive mandate (*Burwell v. Hobby Lobby*). That means that 80 percent of judgments were either unanimous or 5-4, beating last term's 78 percent and significantly higher than the 64.5 percent average of the preceding four terms. In other words, the Court is of one mind on most issues—including important rulings against outlandish assertions of federal power—but continues to be split on constitutional rights and civil liberties, as well as certain types of criminal procedure cases that produce heterodox but consistent divisions.

The Court reversed or vacated 55 lower-court opinions (73 percent), which is essentially the same as last term and in line with recent years. Of the lower courts with significant numbers of cases under review, the U.S. Court of Appeals for the Ninth Circuit attained a 1-11 record (92 percent reversal), decisively beating its traditional rivals the Sixth Circuit (2-9, 82 percent) and Federal Circuit (1-5, 83 percent)—as well as new contender the Fifth Circuit (1-6, or 86 percent)—for the title of "biggest loser."

---

[2] See, e.g., Adam Liptak, Compromise at the Supreme Court Veils Its Rifts, N.Y. Times, July 1, 2014, available at http://www.nytimes.com/2014/07/02/us/supreme-court-term-marked-by-unanimous-decisions.html.

Anthony Kennedy was yet again the justice most often in the majority (69 of 73 cases, or 95 percent), followed by the chief justice (92 percent). Even more significantly, Kennedy was on the winning side in all 10 of the 5-4 decisions—four times with the "conservatives," twice with the "liberals," and four times in "unconventional" alignments. The second-most winner of 5-4 cases was the chief justice—which may seem unsurprising, except that it was Justice Clarence Thomas who was runner-up to Justice Kennedy in each of the previous four terms. Interestingly, Justices Samuel Alito, Kagan, and Kennedy combined to author 8 of the 10 majority opinions in the 5-4 cases, with Kagan authoring 60 percent of the 5-4 opinions in cases where she was in the majority (up from 10, 17, and 0, respectively, in her previous three terms). Most notably, Justice Alito wrote the majority opinions in both *Harris v. Quinn* and *Hobby Lobby*—both decided on the last day of term, June 30—while Justice Kagan wrote the leading dissents in *Harris v. Quinn* and *Town of Greece*. I'm not the only observer to note that both of these justices, who are the most junior of their respective ideological blocs, are coming into their own.

Justice Sotomayor took over from Justice Scalia as the justice most likely to dissent (18 percent of all cases and 54 percent of cases that had dissenters)—most memorably in *Schuette v. Coalition to Defend Affirmative Action*. This was the first time she has been in this position, but she's come close in previous years.

The justice pairings most likely to agree, at least in part, were Justices Thomas and Alito (69 of 72 cases, or 95.8 percent), followed by Justices Scalia and Thomas (69 of 73, or 94.5 percent) and last year's winners Justices Ginsburg and Kagan (67 of 71, or 94.4 percent). Curiously, the Roberts-Alito pairing, which had traded off with Scalia-Thomas for several years, dropped out of the top 10. Justices Alito and Sotomayor voted together less than anyone else (in only 53 of 71 cases, or 74.6 percent), followed very closely by Justices Thomas and Sotomayor (54 of 72, or 75 percent), Justices Ginsburg and Alito (same), and Justices Thomas and Ginsburg (55 of 73, or 75.3 percent). Seen another way, the top two pairings who were least likely to agree included Justice Sotomayor, while the next three included Justice Ginsburg.

My final statistics are more whimsical, relating to the number of questions asked at oral argument. Justice Scalia regained his perch as the Supreme Court's most frequent interlocutor—Justice Sotomayor edged him out last year—with an average of 19.6 questions per argument. That was below his 25.8 average from two terms ago, but it still made Scalia the top questioner in 36 percent of cases and put him in the top three 69 percent of the time. Justice Ginsburg again asked the first question most often (in 31 percent of cases), followed by Sotomayor (20 percent). Justice Thomas continued his non-questioning ways. Finally, it's safe to say that Scalia remains the funniest justice, easily generating the most transcript notations of "[laughter]" per argument.

Before turning to the *Review*, I would be remiss if I didn't say a few words about what some people are calling the Court's libertarian turn—both those alarmed and heartened by this development.[3] While some commentators have long accused the Court of a pro-business bias, to the extent that's the case, the entire Court is guilty of it, not just the "conservative" cohort. (And for the record, the Chamber of Commerce went 13-4 this term, though most of its wins were in less significant cases.) In terms of a pro-liberty bent—which alas isn't the same thing as being pro-business—that's a more distinct and salubrious trend, but it's also a more complicated story.

In July 2013, the Simon Lazarus of the "progressive originalist" Constitutional Accountability Center sounded the alarm against the growing threat of libertarianism and its "potentially seismic" influence on the Court. The "recent surge of libertarianism among conservative academics, advocates, politicians, and of course, voters," Lazarus wrote, has now "begun to register at the Supreme Court."[4]

There was surely something to that claim. For example, the Court's ruling against the Defense of Marriage Act in *United States v. Windsor* was laden with libertarian legal principles, including Justice

---

[3] See, e.g., Damon Root, The Supreme Court Now Leans Libertarian, Reason. com, July 8, 2014, http://reason.com/blog/2014/07/08/the-supreme-court-now-leans-libertarian. For an examination of the similarities and differences between the conservative and libertarian legal movements, see Damon Root, Conservatives v. Libertarians, Reason, July 2010, also available at http://reason.com/archives/2010/06/08/conservatives-v-libertarians.

[4] Simon Lazarus, Alito Shrugged, New Republic, July 28, 2013, http://www.newrepublic.com/article/114059/supreme-court-libertarianism-ron-pauls-bench (subtitle: "Libertarianism has won over the Supreme Court conservatives"). For one analysis of Lazarus's claims, see Ilya Shapiro, "Libertarianism Has Won Over Supreme Court Conservatives," Cato at Liberty, July 30, 2013, http://www.cato.org/blog/libertarianism-has-won-over-supreme-court-conservatives.

Kennedy's favorite theme of how federalism operates to protect for individual liberty. Cato went 15-3 that term, and we were the only organization in the country to file on the winning side of the three blockbusters: *Fisher v. UT-Austin* (racial preferences), *Shelby County v. Holder* (voting rights), and *United States v. Windsor* (DOMA).

That libertarian trend accelerated this term, as the Court issued one broadly freedom-protecting ruling after another, voting against aggregate limits on campaign spending; in favor of a legal challenge to Ohio's truth commission; against warrantless cellphone searches; against compelled unionization; and against executive overreach in a host of ways. So Lazarus was right to worry—and he's even more worried now: Roughly a year after his last jeremiad, he took to the pages of the *New Republic* again to decry that "radical libertarianism is reshaping the bench." He wrote:

> It is not just about reclaiming what Randy Barnett famously called the "lost Constitution." Less visibly but often more consequentially, libertarian academics, advocates, and judges have long advocated thrusting the courts into much more aggressive roles in resolving the details of messy non-constitutional disputes—in interpreting statutes, and, in particular, in scrutinizing and micro-managing executive and regulatory agencies' applications of the laws they administer.[5]

Well, yes. Much as it might frustrate Barack Obama, there's no "if Congress won't act, the president and executive agencies get extra powers" clause in the Constitution. The latest confirmation of that truism came in the unanimous ruling in *Noel Canning*, which invalidated our constitutional-scholar-in-chief's so-called recess appointments of January 2012. For the 13th time since those ill-fated National Labor Relations Board nominations, the Obama Justice Department lost unanimously at the Supreme Court. Each time, the government argued for a radically expansive federal—and especially executive— power and each time not a single justice agreed. In areas of law ranging from criminal procedure to securities regulation, immigration to religious liberty, Obama couldn't even get the votes of the justices

---

[5] Simon Lazarus, John Roberts' Supreme Court Is the Most Meddlesome in History, The New Republic, July 10, 2014, http://www.newrepublic.com/article/118648/john-roberts-supreme-court-most-meddlesome-us-history (subtitle: "How radical libertarianism is reshaping the bench").

he himself appointed. In other words, the Supreme Court is increasingly embracing the Constitution's structural and rights-based protections for individual freedom and self-governance. Not in every case and not without fits and starts, but on the whole the justices are moving in a libertarian direction.

Accordingly, Cato again did swimmingly, compiling a 10–1 record for the year. And, similar to last year, Cato was the only group that filed on the winning side of this term's three highest-profile 5-4 cases: *McCutcheon, Harris v. Quinn*, and *Hobby Lobby*. Notably, we again vastly outperformed the solicitor general's office, which went 11–9. While an improvement over last year, when the government failed to win even 40 percent of its cases—against a historical norm of 70 percent—it still wasn't a good performance. As Miguel Estrada commented when summarizing the government's abysmal results last term, "when you have a crazy client who insists you make crazy arguments, you're gonna lose some cases."[6] Perhaps the government would be better served following Cato's lead on constitutional interpretation, advocating positions that reinforce our founding document's role in securing and protecting liberty.

* * *

Turning to the *Review*, the volume begins as always with the previous year's B. Kenneth Simon Lecture in Constitutional Thought, which in 2013 was delivered by Senior Judge David Sentelle of the U.S. Court of Appeals for the D.C. Circuit. Judge Sentelle's address was a pithy yet trenchant look at a part of the First Amendment not often examined in any depth, even in scholarly circles: the freedom of the press. That is, the Supreme Court's docket sees a steady stream of free-speech and religion cases—some of which are detailed in these pages—and the idea that free people should have the rights "peaceably to assemble" and "to petition the Government for a redress of grievances" is intuitive in a democratic society. But what is this press freedom that we all support unflinchingly? We recognize the importance of a fourth estate to provide a further check on our government,

---

[6] 2013 Annual Supreme Court Roundup, Speech to the Federalist Society's Washington Lawyers Chapter, July 8, 2013, http://www.fed-soc.org/events/detail/2013-annual-supreme-court-round-up.

but is there a media officialdom that gets more freedom along with that responsibility? Did colonial pamphleteers—and then men running around in fedoras with "press" tags—get special rights, so that now the law's main challenge is to draw a line between "legitimate" new media and a motley crew of celebri-tweeters and kitty bloggers? No, says Sentelle in his typically engaging manner, because the Press Clause protects a "method of communication" not a "privileged class of communicators"—the "dissemination of information or opinion by anyone, not just the institutional press."

We move then to the 2013–2014 term, starting with two articles on religious liberty, which came to the Court in very different ways. First we have the libertarian legal world's indomitable lion—and a member of our editorial board, and my former professor—Richard Epstein, with his characteristically unique take on *Burwell v. Hobby Lobby*. He first notes that this would've been a much different case had Obamacare's contraceptive mandate actually come from the text of the Affordable Care Act rather than in an implementing regulation. As it turned out, however, it became a fairly simple exercise in interpreting the Religious Freedom Restoration Act.[7] Epstein thinks that the Supreme Court got this case right, but for the wrong reason: after finding that the mandate imposed a substantial burden on religious exercise, the Court should've considered whether the government nevertheless advanced a compelling interest—rather than assuming that it did—before moving to the question of whether it had used the least-restrictive means to achieve it. He writes that Justice Alito's "intellectual mistake was to think that it is possible to leap from the first to the third question under RFRA without addressing this middle question."

Then we have Eric Rassbach of the Becket Fund for Religious Liberty, who contributes a fascinating article on the Court's rediscovery of historical analysis in its interpretation of the constitutional prohibition on the government's "establishment" of religion. He writes this in the context of *Town of Greece v. Galloway*, the term's legislative-prayer case. The Court's Establishment Clause jurisprudence has

---

[7] I've said all along that this case wasn't that big a deal, at least not for legal doctrine—or Obamacare, for that matter, let alone for "women's rights," since access to birth control was never in question—but instead was a straightforward application of a clear statute. See David H. Gans & Ilya Shapiro, Religious Liberties for Corporations? Hobby Lobby, the Affordable Care Act, and the Constitution? (forthcoming 2014).

long been muddled, but "the process of historical examination that *Town of Greece* has set in motion will continue to reshape how these cases are decided for years to come." Indeed, municipalities' ability to continue opening sessions with invocations is but the smallest consequence of the Court's ruling. Lower courts will now have to "look for historical support (or lack thereof) for particular government practices." This is a healthy development because, instead of forcing judges "into the uncomfortable and irreducibly subjective role of psychological representative of society, the historical approach gives judges objective facts to work with."

Staying within the First Amendment but moving to the Free Speech Clause, newlywed Allen Dickerson of the Center for Competitive Politics analyzes *McCutcheon v. FEC*. While exercised progressives painted this campaign finance case as *Citizens United* redux, any observer who took a moment to read up on the case could see that it's actually the flip side of that misunderstood ruling. Instead of corporate/union/organizational interests, here we had an individual. Instead of independent spending on political speech of various kinds, here we had donations to candidates and parties. Moreover, this case didn't even challenge "base limits"—how much a donor can give to a particular candidate—but only "aggregate limits." In effect, why is it okay (not corrupting) to "max out" to 9 candidates but, once you start on the 10th, it's the end of the Republic? The Court struck down this illogical restriction, which Dickerson says is a "narrow" holding that "clarified that exacting scrutiny requires searching review that pays close attention to the 'fit' between the asserted government interest and Congress's policy choices."

Sticking with election regulation, the next article is under my byline, although I claim it on behalf of my colleagues and all that is true and beautiful. Let me explain: if you followed the Supreme Court this past year, you may have heard of a case involving an Ohio law that *sends you to jail for making "false statements" about politicians*. (As Dave Barry would say, I'm not making this up!) Even if you weren't following the Court, however, you may have heard of the "funniest brief ever" or the "best amicus brief ever." Well, that's where I take my (partial) credit. My brief, co-authored by Trevor Burrus and Gabriel Latner and joined by Cato's esteemed H.L. Mencken Research Fellow, one P.J. O'Rourke, defended truthiness, satire, and the American way of public discourse. Accordingly, instead of analyzing the case in any depth—it turned on rather technical issues of civil procedure—I provide a sketch of it followed by a reprint of the brief. It all goes to show that criminalizing political speech is no laughing matter.

In dealing with another kind of speech—"sidewalk counseling"—the Court provided another narrow holding in *McCullen v. Coakley*, the abortion-clinic buffer zone case. This is one of the notable cases this term where the justices were unanimous in judgment—here striking down a Massachusetts law—but starkly divided in reasoning. Our own Trevor Burrus tackles the case, with a rollicking historical examination of "injordinances," which are a combination of injunctions and ordinances that were originally applied to labor pickets during the Progressive Era and have since moved to modern culture wars. "An injordinance resembles a law in most regards—it is passed by a legislative body and is enforced through criminal sanctions against the general public—but it resembles an injunction in that it applies to specific places and proscribes specific conduct around that space." Regardless of whether you agree with Chief Justice Roberts's measured majority opinion or Justice Scalia's emperor-has-no-clothes ~~dissent~~ concurrence, there's much to learn at the intersection of First Amendment jurisprudence and injordinances used to ensure public safety.

Moving from protections against union pickets to protections against union compulsion, Jacob Huebert of the Illinois Policy Institute—and a year behind me in law school—covers *Harris v. Quinn*. *Harris* came out on the last day of term and was thus overshadowed by *Hobby Lobby*, but some years hence, when the contraceptive mandate is a footnote to the decade's political narrative, we could be talking about this case as the big one from the October Term 2013. Huebert rightly begins his essay by asking the fundamental question, "When can the government force someone to give money to a union to speak on his or her behalf?" The Court ruled that, when it comes to home health aides whose terms of employment are controlled by people they care for, the mere fact that their compensation comes from state Medicaid funds doesn't turn them into state employees who can be coerced into unionization. While Justice Alito's magisterial opinion left in place the 1977 case of *Abood v. Detroit Board of Education*—which enables the compulsion of public-sector employees in states that go in for that sort of thing—it cast as much doubt on its logic as possible without overruling it.

Another constitutional case affecting labor relations was *National Labor Relations Board v. Noel Canning*, a challenge to President Obama's purported use of his recess-appointment power in the context of three NLRB nominations in January 2012, when the Senate didn't consider itself to be in recess. A member of Jones Day's victorious legal team in that case, Bryan Leitch, presents a tour de force of legal scholarship and litigation strategy. The Supreme Court unanimously found executive excess here, albeit again with a blistering Scalia concurrence—which he read from the bench!—about the majority's theory of the executive's "acquiring power by adverse possession." "Going beyond the propriety of one presidential action," Leitch writes, "*Noel Canning* highlighted important jurisprudential debates and brought to the fore the intricate institutional relationships among the federal branches—illustrating the ways in which the Constitution advantages and disadvantages each in the performance of its essential functions."

Next comes George Mason law professor David Bernstein, another member of our editorial board, with a characteristically provocative exposé of a case that provoked great emotions on both sides. Bernstein's title bears noting: "'Reverse *Carolene Products*,' the End of the Second Reconstruction, and Other Thoughts on *Schuette v. Coalition to Defend Affirmative Action*." There's a lot to unpack in this article, which challenges the conventional wisdom about whether and when it might be appropriate to use race in university admissions and other areas of public policy. Indeed, it even challenges what "race" is and whether the Supreme Court doctrines that have arisen to protect the supposed political interests of racial minorities actually do the reverse. "The political process doctrine has become entirely unstable," he explains, "both because of a huge decline since the 1960s in racist attitudes by whites and because issues have changed from rectifying overt racial discrimination to more complex social policies."

Cato senior fellow Nicholas Quinn Rosenkranz, whose day job is as a Georgetown law professor, contributes an essay analyzing *Bond v. United States*—that typical case of federalism, adultery, and chemical weapons. This is the second time that *Bond* has come before the Court and the second time that the government's position has lost unanimously. It was Rosenkranz's scholarship that planted the seed for this case, which challenged the idea that the federal government could gain extra powers—beyond those constitutionally enumerated—pursuant to a duly ratified treaty. Chief Justice Roberts, writing for the majority, didn't go so far as to reject that principle or cabin its application. Instead he rewrote the statute at issue such that Mrs. Bond's use of chemicals was a tax beyond its reach. Justices Scalia, Thomas, and Alito would've gone further and struck down the law on constitutional grounds. As Rosenkranz puts it, their "powerful concurrences went unanswered, and they may well provide a roadmap in a future case."

Our final article about the term just past concerns yet another unanimous ruling, this one without multiple opinions splintering the unified judgment. In a bout of refreshing boldness, the Court held in *Riley v. California* that police can't automatically search the digital contents of a cell phone seized from an arrested suspect. Mayer Brown's Andrew Pincus explains that the "Court refused simply to extend to this new technology the exception to the Fourth Amendment's general requirement of a warrant based on probable cause that had been developed in the pre-digital era." Instead it looked to the "practical, real-world intrusion on long-standing legitimate privacy expectations that would result from taking that step and [rejected] the less-protective standard developed for the pre-digital environment." Pincus runs through the Court's major recent decisions regarding new technologies and concludes that the justices have "charted a course . . . to safeguard Americans' privacy against arbitrary invasion through abuse of government power."

The volume concludes with a look ahead to October Term 2014 by Miguel Estrada and Ashley Boizelle, who are appellate lawyers at the Washington office of Gibson, Dunn & Crutcher. As of this writing, the Court has 39 cases on its docket, down from last year but on par with recent practice, such that we can expect about 75 opinions at term's end. Here are some of the issues: whether a police officer's mistaken belief that someone had committed a traffic violation can form the basis for a lawful search (*Heien v. North Carolina*); whether a prison can prohibit a Muslim inmate from growing a beard (*Holt v. Hobbs*); whether a fisherman can be prosecuted under Sarbanes-Oxley's record-keeping provision for throwing undersized fish overboard (*Yates v. United States*) (again, not making this up); whether Congress can force the State Department to recognize Jerusalem as part of Israel on U.S. passports (*Zivotovsky v. Kerry*); and the circumstances under which criminal charges can attach to Facebook posts

(*Elonis v. United States*). These cases don't yet reach the high profile of recent terms, but if the Court takes up one of the same-sex marriage or Obamacare lawsuits now at its doorstep, all bets are off. As Estrada and Boizelle conclude, "after a 2013 term that featured several controversial decisions and kept commentators on their toes, all eyes will be on the Court again in October."

*   *   *

This is the seventh volume of the *Cato Supreme Court Review* that I have edited, which means that, for good or ill, I've now been responsible for a majority of the volumes. I'll take all the credit but am happy to share the blame with many people. I first need to thank our authors, without whom there would literally be nothing to edit or read. My gratitude also goes to my colleagues Trevor Burrus, Bob Levy, Tim Lynch, and Walter Olson, who provide valuable counsel and editing in legal areas in which I can't even feign expertise. I joke that research associate Jonathan Blanks "makes the trains run on time" in Cato's Center for Constitutional Studies, but he really does more than that for the *Review*, including many steps in the process that I'm sure I've forgotten about. Jon makes all of us look good and, most importantly, keeps track of legal associates Julio Colomba (making his second appearance in these acknowledgments) and Olivia Grady, along with interns Jack Bussell and Carolyn Iodice—who in turn performed many thankless tasks without complaint. Neither the *Review* nor our Constitution Day symposium would be possible without them.

Finally, thanks to Roger Pilon, the founder of Cato's Center for Constitutional Studies, who I know is pleased with how this journal has turned out so many years after he created it. Roger has advanced liberty and constitutionalism for longer than I've been alive, and I've benefited greatly from the high standard of excellence he's set on those fronts. He's also a *mensch*.

I reiterate our hope that this collection of essays will secure and advance the Madisonian first principles of our Constitution, giving renewed voice to the Framers' fervent wish that we have a government of laws and not of men. In so doing, we hope also to do justice to a rich legal tradition in which judges, politicians, and ordinary citizens alike understand that the Constitution reflects and protects the natural rights of life, liberty, and property, and serves as a bulwark against the abuse of government power. In these heady times when the People are beginning to demand an end to unconstitutional government actions and expansions of various kinds, it's more important than ever to remember our proud roots in the Enlightenment tradition.

We hope you enjoy this 13th volume of the *Cato Supreme Court Review*.

Freedom of the Press: A Liberty for All or a Privilege for a Few?

David B. Sentelle*

I. Introduction

On the 17th of September, 1787, the Constitutional Convention sent forth a proposed Constitution that became recognized over the ages as the greatest governing document in the history of the world, providing for liberty and equality. It contained in it a provision that "no Title of Nobility shall be granted by the United States."[1] The original Constitution did not provide enough protection for liberty and equality to satisfy some Americans of the day. Two years and eight days later, the new Congress transmitted to the state legislatures 12 proposed amendments, 10 of which were ratified, effective December 15, 1791. The Fifth Amendment provided for the protection of "due process of law," which is generally recognized as containing an equal protection concept to protect against the unequal operation of federal law, comparable to the protection against the unequal operation of state law later provided by the Fourteenth Amendment.[2]

More directly on point with our subject, the First Amendment to the Constitution provided:

> Congress shall make no law respecting an establishment of religion, or prohibiting the free exercise thereof; or abridging the freedom of speech, or of the press, or the right of the people

*Senior Judge, U.S. Court of Appeals for the D.C. Circuit. This is the 12th annual B. Kenneth Simon Lecture in Constitutional Thought, delivered at the Cato Institute on September 17, 2013. I wish to acknowledge my reliance on the research and writings of Eugene Volokh and the assistance provided by my former law clerk, Christopher Mills.

[1] U.S. Const. art. I, § 9, cl. 8.

[2] See, e.g., Bolling v. Sharpe, 347 U.S. 497, 498 (1954); see also United States v. Windsor, 133 S. Ct. 2675, 2693 (2013).

peaceably to assemble, and to petition the Government for a
redress of grievances.

In this great amendment, the Framers and ratifiers of the Constitution provided for what has become known as the five freedoms: that is, the freedoms of speech, press, religion, petition, and assembly. The question we address today is to whom does the Constitution afford these freedoms, or at least one of them.

Omitting the one as to which a question may have arisen, let us examine the other four. First, as to speech: while the time, place, and manner of speech may be restricted, freedom of speech belongs to every person within the jurisdiction of the United States or the states. This view, as set forth by Justice Louis Brandeis's concurrence in *Whitney v. California*,[3] springs from the proposition that under the First Amendment, "the public has a right to every man's views and every man the right to speak them."[4] While some cases may have cast doubt on that proposition, including *American Communications Association*, in the end it is generally accepted that every person—to abandon what might now be sexist language—has the same protection for free speech as any other.

As to freedom of religion: the constitutional protection of religious liberty extends not only to the professional clergy or to adherents of majority faiths, but "liberty and social stability demand a religious tolerance that respects the religious views of all citizens."[5] The Free Exercise Clause provides and protects religious freedom not only for the adherents of majority religions but even for the practitioners of rituals that "may seem abhorrent to some."[6] The Supreme Court has expressly stated that "religious beliefs need not be acceptable, logical, consistent, or comprehensible to others in order to merit First Amendment protection."[7] Unquestionably, the Free Exercise Clause provides religious liberty to all, not to a favored class.

---

[3] 274 U.S. 357, 373 (1927).

[4] American Commc'ns Ass'n v. Douds, 339 U.S. 382, 395 (1950) (citing Whitney at 373) (Brandeis, J., concurring).

[5] McCreary County, Ky. v. ACLU of Ky., 545 U.S. 844, 860 (2005) (quoting Zelman v. Simmons-Harris, 536 U.S. 639, 718 (2002) (Breyer, J., dissenting)).

[6] Church of Lukumi Babalu Aye, Inc. v. City of Hialeah, 508 U.S. 520, 531 (1993).

[7] Thomas v. Review Bd. of Indiana Emp't Sec. Div., 450 U.S. 707, 714 (1981).

Freedom to petition: Like the other clauses, the clause of the First Amendment protecting the right to petition for a redress of grievances extends to all. As the Supreme Court has recently reminded us, "the First Amendment protects the right of [even] corporations to petition legislative and administrative bodies."[8]

Freedom of assembly: Again, the First Amendment protects the freedom of all to assemble. In *NAACP v. Alabama*, the Supreme Court recognized the availability of that protection to all without regard to the assemblers' identities.[9] They did not need to be members of any particular group. Indeed, the Freedom of Assembly Clause protects those who wish to assemble in privacy and with anonymity. The freedom of assembly belongs to all.

And yet in the face of all this evidence of egalitarianism and the protection of universal right, there is an insistence among some that the First Amendment, by providing that "Congress shall make no law . . . abridging the freedom . . . of the press," created a special class *of privileged persons bearing the noble title* "the press," and not equal protection for everyone who uses a communication method known as "the press"—protection paralleling the freedom of speech afforded to all by the two words that are separated from "the press" by only a comma.

Of course, the first question in determining whether "the press" refers to a method of communication or a privileged class of communicators is: What did the Framers intend in the adoption of the Bill of Rights? The First Amendment, along with the rest of the Bill of Rights, was added to the Constitution after the Anti-Federalists objected to the absence of such a listing of rights in the original Constitution. One of the Anti-Federalist objections was captured well by James Lincoln, a delegate to the South Carolina Convention that considered the Constitution in 1788. Lincoln, from the town of Ninety Six, South Carolina, stood to ask why the freedom of the press was not guaranteed in the Constitution, memorably stating, "The liberty of the press was the tyrant's scourge—it was the true friend and firmest supporter of civil liberty; therefore why pass it

---

[8] Citizens United v. FEC, 558 U.S. 310, 355 (2010) (quoting First Nat'l Bank of Boston v. Bellotti, 435 U.S. 765, 792 n.31 (1978)).

[9] 357 U.S. 449 (1958).

by in silence?"[10] The Federalists eventually agreed to the adoption of the Bill of Rights, passing a First Amendment that proscribes laws "abridging the freedom of speech, or of the press."

So what does the phrase "the press" refer to in the First Amendment? The first conception is that "the press" refers to the media as an institution, a type of fourth branch that provides an independent check on the three branches of government. The most famous expositor of this view was Justice Potter Stewart. Justice Stewart explained his view in a 1974 lecture at Yale Law School. According to Justice Stewart:

> [T]he Free Press Clause extends protection to an institution. The publishing business is, in short, the only organized private business that is given explicit constitutional protection. This basic understanding is essential, I think, to avoid an elementary error of constitutional law. It is tempting to suggest that freedom of the press means only that newspaper publishers are guaranteed freedom of expression. They *are* guaranteed that freedom, to be sure, but so are we all, because of the Free Speech Clause. If the Free Press guarantee meant no more than freedom of expression, it would be a constitutional redundancy. Between 1776 and the drafting of our Constitution, many of the state constitutions contained clauses protecting freedom of the press while at the same time recognizing no general freedom of speech. By including both guarantees in the First Amendment, the Founders quite clearly recognized the distinction between the two. . . . In setting up the three branches of the Federal Government, the Founders deliberately created an internally competitive system. . . . The primary purpose of the constitutional guarantee of a free press was a similar one: to create a fourth institution outside the Government as an additional check on the three official branches. . . . The relevant metaphor, I think, is the metaphor of the Fourth Estate.[11]

The second conception is that "the press" refers to the press as a medium of communication. Under this interpretation, the freedom of the press protects all individuals' written expression and is

---

[10] 4 Jonathan Elliot, The Debates in the Several State Conventions on the Adoption of the Federal Constitution 314 (1876).

[11] Potter Stewart, Or of the Press, 26 Hastings L.J. 631, 633–34 (1975), reprinted in 50 Hastings L.J. 705 (1999) (emphasis added).

complementary to the freedom of speech. A well-known expositor of this view was Chief Justice Warren Burger, who wrote in response to the press-as-institution view:

> I perceive two fundamental difficulties with a narrow reading of the Press Clause. First, although certainty on this point is not possible, the history of the Clause does not suggest that the authors contemplated a "special" or "institutional" privilege. . . . [M]ost pre-First Amendment commentators "who employed the term 'freedom of speech' with great frequency, used it synonymously with freedom of the press." . . . Those interpreting the Press Clause as extending protection only to, or creating a special role for, the "institutional press" must either (a) assert such an intention on the part of the Framers for which no supporting evidence is available . . . ; (b) argue that events after 1791 somehow operated to "constitutionalize" this interpretation . . . ; or (c) candidly acknowledging the absence of historical support, suggest that the intent of the Framers is not important today. . . . The second fundamental difficulty with interpreting the Press Clause as conferring special status on a limited group is one of definition. . . . The very task of including some entities within the "institutional press" while excluding others, whether undertaken by legislature, court, or administrative agency, is reminiscent of the abhorred licensing system of Tudor and Stuart England—a system the First Amendment was intended to ban from this country. . . . In short, the First Amendment does not "belong" to any definable category of persons or entities: It belongs to all who exercise its freedoms.[12]

Perhaps it is this problem of definition raised by Chief Justice Burger that best illustrates the difficulty with the proposition that the freedom of the press protects a class of persons rather than all persons. Such a view raises the question: Who will define the class? Does it not seem at least passing strange that a Constitution that explicitly refuses to establish a religion would at the same time establish a professional class? Does it not seem at least passing strange that such a Constitution would afford the right to every citizen to express his or her views in speech, but at the moment that the citizen chose to commit those thoughts to writing, that constitutional protection

---

[12] Bellotti, 435 U.S. at 798–802 (Burger, C.J., concurring).

would vanish unless the speaker/writer belonged to the privileged profession?

I will interrupt the flow of my remarks on this subject to add that I am aware that the Congress is currently considering this definitional problem under the rubric of a shield statute. As to that, I will only say that I am not here to address the statutory problem, but only the constitutional problem. Back to my original topic.

Various justices and commentators have echoed Burger's concern with how we would define the press if we adopt the press-as-institution interpretation. In *Dun & Bradstreet, Inc. v. Greenmoss Builders, Inc.*, Justice William Brennan, joined in dissent by Justices Thurgood Marshall, Harry Blackmun, and John Paul Stevens, rejected the view that the Free Press Clause is limited to "media" entities because it is "irreconcilable" with First Amendment principles that protect speech, regardless of its origin, and because it would be impossible to define "media" entities.[13] Justice Byron White concurred with the dissent on this point, and the plurality did not reject it, turning its decision instead on the distinction between libelous speech on matters of private concern and libelous speech on matters of public concern.

The class-definition problem created by the press-as-institution interpretation underscores its erroneous nature. It would seem axiomatic that "the First Amendment . . . creates 'an open marketplace' in which differing ideas about political, economic, and social issues can compete freely for public acceptance without government interference."[14] Indeed, the protection of political speech has been repeatedly described by the Supreme Court as the core of the First Amendment.[15] How then is it consistent with First Amendment values to entrust the determination of the scope of free-press protection to the political entities the Framers hoped citizens would be free to criticize, challenge, or advise? How would such an allocation of protection proceed?

---

[13] 472 U.S. 749, 782–83 (1985).

[14] Knox v. SEIU, Local 1000, 132 S. Ct. 2277, 2288 (2012) (quoting New York State Bd. of Elections v. Lopez-Torres, 552 U.S. 196, 202 (2008)).

[15] See, e.g., Brown v. Hartlage, 456 U.S. 45, 52 (1982) ("At the core of the First Amendment are certain basic conceptions about the manner in which political discussion in a representative democracy should proceed.").

Would Congress, or some new undersecretary of the press, decide who is entitled to this press freedom? Could the president make a recess appointment to the official press? This definitional problem poses an insurmountable hurdle to the press-as-institution interpretation.

Before I go further, it is important to note that this debate is not merely academic. For example, recently the North Carolina Board of Dietetics/Nutrition threatened to send a blogger to jail for describing his battle against diabetes and encouraging others to use his diet and lifestyle as an example.[16] The blogger used his website to describe his experience on the "paleo" diet, which apparently is also known as the "caveman" or "hunter-gatherer" diet. On every page of his blog, he includes these words: "I am not a doctor, dietitian, nor nutritionist . . . in fact I have no medical training of any kind."[17] Yet the board conducted a line-by-line red-ink review of the blog site, citing specific words and phrases as impermissible and telling him to remove those lines on penalty of jail.[18] For instance, the board objected to the blogger's providing his daily meal plan on the ground that non-licensed individuals cannot recommend diets to others. According to the board, the blogger "has a First Amendment right to blog about his diet, but he can't encourage others to adopt it unless the state has certified him as a dietitian or nutritionist."[19] The board's director also explained that it would be less likely to prosecute a writer who blogs about vegetarian diets "because a vegetarian is not really like a medical diet."[20] Apparently, the hunter-gathers came up with a medical diet long before penicillin was discovered.

Now, I don't know much about caveman diets, or dinosaur diets, or any other diets, for that matter. But I do know that the North Carolina Board's licensing requirements as applied to this public blog sound suspiciously like the "abhorred" press licensing requirements of old

[16] See Sara Burrows, State Threatens to Shut Down Nutrition Blogger, Carolina Journal, Apr. 23, 2012, available at http://www.carolinajournal.com/exclusives/display_exclusive.html?id=8992.

[17] Id.

[18] See N.C. Bd. of Dietetics/Nutrition Comments on Diabetes-Warrior.net Website, available at http://www.diabetes-warrior.net/wp-content/uploads/2012/01/Website_Review_Cooksey_Jan._2012.pdf.

[19] Burrows, *supra* n. 16.

[20] Id.

England that Chief Justice Burger mentioned. And unless the North Carolina Board has threatened the authors of many of the books on the Amazon bestseller list, the board seems to be applying a different standard to bloggers who write about diets than it does to "professional" authors who write about diets.

The blogger sued in the Western District of North Carolina. After the district court dismissed his claims on justiciability grounds, he appealed to the U.S. Court of Appeals for the Fourth Circuit, represented by the Institute for Justice and supported by amicus American Civil Liberties Union. The Fourth Circuit determined, rightly, that the claims should have been analyzed "under the First Amendment standing framework."[21] A Fourth Circuit panel that included the Honorable Sandra Day O'Connor, sitting by designation, determined that his claim was indeed justiciable and ripe, and remanded the case for appropriate consideration of his First Amendment claims.

While properly analyzing the First Amendment framework, the *Cooksey* decision *sub silentio* highlights another issue. The *Cooksey* panel generally analyzed the blogger's communications under a freedom of speech analysis without distinguishing freedom of the press. This highlights the fact that analysis of freedom of the press involves not only a determination of who enjoys the freedom, but also what means of communication are covered. That is, is the internet (and for that matter, television) a medium for exercising freedom of the press or freedom of speech or what? If we consider freedom of the press to protect all communication rather than the privilege given an institution, it doesn't matter much. If we consider it to protect the activities of a certain class, then it does matter. Under the institutional view, if the blogger not only communicated through the internet but either he or a follower printed out his blog and distributed the printed copies, then the protection would extend to him only if he were in the employ of the *New York Times* or some other representative of the established media but would vanish if he were not.

Back to the general proposition that under the First Amendment, the Constitution protects bad ideas as well as good, for only through the competition of ideas can we determine which ideas are in fact "good." As Justice Oliver Wendell Holmes famously said, "the ultimate good desired is better reached by free trade in ideas[, for] . . .

---

[21] Cooksey v. Futrell, 721 F.3d 226 (4th Cir. 2013).

the best test of truth is the power of the thought to get itself accepted in the competition of the market."[22] The question we confront today is whether it also protects all the purveyors of those ideas, regardless of their identity or affiliation with the elite media.

II. "The Press" as Originally Understood

As I noted earlier, our basic goal is to determine the original meaning of the Constitution's press protections. The press-as-an-institutional-elite view is inconsistent with the original public meaning of the First Amendment. History supports Chief Justice Burger's view of freedom of the press as extending to all citizens. In the late 18th century, state supreme courts, state constitutions, and commentators uniformly referred to "every man" or "every freeman" or "every citizen's" expressive rights, usually using words like those in the Kentucky Constitution of 1792: "[E]very citizen may freely speak, write, and print on any subject, being responsible for the abuse of that liberty."[23] As the Pennsylvania Constitution of 1776 shows, freedom of the press described the individual rights of writing and publishing: "That the people have a right to freedom of speech, and of writing, and publishing their sentiments: therefore the freedom of the press ought not to be restrained."[24]

Noah Webster's 1828 dictionary defined, under the word "press," the "[l]iberty of the press, in civil policy" as "the free right of publishing books, pamphlets or papers without previous restraint; or the unrestrained right which every citizen enjoys of publishing his thoughts and opinions, subject only to punishment for publishing what is pernicious to morals or to the peace of the state."[25] Justice Joseph Story, in his famed *Commentaries on the Constitution*, described the First Amendment as providing that "every man shall have a right to speak, write, and print his opinions upon any subject whatsoever, without any prior restraint, so always, that he does not injure any

---

[22] Abrams v. United States, 250 U.S. 616, 630 (1919) (Holmes, J., dissenting).

[23] Ky. Const. of 1792, art. XII, § 7. See generally Eugene Volokh, Freedom for the Press as an Industry, or for the Press as a Technology? From the Framing to Today, 160 U. Pa. L. Rev. 459, 466–68 (2012).

[24] Pa. Const. of 1776, ch. I, para. 12.

[25] 2 American Dictionary of the English Language 333 (1828) (reprinted 1970).

other person."[26] The original meaning of "the press," then, was not limited to an institution called "the press."[27]

The idea that the freedom of the press was intended to protect a right of all people is consistent with the structure of the publishing industry in the late 18th century. There were no large media conglomerates and few journalists as we now conceive of them. But there were individual authors who paid independent printers to print their pamphlets and small newspapers.[28] "[P]amphlets were written by amateur writers who held other occupations as lawyers, ministers, merchants, or planters."[29]

For instance, one of the most successful uses of a printing press in America at the Founding—and indeed in all of our history—was Thomas Paine's pamphlet *Common Sense*. Paine paid a printer to print the pamphlet anonymously and then donated all proceeds and his copyright to the United States for the cause of independence.[30] At the time, Paine was certainly not a member of any institutional press. He was by trade an excise officer and later a bridge designer. Yet his 1809 biographer wrote that *Common Sense* was entirely "unexampled in the history of the press."[31] Thomas Paine was exercising his freedom of the press, even though he was no professional newsman.

The same is conspicuously true of James Madison, Alexander Hamilton, and John Jay, who published *The Federalist Papers* anonymously in various newspapers. They were not part of an institutional press at the time of the Founding. Just try to imagine it. George Washington, holding a press conference before the White House Press Corps' precursor. "Any questions?" "Yes, this is James Madis . . . er, Publius. "What will be your response to the Whiskey Rebellion?" "No

---

[26] 3 Joseph Story, Commentaries on the Constitution of the United States 732 (1st ed. 1833).

[27] If freedom of the press applied only to the elite, Matt Drudge might still be just a guy with an old hat living in his mom's basement, unless, of course, he could scrape together enough to buy a newspaper and proclaim himself part of "the press."

[28] See McIntyre v. Ohio Elections Comm'n, 514 U.S. 334, 360 (1995) (Thomas, J., concurring in the judgment).

[29] Edward Lee, Freedom of the Press 2.0, 42 Ga. L. Rev. 309, 341 (2008) (internal quotation marks omitted).

[30] 1 Moncure Daniel Conway, The Life of Thomas Paine 69–70 (1892) ("[P]eace f[ound] him a penniless patriot, who might easily have had fifty thousand pounds in his pocket.").

[31] *Id.* at 64.

comment. Next question? Brutus? You're awfully quiet today . . . ." It is inconceivable that the ratifying public would have thought that *Common Sense* and *The Federalist Papers* would not be covered by the freedom of the press.

The proposition that freedom of the press does not create a privileged profession is not at all intended to disparage, but rather to underline the importance of that First Amendment protection. The Framers knew full well the dangers against which they were protecting. In the late 17th century, it was a crime in England to publish news without first obtaining a license; "[w]hether the news was true or false, of praise or censure, was immaterial."[32] "[A]uthors and printers of obnoxious works were hung, quartered, mutilated, exposed in the pillory, flogged, or simply fined and imprisoned, according to the temper of the judges; and the works themselves were burned by the common hangman."[33] This law was followed by the Stamp Act, which placed a duty on all newspapers and advertisements. *According to James Madison, the First Amendment's freedom of the press was understood to forbid precisely these types of laws that imposed prior restraints on publications or imposed ex post penalties on them.*[34]

In England, such laws had been regularly applied against individual printers and writers, not just some institutional press.[35] In fact, the strongest opposition to the free press in England came from the governing classes—in other words, the elite.[36] The idea that the First Amendment, then, was designed to protect only the institutional elite has it backwards.

The history of press regulation in the American colonies also reveals early prosecutions that provide support for Burger's interpretation. One printer was arrested in Virginia for publishing the laws

---

[32] Edward Hudon, Freedom of Speech and Press in America 11 (1963).

[33] *Id.* (internal quotation marks omitted).

[34] See 4 Elliot, *supra* n. 10, at 569–70, reprinted from James Madison, Report on the Virginia Resolutions to the House of Delegates (1800) ("This security of the freedom of the press requires that it should be exempt, not only from previous restraint of the executive, as in Great Britain, but from legislative restraint also; and this exemption, to be effectual, must be an exemption, not only from the previous inspection of licensers, but from the subsequent penalty of laws.").

[35] See Hudon, *supra* n. 32, at 10–12; see also Volokh, *supra* n. 23, at 484–88.

[36] See Hudon, *supra* n. 32, at 11.

of that colony without having an appropriate license. (Perhaps he should have read the laws before printing them.) The colonial governor of Virginia a few years prior had expressed the following sentiment: "I thank God, we have no free schools nor printing; and I hope we shall not have these hundred years; for learning has brought disobedience and heresy and sects into the world."[37]

The first newspaper in the colonies was suppressed after its first issue because it mentioned the Indian Wars, raising the question, at what point does printing make one part of the institutional press? If the press-as-institution view prevails, is the printer of a first edition of a newspaper or periodical part of that institutional press or just an aspirant? If not a member, then how many issues does the printer have to issue before being admitted into the protected class? If one issue is enough, then might we not as well go back to Burger's view that the freedom of the press protects everyone who seeks to circulate a view or a report, not just those who do so at some recognized professional level? Given the early prosecutions of individual authors and printers, and the First Amendment's role in preventing such prosecutions, it seems implausible that the "freedom of the press" would apply only to an institutional press. Indeed, the earliest First Amendment cases nowhere suggest that the freedom of the press was so limited, for they apply the freedom of the press to individual writers and printers.[38]

The Supreme Court has held that "The inherent worth of the speech in terms of its capacity for informing the public does not depend upon the identity of its source, whether corporation, association, union, or individual."[39] The same value adheres to written expression, which serves to inform the public no matter its source. In other words, we do not change "freedom of the press" depending on the source's characteristics, its subscribers, or its ratings. Someone at CNN should breathe a sigh of relief.

The grammatical structure of the First Amendment also confirms Burger's interpretation of "the press" as written dissemination of information or opinion by anyone, not just the institutional press. It makes sense that the amendment, which refers to "the freedom of

---

[37] *Id.* at 18.

[38] See Volokh, *supra* n. 23, at 489–98.

[39] Bellotti, 435 U.S. at 777.

speech, or of the press" within the same clause, would extend both rights to everyone who might speak or write. Adopting the press-as-institution interpretation would require the strange assumption that the Framers used "speech" and "press" much differently—one to categorize the type of freedom protected and one to delineate the persons protected by a freedom. Given the history of contemporaneous constitutions protecting every citizen's "right to speak, to write, or to publish," this assumption, required by the press-as-institution view, seems even more strange. Justice Antonin Scalia calls attention to this strangeness in his concurrence in *Citizens United*. "It is passing strange to interpret the phrase 'the freedom of speech, or of the press' to mean, not everyone's right to speak or publish, but rather everyone's right to speak or the institutional press's right to publish."[40]

A potential objection to Burger's interpretation of "the press" is that it would render the freedom of the press superfluous, for anything it protects would already be protected by the freedom of speech. Burger answers this objection by providing some historical context:

> The Speech Clause standing alone may be viewed as a protection of the liberty to express ideas and beliefs, while the Press Clause focuses specifically on the liberty to disseminate expression broadly and "comprehends every sort of publication which affords a vehicle of information and opinion." *Lovell v. Griffin*, 303 U.S. 444, 452 (1938). Yet there is no fundamental distinction between expression and dissemination. The liberty encompassed by the Press Clause, although complementary to and a natural extension of Speech Clause liberty, merited special mention simply because it had been more often the object of official restraints. Soon after the invention of the printing press, English and continental monarchs, fearful of the power implicit in its use and the threat to Establishment thought and order—political and religious—devised restraints, such as licensing, censors, indices of prohibited books, and prosecutions for seditious libel, which generally were unknown in the pre-printing press era. Official restrictions were the official response to the new, disquieting idea that this invention would provide a means for mass communication.[41]

---

[40] Citizens United, 558 U.S. at 390 n.6 (Scalia, J., concurring).

[41] Bellotti, 435 U.S. at 799–801 (Burger, C.J., concurring).

It may well be that we have erred in dividing the Speech and Press Clauses. In the First Amendment, it reads as one clause: "the freedom of speech, or of the press." When we read this complete clause as protecting the individual right to disseminate ideas to the public, it makes sense that the Framers would have included the complementary concepts of speaking and writing. It is unlikely that the public in 1791 understood the "freedom of speech" in the broad way that we understand it today, and therefore it would have been perfectly sensible to explicitly protect both spoken expression and written expression in the First Amendment.[42]

In fact, of speech and press, the Founding generation more often emphasized the freedom of the press than the freedom of speech. Of course, this is reversed today: a recent poll found that 47 percent of Americans named freedom of speech as their most important freedom, while 1 percent named freedom of the press.[43] Only 14 percent of Americans could even name freedom of the press as a freedom protected by the First Amendment.[44]

But to a Founding generation troubled by British regulation of the use of the printing press, the liberty of the press was conspicuously important. It was through the use of the printing press that Protestants spread the Reformation to change the face of religion in Europe. It was the printing press that enabled Thomas Paine to reach a vast proportion of Americans living at the time with his pamphlet decrying British rule. It was with presses that the Federalists and Anti-Federalists conducted a widely followed debate on the merits of the new Constitution. In *Federalist No. 84*, Hamilton responds to the Anti-Federalist objection to the lack of a Bill of Rights in the Constitution. He discusses only one specific liberty, suggesting the importance placed on that liberty. That one liberty was the freedom of the press.[45]

Likewise, in 1774, the Continental Congress sent a letter to the inhabitants of Quebec attempting to enlist their support against the British. That was a year before we undertook a slight change in

---

[42] See Volokh, *supra* n. 23, at 477.

[43] First Amendment Center, State of the First Amendment: 2013, at 2 (July 2013), available at http://www.firstamendmentcenter.org/madison/wp-content/uploads/2013/07/SOFA-2013-final-report.pdf.

[44] *Id.* at 3.

[45] See The Federalist No. 84, at 513–14 (Clinton Rossiter ed., 2003).

strategy and simply invaded our hesitant northern neighbor. The letter, which lauded various rights enjoyed by Americans, contained no mention of the freedom of speech, but it had quite a bit to say about the freedom of the press:

> The last right we shall mention regards the freedom of the press. The importance of this consists, besides the advancement of truth, science, morality, and arts in general, in its diffusion of liberal sentiments on the administration of Government, its ready communication of thoughts between subjects, and its consequential promotion of union among them, whereby oppressive officers are shamed or intimidated into more honorable and just modes of conducting affairs.[46]

Given the importance of the press at that time, it is no surprise to find written expression explicitly protected in the First Amendment. Further, the content of the appeal to the inhabitants of Quebec illustrates once more the extension of the protection of the freedom of the press not to a professional class, but to all who communicate through that technology. While we might perhaps think of the professional journalist as advancing truth, the advancement of "science, morality, and arts in general" suggests the products of a much larger body of communicators. Thus, it should be apparent that the freedom of the press protects not only newspaper personnel, but scientists, moralists, and all engaged in all arts.

But returning to the superfluity question, it seems most likely that the public would have understood "the press" to be referring to all writings, by all citizens, not just those by an elite group that did not even exist in 1791.[47]

[46] Appeal to the Inhabitants of Quebec, 1 Journals of the Continental Congress 105, 108 (1774).

[47] I have not attempted to catalog all of the cases from the early years of the Constitution in support of the definition of "the press" as referring to the means of communication rather than a privileged class. For further explication, I will again commend the exhaustive collection and analysis by Eugene Volokh in his article, Freedom for the Press as an Industry, or for the Press as a Technology? From the Framing to Today, 160 U. Pa. L. Rev. 459 (2012).

III. Applicability of "The Press" to Modern Technologies

Two further questions arise for the originalist who adopts the liberty-for-all interpretation of "the press." First, does the freedom of the press protect only the actual production of written material? Second, if "the press" refers to the printing press, does the freedom of the press also protect blogs and television and all the other forms of communication that do not originate from a printing press?

The answer to the first question is surely no, for the Supreme Court has consistently held that the freedom of the press protects more than the mere writing of a material.[48] As the Court has explained, the freedom of the press would be meaningless without the included rights to write, publish, and circulate. Thus, Justice Scalia wrote in *McConnell v. FEC*: "License printers, and it matters little whether authors are still free to write. Restrict the sale of books, and it matters little who prints them . . . . What good is the right to print books without a right to buy works from authors? Or the right to publish newspapers without the right to pay deliverymen?"[49]

The breadth of the activity protected by the First Amendment's freedom of the press does not suggest, however, that that freedom affords special protection to a universe of acts by members of the professional media that would not be protected if engaged in by others. It is the excessive claims of such protection that first brought the subject to the front of my mind. It has become commonplace for members of the professional media to suppose that their special freedom enjoyed as members of "the press" includes freedom from the obligation to answer subpoenas, testify in court, or put up with all sorts of other things that the common people must endure.

A few years ago in Washington, D.C., a special prosecutor was leading a grand jury investigation of the suspected unlawful disclosure by high government officials of the identity of a covert CIA agent. As part of the investigation, the grand jury issued subpoenas to a *New York Times* reporter named Judith Miller, along with

---

[48] See, e.g., Ex parte Jackson, 96 U.S. 727, 733 (1877) ("Liberty of circulating is as essential to th[e] freedom [of the press] as liberty of publishing; indeed, without the circulation, the publication would be of little value.").

[49] 540 U.S. 93, 251–52 (2003) (opinion of Scalia, J.).

a correspondent for *Time* and the corporate entity producing that magazine.[50] It was undisputed that Miller had obtained information concerning the identity of a high government official who had leaked the name of the CIA agent. Miller, however, refused to provide her evidence to the grand jury, claiming that her information had come from a confidential informant and arguing that the First Amendment freedom of the press created a privilege for reporters to maintain the confidentiality of their sources. A unanimous panel of the D.C. Circuit, consisting of myself, along with Judges Karen Henderson and David Tatel, rejected the proposition that the concept of the "freedom of the press" contemplates protection beyond those actions properly classified as the preparation and circulation of publications. I stand by that today.

Not only did Miller or any of her supporters fail to produce any historical evidence that the concept of a free press at the time of the Framing (or for that matter, long after) included a broad protection of activities that would be unprotected if conducted by anyone other than a professional journalist, but also, as we noted in the *Miller* case, this question was definitively answered by the Supreme Court in *Branzburg v. Hayes*.[51] In *Branzburg*, as in *Miller*, a journalist who concededly had knowledge of criminal activity resisted a subpoena under the claim that the First Amendment provided protection to a journalist against the revelation of his sources. As we later echoed in *Miller*, the Supreme Court held that there is no such protection within the concept of First Amendment freedom of the press. Justice Byron White, writing for the Court, declared that:

> It is clear that the First Amendment does not invalidate every incidental burdening of the press that may result from the enforcement of civil or criminal statutes of general applicability. Under prior cases, otherwise valid law serving substantial public interests may be enforced against the press as against others, despite the possible burden that may be imposed.[52]

---

[50] See In re Grand Jury Subpoena, Judith Miller, 438 F.3d 1141 (D.C. Cir. 2005). Although the other subpoenaed parties participated in the litigation, the relevant opinions principally address the rights claimed by Miller, and no other litigant raised any unique claim.

[51] 408 U.S. 665 (1972).

[52] *Id.* at 682–83.

Justice White went on to drive the point home: "The Court has emphasized that '[t]he publisher of a newspaper has no special immunity from the application of general laws. He has no special privilege to invade the rights and liberties of others.'"[53]

I cannot leave this discussion of *Branzburg* without recalling one other pithy quotation from Justice White's opinion for the majority: "[W]e cannot seriously entertain the notion that the First Amendment protects a newsman's agreement to conceal the criminal conduct of his source, or evidence thereof, on the theory that it is better to write about crime than to do something about it."[54]

In another case involving a claim to special rights for the institutional press, *Flynt v. Rumsfeld*, the publisher of *Hustler* magazine asserted "a First Amendment right for legitimate press representatives to travel with the military, and to be accommodated and otherwise facilitated by the military in their reporting efforts during combat."[55] We rejected that proposition, holding that "[t]here is nothing that we have found in the Constitution, American history, or our case law to support this claim."[56]

The plaintiff appellant in *Flynt* relied on *Richmond Newspapers, Inc. v. Virginia*, in which the Supreme Court recognized, in a plurality opinion, a constitutional right of access to criminal trials for the news media.[57] The plurality in *Richmond* did not recognize a special status of the press under the First Amendment standing alone, however, but grounded its decision in large part on the openness mandated by the "public trial" provisions of the Sixth Amendment. It was only after extended discussion of the open-trial concept that the Court "h[e]ld that the right to attend criminal trials is implicit in the guarantees of the First Amendment."[58] Even then, the Court went on in the same sentence to state that "without the freedom to attend such trials, which people have exercised for centuries, important aspects of freedom of *speech* and 'of the press could be eviscerated.'"[59] Thus,

---

[53] *Id.* at 683 (quoting Associated Press v. NLRB, 301 U.S. 103, 132–33 (1937)).

[54] *Id.* at 692.

[55] 355 F.3d 697, 703 (D.C. Cir. 2004).

[56] *Id.*

[57] 448 U.S. 555 (1980).

[58] *Id.* at 580.

[59] *Id.* (quoting Branzburg at 681) (emphasis added).

even the plurality in *Richmond Newspapers* did not accord a special right to the press as such, but only as representatives of the public, so that even in that case there is no recognition of a special class of persons more protected by freedom of the press than other persons. Admittedly, Justices Brennan and Marshall would have found the right of access to criminal proceedings in the First Amendment of its own force, but even they couched their concurrence in terms of a right of "First Amendment public access," rather than a special status for some specially privileged group called "the press."[60]

I turn now to the question concerning new technologies and the First Amendment. If we take as given that the Constitution means what the ratifying public would have originally understood its words to mean, perhaps the freedom of the press extends only to works produced by a printing press. Needless to say, the ratifying public in 1791 had no conception of iPads or computers or televisions. The question, then, is what does the originalist do when applying constitutional texts to new technologies. The answer is no different from our usual method of applying the Constitution: we determine how the technology fits into the text, sometimes by analogizing to the technology used in 1791. This issue often arises in the Fourth Amendment context, where the Court has applied the Fourth Amendment to dog sniffs, infrared scanners, and other devices unknown to the Founding generation. When the Constitution allocated war powers between the Congress and the executive, there was, of course, no air force. And yet the courts have had no difficulty in treating the president as "Commander in Chief of the Armed Forces," when the facts involved that branch of the service.[61]

In the First Amendment context, Chief Justice Charles Evans Hughes set out a relevant definition of "the press": "The press in its historic connotation comprehends every sort of publication which affords a vehicle of information and opinion."[62] Even the ratifying public probably did not consider the freedom of the press as being limited to works printed *on a printing press*. It strains credulity to suggest that people in 1791 would have considered the freedom of the press not to protect *handwritten* works as well.

[60] *Id.* at 597 (Brennan, J., concurring).

[61] See, e.g., Reid v. Covert, 354 U.S. 1, 38 (1957).

[62] Lovell v. City of Griffin, 303 U.S. 444, 452 (1938).

In 1769, Blackstone wrote that "[e]very freeman has an undoubted right to lay what sentiments he pleases before the public; to forbid this, is to destroy the freedom of the press."[63] Therefore, as Chief Justice Burger wrote, "It is not strange that 'press,' the word for what was then the sole means of broad dissemination of ideas and news, would be used to describe the freedom to communicate with a large, unseen audience."[64] The extension of "the press" to include new forms of communication recognizes that the freedoms of speech and press are complementary ideas contained in the same clause of the First Amendment and serve together to protect an individual right to disseminate ideas. Thus, protecting online posts, on-air statements, and other new forms of publishing technology is consistent with an originalist interpretation of the First Amendment. These new technologies make it even easier for all citizens to exercise their "freedom of the press," ensuring that it remains the "true friend and firmest support of civil liberty" in these United States.

In closing, I recall that in the wake of the Judith Miller decision, Joel Roberts of CBS stated that "[t]o read the other two judges [Sentelle and Henderson], you might think that journalists have the same First Amendment protections as sock puppets."[65] Since both Judge Henderson and I had written in the firm belief that journalists have the same First Amendment protections as all other Americans, the opinion of the CBS newsman must be that not only do the nobles of "the press" have special rights, but also that the rest of us are nothing but sock puppets. So I will end with a comment directed toward Mr. Roberts, CBS, and their colleagues: The inclusion of the words "the press" in the First Amendment does not confer upon you a title of nobility. You have the protection of the rights encompassed in the First Amendment, but so do the rest of us. You are not nobles, and we are not sock puppets.

---

[63] 4 William Blackstone, Commentaries *151.

[64] Bellotti, 435 U.S. at 800 n.5.

[65] Joel Roberts, Punishing Good Journalists, CBS News, February 16, 2005, available at www.cbsnews.com/news/punishing-good-journalists.

The Defeat of the Contraceptive Mandate in *Hobby Lobby*: Right Results, Wrong Reasons

*Richard A. Epstein**

Last But By No Means Least

Decided on the last day of the 2013–2014 term, *Burwell v. Hobby Lobby*[1] is this year's most controversial Supreme Court decision. By a 5–4 vote that broke along conservative–liberal lines, the Court held that the Religious Freedom Restoration Act of 1993 (RFRA) precluded the Department of Health and Human Services (HHS) from issuing regulations under the Affordable Care Act (ACA) that required Hobby Lobby, a family-owned corporation run in accordance with Christian principles, to supply health insurance coverage for contraceptive and abortion services for its female employees at no cost to the employees themselves. RFRA would not have applied at all if the ACA had explicitly required employers to observe the contraceptive mandate, because the latter specific statute would be a congressional trump over the earlier general statute. Indeed, the point is critical because if RFRA had been neutralized by the ACA, *Hobby Lobby* would then have been purely a First Amendment case, where under the pre-RFRA case law it would have had less chance of success. But the ACA's general command called only for employers to supply coverage for preventive care and screenings at

* Laurence A. Tisch Professor of Law, New York University School of Law; the Peter and Kirsten Bedford Senior Fellow, Hoover Institution; and the James Parker Hall Distinguished Service Professor of Law Emeritus and senior lecturer, University of Chicago. I would like to thank William Baude and Dennis Hutchinson for their comments on an earlier draft and Brian Mendick, Chelsea Phyler, Harry Ritter, and Mallory Suede, from the New York University School of Law's class of 2016, and Krista Perry, from the University of Chicago Law School's class of 2016 for their excellent research assistance.

[1] Burwell v. Hobby Lobby Stores, Inc., 134 S. Ct. 2751 (2014).

no cost to female employees, so everyone agreed that RFRA lay at the heart of the legal challenge to the HHS regulations.[2]

RFRA in turn has three requirements:

First, the statute asks whether the government action "substantially burden[s]" a person's exercise of his or her religious rights. This initial test covers both laws directed toward religion and, most critically, laws "of general applicability," such as HHS's contraceptive mandate.

Second, RFRA addresses the choice of *ends*: the government can prevail only if it shows that it advances "a compelling governmental interest."

Third, if the government prevails on the second point, RFRA addresses the question of *means*: the government must choose the "least restrictive means" to further its compelling interest.[3]

This three-part statutory test has evident constitutional overtones, in large measure because RFRA was passed with huge bipartisan support in response to the Supreme Court's 1990 decision in *Employment Division v. Smith,* which involved Smith's use of peyote in a religious rite.[4] *Smith* held that any neutral law of general applicability could not be challenged on the ground of its disparate impact on religious activities. Taken literally, the *Smith* test meant that the U.S. military could require observant Jewish and Muslim soldiers to eat pork under its standard dietary regimen. RFRA was passed to undo *Smith* and to impose by statute what Congress once thought was the appropriate constitutional test under the Free Exercise Clause of the First Amendment.

Although the *Hobby Lobby* decision preferred religious liberty to employer-provided contraceptive services, by its reasoning it also undermined that powerful bipartisan attack against *Smith.* At the same time, the decision has deeply polarized public opinion and led to immediate and harsh denunciations of the Supreme Court. U.S. District Court Judge Richard Kopf, an appointee of George H. W. Bush, pointedly complained that:

---

[2] 42 U.S.C. § 300gg-13(a)(4).

[3] 42 U.S.C. § 2000bb et seq.

[4] 494 U.S. 872 (1990).

> [F]ive male justices of the Supreme Court, who are all members of the Catholic faith and who each were appointed by a president who hailed from the Republican party, decided that a huge corporation, with thousands of employees and gargantuan revenues, was a "person" entitled to assert a religious objection to the Affordable Care Act's contraception mandate because that corporation was "closely held" by family members. To the average person, the result looks stupid and smells worse.[5]

Additionally Senator Mark Udall (D-CO) sponsored a failed legislative attempt to carve out the contraceptive mandate from RFRA, saying:

> The U.S. Supreme Court's Hobby Lobby decision opened the door to unprecedented corporate intrusion into our private lives. Coloradans understand that women should never have to ask their bosses for a permission slip to access common forms of birth control or other critical health services. My common-sense proposal will keep women's private health decisions out of corporate boardrooms, because your boss shouldn't be able to dictate what is best for you and your family.[6]

His co-sponsor, Senator Patty Murray (D-WA), echoed Louis XIV's famous dictum, "I am the state," by writing: "Your health care decisions are not your boss's business. Since the Supreme Court decided it will not protect women's access to health care, I will."[7]

In comparison, the *New York Times* editorial response sounds moderate:

> The Supreme Court violated principles of religious liberty and women's rights in last week's ruling in the *Hobby Lobby* case, which allowed owners of closely held, for-profit corporations

---

[5] Cheryl Chumley, Federal Judge Angered by Hobby Lobby Decision Tells Supreme Court to 'STFU,' Washington Times, July 8, 2014, available at http://www.washingtontimes.com/news/2014/jul/8/nebraska-judge-angered-hobby-lobby-tells-supreme-c.

[6] For one smattering of quotations that reveal the animosity, see Laura Bassett, Democrats Fast-Track Bill to Override Hobby Lobby Decision, Huffington Post (July 8, 2014), http://www.huffingtonpost.com/2014/07/08/hobby-lobby-override_n_5568320.html.

[7] *Id.*

> (most corporations in America) to impose their religious beliefs on workers by refusing to provide contraception coverage for employees with no co-pay, as required by the Affordable Care Act.[8]

These harsh criticisms are way off the mark. The short response is that critics should let Hobby Lobby run its own business. The critics of the decision are guilty of serious intellectual confusion when they equate the simple refusal to deal with coercion—that is, the threat or use of force against another person. It is not as though Hobby Lobby, by not complying with the HHS mandate, is forcing women to either abstain from sex or risk pregnancy. They still retain the option of purchasing contraception independently or switching jobs. Unlike Christians in Mosul, they will not be beheaded or tortured or confined for the exercise of their beliefs.

The more detailed response makes it critical to reconstruct carefully all aspects of *Hobby Lobby*—its historical background, its textual interpretation, its intellectual justifications, and its ultimate consequences. This essay starts with a brief analysis of the constitutional framework that set up the current situation. Section II then parses the application of RFRA to the contraceptive mandate. Section III closes with some general reflections about the current state of the law. My thesis is that the five-member majority reached the right result, albeit for the wrong reasons. Justice Samuel Alito first held correctly that Hobby Lobby had a significant private interest that brought RFRA into play. Second, in a serious mistake, he found it unnecessary to decide whether the government had a compelling state interest in imposing its contraceptive mandate. Third, he then concluded, wrongly, that even if he assumed that the government did have a compelling state interest, it nonetheless failed to choose the least restrictive means for its implementation.

The correct analysis plays out quite differently in the second and third stages. The government has no compelling state interest for imposing the contraceptive mandate. Once it loses at stage two, the question of least restrictive means never arises. The difference in approach turns out to be critical to the proper understanding of RFRA, and it affords the most powerful grounds on which to challenge the

---

[8] Editorial, Hobby Lobby's Disturbing Sequel, N.Y. Times, July 9, 2014, at A20.

oft-mistaken opinion of Justice Ruth Bader Ginsburg for the four liberal dissenters.

I. The Early Constitutional Background

Two powerful constitutional forces shaped the current struggles in *Hobby Lobby*. First, the epic constitutional battles of 1937 systematically rejected any claim that economic liberties were subject to heightened levels of scrutiny under either the Due Process or Takings Clauses. Key decisions in that regard were *West Coast Hotel v. Parrish*,[9] which upheld the constitutionality of a state minimum-wage law for women only, and *NLRB v. Jones & Laughlin Steel*,[10] which upheld mandatory collective bargaining under the National Labor Relations Act. Years later, that state of affairs was in turn strengthened by the Supreme Court's ringing constitutional endorsement of the antidiscrimination provisions concerning employment and public accommodations found in the Civil Rights Act of 1964.[11] These decisions meant that it was a foregone conclusion that any generalized substantive due process challenge to the ACA on economic liberties or freedom of contract grounds would fail, so much so that none of the many challenges pushed that line.[12]

With that issue "settled," constitutional litigation turned to the question of whether some fraction of individual liberty could be afforded protection under the First Amendment's Free Exercise Clause. Two key prior precedents pointed strongly in that direction. In 1963, *Sherbert v. Verner*[13] allowed the plaintiff to claim unemployment benefits when she refused to take a job that required her to work on the Sabbath. In 1972, *Wisconsin v. Yoder* sustained the rights of the Amish to keep their children out of public education.[14] In both of these cases, the Court took the position that the government was required to make some accommodations for religious beliefs in ways

---

[9] 300 U.S. 379 (1937).

[10] 301 U.S. 1 (1937).

[11] 42 U.S.C. § 2000a(a) Tit. VII, § 201(a) (2012).

[12] For an early repudiation of the due process argument, see Florida v. HHS, 716 F. Supp.2d 1120, 1161–62 (N.D. Fla. 2010).

[13] 374 U.S. 398 (1963).

[14] 406 U.S. 205 (1972).

that exempted both Sherbert and Yoder from general laws that could not be challenged on substantive due process grounds.

The pivotal moment in the run-up to RFRA, as mentioned above, was Justice Antonin Scalia's sharp about-face on the Free Exercise Clause in the 1990 case *Employment Division v. Smith*. At issue in *Smith* were the activities that Alfred Smith and Galen Black engaged in during a religious ceremony at their Native American church. Their action constituted intentional possession and use of a "controlled substance," clearly criminal under Oregon law. *Smith*, of course, was *not* a criminal prosecution, but a dispute over unemployment benefits. Oregon's Employment Office refused to pay those benefits because Smith and Black were fired due to drug use from their positions as workers in a private drug rehabilitation office. The Court had to decide whether the men's participation in the religious ceremony had to be exempted from the criminal law in order to accommodate their interest in religious liberty.

A skeptical Justice Scalia, writing for five justices, rejected any version of the compelling state interest test, ordinarily used in religious liberty cases, for the reason that he had no idea how to make the appropriate balance:

> It is no more appropriate for judges to determine the "centrality" of religious beliefs before applying a "compelling interest" test in the free exercise field, than it would be for them to determine the "importance" of ideas before applying the "compelling interest" test in the free speech field. What principle of law or logic can be brought to bear to contradict a believer's assertion that a particular act is "central" to his personal faith?[15]

Justice Scalia then took great pains to distinguish *Sherbert* and *Yoder*, on the grounds that they were "hybrid" free-speech and free-exercise cases.[16] He then added this kicker: "Subsequent decisions have consistently held that the right of free exercise does not relieve an individual of the obligation to comply with a 'valid and neutral law of general applicability on the ground that the law proscribes (or prescribes) conduct that his religion prescribes (or proscribes).'"[17]

[15] 494 U.S. at 886–87.
[16] *Id.* at 882.
[17] *Id.* at 879.

The "subsequent decisions" referred to cases subsequent to *Reynolds v. United States*, which in 1878 upheld a territorial ban on polygamy against charges that it infringed on the religious liberty of members of the Mormon faith.[18]

Smith prompted vigorous disagreement and partial dissent. Justice Sandra Day O'Connor sided with Scalia on the outcome, but she emphatically rejected his neutrality framework. After citing *Yoder*, she concluded that the state had shown its overriding interest in preventing the physical harm caused by the use of a Schedule I controlled substance.[19] She did not, however, explain why the state's interest was so strong that it had to cover specifically this limited religious use of peyote.

In making her claim, she relied (as did Justice Scalia in *Smith*) on *United States v. Lee*, which held that a compelling state interest justified imposing the Social Security tax on Amish who flatly refused to accept any Social Security benefits.[20] Chief Justice Warren Burger thought that the social need to properly fund the Social Security system counted as the compelling state interest. He did not explain, however, why requiring Social Security taxes from those who took no Social Security benefits was a compelling state interest.

Justice O'Connor's argument in *Smith* is also vulnerable to Justice Harry Blackmun's dissent in this case, which Justices William Brennan and Thurgood Marshall joined. Blackmun formulated the issue in ways relevant to *Hobby Lobby*: "A statute [that burdens the free exercise of religion] may stand only if the law in general, and the State's refusal to allow a religious exemption in particular, are justified by a compelling interest that cannot be served by less restrictive means."[21] At this point, he notes that it is odd in the extreme to call the state's interest compelling if the state has decided not to enforce its criminal law: "It is not the State's broad interest in fighting the critical 'war on drugs' that must be weighed against respondents' claim, but the State's narrow interest in refusing to make an exception for the religious, ceremonial use of peyote."[22]

---

[18] 98 U.S. 145 (1878).

[19] Smith, 494 U.S. at 893.

[20] 455 U.S. 252 (1982).

[21] Smith, 494 U.S. at 907.

[22] *Id*. at 909–10.

The case law prior to RFRA thus shows two competing visions of what constitutes a compelling state interest under *Smith*. The first line, embraced by Justice O'Connor in *Smith*, runs from *Reynolds* through *Lee*.[23] The second, endorsed by Justice Blackmun, runs from *Sherbert* through *Yoder*. The former is more favorable to the state than the latter, and both refer to the triad of significant burden, compelling state interest, and least restrictive means. Justice Scalia's competing vision that any valid and neutral law trumps the claim for religious liberty in all cases rejects both the O'Connor and the Blackmun versions of the compelling state interest argument.

The fierce objection to Scalia's approach fueled the passage of RFRA, which received extensive support in both the House and the Senate and was eagerly signed into law by then President Bill Clinton. One key question under RFRA was whether it adopted the O'Connor or Blackmun view of the compelling state interest test.

RFRA answers that question by stating that its purposes are

(1) to restore the compelling interest test as set forth in *Sherbert v. Verner*, 374 U.S. 398 (1963) and *Wisconsin v. Yoder*, 406 U.S. 205 (1972) and to guarantee its application in all cases where free exercise of religion is substantially burdened; and

(2) to provide a claim or defense to persons whose religious exercise is substantially burdened by government.[24]

Sherbert and *Yoder*, not *Reynolds* and *Lee*, govern.[25] It is now time to turn to the two major opinions in *Hobby Lobby* to see how well they fare against RFRA's tripartite standard dealing with substantial burdens, compelling state interest, and least restrictive means.

---

[23] See also, Lyng v. Nw. Indian Cemetery Protective Ass'n, 485 U.S. 439 (1988), in which Justice O'Connor allowed the federal government to run a forest road located on government property through an Indian burial ground, notwithstanding the government's admission that its road-building activities "could have devastating effects on traditional Indian religious practices." *Id.* at 451. *Smith* relied on *Lyng*.

[24] 42 U.S.C. § 2000bb(b).

[25] For the extensive debate on this question, see Will Baude, Is RFRA Limited to Pre-*Smith* Jurisprudence, or Does RFRA Run Through It?, Volokh Conspiracy, Wash. Post (July 9, 2014), http://www.washingtonpost.com/news/volokh-conspiracy/wp/2014/07/09/is-rfra-limited-to-pre-smith-jurisprudence-or-does-rfra-run-through-it.

II. How RFRA Applies to HHS's Contraceptive Mandate

A. Substantial Burdens on the Exercise of Religion: Are Corporations Covered?

The initial question is whether Hobby Lobby, the firm, counts as a "person" entitled to protection under RFRA. The point was not squarely in the minds of the statutory drafters whose language put Smith's personal decision to smoke peyote front and center. It is also true that no corporation, recognized by law as an entity separate from its shareholder owners, celebrates religious holidays, attends church, performs religious rites, or observes various religious laws. Conceptually, it could not be otherwise, because the corporation is essentially a group of individuals who come together for a common venture, protected by the shield of limited liability. So protected, tort and contract creditors can ordinarily reach only the assets of the corporation, not the personal assets of the individual shareholders.

At first blush, this insulation of individuals from financial responsibility could be mistaken for some kind of abuse. But limited liability, rightly understood, is the only way to get people of substantial wealth to commit large sums of capital to common ventures over which they exercise no direct control. That large aggregation often *increases* the pool of assets available to various claimants against the corporation. Contracting parties can then secure guarantees from individual shareholders or third parties if they fear that corporate assets might prove insufficient to cover their potential liabilities. The state can, and often does, require corporations to take out insurance to protect tort creditors, who now gain access to potential funds in the hands of independent third parties that contract creditors are not able to reach. The ubiquity of limited liability offers ample testimony to its efficiency.

One key question to frame the discussion asks what conditions, if any, the state may impose on individual investors who seek to take advantage of the corporate form. As noted, requiring insurance to offset tort liability is perfectly appropriate. So too are rules that require the corporation to register in any state where it does business, so that it can be sued locally. But Justice Alito is correct to insist that additional conditions on incorporation cannot be imposed willy-nilly. A state could not deny a certificate of incorporation to parties who do not make political contributions to the dominant political party. Nor could it deny incorporation rights to individuals who refuse to waive all protections against unreasonable searches and seizures under the Fourth Amendment, or who refuse to waive their right to speak collectively under the First Amendment.

In this context, it is therefore regrettable that Justice Alito did not make explicit reference to the doctrine of unconstitutional conditions, which certainly applies to this case.[26] The individual shareholders, when faced with the monopoly power of the state, can be forced to accept only conditions that offset the privilege they receive, that is, limited liability. This principle is doubly important when the federal government seeks to condition incorporation under state law on the shareholders' willingness to engage in activities that are inconsistent with the religious beliefs of the owners, which for Hobby Lobby were those of its founding couple and their children.

Justice Alito was therefore right to "reject HHS's argument that the owners of the companies forfeited all RFRA protection when they decided to organize their businesses as corporations rather than sole proprietorships or general partnerships."[27] The analysis here follows the form appropriate in antitrust law generally. The inquiry is always whether the condition or restriction is intended to increase the global efficiency of activities in the corporate form or to secure a wealth transfer from one group to another. The former creates a positive-sum game (whereby all parties subject to the regulation are better off) that should be supported, while the latter creates a negative-sum game (whereby the losses to some parties are larger than the gains to others) that should be stoutly opposed. To be sure, this antitrust-type analysis is normally confined to tie-in and exclusive-dealing contracts.[28] And of course, the weak protection of economic liberties under modern law allows the state a free hand in imposing massive transfer payments on various groups, such that corporations are not insulated from that power. But when religious liberty is at issue, RFRA's higher standard of judicial review applies, even as

---

[26] For my extended treatment, see Richard A. Epstein, Bargaining with the State (1993) (stressing the linkage between the doctrine and monopoly power).

[27] Hobby Lobby, 134 S. Ct. at 2759.

[28] A tie-in contract is one in which the seller insists that the buyer buy one product (the tied product) in order to buy a second (the tying product). An exclusive-dealing contract holds that a given buyer must take all goods of a given sort from the seller in order to acquire any such goods.

the antitrust-like critique of monopoly behavior by the state carries over.

Justice Ginsburg in dissent misses that point by claiming to take a leaf from Justice John Paul Stevens's dissent in *Citizens United v. Federal Election Commission*.[29] She observes that corporations "have no consciences, no beliefs, no feelings, no thoughts, no desires."[30] But it hardly follows that they have no rights, given that they succeed to the rights of their shareholders. Confiscation of corporate assets not only harms the corporation, but it also hurts the individual shareholders it wipes out. A law that bars corporations from political speech could force the *New York Times* or *Wall Street Journal* to the unpalatable choice of surrendering the protection of limited liability in order to preserve their right to speak. Previously, in the same vein, Justice Ginsburg had seriously erred in *Christian Legal Society v. Martinez* when she resuscitated the long-discredited right/privilege distinction to hold that Hastings Law School could refuse to allow the tiny Christian Legal Society (CLS) access to the school's normal administrative support services unless it admitted into voting membership people who were hostile to its stated religious mission.[31]

The correct position is that any public institution should be open to all comers on equal terms, just like common carriers. There is no way, one hopes, that the state could keep CLS members off the public roads unless they agreed to abandon their exclusive membership policies. Hastings Law School is unlike the public highways, however, because as a "limited public forum" it can keep non-students out of the school. But owing to its tax-supported position, it must evaluate all eligible applicants on equal terms, just like the highway system. What is true about state power over public highways is true about state power over incorporation. Any exercise of state monopoly power brings the doctrine of unconstitutional conditions into play, especially since the United States can show no connection whatsoever between its desire to impose the contraceptive mandate and the basic reasons for incorporation. In light of that yawning gulf,

29 558 U.S. 310, 466 (2010).

30 Burwell v. Hobby Lobby, 134 S. Ct. at 2794.

31 Christian Legal Soc'y Chapter of the Univ. of Cal., Hastings Coll. of the Law v. Martinez, 561 U.S. 661 (2010). For my criticism, see Richard A. Epstein, Church and State at the Crossroads: *Christian Legal Society v. Martinez*, 2009–2010 Cato Sup. Ct. Rev. 104 (2010).

it only makes sense to conclude that Hobby Lobby did not sacrifice its RFRA protections when it chose to do business in the corporate form.

B. Does the Contraceptive Mandate Impose Substantial Burdens?

The next question is whether the HHS's contraceptive mandate subjects Hobby Lobby to a substantial burden. In *Smith*, Justice Scalia denied that this type of question admitted a principled answer. But that inquiry cannot be ducked under RFRA. Nor is there any reason to do so. Of course, judges should not ask whether anyone's religious beliefs are true. But the centrality of these beliefs to their faith is not a theological inquiry, but instead is a standard evidentiary question that can be answered by examining the central tenets of any given religion. Narrowly stated, the inquiry is whether under RFRA the government imposes a substantial burden on Hobby Lobby's sincere religious beliefs by requiring it to purchase insurance for employees' contraceptives services. Justice Alito attacks this problem in the wrong way when he insists that the cost of noncompliance, measured in fines that can run into the millions, shows that the burden is substantial.[32] The correct analysis does not look at the cost of noncompliance, which may be high, but at the cost of compliance, which in monetary terms is far lower. It is incorrect to insist that the only measure of a substantial burden is the size of the expenditure. Of equal importance is the purpose to which it is put.

In this connection, it is instructive to compare the question of compelled contributions for the purchase of contraceptive insurance to the forced contributions demanded of union members under a collective-bargaining agreement. As is all too typical of the over-compartmentalization of Supreme Court decisions, neither Justice Alito nor Justice Ginsburg refers to the Court's important decision in *Harris v. Quinn*,[33] decided the same day as *Hobby Lobby*. One key issue that bubbled up in *Harris* was whether individual employees should have the right to opt out of any public union on the ground that, in dealing with public bodies, the political and economic interests are so intertwined that any payment of union dues amounts to a form of compelled speech forbidden under First Amendment

[32] 134 S. Ct. at 2759.
[33] 134 S. Ct. 2618 (2014).

law. Justice Alito skirted that question in *Harris* by deciding, correctly in my view, that the so-called "joint employment" arrangement, whereby the state became a second employer of home health care workers, was a sham. Its only function was to allow the Service Employees International Union to run elections that forced Pamela Harris, a mother who cared for her seriously disabled adult child, to be designated in one audacious statutory maneuver as an employee of both her son and of Illinois.

Yet for these purposes, the key concession comes from Justice Elena Kagan, who in dissent in *Harris*, insisted that the 37-year-old rule in *Abood v. Detroit Board of Education*[34] should govern in *Harris*. In her view, *Abood* made the right accommodation for compelled speech insofar as it held that dissenting workers "may constitutionally prevent the Union's spending a part of their required service fees to contribute to political candidates and to express political views unrelated to its duties as exclusive bargaining representative."[35] This decision is yet another application of the doctrine of unconstitutional conditions that "a government may not require an individual to relinquish rights guaranteed him by the First Amendment as a condition of public employment."[36]

Just that principle is at stake here. HHS interprets the ACA as imposing a general mandate under which employers are compelled to contribute money to causes they oppose on religious grounds. That compelled contribution counts as a significant burden for the same reason here that it does in *Abood*: what matters is the cause, not the amount. In dealing with this issue in *Wheaton College v. Burwell*, the follow-up decision to *Hobby Lobby* that involved eleemosynary religious institutions, Justice Sonia Sotomayor dismissed the seriousness of this concern in saying, "But *thinking* one's religious beliefs are substantially burdened—no matter how sincere or genuine the belief may be—does not make it so."[37] Her one-liner hearkens back to the same indefensible skepticism of Justice Scalia in *Smith* on the ability of courts to determine the centrality of certain beliefs to religious people. So long as the compulsion is to make *any* financial

---

[34] 431 U.S. 209 (1977).

[35] *Id.* at 234.

[36] *Id.*

[37] Wheaton Coll. v. Burwell, 134 S. Ct. 2806, 2812 (2014) (emphasis in original).

contribution to a cause that is repugnant to one's religious beliefs, it is a substantial burden. Whether the restriction is justified by some compelling state interest raises a separate question. But it is hard to think that *any* explicit requirement that someone perform an action that violates his or her core religious beliefs could ever be dismissed as an insignificant burden.

This analysis does not render the requirement of a sincere religious belief toothless. In general, virtually any matter that deals with birth, marriage, and death falls within the core area of religious beliefs. It is, for example, these and only these issues that drove the Roman Catholic Church and many evangelical Christian churches in 2009 to issue The Manhattan Declaration, which stresses the sanctity of life, traditional marriage, and religious liberty.[38] That last term is not given a broad construction, but covers only those cases where religious institutions are forced to perform actions that go against conscience in order to remain in business.[39]

So the only remaining question is whether an employer or even a church could claim in good faith that its participation in ordinary business activities deserves protection under RFRA. As an initial point, it is worth noting that no such broader claim has yet to be made under RFRA since its passage in 1993, which is not surprising given that most churches have thicker conceptions of mutual moral obligations than those embodied in any libertarian code that stresses individual autonomy, thereby denying any legal obligation to assist

---

[38] Manhattan Declaration: A Call of Christian Conscience (November 20, 2009), available at http://manhattandeclaration.org/man_dec_resources/Manhattan_Declaration_full_text.pdf. The statement was drafted by Professor Robert George, McCormick Professor of Jurisprudence, Princeton University; Professor Timothy George, Beeson Divinity School, Samford University; and Chuck Colson, Founder, the Chuck Colson Center for Christian Worldview.

[39] See *id.* at 8:

> After the judicial imposition of "same-sex marriage" in Massachusetts, for example, Catholic Charities chose with great reluctance to end its century-long work of helping to place orphaned children in good homes rather than comply with a legal mandate that it place children in same-sex households in violation of Catholic moral teaching. In New Jersey, after the establishment of a quasi-marital "civil unions" scheme, a Methodist institution was stripped of its tax exempt status when it declined, as a matter of religious conscience, to permit a facility it owned and operated to be used for ceremonies blessing homosexual unions.

others in their time of need.[40] Indeed, the more common practice is for many religious groups to champion their conception of social justice, thereby supporting minimum wages and family-leave legislation. It is thus highly unlikely that any religious group would be tempted to make, let alone make in good faith, the claims Justice Ginsburg fears will follow in the wake of *Hobby Lobby*.

Justice Ginsburg does not cite any such example in her opinion, but only asks the question: "Suppose an employer's sincerely held religious belief is offended by health coverage of vaccines, or paying the minimum wage, or according women equal pay for substantially similar work."[41] But there is nothing to her point. The two cases she cites were both decided before *Smith* and before RFRA. Moreover, both claims failed. In *Alamo Foundation*, an employer lost its challenge to a statutory requirement that it fill out the minimum-wage form under the Fair Labor Standards Act (FLSA), in which it vainly insisted that the "application of the Act's record-keeping requirements would have the 'primary effect' of inhibiting religious activity and would foster 'an excessive government entanglement with religion,' thereby violating the Establishment Clause."[42] In *Shenandoah*, the Fourth Circuit held that church-operated schools were covered by the FLSA, making their teachers and staff employees under that law. Citing both *Sherbert* and *Yoder*, it rejected a free-exercise challenge to the FLSA, which it held advanced a compelling state interest.[43]

In my view, the result in *Shenandoah* is not beyond criticism. There is no question that the substantive due process objections to the Fair Labor Standards Act were brushed aside in *United States v. Darby*,[44]

[40] See, e.g., Most Reverend William F. Murphy, Labor Day Statement, A New "Social Contract" for Today's "New Things," available at http://www.usccb.org/issues-and-action/human-life-and-dignity/labor-employment/upload/labor_day_2010.pdf ("Workers need a new 'social contract.' Currently, the rewards and 'security' that employers and society offer workers in return for an honest day's work do not reflect the global economy of the 21st century in which American workers are now trying to compete.").

[41] Hobby Lobby, 134 S. Ct. at 2802 (Ginsburg, J., dissenting) (citing Tony and Susan Alamo Found. v. Sec'y of Labor, 471 U.S. 290, 303 (1985) and Dole v. Shenandoah Baptist Church, 899 F.2d 1389, 1392 (4th Cir. 1990), respectively).

[42] Tony and Susan Alamo Found., 471 U.S. 290 at 305.

[43] Shenandoah Baptist Church, 899 F.2d at 1398.

[44] 312 U.S. 100, 125 (1941).

on the authority of the earlier decision of the Supreme Court in *West Coast Hotel v. Parrish*.[45] *West Coast Hotel* in turn relied on the weaker rational basis formulation in *Nebbia v. New York*.[46] It is therefore at least open to question whether the FLSA does represent a compelling state interest, given its interference with competitive markets,[47] or whether the claim is upgraded solely to meet the religious free-exercise claim, which is judged by some higher standard. But for the moment at least, this issue is dead in the water.

The bottom line, therefore, is that both cases cited by Justice Ginsburg rejected all claims of religious liberty, and there is not a hint anywhere that RFRA was meant to overturn their results. Perhaps some future case under RFRA will raise line-drawing problems, but no such case could call into question the bona fides of Hobby Lobby's religious objections to the contraceptive mandate. The remote danger of some outlandish religious challenge should not gut the protections that religious groups receive under RFRA.

C. Does the Government Nevertheless Have a Compelling Interest in Pursuing the Mandate?

The second question is whether the government has a compelling state interest in forcing Hobby Lobby to comply with its contraceptive mandate. In dealing with this issue, Justice Alito made a serious intellectual and tactical mistake. His intellectual mistake was to think that it is possible to leap from the first to the third question under RFRA without addressing this middle question. The tactical mistake was that the very question he sought to elide was brought front and center in *Wheaton College*, decided within a week after *Hobby Lobby* came down.

In *Wheaton College*, Justice Stephen Breyer joined the five-member majority in *Hobby Lobby* in issuing an "interim order." It said that Wheaton College could have given HHS notice that it refused to supply contraceptive coverage without filling out its required form that also gave notice of its position to its health insurer or third-party administrator. The narrow grounds of the majority's decision was that

---

[45] 300 U.S. 379 (1937).

[46] 291 U.S. 502, 507 (1934) (cited in West Coast Hotel, 300 U.S. at 397–98).

[47] See the discussion in the next section regarding competitive markets and cross-subsidies.

the notice that *Wheaton College* provided was sufficient "to facilitate the provision of full contraceptive coverage under the Act."[48] In essence, the omission was treated as a form of harmless error.

That limited decision provoked an impassioned dissent from Justice Sonia Sotomayor, who pointed out that *Hobby Lobby* had already decided that "[e]ven assuming that the accommodation somehow burdens Wheaton's religious exercise, the accommodation is permissible under RFRA because it is the least restrictive means of furthering the Government's compelling interests in public health and women's well-being."[49] Worse, she claimed that the Court had just resolved this question when "as justification for its decision in *Hobby Lobby*—issued just this week—the very Members of the Court that now vote to grant injunctive relief concluded that the accommodation 'constitutes an alternative that achieves all of the Government's aims while providing greater respect for religious liberty.'"[50]

She may be right about the flip-flop—though Hobby Lobby's owners were never offered the accommodation, so the least-restrictive-alternative argument may have sufficed in their case even if it didn't for Wheaton College. Analytically, however, this line of argument is *not* available if the compelling state interest issue in *Hobby Lobby* had been resolved against the government, as it should have been, because then the question of least restrictive means never comes up. Justice Alito, however, was so convinced that *Hobby Lobby* could be decided on the "least restrictive means" prong of RFRA that he just assumed for the sake of argument, that the advancement of "women's health" was a compelling state interest that warranted the imposition of the contraceptive mandate against Hobby Lobby. That was an important mistake of legal principle. Note that this case does not fit the narrower conception of compelling state interest that was championed by Justice Brennan in *Sherbert* and *Yoder* and Justice Blackmun in *Smith*. In this regard, Blackmun adopted the instructive line taken by Robert Clark:

> The purpose of almost any law can be traced back to one or another of the fundamental concerns of government: public health and safety, public peace and order, defense, revenue.

[48] Wheaton College, 134 S. Ct. at 2807.

[49] *Id.* at 2808 (Sotomayor, J., dissenting).

[50] *Id.*

> To measure an individual interest directly against one of
> these rarified values inevitably makes the individual interest
> appear the less significant.[51]

The last sentence is of special relevance. The global interest in public health and safety may justify the general control of the street and commercial use of drugs under the Controlled Substances Act, but it hardly justifies the restriction as it applies to the ingestion of peyote as part of a religious rite. The interest in general revenues may justify the income taxation from which no one should be immune, but it hardly justifies forcing the Amish to pay into a Social Security system from which they have abjured all benefits. So too in *Hobby Lobby*, whether we speak of "women's health" or "public health," the claim is idle unless it is tested in its concrete instantiation.

One easy test for this exercise is to note the various types of necessity for which there is no simple market-based solution. Just that situation arises in the public-necessity cases, such as war, contagion, fire, floods, earthquakes, and other natural disasters. Similarly, there is no good market solution to murder and theft. The vulnerable position of infants and insane persons is often met by state-regulated guardianship arrangements. A system of general taxation is needed to supply genuine public goods (the form of tax that was *not* at issue in *Lee*); given the collective-action problem, those taxes cannot be raised voluntarily. There is also a compelling government interest, not mentioned by Clark, in the regulation of natural and legal monopolies as with common carriers and public utilities. But contraceptive services don't fit here because they are readily available in the marketplace to all comers at competitive prices. The right of any woman to access these services surely implies for others, including employers, a correlative duty not to interfere. But *Hobby Lobby* is worlds apart from *Griswold v. Connecticut*,[52] which involved a successful challenge to a Connecticut law that forbade the sale of contraceptives between consenting parties. Why must the state compel employers to make payments or public declarations that violate their religious beliefs when the very services at issue are freely available elsewhere?

---

[51] Robert Clark, Guidelines for the Free Exercise Clause, 83 Harv. L. Rev. 327, 330–31 (1969) (cited in Smith, 494 U.S. at 910 (Blackmun, J., dissenting)).

[52] 381 U.S. 479 (1965).

This logic is at no point addressed in Justice Ginsburg's dissent. Instead, she takes the view that the decision of Congress to require key women's health services at no cost is a belated recognition of a looming moral imperative that an all-wise Congress fulfilled. Her evidence starts with the proposition that "[t]he ability of women to participate equally in the economic and social life of the Nation has been facilitated by their ability to control their reproductive lives."[53] No one would care to disagree with a proposition that should play no role in this dispute. Prior to the adoption of the ACA, every woman was entitled to control her reproductive life by whatever means she chose, either at her own expense or with the assistance of other individuals. Justice Ginsburg is right to insist that many prominent health care professionals have concluded that these contraceptive services "are critically important" to women's health. All the more reason for women to spend their own resources to acquire them. But it is no reason to require others to violate their religious views to foot the bill.

It is equally vacuous to conclude, as Justice Ginsburg does, that "Congress left health care decisions—including the choice among contraceptive methods—in the hands of women, with the aid of their health care providers." Both points remain true even if the contraceptive mandate is rejected, just as it was true before the ACA was enacted, and is true today for women in small firms not covered under the ACA. Hobby Lobby doesn't want to make decisions for women. It just wants to make its own business decision not to pay for practices that it opposes on sincere religious grounds. The focus of Justice Ginsburg's argument looks exclusively at the condition and needs of women, which works at far too high a level of abstraction for the compelling state interest test. What she has to do, but does not attempt, is explain why the state has a compelling state interest in imposing the correlative duty on an employer with sincere religious beliefs at the employer's expense.

Her argument gains no further traction with this observation: "Women paid significantly more than men for preventive care, the amendment's proponents noted; in fact, cost barriers operated to block many women from obtaining needed care at all,"[54] especially

---

[53] Hobby Lobby, 134 S. Ct. at 2787 (Ginsburg, J., dissenting) (citing Planned Parenthood of Se. Pa. v. Casey, 505 U.S. 833, 856 (1992)).

[54] *Id*. at 2788.

the expenses associated with pregnancy and childbirth. Her first mistake is to overlook the benefit side of the health care equation. Women pay far more than men for health care during their working years because their medical expenses are on average higher. They pay more because they get more in return, just as they do for health care insurance supplied outside the employment relationship. The differential rates for insurance reflect the simple and desirable dynamic that competitive markets eliminate inefficient cross-subsidies. But where lies the compelling state interest in forcing one group of individuals to pay for benefits received by another?

Just this issue arose in 1976 in *General Electric v. Gilbert*,[55] which sparked a major congressional response when the Court held it was not a form of sex discrimination for General Electric to refuse to provide disability benefits to women "for time lost due to pregnancy and childbirth," on the ground that pregnancy was neither a disability nor an accident. The point was not that women got a raw deal under GE's practices, because the record showed that the cost of coverage for women in the relevant year was, even without pregnancy benefits, close to twice that for men: $82.57 for women as opposed to $45.76 for men in 1970, and $112.91 for women and $62.08 for men in 1971.[56]

Faced with such numbers, *Gilbert*'s economic logic is impeccable. The stability of any insurance plan depends on its ability to guard against cross-subsidies, lest the entire program dissolve by adverse selection, which happens if the parties who are charged excessive premiums leave the plan. The extra sums paid out for pregnant women are not covered by their lower premiums, so their inclusion in the plan should, in economic terms, count as discrimination against men, who receive in aggregate lower benefits than women for each dollar they put into the program. An equal rate of premiums for unequal benefits is in economic terms a form of discrimination against the party who pays extra to secure the health care of others.

It is worth noting that even if *Gilbert* is rejected, the legal definition of discrimination as applied under Title VII *increases* the economic discrimination above and beyond that in the marketplace.[57] Just that

---

[55] 429 U.S. 125 (1976).

[56] *Id.* at 130–31 n.9.

[57] What is true of pregnancy is true of pensions, see L.A. Dep't of Water & Power v. Manhart, 435 U.S. 702 (1978), which requires that pension levels be set equally for

happened when the firestorm of protest against *Gilbert* prompted the swift passage of the Pregnancy Discrimination Act of 1978,[58] which expands the definition of sex discrimination to cover any action "because of or on the basis of pregnancy, childbirth, or related medical conditions; and women affected by pregnancy, childbirth, or related medical conditions." Under the prevailing constitutional view that affords scant protection to economic liberties, no one could mount a viable constitutional challenge against this law, notwithstanding that it increases the wealth transfer from men to women, and from older women to women of childbearing age.

Nonetheless, Justice Ginsburg finishes with a flourish:

> The exemption sought by Hobby Lobby and Conestoga would override significant interests of the corporations' employees and covered dependents. It would deny legions of women who do not hold their employers' beliefs access to contraceptive coverage that the ACA would otherwise secure. See Catholic Charities of Sacramento, Inc. v. Superior Court, 85 P.3d 67, 93 (2004). ("We are unaware of any decision in which . . . [the U.S. Supreme Court] has exempted a religious objector from the operation of a neutral, generally applicable law despite the recognition that the requested exemption would detrimentally affect the rights of third parties."). In sum, with respect to free exercise claims no less than free speech claims, " '[y]our right to swing your arms ends just where the other man's nose begins.' " Chafee, Freedom of Speech in War Time, 32 Harv. L. Rev. 932, 957 (1919).[59]

There are two serious difficulties with this passage. The first relates to Ginsburg's serious misconstruction of the quote from Zechariah Chafee. The full passage relates to his views on the initial post-World War I cases where political protestors claimed their First Amendment protections:

> Or to put the matter another way, it is useless to define free speech by talk about rights. The agitator asserts his

---

men and women even though women as a group live longer than men. The entire enterprise is yet another instance of a statutory cross-subsidy in favor of women. For the economic analysis, see George Benston, The Economics of Gender Discrimination in Employer Fringe Benefits: *Manhart* Revisited, 49 U. Chi. L. Rev. 489 (1982).

[58] Adding section 701(k).

[59] Hobby Lobby, 134 S. Ct. at 2790–91 (Ginsburg, J., dissenting).

> constitutional right to speak, the government asserts its constitutional right to wage war. The result is a deadlock. Each side takes the position of the man who was arrested for swinging his arms and hitting another in the nose, and asked the judge if he did not have a right to swing his arms in a free country. "Your right to swing your arms ends just where the other man's nose begins."[60]

It is quite proper to take Chafee to task for the same kind of linguistic skepticism that infects Justice Scalia's opinion in *Smith*. Chafee is at sixes and sevens in dealing with these great cases of agitation, *Schenck v. United States*,[61] *Frohwerk v. United States*,[62] and *Debs v. United States*,[63] all of which resulted in convictions for agitation or worse under the Espionage Act of 1917. It turns out that Chafee's article, which was published in June 1919, makes no reference to *Abrams v. United States*,[64] which was decided only in November 1919, and which of course is well known for Justice Oliver Wendell Holmes's famous recantation of his earlier opinion in *Schenck*. The difference between *Schenck* and *Abrams* really matters for these purposes. Under the skeptical attitude revealed in the complete Chafee passage, the government will always get the nod, because there is no clear principle to oppose it. But not so with Holmes in *Abrams*:

> But when men have realized that time has upset many fighting faiths, they may come to believe even more than they believe the very foundations of their own conduct that the ultimate good desired is better reached by free trade in ideas—that the best test of truth is the power of the thought to get itself accepted in the competition of the market, and that truth is the only ground upon which their wishes safely can be carried out. That at any rate is the theory of our Constitution. It is an experiment, as all life is an experiment.[65]

Take this point of view with its references to "free trade in ideas" and "competition of the market," and lo and behold, it is possible

[60] Zechariah Chafee, Freedom of Speech in War Time, 32 Harv. L. Rev. 932, 957 (1919).
[61] 249 U.S. 47 (1919).
[62] 249 U.S. 204 (1919).
[63] 249 U.S. 211 (1919).
[64] 250 U.S. 616 (1919).
[65] *Id.* at 630.

to craft a principle that works tolerably well, notwithstanding our inability to predict the future perfectly. The government is allowed to punish conduct "that produces or is intended to produce a clear and imminent danger that it will bring about forthwith certain substantive evils that the United States constitutionally may seek to prevent."[66] Nothing in the potted quotation from Chafee indicates that Justice Ginsburg had any idea about what he was talking about.

Her use of the Chaffee quotation is even odder because, read in isolation, it endorses the very libertarian view that she rejects. For whatever it is worth, Chafee does not get his causation example correct because, in fact, it is possible to tell where one's arm moves and one's nose ends. The basic trespass rule imposes liability on the party who moved his arm into someone else's nose. The exception is where the party who moves has the right of way, as, for example, on public highways. The point of the basic prohibition is to constrain the use of force, which is the ultimate evil when done by way of aggression and *not self-defense. What is so odd about Justice Ginsburg's quotation* is that she wrongly equates the failure to provide the contraceptive benefit required under the ACA with the use of force by a private party. But the entire structure of the common law (to which she implicitly appeals) draws a sharp distinction between the use of force and the refusal to deal with other people. The latter right has to be observed as a general matter, for otherwise any person could compel any other person to enter into a transaction with him on whatever terms he dictates. With that one maneuver, there can never be such thing as a competitive market because now every employer has to submit to any term that Congress mandates.

There are, of course, cases in which the refusal to deal does attract serious attention, but all of them involve common carriers and public utilities in monopoly positions. There, the refusal to deal shuts one person out of the market, so that the legal response is to impose the duty to serve, subject to the correlative duty to pay compensation that covers the fixed and variable costs of service that the ACA, as will become evident, does not even begin to calibrate. The equation of the refusal to deal in a competitive market with the use of force shows just how far off the rails the Ginsburg analysis goes. The only compelling state interest at work in *Hobby Lobby* is to prevent

[66] *Id.* at 627.

government from using its legislative power to make one person pay for the care of another in the supposed name of women's health. Those heavy-handed government exactions may hold up in a rational basis world in which economic liberties and private rights receive limited protection, but they abjectly fail under RFRA, which is by design more stern. The state has no compelling interest in requiring any employer with sincere religious beliefs to subsidize the health of its female—or, for that matter, male—employees.

D. Does the Government Use the Least Restrictive Means to Achieve Its "Compelling" Goal?

The last of the three prongs of RFRA asks whether the ACA regulations adopt the least restrictive alternative to achieve the compelling state interest. On the view just taken, there is no compelling state interest for the government to force those who pay for health care to fund those procedures that they regard as grave moral sins. So long as that is the case, the issue of the least restrictive alternative never arises. But once Justice Alito declines to face that issue head on, he can knock out the ACA regulations on contraception only by showing that the means chosen—having Hobby Lobby pay for the insurance benefits—are not the least restrictive available.

In order to make that showing, he reverts to the basic tripartite scheme of the regulations. In dealing with these accommodations, HHS takes the position that religious houses of worship are exempted from the entire system on the supposed empirical ground that they "are more likely than other employers to employ people of the same faith who share the same objection" so that they "would therefore be less likely than other people to use contraceptive services even if such services were covered under their plan."[67] The regulations then add that the only way that other religious non-profit organizations can lawfully opt out of their ACA duty to provide contraceptive coverage is to certify their religious objections to their insurance administrator or provider. Once done, the plan administrator or provider has to supply the needed coverage at no expense to the female participants in the program, without charging back

[67] Coverage of Certain Preventative Services under the Affordable Care Act, 78 Fed. Reg. 39,870, 39,874 (July 2, 2013).

any of the associated costs to the protected religious institution.[68] No relief of either sort was offered to for-profit corporations like Hobby Lobby, which had to provide the coverage, pay the fine, or abandon the provision of all health care to its employees.

In his analysis, Justice Alito insisted that the accommodation that HHS offered to nonprofit religious organizations should have been made available also to for-profit corporations like Hobby Lobby. From that he concluded that this lesser restrictive alternative could have, and should have, been offered to Hobby Lobby. His argument is at best incomplete because it brought no scrutiny to the overall system that it validated.

The first difficulty comes with HHS's purported rationales for excluding houses of worship from its contraceptive mandate. It is striking that the quoted passages stress the identity of the interests of most employees of these organizations with the religious objectives of their employer. At no point, however, does the regulation answer the obvious objection that, nonetheless, the mandate should be retained if only to protect even a tiny sliver of nonreligious employees. Quite simply, there is no reason to worry about religious employees, for they don't have any interests in need of protection, so why not adopt a rule that lets the few women who work for these institutions get health insurance coverage for contraceptive services that they want? Indeed, the only justification for the blanket exemption of churches is to protect the church as such. Yet the HHS regulation is consciously written to avoid just that conclusion.

The second portion of the purported HHS synthesis is every bit as shaky as the first. The HHS argument is that a covered nonprofit religious institution merely has to sign a certification that it authorizes its insurer or plan administrator to provide the coverage in question. Thereafter, the HHS regulations take steps to ensure that this party is not able, either directly or indirectly, to charge back any portion of those premiums to either the employer or the beneficiaries under the program.[69] The point of this maneuver is to allow the employee to receive the benefits without imposing any costs on the employer.

---

[68] *Id.* at 39,873–76. Accommodations in Connection with Coverage of Preventative Health Services, 29 C.F.R. §§ 2590.715-2713A(b)(1), (b)(2)(i)–(iii), (c)(2) (2013).

[69] Exemption and Accommodations in Connection with Coverage of Preventive Health Services, 45 C.F.R. § 147.131.

This system itself, however, is subject to two strong objections: one for the employer and one for the insurer. The first of these is that the regulations insist that the for-profit religious organization fill out a form that requests that the insurer or the administrator pick up the entire slack. But why require that form at all? If the government wants to impose this regime, it can simply order the insurance carrier or administrator to comply and dispense with asking the for-profit organization to fill out the religious form. The obvious response is that forcing religious institutions to sign these declarations is a minimal burden, but then so too is a requirement that all Jehovah's Witnesses recite the Pledge of Allegiance, which has no financial consequences at all. Does it sound far-fetched? Well, no, given that Justice Scalia's decision in *Smith* contained this passage cited approvingly from Justice Felix Frankfurter's majority opinion in *Minersville School District Board of Education v. Gobitis*:

> Conscientious scruples have not, in the course of the long struggle for religious toleration, relieved the individual from obedience to a general law not aimed at the promotion or restriction of religious beliefs. The mere possession of religious convictions which contradict the relevant concerns of a political society does not relieve the citizen from the discharge of political responsibilities (footnote omitted).[70]

How quickly we forget, it seems, the wiser words of Justice Robert Jackson in *West Virginia Board of Education v. Barnett*:

> If there is any fixed star in our constitutional constellation, it is that no official, high or petty, can prescribe what shall be orthodox in politics, nationalism, religion, or other matters of opinion or force citizens to confess *by word or act* their faith therein. If there are any circumstances which permit an exception, they do not now occur to us.[71]

(c) Contraceptive coverage—insured group health plans—

(2)(ii) With respect to payments for contraceptive services, the issuer may not impose any cost-sharing requirements (such as a copayment, coinsurance, or a deductible), or impose any premium, fee, or other charge, or any portion thereof, directly or indirectly, on the eligible organization, the group health plan, or plan participants or beneficiaries.

[70] 310 U.S. 586, 594–95 (1940).

[71] 319 U.S. 624, 642 (1943) (emphasis added).

The prohibition is absolute, even without any assistance from RFRA.

At this point, the supposed synthesis should fall of its own weight. But there is still more, for Justice Alito's treatment of the issue never once asks whether it is proper for the HHS regulation to impose the costs of the contraception mandate on the insurer or the plan administrator. There are two possible scenarios here. First, notwithstanding the regulation, the insurer charges back all or some portion of the cost of contraception in its general rates, at which point the desired financial separation fails. Second, this division is watertight, at which point the inquiry shifts to asking by what warrant does the ACA force this obligation on this insurer or administrator, instead of bearing the costs itself.

Start with some of the institutional details. The ACA's obligation is, of course, unliquidated, so that it can only be estimated. But the function of insurance is to pool risks and therefore to supply a *precise premium that the employer as the insured party pays the* insurer. The HHS regulation flat-out denies the insurer or administrator any opportunity to collect the premium, but makes no provision for its payment from the public treasury. At this point, the ACA provision looks quite different from the general rate regulations of the insurance industry, which are intended either to prevent excessive rates or to ensure plan solvency. Rather, the HHS regulation can only be described as a naked transfer of funds from the insurer or plan administrator to the women's contraceptive services that the government deems appropriate. Even today's current lax rules on insurance regulation do not let the government require any insurance company to underwrite any government-selected service for free. The insurers are not required to either submit to confiscatory rates or go out of business.[72] That rule applies not only to the regulation of an entire business, but also to a single line.[73] The most relevant precedent is *Armstrong v. United States*, where Justice Hugo Black gave this oft-quoted summation of the central objective of the Takings Clause: "The Fifth Amendment's guarantee that private property shall not

---

[72] Aetna Cas. & Sur. Co. v. Comm'r of Ins., 263 N.E.2d 698, 703 (Mass. 1970). See also Jersey Cent. Power & Light Co. v. Fed. Energy Regulatory Comm'n, 810 F.2d 1168 (D.C. Cir. 1987) (proof of potential bankruptcy not necessary to attack government rate regulation); Calfarm Ins. Co. v. Deukmejian, 771 P.2d 1247, 1253–56 (Cal. 1989) (same).

[73] Brooks-Scanlon Co. v. R.R. Comm'n of La., 251 U.S. 396 (1920).

be taken for a public use without just compensation was designed to bar Government from forcing some people alone to bear public burdens which, in all fairness and justice, should be borne by the public as a whole."[74]

At issue in *Armstrong* was whether a subcontractor who filed a ship's lien against a group of navy vessels could be stripped of an otherwise valid lien for work done when the United States Navy dissolved the lien by sailing its boats out of Maine waters. The repair work on naval vessels was done for all citizens equally and thus should be supported by tax revenues. By forcing the subcontractor to sacrifice his lien, the United States imposed a huge portion of the funding for this public good on a single subcontractor even though its revenues counted for only a tiny fraction of GDP. Why then should circumstances require it to foot a large portion of this repair bill? The public-choice explanation for the *Armstrong* rule is that making—and keeping—all these expenses on the government balance sheet not only prevents the singling out of vulnerable parties, but also reduces the likelihood of unwise expenditures by blocking off-budget exactions from the subcontractor. The *Armstrong* rule thus preserves democratic transparency and prevents the inexorable overconsumption of government services.

One possible ground to distinguish *Armstrong* is that it involves only a lien held by a single party, as opposed to the general regulation that HHS issued. However, any systematic distinction between the discrete and the general cannot survive close examination.[75] To see why, just assume that the government instituted, by regulation, a general program that moved all military vessels subject to valid liens out of state waters. Centralizing the decision does not obviate the wrong. Quite the opposite: institutionalizing this program only multiplies the risks of political misconduct and thus should be subject to, if anything, greater not lesser constitutional control. The situation here stands in sharp contrast with those cases where careful application of a single rule to multiple parties generates *reciprocal* benefits to all concerned. At that point, those benefits then provide implicit-in-kind compensation to each party that offsets its particu-

---

[74] Armstrong v. United States, 364 U.S. 40, 49 (1960).

[75] For a systematic development, see Richard A. Epstein, Takings: Private Property and the Power of Eminent Domain ch. 14 (1985) ("Implicit In-Kind Compensation").

lar loss. But there is not a trace of any return benefit in either *Armstrong* or *Hobby Lobby*.

There is a second difference between *Armstrong* and the ACA regulations that also cuts the wrong way for the government. Under *Armstrong*, no one can deny that the repair of navy vessels counts as a public use. In contrast, the HHS regulations transfer funds from general revenues to particular individuals for private benefit, which provide no nonexclusive benefits to the public at large. In my view, these transfer payments should be blocked whether the matter is treated as a taking or as a tax. With regard to the former, there is no public use, the Supreme Court notwithstanding, in the creation of these private benefits.[76] Under the taxing power, the ACA funds are not spent "to pay the Debts and provide for the common Defence and general Welfare of the United States," where the last term "general welfare" refers to some government-supplied collective good.[77] After the Court's decision in *NFIB v. Sebelius*, these arguments for a limited taxing power gain no traction under current case law.[78] But the *Armstrong* prohibition against massive uncompensated transfers has to be *stronger* for specific payments made to particular persons than it is for providing traditional nonexclusive public goods. Accordingly, even under current law, the government can require companies to fund this obligation only if it is prepared to reimburse them out of general revenues. The off-balance-sheet financing authorized by the HHS regulations cannot be tolerated. If these extra charges can be imposed upon the current insurer or administrator, why can't they be imposed with equal logic upon any insurer or administrator as a condition for getting a license to do any business at all? In both cases, the demand that any insurance carrier or administrator bear this charge in order to remain in business counts as yet another exaction, which should be condemned as illegal under the unconstitutional conditions doctrine. The only reasonable accommodation, therefore, is for the government to foot the entire bill. The total absence of current political support for this proposal offers the

---

[76] See *id.* at ch. 12.

[77] U.S. Const. art. I, § 8, cl. 1. For discussion, *see* Richard A. Epstein, The Classical Liberal Constitution 194–98 (2014).

[78] 132 S. Ct. 2566, 2579 (2012) (Roberts, C.J.).

best reason to reject the HHS accommodation that currently shifts the entire burden to private parties.

To Justice Alito, however, these consequences to third persons form no part of the equation. Instead, he conducts his analysis as follows:

> The effect of the HHS-created accommodation on the women employed by Hobby Lobby and the other companies involved in these cases would be precisely zero. Under that accommodation, these women would still be entitled to all FDA-approved contraceptives without cost sharing.[79]

Justice Alito never explains why accommodation would not also work with houses of worship, whose dissenting women could then get health care benefits for free, courtesy of an insurer or plan administrator. Nor does he recognize that neither churches nor female employees have to pay even if the government bears the total cost of the accommodation of the employer's good-faith religious beliefs.

Instead, he makes these unwise concessions to deflect two complaints by the Ginsburg dissent. The first is designed to prevent the unfortunate situation where for-profit "corporations have free rein to impose "disadvantages . . . on others" or to require "the general public [to] pick up the tab."[80] But this Ginsberg objection gets it exactly backward. Alito's narrative wrongly treats the corporation as imposing the burdens on the public at large, when HHS is doing the imposing—putting its hand into Hobby Lobby's pocket by imposing a mandate inconsistent with the owners' religious beliefs. The Senate, for the time being at least, has rejected on partisan party lines the "Not My Boss's Business Act,"[81] when the only question on the table is whether a modification of RFRA can force Hobby Lobby to make these payments, which are surely part of its business. However, no one has yet proposed the "Not My Employees' Business Act" to recognize the right of any business to decide how to spend its own money. Hobby Lobby is more than happy to stay out of its employees' business so long as the government stays out of Hobby

---

[79] Hobby Lobby, 134 S. Ct. at 2760.

[80] Id.

[81] Kristina Peterson, Senate Bill to Nullify Hobby Lobby Decision Fails, Wall St. J., July 16, 2014, available at http://online.wsj.com/articles/senate-bill-against-hobby-lobby-decision-fails-1405537082.

Lobby's business, which it decidedly will not do. As demonstrated above, the government should never be given free rein in its legislative directives. It *should* pick up the tab if it wants to impose the program in question, for otherwise there is no counterweight to prevent the abuse whereby the government dictates what it wants, free of all financial constraint.

Justice Alito also gives far too much credit to Justice Ginsburg's second point when he writes, "And we certainly do not hold or suggest that 'RFRA demands accommodation of a for-profit corporation's religious beliefs no matter the impact that accommodation may have on . . . thousands of women employed by Hobby Lobby.'"[82] The answer here is again simple: force these items on the public budget, and this concern is solved, without the imposition on Hobby Lobby or anyone else. Keep them on the insurers, and there is an adverse third-party effect, which Justice Ginsburg should take into account, given her reliance on *Catholic Charities of Sacramento*'s holding that no accommodation can work if it "detrimentally affect[s] the rights of third parties."[83] This broad injunction covers *both* the potential beneficiaries under the program *and* the insurance carriers on whom the HHS regulators impose the full cost under the ACA. Only public funding avoids both invidious third-party effects—assuming it can gain a political foothold, which at present it can't.

At this point, the burden shifts to both Justice Alito and Justice Ginsburg to explain why Congress gets the power to impose mandates by fiat. Justice Alito writes:

> The principal dissent raises the possibility that discrimination in hiring, for example on the basis of race, might be cloaked as religious practice to escape legal sanction. Our decision today provides no such shield. The Government has a compelling interest in providing an equal opportunity to participate in the workforce without regard to race, and prohibitions on racial discrimination are precisely tailored to achieve that critical goal.[84]

[82] Hobby Lobby, 134 S. Ct. at 2760.

[83] *Id.* at 2790 (citing Catholic Charities of Sacramento, Inc. v. Superior Court, 32 Cal. 4th 527, 565 (2004)).

[84] *Id.* at 2783.

It is too easy for anyone on either side of this debate to play the race card in a religion case. But once it is laid on the table, it requires a clear response, which neither Justice Alito nor Justice Ginsburg provides. Two questions come to mind: why is there a compelling government interest in prohibiting racial discrimination, and why does the current law choose the right balance?

Justice Alito is wrong on both ends and means. Start with the choice of ends, and test his compelling state interest claim as articulated in the Clark excerpt that Justice Blackmun relied on in *Smith*. In all those cases, a strong competitive market negated any compelling state interest. In civil rights cases, however, there was an absence of a competitive market in 1964 for two reasons: common-carrier status or private abuse of force.[85]

By the first, a common carrier enjoys a natural or legal monopoly in standardized services such as train service and air traffic. Segregation on these facilities was a national disgrace, and the Civil Rights Act did well to rid us of it. Similarly, the organized repressive regimes in the Old South and elsewhere imposed brutal restraints on entry in many markets, including those for labor. The use of a nondiscrimination statute is a perfectly sensible second-best solution, but one that should not be kept in place now that the coercive institutional structure of segregation has been dismantled. Once competitive forces are allowed to work, open entry offers the best protection for all workers regardless of race.

The point becomes clearer when one reflects on the means–ends question. On this score, the transformation of the 1964 Civil Rights Act from a colorblind statute into a two-sided law bears notice. On the one side, strong disparate impact tests first announced in *Griggs v. Duke Power Co.*, with little or no statutory support, resulted in overkill, especially on matters of ability and aptitude testing.[86] On the other side, affirmative action programs were given wide sweep by

[85] I develop these themes most recently in Richard A. Epstein, Public Accommodations under the Civil Rights Act of 1964: Why Freedom of Association Counts as a Human Right, 66 Stan. L. Rev. 1241 (2014). For the earlier version of this argument, see Richard A. Epstein, Forbidden Grounds: The Case against Employment Discrimination (1992).

[86] 401 U.S. 424 (1971). For criticism, see Michael Evan Gold, The Similarity of Congressional and Judicial Lawmaking under Title VII of the Civil Rights Act of 1964, 18 U.C. Davis L. Rev. 721 (1985); Epstein, Forbidden Grounds at 192–200.

equally dubious interpretations of the basic statutory language in *Steelworkers v. Weber.*[87] *Griggs* should be rejected for its distortion of testing markets. *Weber* should be endorsed solely because it amounts in part to a repeal of the Civil Rights Act that has no sensible function in private competitive markets. The law could not have survived if *Griggs*'s "business necessity" standard had been applied to block private affirmative action programs. But given the divergence between *Griggs* and *Weber* on both sides of the ledger, the 1964 Act does not have any sensible fit to the abstract end of eliminating racial discrimination across the board. By repealing the Civil Rights Act, disparate impact would be history, and affirmative action programs could survive to the extent that they can garner private support, which is as it should be.

The point matters. Accept Justice Alito's account of the race discrimination law and then the compelling state interest test expands beyond its proper contours, as demonstrated by his uncritical acceptance of the government accommodation. This one point dooms his argument on the least restrictive alternative. That issue came to a head just three days after *Hobby Lobby*, when Wheaton College claimed that it should not be required to sign any form that authorized the insurance company payouts. Justice Alito should have been trapped given his explicit praise of that solution in *Hobby Lobby*, and Wheaton College sent packing. But no, in *Wheaton College* a cautiously worded opinion led to a temporary injunction, without prejudice on the merits. A fiery dissent by Justice Sotomayor then asked why *Hobby Lobby* did not control, for which there is no good answer. Note that none of these issues could have arisen if Justice Alito had not treated the advancement of women's health under the ACA as a compelling state interest.

III. The Future

The early rounds of jostling over the contraceptive mandate are over, with the battle lines drawn as sharply as ever. Just what will happen next no one knows. Will Congress amend RFRA to force the mandate? That is doubtful, but if so, when the matter goes back to the Court, that selective repeal will ironically be attacked by conservatives as constitutionally infirm along the lines rejected by the

[87] 443 U.S. 193 (1979).

conservative majority in *Schuette v. Coalition to Defend Affirmative Action*.[88] That argument is likely to lose. More likely in my view is that the constitutional issue decided in *Smith* will reappear. Recall that *Gobitis* was overruled by *Barnette*, and in my view it is quite likely that *Smith* will be either overruled or, more probably, qualified to preserve the *Hobby Lobby* result. After all, the last Supreme Court decision to deal with the neutrality principle, *Hosanna-Tabor Evangelical v. EEOC*,[89] made quick work of *Smith* as dealing with "only outward physical acts" rather than "an internal church decision that affects the faith and mission of the church itself."[90] In so doing, the chief justice disregarded the pervasive reach of *Smith's* neutrality rationale. To be sure, Hobby Lobby is no church, but recall that the Free Exercise Clause applies to individuals as well as churches, and their exercise of religion textually covers more than worship. No one can be sure of what will happen, but it is at least even money that *Smith* is further limited, with the reluctant acquiescence of a grumpy Justice Scalia.

Yet the larger issue looms: why this intellectual mess? On this score, note that my own sympathies on the religion issues lie with Justices Blackmun, Brennan, and Marshall, not your typical conservative icons. On these issues at least, their civil libertarian views aligned with libertarian views more generally. But today the American left is far less libertarian, far more impatient, and far more authoritarian than before. And often it is met with equal vehemence by portions of the conservative right. What both sides tend to forget is that live-and-let-live is a central position for any group, libertarian or not, that wants to preserve civil peace. Only if members of group A are willing to understand that members of group B are entitled to take actions that they, as devout members of group A, find deeply offensive can citizens in a widely diverse society live together. Think of the lesson of the flag-burning cases.[91] Modern progressives do not accept that position, and modern conservatives match them stride for stride. But in *Hobby Lobby*, the critical intellectual gaffe comes

---

[88] 134 S. Ct. 1623 (2014).

[89] 132 S. Ct. 694 (2012).

[90] *Id.* at 697.

[91] See Texas v. Johnson, 491 U.S. 397, 414 (1989) ("[T]he government may not prohibit the expression of an idea simply because society finds the idea itself offensive or disagreeable.").

from the progressive wing of the Democratic Party that insists that the refusal to supply a set of legislated benefits in a competitive market is a form of coercion, the proverbial gun to the head. Not so. All Hobby Lobby wants is to be left alone. Unfortunately, two doctrinal developments block that simple demand. First is the weak protection of economic liberties, which opens the field up to massive regulation such as that found in the ACA, and second is the utter unwillingness to make sensible accommodations whenever religious norms conflict with general laws.

It should be otherwise. Any coherent theory of liberty protects business, speech, and religion in roughly the same proportions. The doctrinal developments that have expanded the gaps between different substantive areas have served to make the modern law more treacherous. There is nothing in RFRA's framework of basic rights, compelling state interest, and least restrictive means that cannot be generalized to cover all human activity. The broader the principles are, the fewer the ad hoc judgments, and the more consistent the social commitment will be to individual liberty in all its manifestations. The good news about *Hobby Lobby* is that a bare majority of the Supreme Court stumbled to the right conclusion. The bad news is that the weak doctrinal analysis from the fractured Court has created a legal and political whirlwind from which it will be difficult for this nation to emerge unscathed given the current political tumult.

Town of Greece v. Galloway: The Establishment Clause and the Rediscovery of History

Eric Rassbach*

The thesis of this essay is that *Town of Greece v. Galloway* marks a major inflection point in the development of the law of the Establishment Clause.[1] A jurisprudence that had been oddly untethered from history has come to embrace it. Going forward, the language of the decision itself will cause great changes in how Establishment Clause cases are decided. But even more important, the process of historical examination that *Town of Greece* has set in motion will continue to reshape how these cases are decided for years to come.

The essay has four parts. First, I describe the general trend of renewed judicial focus on the history of the Bill of Rights. Second, I provide a summarized narrative of how Establishment Clause cases have typically treated history and historical government practice. Third, I set out what *Town of Greece* says about history and what this means for Establishment Clause cases. Fourth, I predict how the

* Deputy General Counsel, Becket Fund for Religious Liberty. The Becket Fund for Religious Liberty is a nonprofit law firm that represents people of all religious traditions, including Buddhists, Christians, Hindus, Jews, Muslims, Santeros, Sikhs, and others. The views stated here are my own and do not necessarily reflect the views of the Becket Fund or my clients. Several of the ideas presented here were presented in alternative form in the Becket Fund's amicus brief filed in *Town of Greece v. Galloway*, 134 S.Ct. 1811 (2014) (No. 12-696), available at http://www.becketfund.org/wp-content/uploads/2013/08/Town-of-Greece-v.-Galloway-Becket-Fund-Amicus-Brief-to-SCOTUS.pdf [hereinafter Becket Fund Br.]; a symposium piece on SCOTUSblog, Eric Rassbach, Symposium: *Lemon* Wins a Reprieve, but the End is Near, SCOTUSblog (May. 6, 2014), http://www.scotusblog.com/2014/05/symposium-lemon-wins-a-reprieve-but-the-end-is-near; and the Annual Donald C. Clark, Jr., '79, Endowed Law and Religion Lecture held on March 27, 2014, at Rutgers School of Law–Camden. I thank my colleagues at the Becket Fund for helping me to develop the ideas in this essay, especially Daniel Blomberg, Luke Goodrich, Mark Rienzi, and Diana Verm.

[1] 134 S.Ct. 1811 (2014).

rediscovery of history will play out in the development of Establishment Clause cases.

I. The March of History through the Bill of Rights

It is a peculiar feature of history that the more time that has elapsed since an event, often the more we know about it. We know much more today about the politics of medieval Japan or the economic life of Victorian England than did the medieval Japanese or the 19th-century English, respectively. We even know a lot more about the Vietnam War than did the generation that fought it; for example, we know much more now about the Vietnamese perspective on that conflict than we did even 20 years ago.

This phenomenon—that historical knowledge increases with time—is a function of changes over time in the organization and accessibility of data on the one hand, and changes in perspective on the other. Over time, historians can gather more data about certain events. Documents that were hidden come to light. Data dispersed in many locations can be collated and analyzed. New technologies appear that make information more organized and more accessible.[2]

The increase in chronological distance also gives the latter-day observer a less self-interested perspective of events than those who were personally swept up in them. Few today are personally exercised about the Teapot Dome scandal that aroused great passions in the 1920s; none of the parties involved are still alive. That emotional distance allows us to view the scandal, its causes, and its effects more objectively. In addition, greater chronological distance allows an observer to better determine what the most important factors in any particular sequence of events may be.

This phenomenon is also true of the American Founding, and in particular the adoption of the Bill of Rights. For example, we now know much more about the Founding than did observers 70 or 80 years ago when the Bill of Rights was being incorporated against the states. The information we have about the Founding is better organized and accessible. And we have a better idea of which historical details from the time were important and which were not.

---

[2] See, e.g., Google, Company Overview, https://www.google.com/about/company ("Google's mission is to organize the world's information and make it universally accessible and useful."); see also *infra* note 47.

This increased historical knowledge about the history of the Founding era has important effects on the law. Because constitutional jurisprudence is particularly attuned to history, any changes in our historical knowledge of the Founding can have significant effects on Bill of Rights jurisprudence.[3]

Indeed, in recent years the expansion and organization of historical data concerning the Bill of Rights has worked great changes in constitutional law. Amendment by amendment, the Supreme Court has reinterpreted the Bill of Rights in the light of this new historical data, specifically historical data concerning the Anglo-American law, the American colonies, and the Founding itself.

Many examples demonstrate the trend. In 2000, the Court recast the Sixth Amendment right to trial by jury by examining "the practice of criminal indictment, trial by jury, and judgment by court as it existed during the years surrounding our Nation's founding."[4] In 2004, the Court made fundamental changes to the Sixth Amendment's protection of a criminal defendant's right to confront the witnesses testifying against him by looking to "the historical background of the [Confrontation] Clause to understand its meaning."[5] In 2008, the Court decided the landmark *District of Columbia v. Heller*, initiating the modern era of Second Amendment litigation.[6] Both the *Heller* majority and its dissent focused on history to reach their conclusions.[7] The disagreement was not about the importance of history in interpreting the Second Amendment, but what that history

---

[3] Note that by "history," I do not mean any of the different originalist theories of constitutional interpretation or their competitors. I mean instead the use of history as part of the interpretive process, which is common to most interpretive schools. See, e.g., Jack M. Balkin, Alive and Kicking, Slate.com (Aug. 29, 2005), http://www.slate.com/articles/news_and_politics/jurisprudence/2005/08/alive_and_kicking.single.html ("Living constitutionalists draw upon precedent, structure, and the country's history to flesh out the meaning of the text. They properly regard all of these as legitimate sources of interpretation.").

[4] Apprendi v. New Jersey, 530 U.S. 466, 478 (2000).

[5] Crawford v. Washington, 541 U.S. 36, 43 (2004).

[6] 554 U.S. 570 (2008).

[7] See *id.* at 598 (examining "the history that the founding generation knew" to interpret the Second Amendment); *id.* at 642 (Stevens, J., dissenting) (examining "contemporary concerns that animated the Framers").

demonstrated. Similarly, the Fourth Amendment has long been rooted in historical understandings.[8]

This trend has in recent years begun to reach the Religion Clauses. In 2012, the Court decided *Hosanna-Tabor Evangelical Lutheran Church and School v. Equal Employment Opportunity Commission*, which relied on both the Free Exercise Clause and the Establishment Clause to declare the existence of a "ministerial exception" to employment discrimination laws.[9] Chief Justice John Roberts, writing for a unanimous Court, began his constitutional analysis with a lengthy discussion of English and colonial government practices concerning the hiring of church ministers, including extensive interference with the selection of clergy.[10] The Court then applied this historical reality to explain what the Religion Clauses mean today:

> It was against this background that the First Amendment was adopted. Familiar with life under the established Church of England, the founding generation sought to foreclose the possibility of a national church. . . . By forbidding the "establishment of religion" and guaranteeing the "free exercise thereof," the Religion Clauses ensured that the new Federal Government—unlike the English Crown—would have no role in filling ecclesiastical offices. The Establishment Clause prevents the Government from appointing ministers, and the Free Exercise Clause prevents it from interfering with the freedom of religious groups to select their own.[11]

Hosanna-Tabor thus stands not just for the proposition that there is a constitutionally mandated ministerial exception. It stands also for a principle of judicial method: that the historical background of the religion clauses serves to delineate their scope today.

From the data above, the trend is clear: in Bill of Rights cases generally and the religion clauses specifically, history has become an

---

[8] See, e.g., United States v. Jones, 132 S. Ct. 945, 950 & n.3 (2012) (examining the "original meaning of the Fourth Amendment," because "we must assur[e] preservation of that degree of privacy against government that existed when the Fourth Amendment was adopted").

[9] 132 S.Ct. 694, 702 (2012). The Becket Fund was counsel to the petitioner, Hosanna-Tabor Evangelical Lutheran Church and School, in the appeal.

[10] *Id.* at 702–04.

[11] Hosanna-Tabor, 132 S.Ct. at 703.

increasingly important interpretive tool, not just for one wing or the other of the Court, but for all of the justices.

II. History and the Establishment Clause 1947–2014

However clear the trend may be in the context of Bill of Rights cases generally, it is impossible to understand *Town of Greece* and the significance of the case's treatment of history unless one is familiar with the tensions within Establishment Clause jurisprudence.

Modern Establishment Clause jurisprudence has had a garbled and, at times, admittedly confused approach toward history as an interpretive tool. To see why, we have to look back at how the Court has treated history and the Establishment Clause from 1947 until 2014. The narrative divides into two phases.

A. *The First Phase*: Everson

The first phase began 67 years ago, with *Everson v. Board of Education of Ewing Township,* a case that dealt with the busing of students to religious schools.[12] *Everson* marks the first time that the Supreme Court decided a claim concerning an establishment of religion by a non-federal entity, and resulted in the incorporation of the Establishment Clause against the states. The case launched modern Establishment Clause jurisprudence.

Everson also marks the first time that the Court discussed history and the Establishment Clause.[13] But as Professor Michael McConnell has pointed out, the *Everson* Court's "careless description of history" left much to be desired.[14] McConnell notes that the *Everson* Court gave a "truncated" account of the history behind the adoption of the Establishment Clause that relied far too heavily on the 1785 rejection of Patrick Henry's Assessment Bill in Virginia and the enactment of Thomas Jefferson's Bill for Establishing Religious Freedom instead.[15] The *Everson* Court looked at only a tiny part of the history and thus focused too exclusively on the reasons offered against establishment,

---

[12] 330 U.S. 1 (1947).

[13] An earlier Establishment Clause case involving the federal government did not include any discussion of history. Bradfield v. Roberts, 175 U.S. 291 (1899).

[14] Michael W. McConnell, Establishment and Disestablishment at the Founding, Part I: Establishment of Religion, 44 Wm. and Mary L. Rev. 2105, 2108 (2003).

[15] *Id.*

without taking into account either the pro-establishment side of the debate or the process of disestablishment that was going on in the states before, during, and after the Founding.[16] Most important, it meant that the Court ignored the question of what an "establishment of religion" actually was.

Everson's approach to history set the tone for Establishment Clause cases decided throughout the 1950s and 1960s. Although cases such as *McGowan v. Maryland* looked in detail at specific practices at the time of the Founding, the analysis consistently circled back to *Everson*'s treatment of the Virginia debate over assessments as the paradigmatic statement of the historic meaning of the Establishment Clause.[17]

B. The Second Phase: Lemon

But 24 years after *Everson*, the Supreme Court adopted a very different approach to history. In *Lemon v. Kurtzman*, the Court did not rely on *Everson*'s version of history but instead specifically stated that it could not know either the history behind the Establishment Clause or consequently what it meant.[18] Thus Chief Justice Warren Burger began his discussion with this confession: "Candor compels acknowledgment . . . that we can only dimly perceive the lines of demarcation in this extraordinarily sensitive area of constitutional law."[19] Then later, "The language of the Religion Clauses of the First Amendment is at best opaque, particularly when compared with other portions of the Amendment."[20] The Court then surrenders, stating that "[i]n the absence of precisely stated constitutional prohibitions, we must draw lines."[21] The *Lemon* Court then drew those lines not by looking to the history of religious establishments in the Founders' experience, or even the state religious establishments that lasted for decades after

---

[16] *Id.*

[17] 366 U.S. 420, 437–40, 442–44 (1961); see also Ill. ex rel. McCollum v. Board of Ed. of Sch. Dist. No. 71, 333 U.S. 203, 210–12 (1948); Zorach v. Clauson, 343 U.S. 306, 312 (1952); Torcaso v. Watkins, 367 U.S. 488, 492–94 (1961); Engel v. Vitale, 370 U.S. 421, 428 n.11 (1962); Sch. Dist. of Abington Twp. v. Schempp, 374 U.S. 203, 216–17 (1963); Walz v. Tax Comm'n, 397 U.S. 664, 667–68 (1970) (all relying on *Everson*'s account).

[18] 403 U.S. 602 (1971).

[19] Lemon, 403 U.S. at 612.

[20] *Id.*

[21] *Id.*

the Founding. Instead, the Court looked to the "cumulative criteria developed by the Court" during the 24 preceding years of Establishment Clause cases to "glean[]" *Lemon's* now-familiar three-prong test, which examines the purpose of the government action at issue, its effects, and whether it unduly entangles the government in religion.[22] Thus the currently governing Establishment Clause standard in all of the lower courts was born as an *ipse dixit* derived from a patently impressionistic survey of just 24 years of precedent.

It is hard to overstate the impact that this move had on how the lower courts processed Establishment Clause claims. *Lemon* created a single, universally applicable Establishment Clause standard while at the same time detaching Establishment Clause analysis (in the lower courts) from the examination of historical practice.[23] The three-pronged *Lemon* test—purpose, effects, entanglement—has staying power in the lower courts for several reasons. It is simple on its face: it provides the sort of test that those courts are used to applying. It doesn't have any strong competitor tests that the Supreme Court has set forth. And it privileges judicial power because the abstract terms of the test give courts license to reframe legislative and even executive action in ways that could reflect personal policy choices.[24] Put another way, if the *Lemon* test were a municipal ordinance rather than a doctrine developed by the Supreme Court, it might well be struck down as void for vagueness.[25]

---

[22] *Id.* at 612–13. Justice Brennan later quoted this "gleaning" language in his dissent in *Marsh v. Chambers*. See discussion in the section immediately following this one.

[23] I do not claim that once *Lemon* was decided, the Supreme Court stopped referring to history in Establishment Clause cases—far from it. Instead, my argument is that *Lemon* marked a shift from one way of thinking about history and the Establishment Clause to another. More importantly, in the lower courts *Lemon* almost completely displaced history as a mode of Establishment Clause analysis.

[24] This is true even when courts do not want that level of unbridled judicial discretion. For example, just last month a federal judge reluctantly ordered a Ten Commandments monument removed from the lawn of the city hall in Bloomfield, New Mexico, stating that "in performing the role of [the endorsement test's reasonable] observer, the Court is thrust into a realm of pretend and make-believe, guided only by confusing jurisprudence and its own imagination." Felix v. City of Bloomfield, 2014 WL 3865948 at *10 (D.N.M. Aug. 7, 2014).

[25] The void-for-vagueness doctrine prohibits laws that do not provide sufficient guidance to those they regulate: "[A] statute which either forbids or requires the doing of an act in terms so vague that men of common intelligence must necessarily guess at its meaning and differ as to its application, violates the first essential of due process

The *Lemon* test's staying power is doubly ironic. First, the test has been heavily criticized for most of its existence.[26] Given the ongoing criticism of the test, it is surprising to some that it has lasted as long as it has. Second, the test provides a decapitated kind of guidance. The Supreme Court has in recent years almost routinely ignored the test. But because it has never expressly overruled *Lemon*, *Lemon* remains the law of the land in all 12 of the regional circuits. Put another way, *Lemon* will remain the law until the Supreme Court specifically abrogates it.

C. The Second Phase and Legislative Prayer: Marsh v. Chambers

Twelve years after *Lemon*, the Court confronted for the first time the constitutionality of legislative prayer. *Marsh v. Chambers* was a challenge to the Nebraska legislature's practice of having a paid chaplain (in this case, a Presbyterian) deliver prayers at legislative sessions, a practice that every other state legislature and both houses of Congress had engaged in.[27] The Supreme Court upheld the practice in an opinion written, like *Lemon*, by Chief Justice Warren Burger. The Court upheld the practice, relying principally on the fact that legislative prayer was an accepted practice at the time of the Founding and indeed was something the Framers themselves practiced when they met.[28] Three justices—William Brennan, Thurgood Marshall, and John Paul Stevens—dissented. Justice Brennan stated in his opinion that

> The Court makes no pretense of subjecting Nebraska's practice of legislative prayer to any of the formal "tests" that have traditionally structured our inquiry under the Establishment Clause. That it fails to do so is, in a sense, a good thing, for it simply confirms that the Court is carving

---

of law" FCC v. Fox Television Stations, Inc., 132 S.Ct. 2307 (2012) (quoting Connally v. Gen. Constr. Co., 269 U.S. 385, 391 (1926)).

[26] See *infra* subsection titled "General Dissatisfaction with Establishment Clause Precedent."

[27] 463 U.S. 783 (1983). In 2011, the Hawaii Senate had ceased holding legislative prayer after the threat of a lawsuit; in the wake of *Town of Greece*, it now may apparently consider reinstituting the practice. Catherine Cruz, Legislature, Council Weighs High Court Prayer Ruling, KITV.com (May 5, 2014), http://www.kitv.com/news/legislature-council-weighs-high-court-prayer-ruling/25827358.

[28] Marsh, 463 U.S. at 790–92.

out an exception to the Establishment Clause, rather than reshaping Establishment Clause doctrine to accommodate legislative prayer.[29]

Justice Brennan was right: the opinion did not explain how the rule set forth in *Marsh* fit together with the rest of Establishment Clause jurisprudence. It dealt instead with the discrete issue of legislative prayer, in effect saying that "the Framers did it so it must be permissible," and not much else. The lack of overt connection between the *Lemon* line of precedent and the *Marsh* line of precedent set up the conflict that led to *Town of Greece*.[30]

D. The Endorsement Test Corollary to Lemon

Meanwhile, the *Lemon* test continued to expand. In 1984, a year after *Marsh* was decided, the Supreme Court expanded the *Lemon* test significantly. In her concurring opinion in *Lynch v. Donnelly*, Justice Sandra Day O'Connor posited what became a corollary to the *Lemon* test, at least as the lower courts applied Establishment Clause precedent: the endorsement test.[31] The test states that a "second and more direct infringement [of the Establishment Clause] is government endorsement or disapproval of religion. Endorsement sends a message to nonadherents that they are outsiders, not full members of the political community, and an accompanying message to adherents that they are insiders, favored members of the political community. Disapproval sends the opposite message."[32]

Since Justice O'Connor first proposed that gloss on *Lemon*, the Supreme Court has found "endorsement" in just six cases.[33] And it has ignored it in many others where the test might have been expected to apply if it were truly a test of general application.[34] However, as

[29] *Id.* at 796 (Brennan, J., dissenting).

[30] See *infra* subsection entitled *"Lemon* and *Marsh* in Conflict."

[31] 465 U.S. 668 (1984).

[32] *Id.* at 688 (O'Connor, J., concurring).

[33] Wallace v. Jaffree, 472 U.S. 38, 59–60 (1985); Sch. Dist. of City of Grand Rapids v. Ball, 473 U.S. 373, 392 (1985), overruled by Agostini v. Felton, 521 U.S. 203 (1997); Edwards v. Aguillard, 482 U.S. 578, 593 (1987); Cnty. of Allegheny v. ACLU, 492 U.S. 573, 599 (1989); Doe. v. Santa Fe Indep. Sch. Dist., 530 U.S. 290, 308 (2000); McCreary Cnty. v. ACLU of Ky., 545 U.S. 844, 866 (2005).

[34] See, e.g., Van Orden v. Perry, 545 U.S. 677, 686 (2005) (plurality op.) (Ten Commandments case decided the same day as the McCreary Ten Commandments

with the original *Lemon* test, the endorsement test has become one that the lower courts feel duty-bound to apply, even if the Supreme Court does not feel so obligated. Thus the endorsement test has in most lower courts become part of the second prong of the *Lemon* test—"effects."[35]

E. General Dissatisfaction with Establishment Clause Precedent

The result of this headless jurisprudence has been widespread dissatisfaction among academics, lawyers, and judges alike.

Professors specializing in law and religion issues aren't satisfied and frequently publish critiques of the Supreme Court's Establishment Clause decisions.[36] Church-state litigators aren't satisfied either. Individual decisions are welcomed by one side or the other, but few litigators if any would say that they are satisfied with Establishment Clause jurisprudence as a whole, regardless of where they are on the ideological spectrum.

Lower court judges certainly aren't satisfied. There have been numerous lower court opinions openly prodding the Supreme Court to fix the jurisprudence in this area of the law. Judge Frank Easterbrook of the U.S. Court of Appeals for the Seventh Circuit has written:

> Standards such as those found in *Lemon* . . . and the "no endorsement" rule, not only are hopelessly open-ended but also lack support in the text of the first amendment and do not have any historical provenance. They have been made up by the Justices during recent decades. The actual Establishment Clause bans laws respecting the establishment of religion— which is to say, taxation for the support of a church, the employment of clergy on the public payroll, and mandatory attendance or worship. See generally Leonard W. Levy, The Establishment Clause: Religion and the First Amendment (2d ed. 1994); Philip Hamburger, Separation of Church and State 89–107 (2002); Michael W. McConnell, Establishment

---

case, but ignoring the *Lemon* and endorsement tests); *id.* at 700 (Breyer, J., concurring) (in controlling concurrence, declining to apply the *Lemon*/endorsement test and seeing "no test-related substitute for the exercise of legal judgment").

[35] Am. Atheists, Inc. v. Port Authority of N.Y. and N.J., 2014 WL 3702452 at *9 (2d Cir. July 28, 2014) (applying endorsement test as part of *Lemon*'s second prong).

[36] See, e.g., Michael W. McConnell, Religious Freedom at a Crossroads, 59 Univ. Chi. L. Rev. 115 (1992); Jesse H. Choper, The Endorsement Test: Its Status and Desirability, 18 J.L. & Pol. 499 (2002).

and Disestablishment at the Founding, Part I: Establishment of Religion, 44 Wm. & Mary L. Rev. 2105 (2003). Holding a high school graduation in a church does not "establish" that church any more than serving Wheaties in the school cafeteria establishes Wheaties as the official cereal. See also Michael W. McConnell, Coercion: The Lost Element of Establishment, 27 Wm. & Mary L. Rev. 933 (1986).[37]

Fellow Seventh Circuit Judge Richard Posner added his own criticism: "The case law that the Supreme Court has heaped on the defenseless text of the establishment clause is widely acknowledged, even by some Supreme Court Justices, to be formless, unanchored, subjective and provide no guidance."[38]

Perhaps the most memorable statement in this vein was from Judge Ferdinand Fernandez, who wrote a concurring opinion in a 2008 appeal to the Ninth Circuit:

> I applaud Judge [Kim McLane] Wardlaw's scholarly and heroic attempt to create a new world of useful principle out of the Supreme Court's dark materials. Alas, even my redoubtable colleague cannot accomplish that. The still stalking *Lemon* test and the other tests and factors, which have floated to the top of this chaotic ocean from time to time in order to answer specific questions, are so indefinite and unhelpful that Establishment Clause jurisprudence has not become more fathomable. Would that courts required neutrality in the area of religion and nothing more or less.[39]

This sort of open criticism of Supreme Court precedent from court of appeals judges is unusual and infrequent—in most areas of the law. In Establishment Clause decisions, it has become commonplace, however, as the lower courts attempt to reconcile seemingly contradictory strands of Supreme Court precedent and express their resentment that the Court has made their task so difficult.

Most important, the justices themselves have expressed their dissatisfaction with the current state of Establishment Clause

---

[37] Doe ex rel. Doe v. Elmbrook School Dist., 687 F.3d 840, 869 (7th Cir. 2012) (Easterbrook, J., dissenting).

[38] *Id.*, at 872 (Posner, J., dissenting).

[39] Card v. City of Everett, 520 F.3d 1009, 1023–24 (9th Cir. 2008) (Fernandez, J., concurring).

precedent—and in particular the *Lemon* test and its endorsement corollary—be it in concurrences or dissents.[40]

F. Lemon *and* Marsh *in conflict*

Into this general dissatisfaction with the Establishment Clause, and the tension between *Lemon* and *Marsh* specifically, came an effort by Americans United for Separation of Church and State and the American Civil Liberties Union to bring test cases concerning municipal legislative prayer. [41] The apparent rationale behind this effort was that *Marsh* was viewed as an aberration and *Lemon*/endorsement the norm. The strategy behind the ACLU/AUSCS initiative was to pick off what could be viewed as an outlier doctrine that allowed legislative prayer to persist. In this point of view, *Marsh's* blessing of legislative prayer ran directly counter to the way most Establishment Clause cases were decided under the *Lemon*/endorsement test. And municipalities were a much easier target than state legislatures, both because they'd be more likely to roll over after being sued and because *Marsh* itself concerned the practices of a state legislature.

The tension that the ACLU and AUSCS saw was a real one—*Lemon* and *Marsh* had quite different approaches to analysis of Establishment Clause claims. *Lemon* dictated an abstract, anti-historical

---

[40] See, e.g., Utah Highway Patrol Ass'n v. Am. Atheists, Inc., 132 S.Ct. 12, 12–23 (2011) (mem.) (Thomas, J., dissenting from denial of cert.) (collecting cases and criticizing *Lemon* and endorsement tests); Cnty. of Allegheny v. ACLU, 492 U.S. 573, 669 (1989) (Kennedy, J., dissenting) (criticizing endorsement test "flawed in its fundamentals and unworkable in practice"); Capitol Square Review & Advisory Bd. v. Pinette, 515 U.S. 753, 768 n.3 (1995) (plurality opinion, Scalia, J., joined by Rehnquist, C.J., Kennedy and Thomas, JJ.) ("[The endorsement test] supplies no standard whatsoever . . . . It is irresponsible to make the Nation's legislators walk this minefield."); Salazar v. Buono, 130 S. Ct. 1803, 1819 (2010) (Kennedy, J., joined by Roberts, C.J., and Alito, J.) ("Even if [the endorsement test] were the appropriate one, but see [*Allegheny* and *Pinette*]"); *id.* at 1824 (Alito, J., concurring) ("Assuming that it is appropriate to apply the so-called 'endorsement test,' this test would not be violated [here]."); Van Orden v. Perry, 545 U.S. 677, 700 (2005) (Breyer, J., concurring) (declining to apply the *Lemon* and endorsement tests and stating that "I see no test-related substitute for the exercise of legal judgment").

[41] Americans United was founded as an anti-Catholic organization known as "Protestants and Other Americans United for Separation of Church and State." See, e.g., Protestants and Other Ams. United for Separation of Church and State v. O'Brien, 272 F.Supp. 712 (D.D.C. 1967). AUSCS has never publicly disavowed its anti-Catholic origins.

approach to deciding Establishment Clause questions, while *Marsh* took a concrete historically rooted approach.

Indeed, *Lemon*'s three questions are quite abstract: Does government have the purpose of promoting or discouraging religion? Does the government action in question have the effect of promoting or discouraging religion? And does the government action in question excessively entangle government with religion?

By contrast, *Marsh* relies entirely on historical practice and very little other reasoning. As Chief Justice Burger wrote in the opinion, the existence of the historical practice of legislative prayer is, standing alone, sufficient grounds to uphold the practice.[42] There is no effort in the opinion to delineate any broader, principled framework for deciding Establishment Clause cases. And we don't find out anything about how the Founders thought about establishments generally; the focus is strictly on legislative prayer. Thus, if anything, *Marsh* is *overly* concrete.

Lemon and *Marsh* have something in common—they have *ipse dixits* at their core. *Lemon*'s very brief canvassing of Establishment Clause jurisprudence of the preceding 24 years leaps to an announcement of the three prongs. And *Marsh* announces that the Framers practiced legislative prayer, so it must be permissible, without situating that claim in a broader framework for deciding constitutional claims. Neither approach is terribly helpful to lower court judges who have to apply principles to a wide variety of facts. *Lemon*'s prongs are too abstract to be true principles, while *Marsh*'s focus on the specific history of legislative prayer is too concrete to be applied to fact scenarios outside the immediate context of legislative prayer.

But these differences explain how the lower courts have applied the two cases. It is *Lemon*'s abstract nature and *Marsh*'s concrete nature that has dictated their very different careers in the lower courts. *Lemon* purports to provide a comprehensive test for Establishment Clause cases, and that claim to comprehensiveness is a useful tool for lower courts. It gives judges elements to work with, even if the prongs themselves are far too abstract to provide consistent results in different courts dealing with different factual scenarios. By contrast, *Marsh*'s exclusive focus on legislative prayer means that it is applied by courts in that context only.

---

[42] Marsh, 463 U.S. at 790–92.

In any event, it is this tension that the ACLU and AUSCS attempted to exploit by bringing municipal prayer cases. Their hope would have been that municipal prayer might fall sufficiently outside the scope of *Marsh* that they could get courts to apply the *Lemon*/endorsement test instead. They succeeded in the lower courts in several cases, including *Town of Greece*—the Second Circuit ruled in AUSCS's clients' favor, on grounds that the town's prayer practices violated the endorsement test.[43] Thus the stage was set for a remarkable convergence of the *Lemon* test, the endorsement test corollary, *Marsh*, and the rise of history in Bill of Rights litigation.

III. *Town of Greece*: A Third Phase?

The case did not disappoint. Although the Supreme Court did not overrule the endorsement test or *Lemon*, in *Town of Greece* it marked a very big change in how the Court deals with history in Establishment Clause cases.

A. The Majority Opinion

Justice Anthony Kennedy, writing for the majority, rejects Justice Brennan's suggestion in his *Marsh* dissent that *Marsh* "'carv[ed] out an exception' to the Court's Establishment Clause jurisprudence[,]" stating that "*Marsh* stands for the proposition that it is not necessary to define the precise boundary of the Establishment Clause where history shows that the specific practice is permitted. *Any* test the Court adopts must acknowledge a practice that was accepted by the Framers and has withstood the critical scrutiny of time and political change."[44]

This statement means at least two remarkable things. First, in the conflict between *Lemon* and *Marsh*, *Marsh* is not so much the exception as it is the rule. *Marsh*'s historical analysis trumps the *Lemon* test, not the other way around. Second, the Court introduces a "historical override" to all Establisment Clause claims. "Any test" a lower court applies must be accompanied by (or probably *preceded* by) a historical analysis, and that analysis trumps the other considerations. This use of history is not reflexive: "Yet *Marsh* must not be understood as permitting a practice that would amount to a constitutional violation

---

[43] Galloway v. Town of Greece, 681 F.3d 20 (2d Cir. 2012).

[44] Town of Greece, 134 S. Ct. at 1819 (emphasis added; citations omitted).

if not for its historical foundation. The case teaches instead that the Establishment Clause must be interpreted 'by reference to historical practices and understandings.'"[45]

The Court later expands on the point:

> The prayer opportunity in this case *must* be evaluated against the backdrop of historical practice. As a practice that has long endured, legislative prayer has become part of our heritage and tradition, part of our expressive idiom, similar to the Pledge of Allegiance, inaugural prayer, or the recitation of "God save the United States and this honorable Court" at the opening of this Court's sessions.[46]

Thus, the particular governmental practice being challenged under the Establishment Clause must be evaluated "against the backdrop of historical practice." And those practices that have "long endured" and become "part of our heritage and tradition" should be upheld, even if they were practices, such as recitation of the Pledge of Allegiance in schools, that were not practiced at the time of the Founding.[47]

The *Town of Greece* majority also went out of its way to reject a specific dictum from *County of Allegheny v. ACLU* that has plagued

---

[45] *Id.* (citing Cnty. of Allegheny, 492 U.S. at 670 (Kennedy, J., concurring in judgment in part and dissenting in part)).

[46] *Id.* at 1825 (emphasis added).

[47] *Id. Town of Greece's* treatment of history also contains confirmation of the phenomenon of the increase of historical knowledge over time. See *supra* note 2. The Court states:

> Although no information has been cited by the parties to indicate how many local legislative bodies open their meetings with prayer, this practice too has historical precedent. See Reports of Proceedings of the City Council of Boston for the Year Commencing Jan. 1, 1909, and Ending Feb. 5, 1910, pp. 1–2 (1910) (Rev. Arthur Little) ("And now we desire to invoke Thy presence, Thy blessing, and Thy guidance upon those who are gathered here this morning . . .").

Id. at 1819. The quote derives from a source—Boston City Council Proceedings in 1909–1910—cited in the Becket Fund's amicus brief. See Becket Fund Br. at 15–16. The Becket Fund found this resource by using Google Books. Thus had Google Books not yet existed, this point might not have been made in the Becket Fund's brief or in the Court's opinion.

many lower court Establishment Clause decisions:

> However history may affect the constitutionality of nonsectarian references to religion by the government, history cannot legitimate practices that demonstrate the government's allegiance to a particular sect or creed . . . . The legislative prayers involved in *Marsh* did not violate this principle because the particular chaplain had "removed all references to Christ."[48]

The *Town of Greece* Court rejected that reasoning:

> This proposition is irreconcilable with the facts of *Marsh* and with its holding and reasoning. *Marsh* nowhere suggested that the constitutionality of legislative prayer turns on the neutrality of its content. . . . Nor did the Court imply the rule that prayer violates the Establishment Clause any time it is given in the name of a figure deified by only one faith or creed. . . . To the contrary, the Court instructed that the "content of the prayer is not of concern to judges," provided "there is no indication that the prayer opportunity has been exploited to proselytize or advance any one, or to disparage any other, faith or belief."[49]

The Court thus expressly rejects the idea that courts must weed out those historical practices that refer to a specific religious faith. The required historical analysis announced by the Court is not to be subjected to a rule of proportional representation enforced against the challenged practice.[50]

B. The Other Opinions

The foregoing understanding of the meaning of *Town of Greece* is borne out by the principal dissent by Justice Elena Kagan and the concurrences by Justices Samuel Alito and Clarence Thomas, respectively. Thus Justice Alito wrote:

> In the case before us, the Court of Appeals appeared to base its decision on one of the Establishment Clause "tests" set out in the opinions of this Court, but if there is any inconsistency

---

[48] 492 U.S. 573, 603 (1989) (quoting Marsh, 463 U.S. at 793, n.14).

[49] Town of Greece, 134 S.Ct. at 1821–22 (quoting Marsh, 463 U.S. at 794–95).

[50] The majority opinion contains a number of other conclusions that will have great effects on Establishment Clause jurisprudence but are not related to the issue of history. For example, the Court rejected the idea that mere offense can constitute forbidden coercion. *Id.* at 1826 ("Offense, however, does not equate to coercion.").

between any of those tests and the historic practice of
legislative prayer, the inconsistency calls into question the
validity of the test, not the historic practice.[51]

Similarly, Justice Thomas's concurring opinion focused squarely on
historical practices at the Founding: "the municipal prayers at issue
in this case bear no resemblance to the coercive state establishments
that existed at the Founding."[52] He also suggested that the crucial
question in future Establishment Clause cases would be *"what constituted an establishment."*[53]

Importantly, Justice Kagan's principal dissent also agreed that history had an important role to play. In the context of legislative prayer,
Kagan referred to "the protective ambit of *Marsh* and the history on
which it relied."[54] The principal dissent's primary disagreement
with the majority opinion was thus not about whether historical
practice provided a justification for legislative prayer, but whether
the specific facts presented in *Town of Greece* fell within the scope
of that historical practice. Justice Kagan also engaged in an extensive historical discussion of the treatment of religious minorities and
demonstrated (correctly) that concern for the protection of religious
minorities was part of the Founders' religious settlement. Indeed,
history is so pervasive a theme in the opinions issued by the justices
that the only opinion that does not mention history at all is Justice
Stephen Breyer's short stand-alone dissent.

The most remarkable aspect of the differences of opinion among
the justices in *Town of Greece*, especially given the tone of the opinions, is their fairly broad-based agreement. The majority and the
principal dissent do not differ all that much when it comes to the
overarching structure of the law concerning legislative prayer. Both
agree that legislative prayer is constitutional under some circumstances; there are now nine votes for legislative prayer instead of
the six in *Marsh*. Both agree that faith-specific legislative prayer is
also constitutional under some circumstances. Both agree that plu-
ralism and the protection of religious minorities are important First
Amendment values. And both agree that history is a guide to the

[51] *Id.* at 1834 (Alito, J., concurring) (internal citation omitted).

[52] *Id.* at 1837 (Thomas, J., concurring).

[53] *Id.* at 1838 (emphasis in original).

[54] *Id.* at 1849 (Kagan, J., dissenting).

perplexed judge who confronts an Establishment Clause challenge. The remaining difference is over the *subtests* within that historical analysis and how the historical analysis applies to the specific practice of municipal prayer. The dissent believes the historical record does not favor prayer practices like Greece's, while the majority disagrees. But that is a relatively small area of disagreement. That the justices could agree on so much in this fraught area of the law augurs well for the prospects of an eventual consensus position on the Court regarding how to approach Establishment Clause cases.

IV. Conclusion: What Does *Town of Greece* Say and What Does That Mean?

A. What Does Town of Greece *Say About the Role of History?*

To sum up, the majority opinion in *Town of Greece* resolved several major points concerning the role history has to play in Establishment Clause analysis:

- The case continued the trend toward reliance on history in Bill of Rights cases. The Establishment Clause, like the Second Amendment, the Fourth Amendment, the Fifth Amendment, and the Sixth Amendment, is defined, at least in part, by what the Framers thought.
- The case also resolved the conflict between *Lemon* and *Marsh* in favor of *Marsh*. *Marsh*'s historical approach trumps *Lemon*'s abstract approach.
- In fact, courts *must* apply the historical analysis in deciding Establishment Clause cases. Looking at history is logically the first step in any Establishment Clause analysis.
- Evidence of historical practice is not to be used in an uncritical fashion; but by the same token, historical practices need not be religiously neutral to be upheld.
- Particular practices that have long endured—such as the Pledge of Allegiance, inaugural prayer, or the recitation of "God save the United States and this honorable Court"—should be upheld, even if the Framers themselves did not participate in them.
- Perhaps most important, the Court does not simply make findings regarding how particular historical data could be applied to particular facts in the case before it. Instead the Court sets out a methodology for lower courts to integrate history into *their* analysis of Establishment Clause cases.

- There is broad support on the Court for the historical approach, although the justices differ strongly over how it should be applied to the specific practice of municipal legislative prayer.

Town of Greece can thus be said to mark a major inflection point—the beginning of a third phase—in the treatment of history in Establishment Clause cases, both at the Supreme Court and in the lower courts. The first phase, from 1947 until 1971, involved *Everson's* truncated account of the history of the Establishment Clause and thereby reserved most if not all of the historical analysis to itself. The second phase, from 1971 until 2014, was dominated by *Lemon's* know-nothing approach to the history of the Establishment Clause. By "gleaning" three abstract principles from 24 years of precedent, the Court made it almost impossible for lower courts to integrate historical analysis into their decisionmaking processes, and bound them to a *Lemon*/endorsement test that the Court itself did not follow. In the third phase, the Court commands lower courts to conduct historical analysis and gives them a methodology for doing so. As set forth below, this will have significant effects on future Establishment Clause cases.

B. *How Will* Town of Greece *Affect Future Establishment Clause Cases?*

There are several likely results from the *Town of Greece* decision.

1. *Municipalities are likely to win legislative prayer cases.* First, within the narrow confines of legislative prayer litigation, municipalities are likely to win cases in all three categories of legislative prayer case—rotating volunteer prayer-givers, paid chaplain, and councilmember-led. *Town of Greece* means that municipalities with rotating non-official prayer-givers are more likely to win. Only if a municipality decides to adopt an express preference for a particular religious tradition will it be in danger of liability. Paid chaplains are rare when it comes to municipalities, but they likely remain protected by *Marsh*, as they were before *Town of Greece* was issued. Councilmember-led prayers are an interesting category because they have not yet been fully litigated. As a category they fall in between rotating volunteers and paid chaplains, however, so they too are likely to be upheld, particularly if the council (or equivalent body) does not adopt an express preference for a particular religious tradition.

2. Lemon/*endorsement is on its last legs.* The majority opinion goes out of its way to negate the *County of Allegheny* dictum, and the Court's tone does not make it sound as if *County of Allegheny*, perhaps the leading endorsement case, is likely to last much longer. Perhaps the most telling fact is that neither the majority opinion nor the principal dissent relies on or applies the *Lemon* or endorsement tests, although Justice Kagan does refer in passing to the "imprimatur" concept associated with endorsement, and the three-justice part of Justice Kennedy's opinion refers to the "reasonable observer." Indeed, the only citation to *Lemon* is in Justice Breyer's stand-alone dissent, and even that makes no mention of *Lemon*'s three-prong test. That neither the majority nor the dissent applied the *Lemon*/endorsement framework to decide an important Establishment Clause case that the lower courts decided using precisely that framework is an indication that the test is lacking viability. Given the proper set of facts, the Court is likely to discard the test.

3. *Outcomes in Supreme Court cases will not change much; lower court outcomes will.* Importantly, as we pointed out in the Becket Fund's amicus brief, the historical approach we advocated and *Town of Greece* adopted will change Establishment Clause *doctrine* but would not have changed *outcomes* in previously decided Supreme Court cases. Cases like *Texas Monthly*,[55] *Kiryas Joel*,[56] *Torcaso*,[57] and *Hosanna-Tabor* would have come out the same way, but the jurisprudential superstructure in which those decisions were embedded would have been entirely different.[58] The change would of course make a major shift in the outcomes in the lower courts, which until now have been bound by the anti-historical *Lemon*/endorsement test, but the law at the Supreme Court level would change surprisingly little.

---

[55] Texas Monthly v. Bullock 489 U.S. 1 (1989) (overturning a Texas statute that exempted religious publications from paying state sales tax).

[56] Bd. of Educ. of Kiryas Joel Vill. Sch. Dist. v. Grumet, 512 U.S. 687 (1994) (holding that school district coinciding with the neighborhood boundaries of a religious group was an unconstitutional aid to religion).

[57] Torcaso v. Watkins, 367 U.S. 488 (1961) (reaffirming that Constitution prohibits states and federal government from requiring any kind of religious test for public office—in this specific case, as a notary public).

[58] See Becket Fund Br., *supra* note*, at 20–27.

4. *Lower courts will examine history in Establishment Clause cases.* As noted above, under the *Lemon*/endorsement regime, lower courts were largely unable to address historical arguments. With *Town of Greece*, they have now not only been empowered to look for historical support (or lack thereof) for particular government practices, but also have been commanded to consider historical practice. There are several advantages to this development. Instead of applying the endorsement test, which forces judges into the uncomfortable and irreducibly subjective role of psychological representative of society, the historical approach gives judges objective facts to work with. The context for any given practice that is challenged is no longer the judge's mind, but the ascertainable facts of historical tradition. Moreover, courts will be able to take advantage of the huge amount of historical scholarship that has been developed in the 43 years since *Lemon* was decided. That will provide further context to the claims before the court.

5. *Lower courts will begin answering the question: "What constitutes an establishment?"* In his *Town of Greece* concurrence, Justice Thomas posed the question of *"what constituted an establishment."* The majority's opinion empowers lower courts to begin this historical inquiry into a feature of public life far more familiar to the Framers than it is to us today. In particular, courts will begin to determine the *categories* of establishment. We pointed out in our *Town of Greece* amicus brief that—at least based on the historical data we have today—there are four rough categories of establishment: government coercion, government control of churches, government funding of churches, and government delegation of powers to churches.[59] We expressly based these categories on Prof. McConnell's seminal history of establishment at the Founding.[60] McConnell identified these different features of an establishment of religion, and in exhausting detail (and over 580 footnotes) described how these establishments functioned in the colonial period, including the differences between the various colonies. He grouped them differently in "Establishment and Disestablishment" than we did—we put three of his categories under the more general heading of "government coercion"—but otherwise the

[59] *Id.* at 17–22.
[60] McConnell, Establishment and Disestablishment at the Founding, *supra* note 14.

historical understanding is common to his article and our brief. The part new to our brief is that we suggested dispensing with *Lemon* and relying on the historical approach instead. And under our approach, if a government action falls into one of these categories, then it can run afoul of the Establishment Clause. If it doesn't fall into any of these categories, then it isn't an establishment of religion and there is no violation.[61]

In practice, this would mean that the first questions a judge would ask when confronted with an Establishment Clause claim are "What category or categories of establishment are being claimed here?" and "Does the challenged government action fall within those categories?" For example, in the case of a challenge to a government-funding program, the judge would ask, "Is this program similar to the kinds of government financial support of churches that the Founders knew?" rather than the almost-philosophical questions of "Does this have the effect of advancing religion?" or "Is the government endorsing religion?" And judges would have source material to grapple with: the Founders' now well-documented understanding of what sort of government funding contributed to an "establishment of religion." That will allow judges to make concrete applications of law to facts, and in the process lead to a more coherent Establishment Clause jurisprudence over time.

6. *There will be less disagreement about church and state.* In the end, the historical approach that we advocated for in our amicus brief and that the Court inaugurated in *Town of Greece* is likely to create much more consensus on Establishment Clause issues. That is especially likely because of the narrowness of the disagreement between the majority opinion and the principal dissent in *Town of Greece*.

*   *   *

The historical approach that the Court employed in *Town of Greece* will probably make activists at both ends of the political spectrum

---

[61] At the Clark Lecture in March 2014, *supra* n.*, Prof. Perry Dane suggested that the four forms of establishment we identified in our *Town of Greece* amicus brief left out an important form of establishment: the government's official proclamation of a "church by law established." See McConnell, *supra* n.14, at 2108. I suspect that this would also have been viewed as a characteristic of an establishment by the Founders.

unhappy, because their preferred policies would not be the law. Those who believe that the United States should be officially proclaimed a "Christian nation" will have to give up on that, short of a constitutional amendment. Others—like AUSCS—who don't like "under God" in the Pledge of Allegiance, "In God We Trust" on the coinage, or legislative prayers like those in *Town of Greece* itself will have to rely on the legislative process rather than litigation to obtain their preferred policy outcomes. But for those in the middle, the historical approach promises to turn down the temperature on this corner of the culture wars. That is something we should all welcome.

McCutcheon v. FEC and the Supreme Court's Return to Buckley

*Allen Dickerson**

Widely hailed (and derided) as the "next *Citizens United*," the Supreme Court's most recent campaign finance ruling has ignited predictable heat and little light. What should have been a relatively modest as-applied challenge to a single restriction, the case instead spawned an impassioned fight over the form and extent of corruption in American government. Ultimately, the controlling opinion marked a decisive step toward straightforward and predictable constitutional analysis.[1] It restored, in important part, the jurisprudence of the seminal *per curiam* decision of *Buckley v. Valeo*, decided in 1976 at a low point in American political history.[2] In doing so, the Court made campaign finance law a simpler, if no less controversial, discipline.

American elections are largely private affairs, with the appeals of candidates and political parties paid for by contributions from individuals. The amount of such contributions has long been limited: individual Americans may contribute a set maximum to each candidate, political party, or political action committee (PAC), on the theory that large contributions from individuals directly to officeholders will create opportunities for corrupt exchanges. In addition, Congress limited the *total* amount that an individual may contribute to all candidates, parties, and PACs in the aggregate. It is this last aggregate limit that was the subject of *McCutcheon v. Federal Election Commission*.

---

* Legal Director, Center for Competitive Politics, Alexandria, Virginia.

[1] McCutcheon v. FEC, 134 S. Ct. 1434 (2012). Authored by Chief Justice John Roberts and joined by Justices Antonin Scalia, Anthony Kennedy, and Samuel Alito. Justice Clarence Thomas's concurring opinion would have gone further, imposing strict scrutiny and overruling contrary precedent, but he nevertheless voted with the majority and patently prefers the plurality's reasoning to that of the dissent.

[2] Buckley v. Valeo, 424 U.S. 1, 26–27 (1976).

The Court began with the largely uncontroversial position that the spending of money—while not itself speech—is necessary for effective advocacy in the United States. As the Court has long recognized, "virtually every means of communicating ideas in today's mass society requires the expenditure of money."[3] Money is not speech, nor is oxygen fire, but in both cases the connection is apparent. Just as a restriction on the use of printing presses or blogging software would be evaluated through a First Amendment freedom-of-speech lens, so too must money that facilitates political expression.[4]

The Court went on to apply the now-familiar, two-part test regarding government infringements on fundamental rights: (1) has the state articulated an important-enough interest to justify infringing upon constitutional liberties, and (2) is its chosen policy appropriately tailored to that interest? This analysis ought to be straightforward and familiar after 40 years of regular Supreme Court rulings on the constitutionality of various campaign finance regulations. But Justice Antonin Scalia spoke for many when he stated at oral argument that "campaign finance law is so intricate that I can't figure it out."[5]

Given this muddled state of affairs, *McCutcheon* made two important doctrinal contributions, one with respect to each of the two prongs of this First Amendment analysis.

First, it clarified that contribution limits must be justified by the government interests in preventing the corruption of officeholders or the appearance of such corruption. It further clarified that when the Court says "corruption," it means "quid pro quo arrangements," and not an amorphous concept of influence or access (much less a generalized understanding of speaker equality). Second, it found that while the base limits on contributions to particular political entities may be justified, aggregate limits paint with too broad a brush. If "it is perfectly fine to contribute $5,200 to nine candidates, [how is it] somehow corrupt to give the same amount to a tenth[?]"[6]

---

[3] *Id.* at 19.

[4] See, e.g., Ilya Shapiro, Wisconsin's Progressive Police State Betrays Campaign Finance Folly, Forbes, July 7, 2014, http://www.forbes.com/sites/ilyashapiro/2014/05/28/wisconsins-progressive-police-state-betrays-campaign-finance-folly.

[5] Transcript of Oral Argument at 17, McCutcheon v. FEC, 134 S. Ct. 1434 (2014) (No. 12-536).

[6] McCutcheon, 134 S. Ct. at 1451.

Thus, in *McCutcheon* the Court provided some much-needed clarity by returning to its roots in *Buckley*, thereby resurrecting a narrower—and hopefully both predictable and familiar—approach to campaign finance regulation.

I. A Brief History of Campaign Finance Regulation

Critics have frequently lumped *McCutcheon* together with the Court's 2010 ruling in *Citizens United*, but it has little in common with that much-discussed (and largely misunderstood) case.[7] That case asked whether the government could ban corporations from running advertisements that advocate—even implicitly—the election or defeat of candidates. Citizens United is a nonprofit advocacy corporation that wished to air a film critical of then-candidate Hillary Clinton. Shaun McCutcheon, by contrast, was an individual (not a corporation) wishing to contribute directly to candidates, parties, and PACs. He hoped to give $1,776 to each of 28 candidates and $25,000 to each of the three Republican national party committees, but the aggregate limits applicable to individual contributors prevented this.[8]

McCutcheon and *Citizens United* thus sit on opposite sides of two important factual divides. First, *McCutcheon* involved individual political activity, not the collective activity of corporations and unions. Second, *McCutcheon* involved direct contribution of money to political actors, not independent spending to comment upon politicians.

These distinctions are important and longstanding. *McCutcheon* is the latest in a line of cases, more or less regularly decided, stretching back to the Supreme Court's 1976 *Buckley v. Valeo* decision.[9] *Buckley* was an omnibus challenge to the Federal Election Campaign Act (FECA). Though there have been subsequent changes to federal campaign finance law, *Buckley* has remained the preeminent articulation of the First Amendment interests that such regulation implicates, and has provided the analytical underpinning for every campaign finance case decided in the past 40 years.

[7] Citizens United v. FEC, 558 U.S. 310 (2010).

[8] McCutcheon, 134 S. Ct. at 1443.

[9] As they must be; Congress has required the Court to review certain challenges to federal campaign finance statutes. McCutcheon, 134 S. Ct. at 1444 ("we ha[ve] no discretion to refuse adjudication of the case on its merits") (citation and internal quotation marks omitted).

A. Buckley v. Valeo

In 1974, in the wake of the Watergate scandal, Congress amended FECA to limit "individual political contributions . . . to $1,000 to any single candidate per election, with an overall annual limitation of $25,000 by any contributor."[10] The amendments also capped "independent expenditures by individuals and groups 'relative to a clearly identified' candidate" at $1,000.[11] The *Buckley* Court recognized differences between expenditures and contributions, and treated the limits on each differently for purposes of constitutional analysis.

Observing that "virtually every means of communicating ideas in today's mass society requires the expenditure of money," the Court pointed out the obvious consequence: limitations on the amount a candidate or group could expend would necessarily "reduce[] the quantity of expression."[12] Considering voters' "increasing dependence on television, radio, and other mass media for news and information," the Court recognized that "effective political speech" might often be expensive.[13]

Given this reality, the Court was particularly troubled by the "$1,000 ceiling on spending 'relative to a clearly identified candidate.'"[14] Such a low expenditure limit "would appear to exclude all citizens and groups except candidates, political parties, and the institutional press from any significant use of the most effective modes of communication."[15] This reduced quantity of speech—and smaller pool of speakers—undermined fundamental democratic principles. To illustrate this concern, the Court noted that it would be "a federal criminal offense for a person or association to place a single one-quarter page advertisement 'relative to a clearly identified candidate' in a major metropolitan newspaper."[16] (Indeed, this same concern about excluding a broad range of potential speakers would be echoed decades later, when *Citizens United* scaled back

---

[10] Buckley, 424 U.S. at 7.

[11] *Id.*

[12] *Id.* at 19.

[13] *Id.*

[14] *Id.*

[15] *Id.* at 19–20.

[16] *Id.* at 40 (citations omitted).

disparate treatment of corporate speakers wishing to make independent expenditures.)[17]

The Court attempted to prevent this result by narrowing the statute's reach. Because it would be unconstitutionally vague and overbroad to regulate all speech "relative to a clearly identified candidate," the Court limited the definition of "expenditure" to speech "expressly advocat[ing] the election or defeat of a clearly identified candidate."[18] But even so limited, the Court struck down FECA's expenditure limits. Congress could not eliminate political speech by essentially all speakers except the conventional media, the institutional political parties, and the candidates themselves.

"By contrast with a limitation upon expenditures for political expression," the Court explained, "a limitation upon the amount that any one person or group may contribute to a candidate or political committee entails only a marginal restriction upon the contributor's ability to engage in free communication."[19] The Court's rationale is worth quoting in its entirety and further illustrates the foundational distinction between contributions and expenditures:

> A contribution serves as a general expression of support for the candidate and his views, but does not communicate the underlying basis for the support. The quantity of communication by the contributor does not increase perceptibly with the size of his contribution, since the expression rests solely on the undifferentiated, symbolic act of contributing. At most, the size of the contribution provides a very rough index of the intensity of the contributor's support for the candidate. A limitation on the amount of money a person may give to a candidate or campaign organization thus involves little direct restraint on his political communication,

---

[17] Citizens United v. FEC, 558 U.S. 310, 352 (2010) ("With the advent of the Internet and the decline of print and broadcast media . . . the line between the media and others who wish to comment on political and social issues becomes far more blurred."). See also Michael W. McConnell, Reconsidering *Citizens United* as a Press Clause Case, 123 Yale L. J. 412, 435 (2013) ("[T]he publication of criticism of a public official is protected whether published by a for-profit media corporation or by persons who are 'not members of the press' in the form of a paid advertisement. That covers both bases of the *Citizens United* problem: the freedom to publish criticisms of public officials and candidates is not lost by virtue of either corporate status or non-membership in the institutional news media.").

[18] Buckley, 424 U.S. at 42.

[19] *Id.* at 20–21.

> for it permits the symbolic expression of support evidenced by a contribution but does not in any way infringe the contributor's freedom to discuss candidates and issues. While contributions may result in political expression if spent by a candidate or an association to present views to the voters, the transformation of contributions into political debate involves speech by someone other than the contributor.[20]

In short, while limiting the expenditure of money for political advocacy will, mathematically, limit the quantity of such expression, the same is not precisely true for contribution limits.

From *Buckley*, then, stems the Court's long-standing distinction between laws that restrict expenditures—like the ban on collective independent expenditures invalidated in *Citizens United*—and those that restrict contributions—like the aggregate limit challenged in *McCutcheon*. Though often conflated in popular discussion, these two categories were set apart more than 40 years ago, and the Court continues to distinguish between them today.

B. *Political Spending after* Buckley

Post-*Buckley* challenges to the constitutionality of campaign finance laws have generally been as-applied cases, limited to particular factual scenarios. Perhaps because of this, the Court's expenditure jurisprudence has been less than uniform. While the Court has purported to apply strict scrutiny to laws that burden independent expenditures, the applicable standard of review—and its application across various contexts—has remained in flux. [21]

---

[20] *Id.* at 21.

[21] See, e.g., Austin v. Michigan Chamber of Commerce, 494 U.S. 652, 669 (1990) (upholding state law forbidding corporations from making independent expenditures out of general treasury funds); FEC v. Wisc. Right to Life, 551 U.S. 449 (2007) ("WRTL II") (striking down federal prohibition on corporate independent expenditures for electioneering communications introduced by the Bipartisan Campaign Reform Act of 2002, but not adopting a uniform rationale for doing so. See *id.* at 483–504 (Scalia, J., dissenting)); McConnell v. FEC, 540 U.S. 93 (2003) (upholding BCRA—including its electioneering communications provisions—on its face); Citizens United, 558 U.S. at 341 (purporting to apply the same scrutiny, but overruling *Austin* and going further than *WRTL II* by concluding that, insofar as BCRA banned corporate independent expenditures, it was unconstitutional).

Fortunately, unlike expenditure cases,[22] the Court's resolution of cases about contribution limits, up to and including *McCutcheon*, has been largely consistent with *Buckley*. In particular, the Court has been clear on three points. First, contribution limits are permitted because they help protect against corruption and its appearance. Second, such limits nonetheless implicate associational (and to a lesser extent speech) liberties.[23] And third, while contribution limits must be reasonable, legislatures will be accorded substantial deference in setting them.

Decisions applying these principles have also been comparatively clear. *Nixon v. Shrink Missouri Government PAC*, for example, upheld Missouri's contribution limits. Reiterating that the government's anti-corruption interest could indeed justify such limits,[24] the Court nonetheless considered their impact on First Amendment rights,[25] while noting that "[t]he quantum of empirical evidence needed to satisfy heightened judicial scrutiny of legislative judgments will *vary up or down with the novelty and plausibility of the justification* raised."[26] The Court applied the same analysis when it later *invalidated* state contribution limits in *Randall v. Sorrell*, recognizing that, "contribution limits might sometimes work more harm to protected First Amendment interests than their anti-corruption objectives

---

[22] And cases turning on whether a particular payment is an expenditure or a contribution, see, e.g., Colo. Republican Fed. Campaign Comm. v. FEC, 518 U.S. 604 (1996).

[23] Although these two liberties are related: "'effective advocacy of both public and private points of view, particularly controversial ones, is undeniably enhanced by group association.'" Buckley, 424 U.S. at 15 (quoting NAACP v. Alabama, 357 U.S. 449, 460 (1976)) (alterations omitted).

[24] 528 U.S. 377, 388–89 (2000) ("Of almost equal concern as the danger of actual quid pro quo arrangements is the impact of the appearance of corruption stemming from public awareness of the opportunities for abuse inherent in a regime of large individual financial contributions . . . Congress could legitimately conclude that the avoidance of the appearance of improper influence 'is also critical . . . if confidence in the system of representative Government is not to be eroded to a disastrous extent'") (quoting Buckley, 424 U.S. at 27; in turn quoting Civil Service Comm'n v. Letter Carriers, 413 U.S. 548, 565 (1973); collecting cases).

[25] *Id.* at 388 ("While we did not attempt to parse distinctions between the speech and association standards of scrutiny for contribution limits, we did make it clear that those restrictions bore more heavily on the associational right than on freedom to speak.") (citing Buckley, 424 U.S. at 24–25).

[26] *Id.* at 391.

[can] justify."[27] Noting that "ordinarily we have deferred to the legislature's determination of such matters," the Court concluded that, in that particular case, the legislature had gone too far and the limits were too low.[28] "[W]e must recognize the existence of some lower bound. At some point the constitutional risks to the democratic electoral process become too great."[29]

Thus the law stood when Shaun McCutcheon's challenge to the individual aggregate contribution limits reached the Supreme Court. Contribution limits had been recognized as a generally permissible tool. But the government was still required to show that any particular limit did not do more harm to First Amendment interests than could be justified by its utility as an anti-corruption measure.

II. *McCutcheon* and Aggregate Contribution Limits

Federal campaign finance statutes impose two types of contribution limits. The first, known as base limits, "restrict[] how much money a donor may contribute to a particular candidate or committee."[30] The second "restrict[] how much money a donor may contribute in total to all candidates or committees."[31] Only the latter type—aggregate limits—were at issue in *McCutcheon*.

The limits challenged in *McCutcheon* in fact contained three distinct aggregate limits. The first of these capped a donor's total contributions to all candidates for federal office at $48,600.[32] In addition, the same donor could contribute up to $74,600 to a combination of political parties and PACs.[33] Of this $74,600, a total of $26,000 was set

---

[27] 548 U.S. 230, 247–48 (2006) (citing Shrink Mo., 528 U.S. at 395–397; Buckley, 424 U.S. at 21).

[28] *Id.* at 248.

[29] *Id.*

[30] McCutcheon v. FEC, 134 S. Ct. 1434, 1442 (2014) (citing 2 U. S. C. § 441a(a)(1)).

[31] *Id.* at 1442 (citing 2 U.S.C. § 441a(a)(3)).

[32] *Id.* at 1442–43 (citing 2 U.S.C. § 441a(a)(3); 78 Fed. Reg. 8532.).

[33] PACs bundle funds from individual donors to support a common mission through election-related spending, including contributions to candidates. They aren't exactly a creature of federal campaign finance law, but they do illustrate the important principle that banning one avenue of political spending will ultimately result in the same dollars being spent via other channels. Indeed, the first "political action committee" was formed by the Congress of Industrial Organizations in response to the newly enacted ban on campaign contributions by labor organizations. For a more complete history of

aside exclusively for the national political parties.[34] (In other words, only $48,600 of the $74,600 could be given to PACs and state/local parties.) Taken together, the result was an overall aggregate limit of $123,200—though that amount was further subdivided among candidates, parties, and PACs, as just described.[35]

The *McCutcheon* holding is simply stated: because they "do little, if anything" to combat corruption, aggregate limits are unconstitutional.[36] The plurality's reasoning is also straightforward: Congress determined that a particular amount of money will not corrupt a given candidate. How, then, could that same amount of money become corrupting if also contributed to another candidate? Or if given to nine? Or a tenth?

In defending the aggregate limits, the government argued that the danger wasn't so much the corruption of the tenth versus ninth candidate, but the risk that those contributing large amounts in the aggregate would devise circumvention schemes, allowing them to funnel an amount of money that *is* corrupting to a chosen candidate.

Buckley could indeed be read to lend support to the proposition that aggregate limits help prevent circumvention of base limits. Though it noted that the question had not been briefed, the *Buckley* Court ruled that FECA's $25,000 aggregate limit on all contributions to candidates, parties, and PACs was "no more than a corollary" of base limits.[37] In particular, there was a danger that the base limits would be circumvented when "'massive amounts of money [were given] to a particular candidate through the use of unearmarked contributions' to entities that are themselves likely to contribute to" a particular candidate.[38]

---

the development of PACs, see Allison R. Hayward, Revisiting the Fable of Reform, 45 Harv. J. on Legis. 421, 448–456 (2008).

[34] McCutcheon, 134 S. Ct. at 1442–43 (citing 2 U.S.C. § 441a(a)(3); 78 Fed. Reg. 8532.).

[35] In a related case filed shortly after *McCutcheon*, an individual contributor brought suit under the theory that, even if the overall aggregate limit were a constitutional exercise of congressional power, these discriminatory sub-limits—which forced a contributor to funnel a portion of the $123,200 maximum through parties and PACs—furthered no constitutionally sufficient government interest. James v. FEC, 134 S. Ct. 1806 (2014). The author represented the plaintiff in the *James* litigation.

[36] McCutcheon, 134 S. Ct. at 1442.

[37] Buckley, 424 U.S. at 38.

[38] McCutcheon, 134 S. Ct. at 1446 (quoting Buckley, 424 U.S. at 38).

The *McCutcheon* Court acknowledged and rejected *Buckley's* three-sentence analysis, noting that the Bipartisan Campaign Reform Act (McCain-Feingold) "is a different statutory regime, and the aggregate limits it imposes operate against a distinct legal backdrop."[39] Beyond recognizing that *Buckley's* brief mention of aggregate limits under an out-of-date statute was not controlling, the *McCutcheon* Court considered a number of laws and regulations adopted after *Buckley*, which made it unlikely that funds could in fact be funneled to defeat the base contribution limits or raise the specter of quid pro quo corruption.

A. Standard of Review

Expenditure limitations are generally subject to "strict scrutiny," while other laws that burden expressive political activity—including contribution limits—are subject to less-searching review, often labeled "exacting scrutiny."[40] But there is much confusion regarding what this "exacting scrutiny" standard requires.

In *Worley v. Cruz-Bustillo*, for example, the U.S. Court of Appeals for the Eleventh Circuit upheld Florida's reporting and disclosure requirements as applied to a group of individuals that wanted to purchase $600 worth of radio ads.[41] In failing to require more than the state's assertion of an "informational interest" to justify a speech-suppressing PAC regime, the Eleventh Circuit set a precedent that "exacting scrutiny" is little (if anything) more than simple rational basis review.

By contrast, at least one Tenth Circuit judge has concluded that exacting scrutiny instead means a level of review just shy of *strict* scrutiny. In *Riddle v. Hickenlooper*, a challenge to a Colorado law imposing different contribution limits upon major party and non-major party candidates, Judge Neil Gorsuch began by "confess[ing] some uncertainty about the level of scrutiny the Supreme Court wishes us to apply to this contribution limit challenge."[42] He endorsed the plaintiff's view:

> that contributing in elections implicates a fundamental
> liberty interest, that Colorado's scheme favors the exercise

39 *Id.*

40 See, e.g., Citizens United v. FEC, 558 U.S. 310, 369 (2010) ("[t]he Court has explained that disclosure is a less restrictive alternative to more comprehensive regulations of speech") (citing FEC v. Mass. Citizens For Life, Inc., 479 U.S. 238, 262 (1986)).

41 717 F.3d 1238 (11th Cir. 2013).

42 742 F.3d 922, 930 (10th Cir. 2014).

of that fundamental liberty interest by some at the expense of others, and for this reason warrants the most searching level of judicial scrutiny. For my part, I don't doubt this line of argument has much to recommend it. *The trouble is, we have no controlling guidance on the question from the Supreme Court. And in what guidance we do have lie some conflicting cues.*[43]

Judge Gorsuch's explanation of this conflicting Supreme Court precedent—and the resulting confusion—bears repeating:

No one before us disputes that the act of contributing to political campaigns implicates a "basic constitutional freedom," one lying "at the foundation of a free society" and enjoying a significant relationship to the right to speak and associate—both expressly protected First Amendment activities. Even so, the Court has yet to apply strict scrutiny to contribution limit challenges—employing instead something pretty close but not quite the same thing. Some have questioned whether contribution limits should be subject to strict scrutiny. The Court itself now has under consideration a case in which it may (or may not) choose to address the question. But, to date at least, the Court hasn't gone so far.[44]

In short, even sophisticated advocates and judges have struggled to answer this important question, with weighty constitutional implications: what is "exacting scrutiny"?

Thus, *McCutcheon* was a significant clarification. While it declined to venture into the realm of strict scrutiny, *McCutcheon* returned "exacting scrutiny" to its proper place.[45] The chief justice was clear: "ex-

---

[43] *Id.* at 930–31 (emphasis added).

[44] *Id.* at 931 (citing Buckley v. Valeo, 424 U.S. at 25 (applying a "closely drawn" rather than strict scrutiny standard); Davis v. FEC, 554 U.S. 724, 740 n.7 (2008); Republican Party of N.M. v. King, No. 12–2015, 741 F.3d 1089, 2013 U.S. App. LEXIS 25084 at *9 (10th Cir. Dec. 18, 2013); Randall v. Sorrell, 548 U.S. 230, 266–67 (2006) (Thomas, J., concurring in the judgment); Buckley, 424 U.S. at 241–45 (Burger, C.J., concurring in part and dissenting in part); McCutcheon v. FEC, 133 S. Ct. 1242 (2013) (noting probable jurisdiction in a challenge to aggregate contribution limits; oral argument was held October 8, 2013); Citizens United v. FEC, 558 U.S. 310, 359 (2010)). The judge was speaking of *McCutcheon*, which indeed declined to impose strict scrutiny.

[45] This makes perfect sense. The term "exacting" implies something significantly more robust than mere intermediate scrutiny. Indeed the concept of "exacting scrutiny" has its origin in a line of cases from the civil rights era, wherein the Court blocked

acting scrutiny [is] applicable to limitations on core First Amendment rights of political expression."[46] And this test is familiar: "Under exacting scrutiny, the Government may regulate protected speech only if such regulation promotes a compelling interest and is the least restrictive means to further the articulated interest."[47]

Having resolved a significant source of confusion in the context of expenditure limits, the plurality next explored the lower standard of scrutiny applicable to contribution limits. Because such limits "impose a lesser restraint on political speech"[48] than do limits on expenditures, on the theory that contributions are not themselves speech but rather a "symbolic expression of support"[49] for a candidate or cause, they are subject to a "lesser but still rigorous standard of review."[50] Specifically, "even a significant interference with protected rights of political association may be sustained if the State demonstrates a sufficiently important interest and employs means closely drawn to avoid unnecessary abridgment of associational freedoms."[51] This "'closely drawn' test" is now the bedrock of analysis in contribution limit cases.[52]

---

attempts by various state governments to obtain donor or membership lists from civil rights organizations operating in segregated states. In reviewing those states' attempts to compel disclosure of the NAACP's donor lists, for example, the Court noted a fundamental principle that rings true today: "Of course, it is immaterial whether the beliefs sought to be advanced by association pertain to political, economic, religious or cultural matters, and state action which may have the effect of curtailing the freedom to associate is subject to the closest scrutiny." NAACP v. Ala. ex rel. Patterson, 357 U.S. 449, 460–61 (1958). *Buckley* characterized this "closest scrutiny" as "exacting," suggesting that exacting scrutiny is indeed merely a linguistic twist on the familiar strict scrutiny standard. Buckley, 424 U.S. at 64 ("Since *NAACP v. Alabama* we have required that the subordinating interests of the State must survive exacting scrutiny.").

[46] McCutcheon, 134 S. Ct. at 1444 (quoting Buckley, 424 U.S. at 44–45).

[47] *Id.* (quoting Sable Communications of Cal., Inc. v. FCC, 492 U.S. 115, 126 (1989)).

[48] McCutcheon, 134 S. Ct. at 1444.

[49] *Id.* (quoting Buckley, 424 U.S. at 21).

[50] *Id.* (quoting Buckley, 424 U.S. at 29).

[51] *Id.* (quoting Buckley, 424 U.S. at 25 (quoting Cousins v. Wigoda, 419 U.S. 477, 488 (1975))).

[52] *Id.* at 1445 (citation omitted).

B. *The Government Interest: Quid Pro Quo Corruption and Its Discontents*

The first step of the constitutional analysis is to determine whether the government has asserted a sufficiently important interest. That step ought to be reasonably simple, as the Supreme Court has recognized only one such interest as regards contribution limits: preventing corruption or its appearance. In practice, however, the definition of "corruption" is highly contested, a conflict demonstrated by the sharp conflict between the *McCutcheon* plurality and dissent on this point.

At the heart of this dispute is the concept of "quid pro quo" corruption, or, as the *McCutcheon* plurality described it, the notion of a direct exchange of an official act for money. "The hallmark of corruption is the financial quid pro quo: dollars for political favors."[53] The Court further explained that "[c]ampaign finance restrictions that pursue other objectives . . . impermissibly inject the Government into the debate over who should govern. And those who govern should be the *last* people to help decide who *should* govern."[54]

This understanding of corruption comes straight from *Buckley*.[55] But when is a campaign finance law in fact aimed at quid pro quos, and when is it seeking another end—perhaps to "level the playing field," or "level electoral opportunities," or "equalize the financial resources of candidates"[56]—while masquerading as an anti-corruption tool? This is the essence of the debate, and answering this question requires a further discussion of the legislative and judicial history.

1. *Quid pro quo corruption: A concept born of* Buckley

Buckley began by defining the government's interest as "the prevention of corruption and the appearance of corruption spawned by the real or imagined coercive influence of large financial contributions

[53] *Id.* at 1441 (quoting FEC v. Nat'l Conservative PAC, 470 U.S. 480,497 (1985)).

[54] *Id.* (emphasis in original).

[55] Buckley, 424 U.S. at 26–27 ("To the extent that large contributions are given to secure political quid pro quo's from current and potential office holders, the integrity of our system of representative democracy is undermined.")

[56] McCutcheon, 134 S. Ct. at 1450 (quoting Arizona Free Enterprise Club's Freedom Club PAC v. Bennett, 131 S. Ct. 2806, 2825–26 (2011); Davis, 128 S. Ct. at 741–742; Buckley, 424 U.S. at 56).

on candidates' positions and on their actions if elected to office."[57] Notice two things. First, the danger recognized in *Buckley* isn't generic influence. Rather, it's *coercive* influence. Second, the thing that may be coerced in a corrupt bargain is the "candidates' positions . . . and actions."[58]

Having articulated the government's interest, the *Buckley* Court devoted two paragraphs to exploring its contours. With respect to actual "corruption," the Court imagined "a candidate lacking immense personal or family wealth [who] must depend on financial contributions from others to provide the resources necessary to conduct a successful campaign."[59] In such cases, where fundraising is an "essential ingredient of an effective candidacy," there may be a risk of coercion.[60] But, for purposes of regulation, such corruption exists only "*to the extent* that large contributions are given to secure a political *quid pro quo* from current and potential office holders."[61]

The Court then turned to "the appearance of corruption stemming from public awareness of the opportunities for abuse inherent in a regime of large individual financial contributions."[62] It took pains to explicitly contrast this apparent corruption with "the danger of actual *quid pro quo* arrangements" described in the previous paragraph.[63]

This compels two results. First, "actual quid pro quo arrangements" are the "corruption" the Court was talking about when it mentioned "corruption and the appearance of corruption." Second, the "appearance of corruption" and "opportunities for abuse" included only opportunities for those same quid pro quo exchanges. That is, the appearance that such exchanges might have taken place, even if they cannot be proven.

Having defined the government's interest in a contribution context, the *Buckley* Court explicitly reiterated this formulation vis-à-vis expenditures. The Court "assum[ed] *arguendo,* that large independent expenditures pose the same dangers of actual or apparent *quid*

---

[57] Buckley, 424 U.S. at 25.

[58] *Id.*

[59] *Id.* at 26.

[60] *Id.*

[61] *Id.* (emphasis added).

[62] *Id.* at 27.

[63] *Id.*

pro quo arrangements as do large contributions,"[64] but ultimately determined that even that assumption was insufficient to save expenditure limits. This was because "absence of prearrangement and coordination of an expenditure with the candidate or his agent . . . alleviates the danger that expenditures will be given as a *quid pro quo* for improper commitments from the candidate."[65]

The *McCutcheon* dissenters would disagree. Although they agree that corruption is the correct governmental interest, they define it differently. For them, corruption is not limited to *Buckley*'s quid pro quo understanding, but is that which "breaks the constitutionally necessary 'chain of communication' between the people and their representatives."[66] Justice Stephen Breyer elaborated:

> Where enough money calls the tune, the general public will not be heard. Insofar as corruption cuts the link between political thought and political action, a free marketplace of political ideas loses its point. That is one reason why the Court has stressed the constitutional importance of Congress' concern that a few large donations not drown out the voices of the many.[67]

To support this statement, Justice Breyer cites pages 26–27 of *Buckley*. This is mystifying, because those pages contain the numerous references to quid pro quo arrangements just discussed, and say nothing about drowning out other voices.

Buckley did acknowledge the government's argument that "the limits serve to mute the voices of affluent persons and groups in the election process and thereby to equalize the relative ability of all citizens to affect the outcome of elections."[68] But the Court considered this a merely "ancillary" argument and did not rely upon it.[69] Thus, *Buckley*'s treatment of corruption—even considering the exact pages

---

[64] *Id.* at 45.

[65] *Id.* at 47.

[66] McCutcheon, 134 S. Ct. at 1467.

[67] *Id.* at 1467–68 (citing Buckley, 424 U.S. at 26–27).

[68] Buckley, 424 U.S. at 25.

[69] *Id.* at 25–26 ("It is unnecessary to look beyond the Act's primary purpose—to limit the actuality and appearance of corruption resulting from large individual financial contributions.").

cited by Justice Breyer—does not seem to support the *McCutcheon* dissenters' broad pronouncement.

2. The McCutcheon *Dissent and the Court's Historical Understanding of Corruption*

In fairness to the dissenters, however, they do cite additional cases suggesting a broader understanding of corruption. But a close reading of those authorities does not get them as far as they would wish, nor does it change the fact that the plurality's understanding of corruption is well rooted in *Buckley* itself.

a. Beaumont

In *FEC v. Beaumont*, the Court upheld a ban on corporate contributions and expenditures "in connection with" certain federal elections.[70] It explicitly reiterated that "limits on contributions are more clearly justified by a link to political corruption than limits on other kinds of . . . political spending are (corruption being understood not only as quid pro quo agreements, but also as undue influence on an officeholder's judgment, and the appearance of such influence)."[71] Of course, the issue of whether corporations may make contributions was not at issue in *McCutcheon*, which may explain why the plurality didn't cite the case.

b. Colorado II

The dissenters also relied upon *FEC v. Colorado Republican Federal Campaign Committee (Colorado II)*, where "the Court upheld limits imposed upon coordinated expenditures among parties and candidates because it found they thwarted corruption and its appearance, again understood as including 'undue influence' by wealthy donors."[72] While this citation is correct, it is not at all clear that *Colorado II* in fact turned on the distinction between quid pro quo arrangements and other, lesser forms of "influence." *Colorado II*—a facial challenge—turned instead on the issue of base-limit *circumvention*, not the nature of the anti-corruption interest those base limits are supposed to serve in the first place.

[70] 539 U.S. 146 (2003).

[71] *Id.* at 155–56 (citing Colorado II, 533 U.S. at 440–41) (alterations in original).

[72] McCutcheon, 134 S. Ct. at 1469 (Breyer, J., dissenting) (citation omitted).

Colorado II rejected the argument that, because spending coordinated with candidates comprises a substantial portion of political party activity, limits on coordinated spending impose a special burden upon parties. The Court concluded that, just as political parties could not be subject to special restrictions upon independent expenditures, neither were they entitled to special privileges. In doing so, the Court necessarily asked whether limits on coordinated expenditures served an anti-corruption purpose. But the central question was not the scope of that corruption interest, but whether "unlimited coordinated spending by a party raises the risk of corruption (and its appearance) through circumvention of valid contribution limits."[73]

There is consequently a tension in *Colorado II*. On one hand, the Court spoke in broad terms of a favored candidate's "obligation" to contributors, and of the parties' role as "agents for spending on behalf of those who seek to produce obligated officeholders."[74] On the other, the particular relationship between donors funneling money to a given candidate's committee, and that specific candidate, is irrelevant to the Court's ruling. What was really at stake was that "an increased opportunity for coordinated spending would aggravate the use of a party to funnel money to a candidate from individuals and nonparty groups, who would thus bypass the contribution limits that Buckley upheld."[75]

The touchstone, again, was *Buckley*. And since *Buckley* upheld limits on the contributions to particular candidates, preventing circumvention of those limits was, in *Colorado II*, itself a sufficient governmental interest. The Court's *characterization* of the corruption interest is not necessary to the holding. Moreover, while the Court made only limited reference to the record (and even then, did so almost solely to demonstrate the possibility of circumvention), that record was consistent with a quid pro quo understanding of corruption.[76]

In sum, while *Colorado II* contains language that suggests a corruption interest broader than quid pro quo, that language is dicta from

[73] Colorado II, 533 U.S. at 456.

[74] *Id.* at 452.

[75] *Id.* at 447.

[76] Colorado II, 533 U.S. at 451, n.12 (noting Senator Paul Simon's claim that "people contribute to party committees on both sides of the aisle . . . because they want favors. There is an expectation that giving to party committees helps you legislatively") (citation omitted). Also consider the heavy emphasis on "tallying."

an opinion that was really about the problem of circumvention. This distinction is particularly relevant in *McCutcheon,* another circumvention case. In any event, *Colorado II* cannot take Justice Breyer as far as he would wish.

c. Shrink Missouri

The *McCutcheon* dissent also noted that, in *Shrink Missouri,* "the Court upheld limitations imposed by the Missouri legislature upon contributions to state political candidates, not only because of the need to prevent bribery, but also because of 'the broader threat from politicians too compliant with the wishes of large contributors.'"[77] The *Shrink Missouri* Court indeed interpreted *Buckley* to address "the power of money 'to influence governmental action' in ways less 'blatant and specific' than bribery."[78] In part because Missouri had not preserved its legislative history, however, the Court relied to an unusual degree on the *appearance* of corruption.[79] Its discussion of apparent corruption evidences a concern shared by the *McCutcheon* dissent—that "the general public will not be heard."[80]

The *Shrink Missouri* Court explained that concern as follows:

> Leave the perception of impropriety unanswered, and the cynical assumption that large donors call the tune could jeopardize the willingness of voters to take part in democratic governance. Democracy works "only if the people have faith in those who govern, and that faith is bound to be shattered when high officials and their appointees engage in activities which arouse suspicions of malfeasance and corruption."[81]

Of course, the contours of this "impropriety" are unclear from the *Shrink Missouri* opinion itself. It is possible that Missourians were concerned about actual quid pro quo arrangements—and that they might stem from "munificent" contributions—rather than a generalized theory of influence. It is difficult to know, however, because the only evidence on this point was a single affidavit from a single

[77] McCutcheon, 134 S. Ct. at 1469 (quoting Nixon v. Shrink Mo. Gov't PAC, 528 U.S. 377, 389 (2000)).

[78] Shrink Mo., 528 U.S. at 389 (quoting Buckley, 424 U.S. at 28).

[79] *Id.* at 393.

[80] McCutcheon, 134 S. Ct. at 1467.

[81] Shrink Mo., 528 U.S. at 390 (citation omitted).

state senator and some newspaper reports relied upon by the district court.[82]

Nevertheless, *Shrink Missouri* could be read as expanding *Buckley*'s understanding of corruption beyond quid pro quo arrangements. Certainly, Justice Clarence Thomas's spirited dissent read the majority opinion as doing precisely that:

> [I]nvoking *"Buckley*'s standard of scrutiny," the Court proceeds to significantly extend the holding in that case. The Court's substantive departure from *Buckley* begins with a revision of our compelling-interest jurisprudence. In *Buckley*, the Court indicated that the only interest that could qualify as "compelling" in this area was the government's interest in reducing actual and apparent corruption. And the Court repeatedly used the word "corruption" in the narrow quid pro quo sense, meaning "perversion or destruction of integrity in the discharge of public duties by bribery or favour."[83]

Of course, *Shrink Missouri* involved a challenge to base limits, the campaign finance restriction that—going back to *Buckley*—has generally enjoyed the greatest deference.[84] And while the *Shrink Missouri* Court did suggest a broad understanding of the corruption interest, it is far from clear that such a reading was central to its holding.

Moreover, even in *Shrink Missouri*, the Court noted that it "ha[s] never accepted mere conjecture as adequate to carry a First Amendment burden.'"[85]

d. McConnell

Justice Breyer's strongest argument comes from *McConnell v. FEC*.[86] In that sprawling challenge to McCain-Feingold, the Court reviewed limits on "soft money" contributions to political parties. Such funds were contributed directly to parties "but could be used for activities such as voter registration, get out the vote drives, and advertising that did not expressly advocate a federal candidate's

---

[82] *Id.* at 393–94.

[83] *Id.* at 422 (citations omitted).

[84] See, e.g., *id.* at 403–04; Buckley, 424 U.S. at 22.

[85] Shrink Mo., 528 U.S. at 392.

[86] 540 U.S. 93 (2003).

election or defeat."[87] A majority of the "Court found they 'thwarted a significant risk of corruption—understood not as quid pro quo bribery, but as privileged access to and pernicious influence upon elected representatives.'"[88] That understanding of "access and influence" is not only clearly broader than quid pro quo arrangements, it also expresses the concept more concretely than the other cases the *McCutcheon* dissenters cite.

McConnell is notable for its substantial record, amassed before a special three-judge panel of the D.C. district court. "That record consisted of over 100,000 pages of material and included testimony from more than 200 witnesses."[89] While not "a single discrete instance of quid pro quo corruption" was identified as a result of a soft-money contribution, the *McConnell* Court found that "[t]here was an indisputable link between generous political donations and opportunity after opportunity to make one's case directly to a Member of Congress."[90]

The plaintiffs argued that, because there was no evidence "of an instance in which a federal officeholder has actually switched a vote in exchange for soft money,"[91] the limit on soft money contributions was necessarily unconstitutional, as Congress had failed to demonstrate corruption or its appearance. The Court disagreed. Departing from *Buckley*, it viewed the relevant interest as "extend[ing] beyond preventing simple cash-for-votes corruption to curbing 'undue influence on an officeholder's judgment, and the appearance of such influence.'"[92] Put differently, "the danger [was] that officeholders will decide issues not on the merits or the desires of their constituencies, but according to the wishes of those who have made large financial contributions valued by the officeholder."[93]

There is little doubt that *McConnell* helps Justice Breyer's position in *McCutcheon*—at least insofar as it reads corruption more broadly than quid pro quo arrangements. Nevertheless, his application of *McConnell* goes too far for two reasons. First, *McConnell* dealt with both

---

[87] McCutcheon, 134 S. Ct. at 1469 (Breyer, J. dissenting).

[88] *Id.* (citation omitted).

[89] *Id.*

[90] *Id.* at 1469–70 (Breyer, J. dissenting) (citations omitted).

[91] *Id.* at 1470 (quoting McConnell, 540 U.S. at 146, 149–50).

[92] *Id.*

[93] *Id.* (quoting McConnell, 540 U.S. at 153).

a facial challenge and a substantial evidentiary record. The plaintiffs argued that—absent evidence that some politician had changed his or her vote in consideration of a contribution—there was no situation whatsoever in which the government could limit political party contributions. That claim is vastly broader than Mr. McCutcheon's and extends far beyond the plurality's narrow holding. Second, *McConnell* upheld the "soft money" ban, a *base* limit on a particular individual's contribution to a political party. *McCutcheon* does nothing to disturb that holding.[94]

e. Austin

Thus, we turn to the case that would provide Justice Breyer's dissent with the clearest support: the since-overruled *Austin v. Michigan Chamber of Commerce* decision, which upheld a state ban on corporate independent expenditures. That case saw corruption not only in quid pro quo arrangements, but also in "the corrosive and distorting effects of immense aggregations of wealth that are accumulated with the help of the corporate form."[95] Yet even the *Austin* Court was careful to note that it was not "attempt[ing] to equalize the relative influence of speakers on elections" but was instead fighting the "unfair[] influence" of corporate wealth that might not "reflect actual public support for the political ideas espoused by corporations."[96]

Austin was overruled by *Citizens United*. As Justice Kennedy (who wrote an impassioned dissent in *Austin*) reiterated in *Citizens United*:

> The *Buckley* Court explained that the potential for *quid pro quo* corruption distinguished direct contributions to candidates from independent expenditures. The Court emphasized that "the independent expenditure ceiling . . . fails to serve any substantial governmental interest in stemming the reality or appearance of corruption in the electoral process," because "[t]he absence of prearrangement and coordination . . . alleviates the danger that expenditures will be given as a *quid pro quo* for improper commitments from the candidate."[97]

---

[94] *Id.* at 1451 n. 6.

[95] 494 U.S. 652, 660 (1990) (overruled parenthetical).

[96] *Id.* (citations and quotation marks omitted).

[97] Citizens United, 558 U.S. at 345 (citations omitted) (alterations in original).

Nevertheless, *Austin's* concern that speech would be "corrosive and distorting" if it did not "correlat[e] to the public's support for the corporation's political ideas"[98] finds an echo in Breyer's fear that "a few large donations [may] drown out the voices of the many," which will in turn "cut[] the link between political thought and political action."[99]

But certainly that was a broad—and possibly creative—theory of corruption when *Austin* was decided. In dissent, Justice Scalia dubbed it "the New Corruption."[100] He noted that *Austin* was about corporate speech but asked how this expansive view of corruption could find a limit. If corporations could be limited on this basis, he asked, "[w]hy is it perfectly all right if advocacy by an individual billionaire is out of proportion with 'actual public support' for his positions?"[101] Justice Breyer, of course, answers that question in his *McCutcheon* dissent: it is *not* perfectly all right. Allowing that billionaire (or even a millionaire) to give to a sufficiently wide number of candidates and political committees will drown out those who do not "publicly support" his views.

Justice Breyer concedes that that view was rejected in *Citizens United* and Justice Scalia's *Austin* dissent illustrates precisely why: it is so sweeping an interest as to be essentially limitless.

Consequently, *McCutcheon* clarified the law and halted the Court's movement away from *Buckley's* understanding of corruption. The relevant governmental interest is the avoidance of quid pro quo corruption and the appearance of such arrangements. The government may not regulate to limit mere access or influence that falls short of this standard.

f. After McCutcheon

The quid pro quo standard may not, in the end, be as narrow as the *McCutcheon* dissenters lament. Previous cases have expressed concern about the chain from large contributions, to access, to influence, and, ultimately, to favors. Similarly, previous Court majorities have worried that such "access and influence" will convince individuals

---

[98] Austin v. Mich. Chamber of Commerce, 494 U.S. 652, 660 (1990).

[99] McCutcheon, 134 S. Ct. at 1467–68.

[100] Austin, 494 U.S. at 691 (Scalia, J., dissenting).

[101] *Id.* at 685.

that their voices don't matter, causing them to drop out of our democratic system. But vindication of that first concern is entirely consistent with Chief Justice Roberts's view. And the second is, in many ways, a self-fulfilling prophecy.

The majority's concern is clear. Justice Breyer would "separate[] corruption from its quid pro quo roots and give[] it a new, far-reaching" meaning while "casting aspersions on 'politicians too compliant with the wishes of large contributors.'"[102] While not explicitly stating that this theory would "equalize the voices of citizens"—a proposition "*Buckley* rejected out of hand"[103]—the dissenters nonetheless fail to state the boundaries of their theory of corruption or how it differs, in practice, from an equalizing interest.

The dissenters missed an opportunity to address this concern and suggest an alternative theory of corruption—one subject to *some* limiting principle. Instead, Justice Breyer posited possibly the broadest theory since *Austin*, one with little chance of being adopted by a majority concerned with governmental overreach.

In any event, the dissent misunderstands the relevant interest when it conflates quid pro quo corruption with bribery. The Court has never held that criminal penalties for actual corrupt arrangements are the outer limit of congressional power. As the chief justice stated:

> It is worth keeping in mind that the base limits themselves are a prophylactic measure. As we have explained, "restrictions on direct contributions are preventative, because few if any contributions to candidates will involve quid pro quo arrangements." The aggregate limits are then layered on top, ostensibly to prevent circumvention of the base limits. This "prophylaxis-upon-prophylaxis approach" requires that we be particularly diligent in scrutinizing the law's fit.[104]

That "fit" is *McCutcheon*'s big question. And the plurality distinguished the dissenters' central concern—that base limits are

---

102 Shrink Mo., 528 U.S. at 423–24 (Thomas, J., dissenting) (internal quotation marks omitted).

103 *Id.* at 424.

104 McCutcheon, 134 S. Ct. at 1458 (citing Citizens United, 558 U.S. at 357; Wisconsin Right to Life, 551 U.S. at 479 (opinion of Roberts, C. J.); McConnell, 540 U.S. at 268–69 (opinion of Thomas, J.)).

necessary to prevent circumvention of the ban on soft money—because it nowhere stated that prophylactic rules are improper. The question is one of degree. Where Justice Breyer could have suggested a way to limit the risk of such circumvention, he instead went "all in"—choosing to largely reject any categorical limit on the government's power to regulate in this area. Had he provided such an alternative, it may have garnered a majority.

C. Tailoring

Having determined that the proper governmental interest is the prevention of corruption narrowly defined, but having allowed that prophylactic rules will be necessary to accomplish that goal, the majority asked the simple question at the heart of the *McCutcheon* dispute: were the aggregate limits "closely drawn" to help the government prevent quid pro quo corruption?

The district court believed they were, and

> imagined a hypothetical scenario that might occur in a world without aggregate limits. A single donor might contribute the maximum amount under the base limits to nearly 50 separate committees, each of which might then transfer the money to the same single committee. That committee, in turn, might use all the transferred money for coordinated expenditures on behalf of a particular candidate, allowing the single donor to circumvent the base limit on the amount he may contribute to that candidate.[105]

The district court conceded that such a scenario "seem[s] unlikely," since "so many separate entities [must] willingly serve as conduits."[106] Nevertheless, because it found this hypothetical "not hard to imagine," it upheld the aggregate limits.

Such hypotheticals loomed large in *McCutcheon*, as the district court correctly identified the two arguments in play. On one hand, as the dissenters found, the base and aggregate limits together acted "as a coherent system rather than merely a collection of individual limits," and this system, the government argued, was necessary to prevent circumvention of any of its constituent parts.[107] On the other

[105] McCutcheon, 134 S. Ct. at 1443.
[106] Id.
[107] Id. at 1444.

hand, as the plurality concluded, McCain-Feingold's many limits amounted to simply "stacking prophylaxis upon prophylaxis."[108]

At oral argument, the government made two points.

> Aggregate limits combat corruption both by blocking circumvention of individual contribution limits and, equally fundamentally, by serving as a bulwark against a campaign finance system dominated by massive individual contributions in which the dangers of quid pro quo corruption would be obvious and the corrosive appearance of corruption would be overwhelming.[109]

Let's consider each point—the circumvention concern that informed the district court's ruling, and the danger of a system "dominated" by a few wealthy donors—in turn.

1. Circumvention

As previously noted, *Buckley* upheld FECA's aggregate limit as a "mere corollary" of that law's base limits on contributions to candidates. That aggregate limit was acceptable because it helped prevent circumvention of the base limitation by a single donor flooding a political committee with enormous contributions.

When *Buckley* was decided, this was a real danger. While the version of FECA at issue in *Buckley* "had already capped contributions *from* political committees to candidates . . . the 1976 version added limits on contributions *to* political committees."[110] This additional restriction was understood as intended "at least in part to prevent circumvention of the very limitation on contributions . . . upheld in *Buckley*."[111] Consequently, in 1974 a donor very well could "flood [a] committee with 'huge' amounts of money so that each contribution th[at] committee ma[de] [was] perceived as a contribution" from the donor.[112] But after the 1976 amendments imposed a $5,000 limit on contributions from individuals to such committees, this takeover scenario ceased to present the danger of a quid pro quo understand-

---

[108] *Id.*

[109] Transcript of Oral Argument, *supra* note 5, at 27.

[110] McCutcheon, 134 S. Ct. at 1446.

[111] *Id.* (emphasis in original).

[112] *Id.*

ing. Instead, "[l]imits on contributions to political committees . . . create an additional hurdle for a donor who seeks both to channel a large amount of money to a particular candidate and to ensure that he gets the credit for doing so."[113]

This is not the only hurdle. "The 1976 Amendments also added an antiproliferation rule prohibiting donors from creating or controlling multiple affiliated political committees."[114] This prohibition "blocks a straightforward method" of circumventing base limits by "eliminat[ing] a donor's ability to create and use his own political committees to direct funds in excess of the individual base limits."[115]

2. Wild Hypotheticals

The *McCutcheon* dissenters found these checks insufficient. Indeed, the district court originally upheld the aggregate limits on the theory that they prevented complex attempts to defeat the base limits. These included making many (relatively) small contributions to various political committees, which would then forward those contributions to a designated candidate.

Such theories were a mainstay of the government's argument and the dissent's rationale. As articulated by Justice Elena Kagan:

> If you take off the aggregate limits, people will be allowed, if you put together the national committees and all the state committees and all the candidates in the House and the Senate, it comes to over $3.5 million. So I can write checks totaling $3.5 million to the Republican Party committees and all its candidates or to the Democratic Party committees and all its [candidates].[116]

In his eventual dissenting opinion, Justice Breyer posited two circumstances where, absent the aggregate limits, these millions of dollars could be funneled through various entities into the hands of a single candidate.

Justice Breyer imagined a single wealthy donor who first contributes the maximum of $64,800 to all three national party committees.

---

[113] *Id.*

[114] *Id.*

[115] *Id.* at 1447.

[116] Transcript of Oral Argument, *supra* note 5, at 23.

Then he contributes the maximum of $20,000 to each state party committee. Finally, the donor maxes out to each candidate from his party running in every House and Senate election nationwide: $2,600 per election, or $5,200 for both the primary and general elections. This yields a total of $3,628,000 over two years.

But how would this money, distributed among 521 separate committees, be funneled to a particular candidate? Justice Breyer noted that each of a party's 435 House and 33 Senate candidates can write checks of up to $4,000 to each other. And each state and national party committee may write checks of up to $10,000 to a candidate. Taken together, "[t]his yields a potential $1,872,000 (from candidates) plus $530,000 (from party committees)."[117] Consequently, these 521 committees can collude to each redirect $2.37 million of the hypothetical $3.6 million check directly to a favored candidate.

Of course, this can only be done once, because there are limits on how much each committee may give another. But Justice Breyer *notes that nothing prevents these committees from finding another* $3.6 million donor and making another $2.37 million in contributions to a second candidate, and so on.

This scenario is further limited by the number of potential committees. There are only so many party committees, so many states, and so many seats in Congress. Fine, says Justice Breyer, but what about unaffiliated PACs? That question led to the dissent's second hypothetical:

> Groups of party supporters—individuals, corporations, or trade unions—create 200 PACs. Each PAC claims it will use the funds it raises to support several candidates from the party, though it will favor those who are most endangered . . . Over a 2-year election cycle, Rich Donor One gives $10,000 to each PAC ($5,000 per year)—yielding $2 million total. Rich Donor 2 does the same. So, too, do [eight other] Rich Donors. This brings their total donations to $20 million, disbursed among the 200 PACs. Each PAC will have collected $100,000, and each can use its money to write ten checks of $10,000 to each of the ten most Embattled Candidates in the party (over two years). Every Embattled Candidate, receiving a $10,000 check from 200 PACs, will have collected $2 million.[118]

---

[117] McCutcheon, 134 S. Ct. at 1474.

[118] *Id.* at 1474–75.

The result is "that ten Rich Donors will have contributed $2 million each, and ten Embattled Candidates will have collected $2 million each."[119]

3. *The FEC and the limits of prophylaxes*

The plurality called these hypotheticals "illegal under current campaign finance laws," "implausible," and "divorced from reality." It relied heavily upon the existence of the FEC and its "intricate regulatory scheme."[120] In particular, the FEC has enacted broad regulations designed to prevent other vehicles, such as PACs or joint fundraising committees (JFCs), from being used to circumvent contribution limits.[121]

The government, the opinion below, and the dissent all raised the troubling prospect of millions of dollars being passed through sham organizations directly to candidates. But they ignored the fact that this concern—which, of course, dates back to *Buckley* and FECA's 1976 amendments—is already addressed by the FEC's existing regulatory paradigm.

The FEC's anti-proliferation rules "prohibit[] donors from creating or controlling multiple affiliated political committees."[122] Commission regulations permit the FEC to weigh a number of factors in determining if a political committee is "affiliated" with another PAC or candidate.[123] For instance, the commission may consider "[w]hether a [non-joint fundraising] sponsoring organization, or committee, causes or arranges for funds in a significant amount or on an ongoing basis to be provided to another sponsoring organization or committee."[124]

---

[119] *Id.* at 1475.

[120] *Id.* at 1447; See 11 C.F.R. § 100, et. seq.

[121] 11 C.F.R. 113.1(g) covers one of the most pernicious situations that confronted the *Buckley* Court. Before 1980, it was perfectly legal for campaign funds to be used for a candidate's personal expenses, such as buying groceries, paying college tuition, or covering rent and mortgage payments.

[122] McCutcheon, 134 S. Ct. at 1446–47. Another restriction, which Justice Breyer fails to address, is the federal rule requiring PACs that give to multiple candidates to "have more than 50 contributors." *Id.* at 1442 (referencing 11 C.F.R. § 100.5(e)(3)).

[123] 11 C.F.R. 100.5(4)(i)–(ii).

[124] 11 C.F.R. 100.5(4)(ii)(H).

The FEC's earmarking rules are similarly strict. A contribution is considered earmarked when there has been "a designation, instruction, or encumbrance, *whether direct or indirect*, express or implied, oral or written, which results in all or any part of a contribution or expenditure being made to, or expended on behalf of, a clearly identified candidate or a candidate's authorized committee."[125] Further, if any "intermediary exercises any direction or control over the choice of the recipient candidate, the earmarked contribution shall be considered a contribution by *both* the original contributor and the . . . intermediary."[126]

Moreover, the law prohibits "an individual who has contributed to a candidate also contribut[ing] to a political committee that has supported or anticipates supporting the same candidate, if the individual knows that 'a substantial portion [of his contribution] will be contributed to, or expended on behalf of,' that candidate."[127]

These regulations existed before *McCutcheon*. Notably, even in a world with aggregate limits, it would be possible for an individual conspiring with 15 PACs to funnel $74,600 to a single candidate.[128] Yet, perhaps unsurprisingly, nobody appears to do this—because it would involve breaking an astounding number of federal laws.

The dissenters found this analysis insufficient, largely because they don't trust the FEC. Specifically regarding circumvention, they noted that "the regulation requires a showing that donors have *knowledge* that a substantial portion of their contributions will be used by a PAC to support a candidate to whom they have already contributed. And 'knowledge' is hard to prove."[129] They further noted that, of nine FEC cases referencing the anti-circumvention regulation, eight

---

[125] 11 C.F.R. 110.6(b)(1).

[126] 11 C.F.R. 110.6(b)(2) (emphasis added).

[127] *McCutcheon*, 134 S. Ct. at 1447 (citing 11 C.F.R. 110.1(h)(2)) (brackets in original). See also FEC v. Nat'l Republican Senatorial Comm., 966 F.2d 1471 (D.C. Cir. 1992) (upholding FEC rejection of Common Cause's complaint that the NRSC "exercised direction or control" over contributions raised by a committee that divided the money equally among four candidates). Furthermore, using a PAC to evade base limits would violate 11 C.F.R. 110.4(b)(i): "No person shall make a contribution in the name of another."

[128] See Zac Morgan, *McCutcheon's Wild Hypotheticals*, Center for Competitive Politics, Dec. 11, 2013, http://www.campaignfreedom.org/2013/12/11/mccutcheons-wild-hypotheticals.

[129] *McCutcheon*, 134 S. Ct. at 1477 (Breyer, J., dissenting).

failed to find the requisite knowledge.[130] In the one case that did, the contributors were the receiving candidates' family members who gave to a group of PACs organized by an outside consulting firm.

Justice Breyer made his point clear, quoting Oscar Wilde. "Given this record of FEC (in)activity, my reaction to the plurality's reliance upon agency enforcement of this rule (as an adequate substitute for Congress' aggregate limits) is: 'One must have a heart of stone to read [it] without laughing.'"[131]

The chief justice (necessarily) responded to this bon mot, noting that "[i]t might be that such guilty knowledge could not be shown because the donors were not guilty—a possibility that the dissent does not entertain."[132] Besides, "the donors described in those eight cases were typically alleged to have exceeded the base limits by $5,000 or less."[133] Consequently, there was little in common between a scheme to exceed the base limits by a (relatively) small amount of money and one to route millions of dollars through hundreds of entities. In such cases, an official failing to identify the violation "has not a heart but a head of stone."[134]

This level of sarcasm belies a foundational disconnect between the supporters and opponents of increased campaign finance regulation. To some, the FEC's failure to find a large number of campaign finance violations indicates a lack of concrete evidence that campaign law scofflaws abound, as well as the agency's care in regulating activity that so closely implicates constitutional freedoms. To others, it must be the result of incompetence or unwillingness to enforce the law. As the chief justice noted, for the dissenters, "[t]he dearth of FEC prosecutions . . . proves only that people are getting away with it."[135] And the lack of evidence of such people just shows that "the methods of achieving circumvention are more subtle and more complex" than some appreciate.[136]

---

[130] *Id.* (emphasis added).

[131] *Id.* at 1478.

[132] *Id.* at 1456.

[133] *Id.*

[134] *Id.*

[135] *Id.*

[136] *Id.*

Recall that the question is whether Congress has tailored its response to its interest. In answering, Chief Justice Roberts looked at all the ways Congress has attempted to prevent evasion of the base limits, including not only its own statutory responses (such as prohibitions on circumvention and earmarking), but also its mandate to the FEC, which exercises delegated authority to regulate in this area.

In *Wisconsin Right to Life,* the chief justice—then also writing the controlling opinion—noted that it was impermissible to pile prophylaxis upon prophylaxis,[137] a view he reiterated in *McCutcheon.* But he was prepared to defer to the FEC's regulations and enforcement expertise in the latter case in part *because* the agency itself is a prophylaxis.

This is evident not only in his discussion of FEC enforcement, but also of the government's opportunities to tailor its response to circumvention concerns. While Roberts largely concentrates on actions Congress could take that would work less harm than the overall aggregate limit—including *limitations on transfers between committees*—he also notes that the FEC can construct regulatory checks, such as "defining how many candidates a PAC must support in order to ensure that 'a substantial portion' of a donor's contribution is not rerouted to a certain candidate."[138]

Thus, the plurality sees the existence of the FEC—with its regulations, enforcement powers, and rulemaking authority—as itself a step taken by Congress to prevent circumvention of statutory contribution limits. The dissenters disagree, seeing in the FEC only an empty shell. But the plurality's ruling raises the intriguing possibility that, at least in the context of First Amendment challenges, Congress's decision to delegate authority to an administrative agency may itself inform the tailoring analysis.

4. Non-circumventing corruption: The $3.6 million check

The district court upheld the statute under a theory of circumvention, as originally articulated by *Buckley,* and the government's briefing largely followed that reasoning. But at oral argument, the government shifted its focus to an argument that the aggregate

---

[137] *Id.* at 1458.
[138] *Id.* at 1459.

limits deter corruption regardless of whether they prevent circumvention.[139] This is, in essence, because joint fundraising committees exist. Such entities allow various committees—candidate, party, and PAC—to share the costs of fundraising and split the proceeds pro rata. Thus, a single officeholder could solicit a large check from a single donor, later dividing that contribution among the various entities in the joint committee. As the solicitor general explained, the heads of such committees might solicit very large checks, which in his view raised its own concerns:

> The very fact of delivering the $3.6 million check to the whoever it is, the Speaker of the House, the Senate Majority Leader, whoever it is who solicits that check, the very fact of delivering that check creates the inherent opportunity for quid pro quo corruption, exactly the kind of risk that the Court identified in *Buckley*, wholly apart from where that money goes after it's delivered.[140]

The dissent's clearest articulation of this concern came in the context of a hypothetical contributor giving to a "Joint Party Committee" comprising a party's three national committees and 50 state committees. "[I]n the absence of any aggregate limit, an individual could legally give to the Republican Party or to the Democratic Party about $1.2 million over two years . . . . The titular heads of these joint committees could be the Speaker of the House of Representatives and the Minority Leader of the House."[141]

The dissent then asked (presumably rhetorically) whether "elected officials [will] be particularly grateful to the large donor, feeling obliged to provide him special access and influence, and perhaps even a quid pro quo legislative favor?"[142] They posited that because the soliciting officeholder will "become a player [in his party] beyond his own race" by raising such large sums, "the donor's influence is multiplied."[143] As Justice Kagan put it, with such a large check "you get a very, very special place at the table."[144]

---

[139] Transcript of Oral Argument, *supra* note 4, at 29–30, 50–52.

[140] *Id.* at 29.

[141] McCutcheon, 134 S. Ct. at 1472.

[142] *Id.*

[143] *Id.* at 1473.

[144] Transcript of Oral Argument, *supra* note 5, at 24.

The plurality disagreed. Obviously, monies that pass through joint fundraising committees are still subject to the base limits. More pointedly, "*Buckley* made clear that the risk of corruption arises when an individual makes large contributions to the candidate or officeholder himself. *Buckley*'s analysis of the aggregate limit under FECA was similarly confined. The Court noted that the aggregate limit guarded against an individual's funneling—through circumvention—'massive amounts of money to a particular candidate.'"[145]

Besides precedent, the plurality dismissed the dissent's view of gratitude on practical grounds, demanding "a clear, administrable line between" money given directly to a candidate and "money beyond the base limits given widely to a candidate's party."[146] In the latter case, gratitude is widely shared within the party, and while "the leaders of the party or cause may feel particular gratitude" to "recast such shared interest, standing alone, as an opportunity for quid pro quo corruption would dramatically expand government regulation of the political process."[147]

If its standard of corruption is inherently unworkable, the government did "suggest[] that it is the *solicitation* of large contributions that poses the danger of corruption."[148] But having tendered a startlingly broad theory of corruption, the fact remained that the aggregate limits were not limited to solicited contributions. As the majority noted, after an exhausting disagreement over the proper role of the government in preventing corruption, "it is enough that the aggregate limits at issue are not directed specifically to candidate behavior" like solicitations.[149]

5. Questions of fact versus questions of law?

Having disagreed about both the appropriate understanding of corruption and the "fit" between that interest and the aggregate limits, both sides at least agreed on the legal question: whether the aggregate limits are closely drawn to further a compelling governmental

---

[145] McCutcheon, 134 S. Ct. at 1460.

[146] *Id.* at 1461.

[147] *Id.*

[148] *Id.*

[149] *Id.* (emphasis in original).

interest.[150] Both the plurality and the government, which brought the case to the Supreme Court on cross-motions for summary judgment, saw this as a question of law. The dissenters had a different view.

To Justice Breyer, that legal question "turn[ed] on factual questions about whether corruption, in the absence of such limits, is a realistic threat to our democracy."[151] He favored a remand for development of a factual record to help "determine whether or the extent to which [the Court] should defer to Congress' own judgments."[152] And he suggested that disagreements "on the possibilities for circumvention of the base limits" and "how effectively the plurality's alternatives could prevent evasion" explained the different results reached by the plurality and the dissent.[153]

It is unclear how—apart from the discussion *McCutcheon* already contains—such a counterfactual could be shown. (Indeed, the plurality and dissent read even the facts of the FEC's public enforcement record quite differently.) Justice Breyer apparently had in mind a record "contain[ing] testimony from Members of Congress (or state legislatures) explaining why Congress (or the legislature) acted as it did."[154]

But creating such a record is expensive, and requiring one threatens to foreclose future challenges to campaign finance laws. The *McConnell* record was, famously, over 100,000 pages long. Many attorneys would recognize that "amassing" such a record, to borrow the justice's apt word, would render many cases impracticable.

But Justice Breyer's preference for a record does not extend to the probability of base-limit circumvention:

> Determining whether anticorruption objectives justify a particular set of contribution limits requires answering empirically based questions, and applying significant discretion and judgment. To what extent will unrestricted giving lead to corruption or its appearance? What forms will any such corruption take? To what extent will a lack of

[150] *Id.* at 1480.
[151] *Id.*
[152] *Id.*
[153] *Id.*
[154] *Id.* at 1479.

regulation undermine public confidence in the democratic system? To what extent can regulation restore it? These kinds of questions, while not easily answered, are questions that Congress is far better suited to resolve than are judges.[155]

This may be true, but the burden of demonstrating appropriate tailoring falls upon the government. If Congress had sophisticated, evidence-based reasons for adopting the aggregate limits, it could have articulated them as part of passing BCRA.[156] There is little evidence that it had such a purpose or such evidence. If the government was nonetheless willing to bring the case to court as a purely legal question, and Congress was willing to pass legislation with little evidence of considered analysis along the lines Justice Breyer suggests, why should the Court decline to rule?

Conclusion

McCutcheon could have been a straightforward case. *Buckley*, with little analysis, upheld aggregate contribution limits as a "corollary" needed to safeguard against circumvention of base limits. The question was simple: with the benefit of briefing and argument on the topic, were the limits in fact closely drawn to prevent corruption?

The plurality saw this is as inquiry rooted in *Buckley* itself. If Congress designated a certain amount as, in its judgment, non-corrupting, it could not say that amount of money becomes corrupting if given to too many candidates.

The holding, then, is narrow. *McCutcheon* clarified that exacting scrutiny requires searching review that pays close attention to the "fit" between the asserted government interest and Congress's policy choices. It also clarified that the "corruption" of *Buckley* is

---

[155] *Id.* at 1480.

[156] The dissenters appear willing to accept limitations imposed without evidence, while requiring evidence from those who would challenge such restrictions. This approach finds some support in *Shrink Missouri*'s statement that "[t]he quantum of empirical evidence needed to satisfy heightened judicial scrutiny of legislative judgments will vary up or down with the novelty and plausibility of the justification raised." 528 U.S. at 391. But as *McCutcheon* illustrates, the novelty of the government's interest may itself be disputed. Moreover, because they take a broad view of what is "plausible" in the real world, the dissenters' view would create a one-way ratchet favoring greater regulation. For instance, they credulously accept the government's circumvention hypotheticals without requiring any supporting evidence, and it appears that they would have upheld the challenged statute on that basis alone.

quid pro quo corruption and not a broader understanding of political equality or the need to ensure broader political participation—though that is certainly an interest Congress may pursue through other means. Consequently, the Court rooted its jurisprudence more firmly in *Buckley* and clarified the scope of governmental power in the area of speech regulation. Such clarity, in this confusing area, can only be to the good.

Ohio's Truth Ministry vs. Cato's Truthiness Brief

Ilya Shapiro* et al.**

Introduction to the Background

Believe it or not, Ohio has a law that *criminalizes* knowingly or recklessly making "false" statements about a political candidate or a ballot initiative with the intent to affect an election.[1] My colleagues and I could hardly believe it either when we first heard about this all-too-serious tomfoolery in the context of *Susan B. Anthony List v. Driehaus* ("*SBA List*"), an actual federal case that the Supreme Court heard this past term.[2] For dogged supporters of the First Amendment such as the Cato Institute, Ohio's law seems like it was ripped from the pages of Orwell's *1984*. What's more, around 20 states have similar laws.[3] We couldn't let this darkening bog lie and quickly decided to get involved.

But that's nothing special; in recent years, Cato has filed 30–40 amicus briefs every Supreme Court term (about half at the cert stage,

---

*Ilya Shapiro is a senior fellow in constitutional studies at the Cato Institute and editor-in-chief of the Cato Supreme Court Review.

** Olivia Grady helped outline the case background you see below; Trevor Burrus and Gabriel Latner co-authored the brief you see further below (and aren't yet members of any bar so couldn't have their names on it); P.J. O'Rourke didn't tweak either my jokes or legal analysis in said brief; and Chief Justice John Roberts allowed the brief to be filed despite its footnote 15. All errors are, of course, their fault.

[1] Ohio Rev. Code Ann. § 3517.21(B) (LexisNexis 2014).

[2] Susan B. Anthony List v. Driehaus, 134 S. Ct. 2334 (2014). Curiously, the case ascended to the Court around the time that President Obama's infamous claim that the Affordable Care Act ensures that "if you like your health care plan you can keep it" was publicly adjudged to be the most blatant lie of his administration. See, e.g., Angie Drobnic Holan, Lie of the Year: 'If You Like Your Health Care Plan, You Can Keep It,' Politifact.com (Dec. 12, 2013), http://www.politifact.com/truth-o-meter/article/2013/dec/12/lie-year-if-you-like-your-health-care-plan-keep-it.

[3] Aaron Marshall, Despite Laws against Lying, Tall Tales Have Become the Norm on the Campaign Trail, Experts Say, Cleveland Plain Dealer, Oct. 29, 2012, available at http://www.cleveland.com/open/index.ssf/2012/10/despite_laws_against_lying_tal.html.

half on the merits). What's special is the notice that our merits brief garnered.[4] Although Cato lawyers and scholars have been central to debates over many issues—and our briefs are often referenced by legal analysts and occasionally cited by the Court—never before has one of our filings generated so much attention. Nor had I previously had the opportunity to share a byline with P.J. O'Rourke.[5] It's thus the ridiculous background to the case and Cato's role in it—all illustrating an absurd law—that have inserted *SBA List* into this volume of the *Cato Supreme Court Review*, not its overarching importance or doctrinal innovation.

Indeed, *SBA List* ultimately concerned the ability of certain groups to challenge Ohio's "Pinocchio" law—whether they could get into court even though they aren't currently being prosecuted. The Supreme Court thus didn't reach any of the obvious constitutional defects with the law itself to rule unanimously in favor of these challengers. That consideration of ripeness and standing doctrine, while important for legal practitioners, doesn't normally merit inclusion in these pages.

Accordingly, instead of providing our typical 7,500–12,000-word analysis, for *SBA List* we've decided to simply give you an overview of the case—especially color from briefing and oral argument—before republishing our famous "funny brief" (in the pages that follow this introductory essay). I hope all this gives you not just a laugh, but also pause to reflect on how a democratic society could possibly allow such a law to be passed and enforced. We simply can't let the government determine who can speak, how much they can speak, and on what topic—particularly when it comes to our political discourse.

---

[4] See, e.g., David Lat, Best Amicus Brief Ever, Above the Law (Mar. 3, 2014), http://abovethelaw.com/2014/03/best-amicus-brief-ever; Is It Wise to Criminalise Lies?, The Economist Mar. 8, 2014, available at http://www.economist.com/news/united-states/21598683-challenging-buckeye-states-ban-political-mudslinging-it-wise-criminalise-lies; Adam Liptak, In Ohio, a Law Bans Lying in Elections. Justices and Jesters Alike Get a Say., N.Y. Times, Mar. 25, 2014, at A16.

[5] P.J. O'Rourke and Ilya Shapiro, We Reserve the Right to Lie about Our Politicians, Politico Magazine, Mar. 26, 2014, available at http://www.politico.com/magazine/story/2014/03/supreme-court-lying-politicians-cato-amicus-105050.html. See also Podcast: P.J. O'Rourke, Ilya Shapiro on Lying Politicians, Constitution Daily, National Constitution Center (Apr. 30, 2014), http://blog.constitutioncenter.org/2014/04/podcast-p-j-orourke-ilya-shapiro-on-lying-politicians.

Background

The Susan B. Anthony List (SBA List) and the Coalition Opposed to Additional Spending and Taxes (COAST) are conservative advocacy organizations. Both organizations wanted to target Congressman Steve Driehaus (D-OH) for supporting the Affordable Care Act (ACA)—claiming that this meant that Driehaus voted for taxpayer-funded abortion—but were unable to because of Ohio's false-statement statute. Any person can file a complaint alleging a false statement with the Ohio ~~Truth~~ Election Commission (OEC). To expedite the procedure during elections, however, complaints are first heard by a commission panel to determine whether probable cause exists. If the panel finds probable cause, and if the full commission then finds a violation with clear and convincing evidence, it may refer the case to a prosecutor, who has discretion to prosecute the case.

Rep. Driehaus first threatened legal action against SBA List during the 2010 federal election campaign, which resulted in an advertising company refusing to put up an SBA List billboard. Later that year, Driehaus filed a complaint with the OEC asserting that SBA List's advertisement violated Ohio's false-statement statute. On October 14, 2010—three weeks before the election—a panel found that there was probable cause and referred Driehaus's complaint to the full commission. Four days later, SBA List filed this case in federal district court seeking declaratory and injunctive relief and a temporary restraining order to enjoin the OEC proceeding. The OEC hearing was then postponed till after the election, which Driehaus subsequently lost, at which point he withdrew his complaint. The following month, SBA List amended its complaint to allege that the OEC proceedings chilled its speech and that, because the group was planning to make the same or similar speech in future elections, it feared further actions against it.

Similarly, COAST wanted to criticize Driehaus by writing emails, blogposts, and press releases, as well as publicizing the fact that he had filed the OEC complaint against SBA List. COAST didn't publish these materials, however, and instead sued the commission about a week before the 2010 election, claiming that the SBA List proceedings chilled its own speech. The district court consolidated the two cases and granted defendants' motions to dismiss based on standing and ripeness, as well as the mootness of the SBA List proceeding.

SBA List and COAST appealed those rulings to the U.S. Court of Appeals for the Sixth Circuit, which affirmed the lower court's decision on ripeness grounds.

SBA List and COAST then filed a cert petition, asking the Supreme Court to determine when an individual can sue for a First Amendment violation based on a law that restricts speech. They presented the questions whether a party must prove that authorities would certainly and successfully prosecute him to challenge a speech-suppressive law and whether the Sixth Circuit erred when it held that state laws proscribing "false" political speech are not subject to pre-enforcement First Amendment review so long as the speaker maintains that its speech is true. Petitioners' first argument was that the Sixth Circuit failed to follow seven other circuits by imposing substantial hurdles to the review of speech-suppressive laws. Second, the Sixth Circuit's finding was inconsistent with First Amendment jurisprudence, which allows pre-enforcement review when a law chills speech.[6] Finally, the Sixth Circuit's ruling chills speech in its most important area—the political arena—and leaves no remedy for the speaker's political injury.

Remarkably, Driehaus waived his right to respond to the petition. The Ohio attorney general, however, filed a brief opposing the petition on behalf of the OEC and other state defendants, arguing that a First Amendment challenge isn't ripe when plaintiffs have alleged only a generalized and subjective chill of their speech and don't face any threat of actual criminal prosecution. The brief made several further counterpoints, including that the OEC has only the narrow function of recommending cases to prosecutors, rather than actual enforcement authority.

On January 10, 2014, the Supreme Court took the case. In its opening brief, SBA List argued that it faces a "credible threat of prosecution" under Ohio's law because the OEC had already found probable cause that behavior SBA List regularly engages in runs afoul of the law—and pre-enforcement First Amendment challenges are allowed where there's a "credible threat of prosecution." Moreover, the Sixth Circuit's jurisprudence is contrary to established First Amendment

---

[6] See Babbitt v. United Farm Workers Nat'l Union, 442 U.S. 289 (1979); Virginia v. Am. Booksellers Ass'n. Inc., 484 U.S. 383 (1988); Holder v. Humanitarian Law Project, 130 S. Ct. 2705 (2010).

precedent. For example, the Sixth Circuit, unlike the Supreme Court, requires a plaintiff to show a particularized threat or certainty of prosecution. Finally, the Sixth Circuit's approach impairs free speech in its most important context—politics—by forbidding meritorious challenges to laws that suppress speech.

Many organizations filed amicus briefs in support of the petitioners, including Cato (joined by our own H.L. Mencken research fellow, P.J. O'Rourke). As you'll see below, in our brief we style the question presented as whether a state government can criminalize political statements that aren't 100 percent truthful. We point out that truthiness—"a 'truth' asserted 'from the gut' or because it 'feels right' without regard to evidence or logic"—is an important part of political discourse because it allows the public to hear responses to allegations, thus creating a "self-correcting marketplace of ideas."[7] Moreover, the Supreme Court already held in *United States v. Alvarez* that truthiness and even outright lies are protected by the First Amendment.[8] Finally, the public interest in truthful political discourse is best served by satirists and pundits because it's through humor that political dishonesty is best exposed—and if politicians' lies aren't exposed by satirists or fact-checkers, they certainly won't be by the OEC.

In a development perhaps even rarer than a nationally renowned satirist joining a Supreme Court brief, Ohio Attorney General Mike DeWine filed two briefs. In a maneuver reminiscent of Robert Bork's "Cerberus-headed" actions in the seminal 1976 campaign-finance case of *Buckley v. Valeo*, DeWine filed an amicus brief as Ohio's chief law officer that questioned the constitutionality of Ohio's law—even as he continued representing the OEC.[9] In his amicus brief, DeWine

---

[7] Truthiness, Wikipedia, http://en.wikipedia.org/wiki/Truthiness (last visited Aug. 4, 2014) (describing the term's coinage by Stephen Colbert during the pilot of his show in October 2005). See also Truthiness, Dictionary.com, http://dictionary.reference. com/browse/truthiness (last visited Aug. 4, 2014); Brief for the Cato Institute and P.J. O'Rourke as Amicus Curiae Supporting Petitioners at 7, Susan B. Anthony List v. Driehaus, 134 S. Ct. 2334 (2014) (No. 13-193).

[8] 132 S. Ct. 2537, 2544–45 (2012).

[9] See Marty Lederman, The Return of the Robert Bork "Dueling Briefs" Strategy: *Buckley v. Valeo, Susan B. Anthony List,* and Ohio Attorney General DeWine, SCOTUSblog (Mar. 17, 2014), http://www.scotusblog.com/2014/03/commentary-the-return-of-the-robert-bork-dueling-briefs-strategy-buckley-v-valeo-susan-b-anthony-list-and-ohio-attorney-general-dewine.

argued that the Ohio statute may chill constitutionally protected speech at critical times immediately before elections and may be intentionally used by private actors in order to gain a campaign advantage without ever proving the falsity of the statement at issue. In addition, a probable-cause finding that an individual has made a false statement right before an election would be extremely harmful politically, and this harm can't be remedied after the election. Curiously, the brief is styled as supporting neither party and, rather than calling for the Sixth Circuit to be reversed, coyly concludes that its review of the statute "may be helpful to the Court in considering the questions presented in this case."[10]

Turning to the Ohio attorney general's brief as a party, DeWine's more conventional brief first argued for ripeness as a constitutional and prudential limit on the judiciary: Adequate allegations of a future injury are needed to establish a present controversy and ensure that the case allows the court to resolve the claims. In this case, the brief explained, the plaintiffs' allegations lack concrete form and their threatened injury is too indirect. Moreover, SBA List and COAST allege only a past injury from Driehaus's complaints, and their allegations of future injury are too speculative.

And so the battlefield was set, with oral argument set for April 22, 2014, two months before the end of the Supreme Court term.

At the Supreme Court

The petitioners, represented by seasoned advocate Michael Carvin, first argued that they had a ripe and justiciable controversy because the OEC panel found that their speech likely violated Ohio's false-statement law, thus meeting the "credible threat of enforcement" test. Justices Ruth Bader Ginsburg and Sonia Sotomayor questioned, however, whether COAST had a credible threat of enforcement since no one had filed a complaint against it.[11] Carvin replied that they both had standing because unlike an important precedent calling for courts to abstain from deciding certain cases, the speech of SBA List

[10] Brief for Ohio Attorney General Michael DeWine as Amicus Curiae in Support of Neither Party at 22, SBA List, 134 S. Ct. 2334. The brief is signed not by DeWine himself—as the brief of the state defendants is—but by Erik Jaffe and Bradley Smith, friends of Cato whose writing has appeared in these pages.

[11] Transcript of Oral Argument at 4–7, Susan B. Anthony List v. Driehaus, 134 S. Ct. 2334 (2014) (No. 13-193).

and COAST here was the same.[12] Unconvinced that COAST faced a credible threat of enforcement, Justice Sotomayor then asked why this case was different from a recent First Amendment-standing case called *Clapper v. Amnesty International*.[13] Carvin responded that both petitioners, unlike the *Clapper* petitioners, had actually been harmed by the OEC hearing.

The justices next focused on how the OEC or petitioners could avoid hearings on frivolous claims. Justice Ginsburg suggested that petitioners could have sought an advisory opinion, but Carvin found that to be a non-starter because, in the first place, the "ministry of truth has no ability to judge . . . political speech as falsity."[14] Moreover, "it would be cutting off [their] nose to spite [their] face" to voluntarily invoke this procedure.[15]

Petitioners' counsel also argued that this case is special because its subject matter is political speech, which not only is at the core of the First Amendment but also is unique for being most important during *the period of an election campaign. Because of the short time frame,* one cannot complete a challenge to restrictions on political speech before the election to which it is relevant, so facially unconstitutional laws continue to exist and impose serious burdens on speakers. This essentially becomes a "capable of repetition yet evading review" exception to the mootness doctrine.[16] The justices finally asked about the "credible threat of prosecution," which petitioners defined as: "if the enforcement agency has previously announced that your speech probably violates the law at issue, then you have a credible threat of future enforcement if you repeat that speech."[17]

The United States, arguing as amicus and represented by assistant to the solicitor general Eric Feigin, called for partial affirmance— supporting SBA List's right to make a facial First Amendment claim against the false-statement law and challenge the OEC's enforcement of it, but rejecting certain ancillary claims and defendants. The government first argued that the two critical factors for justiciability

---

[12] Younger v. Harris, 401 U.S. 37 (1971).

[13] Clapper v. Amnesty Int'l USA, 133 S. Ct. 1138, 1147 (2013).

[14] Tr. of Oral Arg. at 9, SBA List, 134 S. Ct. 2334.

[15] *Id.* at 13.

[16] Roe v Wade, 410 U.S. 113, 125 (1973).

[17] Tr. of Oral Arg. at 17, SBA List, 134 S. Ct. 2334.

in this case were the OEC's probable-cause finding and petitioners' intent to repeat their speech. Chief Justice John Roberts then asked whether a probable-cause determination was needed for standing. Feigin argued that without a probable-cause finding, the likelihood of an enforcement proceeding would be too speculative. Roberts seemed skeptical of this response, because, under the law, any person could trigger an enforcement action. Moreover, petitioners aren't going to argue that their speech is false and invite prosecution. Justice Elena Kagan followed up by asking whether it would be enough if Rep. Driehaus had written a letter threatening enforcement. Feigin replied that a letter would be enough to bring suit against Driehaus only. Kagan challenged the government's rule about the need for some tangible threat of prosecution by pointing out that there might be some statements that "given this process, it's just going to require too much fortitude to resist the temptation to bring this in front of this Commission."[18] The government responded that this would still be too speculative, but since this is a "private attorney general statute," the threat-of-prosecution standard might be relaxed.[19]

The respondents, valiantly represented by Ohio solicitor general Eric Murphy, argued that the Sixth Circuit should be affirmed because the petitioners had not established a credible threat of criminal prosecution, and any other injury is not impending. Chief Justice Roberts quickly asked whether the state would take action against petitioners if they repeated their speech in the next election, to which Murphy conceded that he didn't have the authority to disavow such a potential action.[20] It was all downhill from there.

Justice Antonin Scalia offered that the petitioners are complaining not just about the current possible criminal prosecution but also about future commission hearings during election season. Ohio's lawyer replied that the complaint about future hearings is speculative because SBA List was challenging specific congressmen.[21] That is, petitioners targeted only pro-life Democrats who originally voted against the ACA but then later changed their vote.

[18] *Id.* at 24.
[19] *Id.* at 25.
[20] *Id.* at 29–30.
[21] *Id.* at 30–31.

Justice Anthony Kennedy then asked whether there was a serious First Amendment concern with the law—one of the few merits-based questions during the generally technical argument—but Murphy reminded him that the issue here was standing.[22] Justice Stephen Breyer retorted that the harm was the chilling of speech (a First Amendment concern), but Murphy gamely offered that the chilling of speech wasn't a harm because of *Golden v. Zwickler*.[23] Justice Ginsburg jumped in here to distinguish *Golden* because the plaintiff there attacked a specific candidate, not an issue, and he wasn't planning on similar speech in the future. Murphy countered that the *Golden* plaintiff was planning on leafleting in the future but didn't mention specific candidates, just like in this case.[24]

Justice Kagan argued next that the probable-cause finding is a harm because voters don't know that it represents a low standard of proof, that "[t]here are voters out there . . . [who] think probable cause means you probably lied."[25] Murphy similarly replied that petitioners didn't make that argument in the lower courts, and they had told their supporters what a probable-cause finding meant. Chief Justice Roberts then mentioned that the billboard company refused to put up their billboard and that the state's involvement in the probable-cause finding is more meaningful than a possible private defamation suit. As Justice Scalia put it, "The mere fact that a private individual can chill somebody's speech does not say, well, since a private individual can do it, you know, the ministry of truth can do it."[26]

Justice Sotomayor then asked how many cases were fully prosecuted, and Ohio's lawyer replied that only five referrals had been made—in an attempt to show how unlikely criminal prosecution is.[27] Chief Justice Roberts responded that many of the proceedings must have been mooted, although Murphy didn't have data on that front. Justice Samuel Alito then mused that the statistics that respondents

---

[22] *Id.* at 32.

[23] 394 U.S. 103, 109 (1969) (dismissing challenge to an electoral leafleting ban as nonjusticiable because plaintiff's "sole concern was literature relating to the Congressman and his record," and it was "most unlikely that the Congressman would again be a candidate").

[24] Tr. of Oral Arg. at 34–35, SBA List, 134 S. Ct. 2334.

[25] *Id.* at 36.

[26] *Id.* at 38.

[27] *Id.* at 39–40.

provided show a system that limits speech without much of an opportunity for judicial review, with thousands of complaints and few prosecutions. Respondents answered that they are arguing about this case only and that, since the law is unambiguous, petitioners need to allege more than just the possibility of prosecution.[28]

Finally, Justice Breyer expressed concern that elections are coming up, and people need to know what they can say, so perhaps the Court needed to get into the merits. Respondents' counsel suggested that, if he lost and the Supreme Court remanded to the district court, that court could ask the Ohio Supreme Court to clarify the scope of the law. Chief Justice Roberts joked that respondents' suggestion to involve another court system would really "speed things up."[29] Justice Alito asked what narrowing construction could possibly be consistent with *United States v. Alvarez*.[30] Justice Scalia jokingly replied that the statement at issue would have to be "really false."[31] Murphy attempted to distinguish *Alvarez* because that case was "about false statements in the abstract," but Alito corrected him by noting that *Alvarez* concerned "hard factual statements."[32]

On rebuttal, petitioners' counsel argued against Ohio's suggestion of a certification to the state supreme court because that would cause further delay and not solve the questions regarding the constitutionality of the statute. Carvin asked the Court instead to follow *Citizens United* when deciding whether to remand the case for a First Amendment facial challenge because a remand causes further constitutional injury from delay when "our entire point is it's unconstitutional for us to [have to] say, 'Mother, may I?' before we speak."[33]

---

[28] *Id.* at 44.

[29] *Id.* at 47.

[30] 132 S. Ct. 2537 (2012) (striking down the Stolen Valor Act, which criminalized false statements about having won military honors).

[31] Tr. of Oral Arg. at 48, SBA List, 134 S. Ct. 2334.

[32] *Id.* at 48.

[33] *Id.* at 53 (citing Citizens United v. FEC, 558 U.S. 310, 329 (2010)).

The Ruling

To nobody's surprise, the justices unanimously reversed the Sixth Circuit decision and held that a pre-enforcement challenge here was both ripe and justiciable.[34] Justice Clarence Thomas delivered the opinion of the Court, first deciding that SBA List and COAST alleged a credible threat of enforcement that amounts to an Article III injury. After all, both petitioners want to make statements in future elections that are similar to the statements made by SBA List in the 2010 election, and because this is political speech, it is "affected with a constitutional interest."[35] In addition, the intended speech is arguably proscribed by the Ohio statute because the OEC already made a probable-cause finding about the speech—which also makes the threat of enforcement substantial. Further, anyone can file a complaint—including political opponents—making it more likely that a complaint will be filed. Therefore, the Court concluded that the combination of the burdensome OEC proceedings (which occur regularly) and the additional threat of criminal prosecution was enough to get SBA List and COAST their day in court.

I imagine that the lower courts, now sufficiently chastened, will strike down Ohio's law on remand—and we'll never hear of such nonsense again. Still, *SBA List* now joins the motley pantheon of Supreme Court curiosities: little, bizarre cases that will be remembered fondly for the sunlight they brought to absurd legal practices. And if Cato's brief contributed in some small way to this sunlit disinfectant, all the better.[36]

*   *   *

The "Best Amicus Brief Ever"

Since its founding, this country has held as one of its cardinal principles the right of the people to castigate and mock their leaders. The monarchic culture that the Founders chose to break from

---

[34] SBA List, 134 S. Ct. 2334, 2347 (2014).

[35] Babbitt, 442 U.S. at 298.

[36] For a recent (post-decision) local take on Ohio's law, see Scott Blackburn, Ohio's False Statement Law Impedes Political Discourse, Cleveland Plain Dealer, Aug. 1, 2014, available at http://www.cleveland.com/opinion/index.ssf/2014/08/ohios_false_statement_law_scot.html.

recognized a speech-crime known as *lèse-majesté*: any speech or action that insulted the monarchy or offended its dignity was an act of treason. Lest European monarchs grow too proud, however, they would appoint court jesters. These "licensed fools" were granted a special dispensation permitting them to mock their monarchs without fear of death. Like the slave riding behind a Roman general, the fool's role was to remind the king that he too was mortal.

Why did we write the brief? Because in America, *lèse-majesté* is not a crime; we each have the right to be as foolish as we wish. Ohio's law threatens that sacred right, undermining the First Amendment's protection of the serious business of making politics funny.[37]

---

[37] For more on why we filed the brief, see Ilya Shapiro, Trevor Burrus & Gabriel Latner, Truthiness and the First Amendment, 16 U. Pa. J. Const. L. Height. Scrutiny 51 (2014), available at https://www.law.upenn.edu/live/files/3381-shapiro16upajconst lheightscrutiny512014pubpdf.

No. 13-193

In The

$\mathfrak{Supreme}$ Court of the United States

SUSAN B. ANTHONY LIST, ET AL.,

Petitioners,

v.

STEVEN DRIEHAUS, ET AL.,

Respondents.

On a Writ of Certiorari
to the United States Court Of Appeals
for the Sixth Circuit

BRIEF OF *AMICI CURIAE* CATO INSTITUTE
AND P.J. O'ROURKE IN SUPPORT OF
PETITIONERS

ILYA SHAPIRO
Counsel of Record
Cato Institute
1000 Mass. Ave. NW
Washington, DC 20001
(202) 842-2000
ishapiro@cato.org

i

QUESTION PRESENTED

Can a state government criminalize political statements that are less than 100% truthful?

Ohio's Truth Ministry vs. Cato's Truthiness Brief

ii

TABLE OF CONTENTS

Page

iii

TABLE OF AUTHORITIES

Ohio's Truth Ministry vs. Cato's Truthiness Brief

iv

v

1

INTEREST OF *AMICI CURIAE*[1]

Established in 1977, the Cato Institute is a non-partisan public policy research foundation dedicated to advancing the principles of individual liberty, free markets, and limited government. Cato's Center for Constitutional Studies was established in 1989 to help restore the principles of constitutional government that are the foundation of liberty. Toward those ends, Cato holds conferences and publishes books, studies, and the annual *Cato Supreme Court Review*.

P.J. O'Rourke is America's leading political satirist and an H.L. Mencken Research Fellow at the Cato Institute. Formerly the editor of the *National Lampoon*, he has written for such publications as *Car and Driver*, *Playboy*, *Esquire*, *Vanity Fair*, *House & Garden*, *The New Republic*, *The New York Times Book Review*, *Parade*, *Harper's*, and *Rolling Stone*. He is now a contributing editor at *The Atlantic* and *The Weekly Standard*, a member of the editorial board of *World Affairs*, and a regular panelist on NPR's *Wait, Wait . . . Don't Tell Me*. O'Rourke's books have been translated into a dozen languages and are worldwide bestsellers. Three have been *New York Times* bestsellers: *Parliament of Whores*, *Give War a Chance*, and *All the Trouble in the World*. He is also

---

[1] Pursuant to this Court's Rule 37.3(a), letters of consent from all parties to the filing of this brief have been submitted to the Clerk. Pursuant to this Court's Rule 37.6, *amici* state that this brief was not authored in whole or in part by counsel for any party, and that no person or entity other than *amici* made a monetary contribution its preparation or submission. Also, *amici* and their counsel, family members, and pets have all won the Congressional Medal of Honor.

149

2

the author of *Eat the Rich, Peace Kills,* and *Don't Vote: It Just Encourages the Bastards.*

This case concerns *amici* because the law at issue undermines the First Amendment's protection of the serious business of making politics funny.

INTRODUCTION AND
SUMMARY OF ARGUMENT

"I am not a crook."

"Read my lips: no new taxes!"

"I did not have sexual relations with that woman."

"Mission accomplished."

"If you like your healthcare plan, you can keep it."

While George Washington may have been incapable of telling a lie,[2] his successors have not had the same integrity. The campaign promise (and its subsequent violation), as well as disparaging statements about one's opponent (whether true, mostly true, mostly not true, or entirely fantastic), are cornerstones of American democracy. Indeed, mocking and satire are as old as America, and if this Court doesn't believe *amici*, it can ask Thomas Jefferson, "the son of a half-breed squaw, sired by a Virginia mulatto father."[3] Or perhaps it should

---

[2] Apocryphal.

[3] Monticello.org, *Son of a Halfbreed Indian Squaw (Quotation),* http://www.monticello.org/site/son-half-breed-indian-squaw-quotation (last visited Feb. 28, 2014).

Ohio's Truth Ministry vs. Cato's Truthiness Brief

3

ponder, as Grover Cleveland was forced to, "Ma, ma, where's my pa?"[4]

In modern times, "truthiness"—a "truth" asserted "from the gut" or because it "feels right," without regard to evidence or logic[5]—is also a key part of political discourse. It is difficult to imagine life without it, and our political discourse is weakened by Orwellian laws that try to prohibit it.

After all, where would we be without the knowledge that Democrats are pinko-communist flag-burners who want to tax churches and use the money to fund abortions so they can use the fetal stem cells to create pot-smoking lesbian ATF agents who will steal all the guns and invite the UN to take over America? Voters have to decide whether we'd be better off electing Republicans, those hateful, assault-weapon-wielding maniacs who believe that George Washington and Jesus Christ incorporated the nation after a Gettysburg reenactment and that the only thing wrong with the death penalty is that it isn't administered quickly enough to secular-humanist professors of Chicano studies.

---

[4] Answer: "Gone to the White House, ha ha ha!" Elisabeth Donnelly, *Ye Olde Sex Scandals: Grover Cleveland's Love Child*, The Awl, http://www.theawl.com/2010/02/ye-olde-sex-scandals-grover-clevelands-love-child.

[5] Wikipedia.com, *Truthiness*, http://en.wikipedia.org/wiki/Truthiness (last visited Feb. 28, 2014) (describing the term's coinage by Stephen Colbert during the pilot of his show in October 2005). *See also* Dictionary.com, *Truthiness*, http://dictionary.reference.com/browse/truthiness (last visited Feb. 28, 2014).

4

Everybody knows that the economy is better off under [Republican/Democratic] [6] presidents—who control it directly with big levers in the Oval Office—and that:

President Obama is a Muslim.

President Obama is a Communist.

President Obama was born in Kenya.

Nearly half of Americans pay no taxes.[7]

One percent of Americans control 99 percent of the world's wealth.

Obamacare will create death panels.

Republicans oppose immigration reform because they're racists.

The Supreme Court is a purely political body that is evangelically [liberal/conservative].[8]

All of the above statements could be considered "truthy," yet all contribute to our political discourse.

Laws like Ohio's here, which criminalize "false" speech, do not replace truthiness, satire, and snark with high-minded ideas and "just the facts." Instead, they chill speech such that spin becomes silence. More importantly, Ohio's ban of lies and damn lies[9] is inconsistent with the First Amendment.

---

[6] Circle as appropriate.

[7] 47 percent to be exact, though it may be higher by now.

[8] Again, pick your truth.

[9] *Amici* are unsure how much torture statistics can withstand before they too run afoul of the law.

5

This Court has repeatedly held that political speech, including and especially speech about politicians, merits the highest level of protection. *See, e.g., Burson v. Freeman,* 504 U.S. 191, 196 (1992) ("the First Amendment has its fullest and most urgent application to speech uttered during a campaign for political office."). Indeed, quite recently this Court held that the First Amendment protects outright lies with as much force as the truth. *United States v. Alvarez,* 132 S. Ct. 2537 (2012).

It is thus axiomatic—not merely truthy—that speech may only be restricted or regulated where doing so is necessary to further a compelling state interest. But the government has no compelling interest in eliminating truthiness from electioneering and, even if such an interest existed, such laws are unnecessary because any injury that candidates suffer from false statements is best redressed by pundits and satirists—and if necessary, civil defamation suits. Nor is the government well-suited for evaluating when a statement crosses the line into falsehood.[10]

Ohio's law blatantly violates the First Amendment and directly conflicts with *Alvarez.* This Court should terminate it with extreme prejudice.

---

[10] Two Pinocchios out of five is OK, but three is illegal?

6

ARGUMENT

I. TRUTHINESS, INSINUATIONS, AND ALLEGATIONS ARE A VITAL PART OF POLITICAL SPEECH

In the hotly contested election of 1828, supporters of John Quincy Adams called Andrew Jackson a "slave-trading, gambling, brawling murderer." Mac McClelland, *Ten Most Awesome Presidential Mudslinging Moves Ever,* Mother Jones, (October 31, 2008).[11] Jackson's supporters responded by accusing Adams of having premarital sex with his wife and playing the role of a pimp in securing a prostitute for Czar Alexander I. *Id.*

During Thomas Jefferson's presidency, James T. Callender, a pamphleteer and "scandalmonger," alleged that Jefferson had fathered numerous children with his slave Sally Hemings.[12] Callender's allegations would feature prominently in the election of 1804, but it wasn't until nearly two centuries later that the allegations were substantially confirmed.[13]

More recently, we've had discussions of draft-dodging, Swift Boats, and lying about birthplaces[14]—

---

[11] Available at http://www.motherjones.com/mojo/2008/10/ten-most-awesome-presidential-mudslinging-moves-ever.

[12] Monticello.org, *James Callender,* http://www.monticello.org/site/research-and-collections/james-callender.

[13] Monticello.org, *Thomas Jefferson and Sally Hemings: A Brief Account,* http://www.monticello.org/site/plantation-and-slavery/thomas-jefferson-and-sally-hemings-brief-account.

[14] While President Obama isn't from Kenya, he is a Keynesian—so you can see where the confusion arises.

Ohio's Truth Ministry vs. Cato's Truthiness Brief

7

not to mention the assorted infidelities that are a political staple. Any one of these allegations, if made during an Ohio election, could be enough to allow a complaint to be filed with the Ohio Election Commission (OEC) and thus turn commonplace political jibber-jabber into a protracted legal dispute.

When political barbs become legal disputes, the public is denied an important part of political speech, namely, responses to those allegations. "If there be time to expose through discussion the falsehood and fallacies, to avert the evil by the processes of education, the remedy to be applied is more speech, not enforced silence." *Whitney v. California*, 274 U.S. 357, 377 (1927). Inflammatory, insulting, and satirical speech is more likely to produce a response, thus making the back-and-forth of politics a self-correcting marketplace of ideas—except, of course, when candidates can tattle to the government, which then takes away their ~~toys~~ speech.

This case began when Rep. Steven Driehaus responded to an advocacy group's political attack[15] by filing a complaint with the OEC. Cert. Pet. at 2. Resources that could have been spent responding to the petitioner's truthiness were thus redirected to a bizarre legal fight. And this caused a ripple effect: The Coalition Opposed to Additional Spending and Taxes felt sufficiently chilled by Driehaus's actions to refrain from engaging in the campaign at all. *Id.* at

---

[15] Driehaus voted for Obamacare, which the Susan B. Anthony List said was the equivalent of voting for taxpayer-funded abortion. *Amici* are unsure how true the allegation is given that the healthcare law seems to change daily, but it certainly isn't as truthy as calling a mandate a tax.

8

4. Ohio's law thus ultimately weakened the vibrancy of the state's political discourse.

Supporters of Ohio's law believe that it will somehow stop the lies, insults, and truthiness, raising the level of discourse to that of an Oxford Union debate.[16] Not only does this Pollyannaish hope stand in the face of all political history, it disregards the fact that, in politics, truths are *felt* as much as they are *known*. When a red-meat Republican hears "Obama is a socialist," or a bleeding-heart Democrat hears, "Romney wants to throw old women out in the street," he is feeling a truth more than thinking one. No government agency can change this fact, and any attempt to do so will stifle important political speech.

II. THIS COURT HAS ALREADY HELD THAT TRUTHINESS, INSINUATIONS, AND ALLEGATIONS ARE PROTECTED BY THE FIRST AMENDMENT

1. Many campaign statements cannot easily be categorized as simply "true" or "false." According to Politifact.com, President Obama's claim that "if you like your health-care plan you can keep it" was true five years before it was named the "Lie of the Year."[17]

---

[16] *Amici*'s counsel has been to an Oxford Union debate; the level of discourse is not always that high.

[17] Compare Politifact.com, *Obama's Plan Expands Existing System*, Oct. 9, 2008, http://www.politifact.com/truth-o-meter/statements/2008/oct/09/barack-obama/obamas-plan-expands-existing-system, with Politifact.com, *Lie of the Year: 'If you like your health care plan, you can keep it,'* Dec. 12, 2013, http://www.politifact.com/truth-o-meter/article/2013/dec/12/lie-year-if-you-like-your-health-care-plan-keep-it.

9

More importantly, even if such a categorization *could* be made, false (and truthy) speech is protected by the First Amendment, especially if it's political.

In *United States v. Alvarez*, this Court held that there is no "general exception to the First Amendment for false statements." 132 S. Ct. at 2544. In that case, the speech was entirely false, and there was no reasonable way to interpret it as truthful. Yet if *Alvarez* confirmed that the First Amendment protects even blatant lies made in the process of campaigning for office, surely it protects spin, parody, and truthiness.

In declaring unconstitutional an equivalent ban on false campaign speech, the Washington Supreme Court held that the government's claimed interest in prohibiting false statements of fact was invalid, in part because it "presupposes the State possesses an independent right to determine truth and falsity in political debate, a proposition fundamentally at odds with the principles embodied in the First Amendment. Moreover, it naively assumes that the government is capable of correctly and consistently negotiating the thin line between fact and opinion in political speech." *Rickert v. Pub. Disclosure Comm'n*, 168 P.3d 826, 849-850 (Wa. 2007).

This Court has held that as "neither factual error nor defamatory content suffices to remove the constitutional shield from criticism of official conduct, the combination of the two elements is no less inadequate. This is the lesson to be drawn from the great controversy over the Sedition Act of 1798." *N.Y. Times v. Sullivan*, 376 U.S. 254, 273 (1964). By the same logic, false and defamatory statements about politicians' backgrounds—including their

10

voting records—are also constitutionally protected. Statements that are merely false, and not inherently defamatory, must therefore also be protected.

Ohio's law explicitly prohibits not merely *defamatory* falsehoods, but *all of them*—including the sort of self-promoting lies that this Court held to be constitutionally protected in *Alvarez*. And not only does it make no distinction between defamatory and non-defamatory statements, but the petitioners' allegation could not have been inherently defamatory given that more than 78 percent of Americans favor legal abortion in at least some cases.[18]

2. This case began with a claim—"Steve Driehaus voted to fund abortions"—that certainly could have caused consternation if uttered at a bar or dinner party. Surreally, it ended up before the U.S. Supreme Court. Even worse, there is no question whether Driehaus voted for the bill at issue; the only dispute is whether that bill actually provides federal funding for abortions—which is a question of legal, economic, and even theological interpretation.

Statements of this kind—call them truthiness, spin, smear, or anything else—are as politically important as their factually pure counterparts. Democracy is based on the principle that the people elect representatives who reflect their beliefs and values, and whom they trust. Beliefs drive democracy—not some truth as adjudged by Platonic guardians—and there is no law that could make it

---

[18] Gallup.com, *Abortion*, http://www.gallup.com/poll/1576/abortion.aspx (last visited Feb. 28, 2014) (latest poll, from May 2013: 26 percent favoring legal abortion always, 52 percent sometimes, 20 percent never).

11

otherwise. Those voters who believed that the Patient Protection and Affordable Care Act provides federal funding for abortion-on-demand (as many do) were told by the Susan B. Anthony List that one candidate had voted in favor of that law. The voters' *beliefs* were more important and relevant than the technical truths about the underlying legislation.

The Ohio law extends far beyond disputes over interpretation or implication. Its broad language also criminalizes rhetorical hyperbole and political satire. If, instead of a billboard reading "Driehaus voted for federally funded abortion," the petitioners had erected a billboard that said "Driehaus is a baby killer" the law would apply with equal effect. All the statute requires is: (1) that the statement be false; (2) that the speaker knew the statement was false, or spoke with reckless disregard for the truth; and (3) that the statement was made with the intent of impacting the outcome of the election. Ohio Rev. Code § 3517.21(B) It is thus apparently illegal in Ohio for an outraged member of the public to call a politician a Nazi or a Communist—or a Communist Nazi, for that matter. That is no exaggeration: the law criminalizes a misstatement made in "campaign materials," which includes "public speeches." *Id.*

And it is irrelevant that the law is limited to cases where the statements were made "knowingly" or with reckless disregard for the truth. It would not be a total defense to any charge under the law to simply state, "I honestly thought this was true." Instead, some fact-finder (whether the OEC, a judge, or a jury) will have to determine (1) whether the statement was false, and (2) whether the defendant knew it was false, or spoke recklessly.

12

The law also stifles, chills, and criminalizes political satire. For example, it is a crime in Ohio for a late-night talk-show host to say: "Candidate Smith is a drug-addled maniac who escaped from a mental institution." Even satirists and speakers that are clearly attempting primarily to entertain their audiences are subject to prosecution if they intend or expect their statements to impact how the audience perceives a candidate. A publication like *The Onion*—which regularly puts words in political figures' mouths, or makes up outlandish stories about them—could be violating Ohio law by making people think at the same time it makes them laugh.

3. This law is a paradigmatic example of a content-specific speech restriction that the First Amendment protects against. Why should a false or exaggerated statement about a politician attract government sanction, when that same statement made about another public figure would not?

In *Alvarez* this Court expressed its concern that upholding the Stolen Valor Act "would endorse government authority to compile a list of subjects about which false statements are punishable." 132 S. Ct. at 2547. Yet that is precisely what Ohio's legislature has done. While one subsection serves as a catch-all prohibition on all "false" statements made about a candidate, Ohio Rev. Code § 3517.21(B)(10), the majority of the section is devoted to a *specific* list of subjects about which false statements are punishable, including: a candidate's education (2), work history (3), criminal record (4-5), mental health (6), military service (7), and voting record (9).

But wait, there's more! Refraining from stating (arguable) falsehoods is not enough to stay clear of

13

violating the law. For example, the regulation of statements concerning a politician's criminal record requires speakers to actively take steps to avoid even the possibility of misinterpretation. If an Ohio political candidate has been indicted a dozen times on corruption and racketeering charges, you *cannot* lawfully say "Candidate Smith has been repeatedly indicted for corruption" without also saying how those indictments were resolved. Ohio Rev. Code § 3517.21(B)(5). Even if this Court were to reverse itself and hold that false statements are outside the scope of First Amendment protection, there is no question that truthful statements about candidates' criminal records are "at the core of our electoral process and of the First Amendment freedoms." *Williams v. Rhodes*, 393 U.S. 23, 32 (1968).

There is no reason why speech about these topics should be subject to regulation by the state, or why they should only be regulated for the benefit of politicians as opposed to other public figures—like actors, religious leaders, and famous athletes—who are often lied about. *See, e.g., Hustler Magazine v. Falwell,* 485 U.S. 46 (1988) (the First Amendment protects magazine accusing religious leader of a sexual relationship with his mother); *Beckham v. Bauer Publ'g Co.,* 2011 U.S. Dist. LEXIS 32269 (C.D. Cal. Mar. 17, 2011) (a newspaper asserting that famous soccer player had cheated on his wife with a prostitute was protected by both the First Amendment and anti-SLAPP statutes); *N.Y. Times v. Sullivan,* 376 U.S. 254 (1964) (protecting false statements about police officers' conduct). Nor are Ohio politicians so particularly thin-skinned that they require protection that politicians in other states do not. *See, e.g., Judge Dismisses Libel Suit*

14

Against Tenn. Senator, Associated Press, Apr. 26, 2013 (unreported case regarding allegations that a politician's opponent had been arrested on drug charges).[19] "Politics are politics, and it's a big boys' and big girls' game. That's just the way it is." *Id.* (judge's comments in dismissing the suit).

Those cases where the courts have allowed libel suits based on spurious statements about celebrities further demonstrate that the appropriate remedy when it comes to lies about public figures is, if anything, a civil suit. *See, e.g., Burnett v. Nat'l Enquirer,* 144 Cal. App. 3d 991 (Cal. Ct. App. 1983) (publisher can be held civilly liable for defamatory and false speech); *Eastwood v. Nat'l Enquirer,* 123 F.3d 1249 (9th Cir. 1997) (fabrication of public figure's interview answers civilly actionable).

This Court has also limited the remedies states can provide to subjects of false speech. It would be incoherent if states were allowed to apply criminal sanctions—as Ohio attempts to do here—for conduct to which this Court has held the Constitution only permits the attachment of compensatory liability. *See Gertz v. Robert Welch,* 418 U.S. 323 (1974) (even when the subject of false statement is not a public official, liability for anything beyond actual damages can only be established by proof of actual malice).

While the mere fact that the courts have not recognized an exception to the First Amendment in the past does not mean that such an exception does not exist, this Court requires that those advocating

---

[19] Available at http://www.firstamendmentcenter.org/judge-dismisses-libel-case-against-tenn-senator.

Ohio's Truth Ministry vs. Cato's Truthiness Brief

15

for such an exception show "persuasive evidence that a novel restriction on content is part of a long (if heretofore unrecognized) tradition of proscription." *Brown v. Entm't Merch. Ass'n,* 131 S. Ct. 2729, 2734 (2011). In *Alvarez,* this Court held that the government had not proven a longstanding tradition of restricting false statements made by or about a political candidate. 132 S. Ct. at 2548. If the historical record provides evidence for any longstanding tradition in this regard, it is the venerable practice of politicians' lying about themselves and each other with complete impunity.

III. THE PUBLIC INTEREST IN POLITICAL HONESTY IS BEST SERVED BY PUNDITS AND SATIRISTS

This country has a long and estimable history of pundits and satirists, including *amici,* exposing the exaggerations and prevarications of political rhetoric. Even in the absence of the First Amendment, no government agency could do a better job policing political honesty than the myriad personalities and entities who expose charlatans, mock liars, lambaste arrogance, and unmask truthiness for a living.

Just two terms ago, this Court agreed whole-heartedly with that sentiment:

> The remedy for speech that is false is speech that is true. This is the ordinary course in a free society. *The response to the unreasoned is the rational; to the uninformed, the enlightened; to the straight-out lie, the simple truth. See Whitney v. California,* 274 U. S. 357, 377 (1927) (Brandeis, J., concurring) ("If there be time to expose through discussion the

16

falsehood and fallacies, to avert the evil by the processes of education, the remedy to be applied is more speech, not enforced silence"). The theory of our Constitution is "that the best test of truth is the power of the thought to get itself accepted in the competition of the market," *Abrams v. United States*, 250 U. S. 616, 630 (1919) (Holmes, J., dissenting). The First Amendment itself ensures the right to respond to speech we do not like, and for good reason. Freedom of speech and thought flows not from the beneficence of the state but from the inalienable rights of the person. *And suppression of speech by the government can make exposure of falsity more difficult, not less so. Society has the right and civic duty to engage in open, dynamic, rational discourse.* These ends are not well served when the government seeks to orchestrate public discussion through content-based mandates.

Alvarez, 132 S. Ct. at 2550 (emphases added).

As Chief Judge Kozinski argued when *Alvarez* was before the Ninth Circuit, a prohibition on lying devalues the truth: "How can you develop a reputation as a straight shooter if lying is not an option? Even if untruthful speech were not valuable for its own sake, its protection is clearly required to give breathing room to truthful self-expression, which is unequivocally protected by the First Amendment." *United States v. Alvarez*, 638 F.3d 666, 675 (9th Cir. 2011).

No one should be concerned that false political statements won't be subjected to careful examination. As this Court said in *Brown v. Harlage*,

Ohio's Truth Ministry vs. Cato's Truthiness Brief

17

"a candidate's factual blunder is unlikely to escape the notice of, and correction by, the erring candidate's political opponent. The preferred First Amendment remedy of 'more speech, not enforced silence,' thus has special force." 456 U.S. 45, 61 (1982). Recent technological advancements mean that statements by or about candidates will not just attract the attention of his or her opponents—instantly—but that of investigative journalists and professional fact checkers.

Politicians who are caught lying about themselves or others regularly attract more attention from the press than the subject of the original lie. The typical outcome is that the lie or cover up becomes more important than the original accusation or offense. And that dynamic predates smartphones and their latest "apps." The impeachment of President Clinton was not based on any sexual activities he might have engaged in with Monica Lewinsky, but over the attempt to cover it up. Similarly, President Nixon's resignation was prompted by his obfuscations rather than his orchestration of a third-rate burglary. And if this Court isn't yet convinced of this point, *amici* have but two words more on the subject: Anthony Weiner.

If Ohio's concern is that there are abundant lies being told in campaigns that escape media notice—and cannot be proven in a civil defamation suit—wouldn't that same lack of evidence hamstring prosecution under Ohio Rev. Code § 3517.21? Anyone who could fabricate enough evidence to mislead all of the fact-checkers and investigators who scrutinize his fables could surely evade a charge under this law.

18

Adding further penalties will not dissuade successful and talented liars. The only way that such a law could offer the public greater protection from untruthful speech—accepting for the sake of argument that such protection is lawful, desirable, and necessary—would be if it adopted lower standards of proof than those required by civil defamation suits or newspaper editors.

There is no lie that can be told about a politician that will not be more damaging to the liar once the truth is revealed. A crushing send-up on *The Daily Show* or *The Colbert Report* will do more to clean up political rhetoric than the Ohio Election Commission ever could.

CONCLUSION

Criminalizing political speech is no laughing matter, so this Court should reverse the court below.

Respectfully submitted,

ILYA SHAPIRO
Counsel of Record
Cato Institute
1000 Mass. Ave., NW
Washington, D.C. 2000
(202) 842-0200
ishapiro@cato.org

February 28, 2014

Injordinances: Labor Protests, Abortion-Clinic Picketing, and *McCullen v. Coakley*

*Trevor Burrus**

Introduction

In *McCullen v. Coakley*, the Supreme Court invalidated a Massachusetts law that established a 35-foot "speech free" buffer zone around abortion clinics.[1] Specifically, the law prohibited any person from "knowingly enter[ing] or remain[ing] on a public way or sidewalk adjacent to a reproductive health care facility within a radius of 35 feet."[2]

The law was the latest iteration of abortion-clinic buffer zones to reach the Supreme Court. In 2000, in the highly controversial case *Hill v. Colorado*, the Court upheld a so-called "floating buffer zone" that established an 8-foot bubble around those within 100 feet of a medical facility.[3] Whereas that law regulated only speech conduct within 100 feet of a medical facility—it is unlawful to "knowingly approach another person . . . for the purpose of passing a leaflet or handbill to, displaying a sign to, or engaging in oral protest, education, or counseling"[4]—the Massachusetts law made mere public presence in the 35-foot zone a criminal offense.

That sweeping prohibition was a little too much for the Supreme Court, which unanimously struck down the law as an unconstitutional violation of the First Amendment. There was, however, disagreement among the justices as to why the law was unconstitutional. Chief Justice John Roberts was joined in the five-justice majority by

* Research Fellow, Cato Institute Center for Constitutional Studies.

[1] 134 S. Ct. 2518 (2014).

[2] Mass. Gen. Laws, ch. 266, § 120E½(b)(2014).

[3] Hill v. Colorado, 530 U.S. 703 (2000).

[4] Colo. Rev. Stat. § 18-9-122(3).

the "liberal" wing of the Court: Justices Ruth Bader Ginsburg, Stephen Breyer, Sonia Sotomayor, and Elena Kagan. Roberts ruled that the law was neither content-based nor viewpoint-based and therefore need not be analyzed under strict scrutiny.[5] Nevertheless, the breadth of the law's restrictions meant that it "burden[s] substantially more speech than is necessary to further the government's legitimate interests" and was thus unconstitutional.[6]

In a characteristically vehement concurrence—a dissent in all but name—Justice Antonin Scalia, joined by Justices Anthony Kennedy and Clarence Thomas, argued that the majority opinion's "dicta" on content-neutrality was unnecessary to the "not narrowly tailored" holding and, moreover, that the law was in fact content-based and therefore deserved strict scrutiny.[7] Scalia reiterated what he had said in previous abortion-clinic buffer zone cases: that the laws are clearly content-based ordinances that can't survive the heightened scrutiny they deserve.[8]

In this article I will examine the history of laws and injunctions that prohibit picketing and protesting in public places. I will then look at the lessons we can learn from that history and the decision in *McCullen*.

Before abortion became a lively issue, the majority of legal actions that prohibited public picketing were injunctions or ordinances against labor unions. Abortion-clinic buffer zones and labor-picketing ordinances can be seen as "injordinances," a combination of an ordinance and an injunction.[9] An injordinance resembles a law in most regards—it is passed by the legislative body and is enforced through criminal sanctions against the general public—but it resembles an injunction in that it applies to specific places and proscribes specific conduct around that space. Moreover, like an injunction, the injordinance is justified by appeals to prior unlawful actions of a group of people.

[5] McCullen, 134 S. Ct. at 2525–41 (opinion of Roberts, C.J.).

[6] *Id.* at 2535 (citing Ward v. Rock Against Racism, 491 U.S. 781, 799 (1989)).

[7] *Id.* at 2541–49 (Scalia, J., concurring in judgment).

[8] See Hill, 530 U.S. at 741–64 (Scalia, J., dissenting).

[9] Credit for this useful term goes to the amicus brief of the Life Legal Defense Foundation and Walter B. Hoye II. See, Brief for the Life Legal Defense Foundation and Walter B. Hoye II as Amici Curiae Supporting Petitioners at 4, McCullen v. Coakley, 134 S. Ct. 2518 (2014) (No. 12-1168).

Given that injordinances came out of injunctions, exploring the history of labor injunctions allows us to examine Justice Scalia's claim in his dissent in *Hill*, that he has "no doubt that this regulation would be deemed content-based *in an instant* if the case before us involved antiwar protesters, or union members seeking to 'educate' the public about the reasons for their strike."[10]

Is Justice Scalia's claim correct? The controversial issue of abortion and women's reproductive rights sits in the background of cases like *Hill* and *McCullen*. Does this lead more pro-abortion-rights justices to view abortion picketers as a unique type of threat to exercising an important right? Similarly, do anti-abortion-rights justices give abortion picketers more of a free pass when it comes to the state's role in protecting people from unwanted interference in a public place?

These counterfactuals are probably unanswerable, but a careful examination of past jurisprudence on labor injunctions might give us a better window into the questions. Perhaps, at bottom, what re-*ally animates views in this area is a background belief about how* disruptive and violent either (or both) labor picketers and abortion picketers are likely to be. Did justices and judges in past labor-picketing cases, and do justices and judges in current abortion-picketing cases, adopt an unstated position of taking judicial notice that either labor union protesters or abortion protesters are uniquely prone to violent behavior? If either labor protesters or abortion protesters are viewed as a swirling, uncontrollable mob, then it seems far more likely that a judge will uphold laws and injunctions restricting their activities and speech. Otherwise, generally applicable laws such as trespass, assault, and obstruction should be sufficient to deal with the occasional bad apple whose First Amendment-protected speech act turns into unlawful action.

Knowing that such bad apples would be unsympathetic plaintiffs, both labor lawyers of the past and those fighting abortion-clinic buffer zone laws today have tried to choose peaceful clients to bring challenges. For example, septuagenarian grandmother Eleanor McCullen and her friends have moral and religious convictions that abortion is wrong. Like many people with deeply held beliefs, they would like to try to convince others that they are correct and hopefully to help others avoid making a decision that they view as deeply

[10] Hill, 530 U.S. at 742 (emphasis in original).

immoral. To that end, McCullen and others sit outside Massachusetts abortion clinics and try to convince women not to have abortions with "close, kind, personal communication, with a calm voice, a caring demeanor, and eye contact."[11]

Given that modus operandi, Eleanor McCullen has never been arrested. Instead, over the years, she and her husband have spent over $50,000 helping women choose options other than abortion. She has paid for "baby showers, living quarters, furniture, heating oil, electricity, water, gasoline, clothing, food, baby formula, diapers, strollers, or whatever else women needed."[12]

The other petitioners in *McCullen v. Coakley* have similar stories.[13] They style themselves as "counselors" not "protesters," and Chief Justice Roberts accepted that characterization in his majority opinion, as did the four "liberal" justices who joined him. So perhaps *McCullen* is actually about the right to be a decent, lawful, unobtrusive person who counsels people in a time of need. After all, McCullen has good evidence that many women entering abortion clinics are ignorant of other options or have not been fully apprised of the risks. She convincingly argued that, in order to be a better counselor, communication with the women needs to be up close and personal.[14]

In the past, many who challenged labor injunctions were similarly peaceful. Accordingly, the running narrative through these cases is, essentially, how much do peaceful protesters have to suffer under regulations designed to curb non-peaceful protesters?

Labor Law Injunctions

Compared to decades past, today we rarely hear about labor disputes and labor injunctions. But questions about the practices of labor unions were common in the courts from the 19th century through the first decades of the 20th. Prior to abortion controversy engendered by *Roe v. Wade*, the most common form of picketing was in the context of labor disputes. Union members and supporters would picket recalcitrant employers, retailers that sold products of

[11] Petition for Writ of Certiorari at 11, McCullen v. Coakley, 134 S. Ct. 2518 (2014) (No. 12-1168).

[12] Brief for Petitioners at 10, McCullen v. Coakley, 134 S. Ct. 2518 (2014) (No. 12-1168).

[13] See *id.* at 10–11.

[14] *Id.* at 11.

the business, and many other places where they felt their message should be heard. As a consequence, courts often entered injunctions against picketing.

The early labor movement was dogged by many types of antagonistic laws and officials. The first obstacle was simply the illegality of unions as conspiracies in restraint of trade. In 1806, in one of the first American cases arising from a labor strike, a group of Philadelphia cordwainers were prosecuted for striking for higher wages. The charge against them was conspiracy, and they lost.[15] The legal status of labor unions was shaky until Massachusetts Chief Justice Lemuel Shaw ruled that

> associations [unions] may be entered into, the object of which is to adopt measures that may have a tendency to impoverish another, that is, to diminish his gains and profits, and yet so far from being criminal or unlawful, the object may be highly meritorious and public spirited. The legality of such an association will therefore depend upon the means to be used for its accomplishment. If it is to be carried into effect by fair or honorable and lawful means, it is, to say the least, innocent; if by falsehood or force, it may be stamped with the character of conspiracy.[16]

Shaw's reasoning—that unions were not per se illegal but that the means that they use could be illegal—would be applied to cases concerning unions picketing. Each picketing situation would be analyzed individually. Up until the 1930s, many times the unions lost.

Section 20 of the Clayton Act provided some protection for unions that wished to picket outside workplaces. It provides that "no such restraining order or injunction shall prohibit any person or persons, whether singly or in concert . . . from recommending, advising, or persuading others by peaceful means."[17] One of the first cases to analyze Section 20, *American Steel Foundries v. Tri-City Cent. Trades Council*, arose out of a labor dispute in which the business charged "that [a] conspiracy was being executed by organized picketing, accompanied by threats, intimidation and violence toward persons employed or

[15] Clarence E. Bonnett, The Origin of the Labor Injunction, 5 S. Cal. L. Rev. 105, 113 (1931).

[16] Commonwealth v. Hunt, 45 Mass. 111 (1842).

[17] 29 U.S.C § 52 (2012).

seeking employment there."[18] The case is notable not only for the way in which labor picketing is treated as nearly per se illegal, but also for how it nearly entirely ignores the crucial speech values at issue.

Chief Justice William Howard Taft wrote that Section 20 of the Clayton Act added "no new principle into the equity jurisprudence of those courts. It is merely declaratory of what was the best practice always."[19] Equitable injunctive relief against protesters and picketers had always been properly focused on enjoining truly unlawful acts, such as force and intimidation, while letting lawful persuasion run free. With Section 20, "Congress wished to forbid the use by the federal courts of their equity arm to prevent peaceable persuasion by employees, discharged or expectant, in promotion of their side of the dispute, and to secure them against judicial restraint in obtaining or communicating information in any place where they might lawfully be."[20] Section 20 merely underscored and clarified common-law practice.

As would become a common inquiry in cases involving labor injunctions, and also in future cases involving abortion-protesting in-jordinances, the Court asked the key question: "How far may men go in persuasion and communication and still not violate the right of those whom they would influence?"[21]

Taft's answer to this question is relevant to the modern issue of abortion-clinic buffer zones:

> In going to and from work, men have a right to as free a passage without obstruction as the streets afford, consistent with the right of others to enjoy the same privilege. We are a social people and the accosting by one of another in an inoffensive way and an offer by one to communicate and discuss information with a view to influencing the other's action are not regarded as aggression or a violation of that other's rights. If, however, the offer is declined, as it may rightfully be, then persistence, importunity, following and dogging become unjustifiable annoyance and obstruction which is likely soon to savor of intimidation. From all of this

---

[18] 257 U.S. 184, 193 (1921).

[19] *Id.* at 203.

[20] *Id.*

[21] *Id.* at 204.

the person sought to be influenced has a right to be free and
his employer has a right to have him free.[22]

In the end, the Court held that the picketing was unlawful, describing the difficulty in finding a way through the picketers as
"running a gauntlet."[23] The Court continued: "It is idle to talk of
peaceful communication in such a place and under such conditions.
The numbers of the pickets in the groups constituted intimidation.
The name 'picket' indicated a militant purpose, inconsistent with
peaceable persuasion."[24]

In fact, Chief Justice Taft came very close to saying that any picketing worthy of the name is nearly per se unlawful because of the nature of picketing. And if any act of violence or intimidation occurred,
then the entire peaceful, communicative purpose of picketing is
permanently undercut: "When one or more assaults or disturbances
ensued, they characterized the whole campaign, which became effective because of its intimidating character, in spite of the admoni-
tions given by the leaders to their followers as to lawful methods to
be pursued, however sincere. Our conclusion is that picketing thus
instituted is unlawful and can not be peaceable and may be properly
enjoined by the specific term."[25]

Interestingly, Taft took it upon himself to issue a fairly specific and
limiting injunction in the case. The strikers "should be limited to one
representative for each point of ingress and egress in the plant or
place of business" who is authorized by the group to observe, communicate, and persuade in such a way that "shall not be abusive,
libelous or threatening, and that they shall not approach individuals
together but singly, and shall not in their single efforts at communication or persuasion obstruct an unwilling listener by importunate
following or dogging his steps."[26] The behavior Taft describes is not
unlike that of Eleanor McCullen and her friends in front of abortion
clinics.

Overall, in *American Steel* we see the Court dealing with the
scope and purpose of injunctive relief in a relatively hostile and

22 *Id.*
23 *Id.* at 205.
24 *Id.*
25 *Id.*
26 *Id.* at 206–07.

unforgiving manner. Picketing is seen as nearly presumptively wrong due to the "necessary element of intimidation in the presence of groups as pickets," and the speech aspect of picketing is almost ignored completely.[27] This is, of course, understandable given the state of First Amendment jurisprudence at the time.

We also see how the violence associated with labor disputes helped undercut any claim that picketing could remain peaceful. It was "clear from the evidence" that "violent methods were pursued from time to time in such a way as to characterize the attitude of the picketers as continuously threatening," and that the situation was bad enough that "[a] number of employees, sometimes fifteen or more, slept in the plant for a week during the trouble, because they could not safely go to their homes."[28] Again, the situation is quite similar to the violence that surrounds abortion protests, including actual murders of abortion doctors.[29]

In the first decades of the 20th century, state courts often heard cases involving labor-picketing injunctions. Sometimes, injunctions would be upheld against small pickets and nonviolent protests. In Texas, in *Webb v. Cooks', Waiters', and Waitresses' Union*, the court of civil appeals upheld an injunction against those picketing a cafe that refused unionization.[30] The picketing consisted of two or more members at a time, but usually two, "walking back and forward in front of plaintiff's restaurant and handing out to passers-by cards upon which were printed the words: 'This cafe is unfair to organized labor.'"[31] Picketers were also heard to have said, "Please don't go into that café!," "We are working for organized labor!," and "We will win!"[32]

Despite these innocuous pleas, the court railed against the conduct of the picketers, even while conceding that violence was not at issue. "We at least cannot hide nor obscure the truth with the specious contention urged herein that *no open threats or violence was*

[27] *Id.* at 207.

[28] *Id.* at 200.

[29] William Booth, Doctor Killed During Abortion Protest, Wash. Post., Mar. 10, 1993, at A1.

[30] 205 S.W. 465 (Tex. 1918).

[31] *Id.* at 466.

[32] *Id.*

proven. We must know what has frequently been declared in adjudicated cases, that restraint of the mind is just as potent as a threat of physical violence."[33]

In a 1902 New Jersey case, the court was asked whether "one person has a right to *persuade* another to work or not to work."[34] Only "if the other person is willing to listen and be persuaded," said the court, because "no person has a right to speak to another after he knows that his endeavor is unwelcome."[35]

In general, by the 1930s, labor unions were more often on the losing side of challenges to labor injunctions. In the words of one early-'30s commentator, Jerome Hellerstein, "courts have tended without analysis to conclude that everything beyond the stationing of a few pickets who carry banners or in calm terms speak to customers or employees is beyond the lawful ambit permitted the worker."[36] Hellerstein went on to passionately explain how the important message of labor unions depended upon the use of language that the courts had classified as "intimidating":

> Certainly when a picket yells "scab" or curses a strike breaker or a customer, he is unmistakably expressing his contempt for the employee or the customer, and is voicing his vehement disapproval of the latter's conduct. . . . It is exceedingly important to recognize that there is a strong emotional force which can be here exerted, which has no relation to a threat of physical injury or violence, a moral force which labor has every right to exert in industrial struggles, and that it greatly handicaps the worker to deprive him of the use of this weapon.[37]

The *American Steel* decision "dealt a death blow to the legality of mass picketing in this country."[38] Yet labor picketing was resuscitated by the Norris-LaGuardia Act, which limited equity jurisdiction of federal courts to situations where "such action is imperatively

---

[33] *Id.* at 467 (emphasis added).

[34] Frank v. Herold, 63 N.J. Eq. 443 (N.J. Ch. 1902) (emphasis added).

[35] *Id.* at 449–50.

[36] Jerome R. Hellerstein, Picketing Legislation and the Courts, 10 No. Car. L. Rev. 158, 177 (1931).

[37] *Id.* at 178.

[38] *Id.* at 182.

demanded."[39] Specifically, nine activities were insulated from injunction, including work stoppages, union membership, peaceful assembly to promote their "interests in a labor dispute," and, importantly, "[g]iving publicity to the existence of, or the facts involved in, any labor dispute, whether by advertising, speaking, patrolling, or by any other method not involving fraud or violence."[40]

Norris-LaGuardia gave labor a statutory carve-out, but injunctions were still granted against union picketing when "imperatively demanded." Most important, the First Amendment had not yet made a significant appearance in the discussion. In the early 1940s, however, the First Amendment would be applied to picketing that, thereafter, the law around public picketing would change dramatically.

The First Amendment and Labor Injunctions

In his dissent in *Hill*, Justice Scalia rightly admonishes the majority for partially relying on the decision in *American Steel* to support Colorado's anti-abortion picketing statute. In *American Steel*, Scalia writes, "the First Amendment was not at issue, and was not so much as mentioned in the opinion."[41]

In 1921, First Amendment jurisprudence barely existed. Nevertheless, the majority in *Hill* approvingly cited *American Steel* as if subsequent First Amendment decisions did not fundamentally alter the case, and thus did not alter the precedential value of *American Steel*. As the *Hill* majority wrote, while quoting *American Steel*, "None of our decisions has minimized the enduring importance of 'the right to be free' from persistent 'importunity, following and dogging' after an offer to communicate has been declined."[42]

It is shocking to think that a case about labor picketing would fail to even mention the most known and prominent part of the Bill of Rights, but it says something about the state of the First Amendment at the time that it wasn't brought up. Granted, the First Amendment wasn't incorporated against the states until *Gitlow v. New York* in 1925,

---

[39] S. Rep. No. 163, 72d Cong., 1st Sess. 11 (1932).

[40] 29 U.S.C. § 104(e) (2012). For a general discussion of Norris-LaGuardia's affect on labor injunctions, see, Eileen Silverstein, Collective Action, Property Rights and Law Reform: The Story of the Labor Injunction, 11 Hofstra Lab. L. J. 97 (1993).

[41] Hill, 530 U.S. at 753 (Scalia, J., dissenting).

[42] *Id.* at 718 (citing American Steel Foundries, 257 U.S. at 204).

but, even before incorporation, it was not uncommon for a right to be mentioned in order to highlight it as an important value of a free society. Yet in *American Steel*, speech seems to be hardly valued at all.[43] The first question at hand, therefore, is to examine how evolved First Amendment jurisprudence affected the law around labor picketing as well as picketing in general. Second, we must examine how the First Amendment affects, if it does, "common law freedoms in ordinary disputes between private parties."[44]

In *Lovell v. City of Griffin* (1938), the Court overturned a city ordinance that prevented the distribution of "circulars, handbooks, advertising, or literature of any kind . . .without first obtaining written permission from the City Manager."[45] The Court found that "[w]hatever the motive which induced [the ordinance's] adoption, its character is such that it strikes at the very foundation of the freedom of the press by subjecting it to license and censorship."[46]

In *Lovell*, the Court also performed an early version of a "fit" analysis—that is, analyzing whether a law sweeps in too much lawful conduct in the name of prohibiting unlawful conduct. "The ordinance is not limited to 'literature,'" wrote Chief Justice Charles Evans Hughes, "that is obscene or offensive to public morals or that advocates unlawful conduct."[47] Because the ordinance wasn't limited to literature that was feasibly proscribable as "involving disorderly conduct, the molestation of the inhabitants, or the misuse or littering of the streets," then the ordinance had to fall.[48]

Analyzing how a statute "fits" with a legitimate government goal is central to any First Amendment question. In both *Hill* and *McCullen*, the Court examined whether, in attempting to limit unlawful intimidation and molestation, the statutes prohibited the lawful exercise of First Amendment rights. In upholding a First Amendment protection of the right to distribute literature, the *Lovell* Court began to insert the First Amendment into the debate about communications

---

[43] Gitlow v. New York, 268 U.S. 652 (1925).

[44] Richard A. Epstein, Wrong on Abortion Picketing, Defining Ideas (June 30, 2014), http://www.hoover.org/research/scotus-gets-abortion-picketing-wrong.

[45] Lovell v. City of Griffin, 303 U.S. 444, 447 (1938).

[46] *Id.* at 451.

[47] *Id.*

[48] *Id.*

on public streets. Recall that in *American Steel,* such First Amendment analysis is absent. There is some discussion of how many permissible peaceful activities were being enjoined, but there is more focus on the rights of *listeners* to be free from annoying and intimidating speech than there is on the abridgment of a fundamental right of the speaker (freedom of speech). In the words of Chief Justice Taft: "the accosting by one of another in an inoffensive way and an offer by one to communicate and discuss information with a view to influencing the other's action are *not regarded as aggression or a violation of that other's rights.*"[49]

Taft's focus on the listener is understandable given the state of First Amendment jurisprudence at the time. Now, because the freedom of speech has ascended to such a cherished position in our constitutional hierarchy, such language is strange. Freedom of speech, the ability to speak one's mind, is now seen as an essential human right for the *speaker.* Listeners are still important, especially in many campaign finance cases, but freedom from annoyance for the listener is certainly not at the same level in our constitutional hierarchy.

After *Lovell,* the law around handbilling and leafleting continued to evolve. In 1939, the Supreme Court decided *Schneider v. State,* a challenge to four municipal ordinances prohibiting the distribution of handbills on public sidewalks.[50] The Court, in an opinion by Justice Owen Roberts, held that "[a]lthough a municipality may enact regulations in the interest of the public safety, health, welfare or convenience, these may not abridge the individual liberties secured by the Constitution to those who wish to speak, write, print or circulate information or opinion."[51]

In holding this, however, Justice Roberts was quick to point out that the First Amendment did not provide absolute protection to those who were communicating their message by being willfully obstreperous, noisome, and intimidating:

> So long as legislation to this end does not abridge the constitutional liberty of one rightfully upon the street to impart information through speech or the distribution of literature, it may lawfully regulate the conduct of those using

[49] American Steel Foundries, 257 U.S. at 204 (emphasis added).
[50] 308 U.S. 147 (1939).
[51] *Id.* at 160.

the streets. For example, a person could not exercise this liberty by taking his stand in the middle of a crowded street, contrary to traffic regulations, and maintain his position to the stoppage of all traffic; a group of distributors could not insist upon a constitutional right to form a cordon across the street and to allow no pedestrian to pass who did not accept a tendered leaflet; nor does the guarantee of freedom of speech or of the press deprive a municipality of power to enact regulations against throwing literature broadcast in the streets. Prohibition of such conduct would not abridge the constitutional liberty since such activity bears no necessary relationship to the freedom to speak, write, print or distribute information or opinion.[52]

Here, we see further elucidation of the crucial distinction between proscribable, coercive conduct and protected speech. Justice Roberts describes the freedom to pass out literature as a "constitutional liberty" held by the individual, and therefore he focuses less on whether that liberty might annoy others. Stopping traffic and littering are proper objects of state action, but limiting the freedom of speech is not. In *Schneider*, we also see the Court beginning to wrestle with the concept of public forums. "[T]he streets," wrote Justice Roberts, "are natural and proper places for the dissemination of information and opinion."[53]

After *Lovell* and *Schneider*, the stage was set for a constitutional challenge to a pair of labor injordinances. Like the abortion injunctions that would eventually give rise to injordinances, labor injunctions saw the same evolution. In two cases decided the same day, the Supreme Court invalidated labor injordinances designed to curtail labor union speech in specific locations.

In *Thornhill v. Alabama*, the Court overturned the conviction of Byron Thornhill for violating a state law prohibiting people from going "near or loiter[ing] about the premises or place of business of any other person, firm, corporation, or association of people, engaged in a lawful business" with the intent to induce "other persons not to trade with, buy from, sell to, have business dealings with, or be employed by such persons."[54] Testimonial evidence showed that

[52] *Id.* at 160–61.

[53] *Id.* at 163.

[54] Thornhill v. Alabama, 310 U.S. 88, 91 (1940).

Mr. Thornhill had been peacefully picketing. According to one witness, a non-union member who showed up for work, "[n]either Mr. Thornhill nor any other employee threatened me on the occasion testified to. Mr. Thornhill approached me in a peaceful manner, and did not put me in fear; he did not appear to be mad."[55] The Court, in an opinion by Justice Frank Murphy, held that the ordinance violated the First Amendment.

Given that the statute—the injordinance—in *Thornhill* greatly resembled labor injunctions like those in *American Steel*, it is interesting how differently the *Thornhill* Court analyzed the scope of the statute than did the Court in *American Steel*. The *Thornhill* Court was concerned that the statute prohibited too much peaceful speech and thus it would inhibit public debate. As Justice Murphy wrote:

> The range of activities proscribed by § 3448, whether characterized as picketing or loitering or otherwise, embraces nearly every practicable, effective means whereby those interested—including the employees directly affected—may enlighten the public on the nature and causes of a labor dispute. . . . Abridgment of the liberty of such discussion can be justified only where the clear danger of substantive evils arises under circumstances affording no opportunity to test the merits of ideas by competition for acceptance in the market of public opinion. We hold that the danger of injury to an industrial concern is neither so serious nor so imminent as to justify the sweeping proscription of freedom of discussion embodied in § 3448.[56]

In *American Steel*, the Court showed almost no concern that the injunction was too broad.

In *Carlson v. California*, decided the same day as *Thornhill*, the Court overturned the conviction of a man engaged in picketing in front of a tunnel construction work site.[57] The men walked on the edge of the highway for "a distance of 50 to 100 feet" then turned around to retrace their steps.[58] Some held signs, including one that said "This job is unfair to CIO."[59]

---

[55] *Id.* at 94.

[56] *Id.* at 104-05.

[57] Carlson v. California, 310 U.S. 106 (1940).

[58] *Id.* at 110.

[59] *Id.*

Again, Justice Frank Murphy wrote the opinion for the Court. "The sweeping and inexact terms of the ordinance disclose the threat to freedom of speech inherent in its existence," he wrote.[60] He also added a comment about the legitimate role of the state in maintaining public safety:

> The power and duty of the State to take adequate steps to preserve the peace and protect the privacy, the lives, and the property of its residents cannot be doubted. But the ordinance in question here abridges liberty of discussion under circumstances presenting no clear and present danger of substantive evils within the allowable area of state control.[61]

Just one year after *Thornhill* and *Carlson* struck down labor-picketing injordinances, the Court had a chance to revisit the question of traditional labor injunctions in *Milk Wagon Drivers Union of Chicago, Local 753 v. Meadowmoor Dairies*.[62] In *Milk Wagon*, unlike *American Steel*, the Court treated the issue as primarily one of the First Amendment. Just like *American Steel*, however, the Court, in an opinion by Justice Felix Frankfurter, upheld the broad injunction. This time, however, there were vehement and prescient dissents from Justices Hugo Black and Stanley Reed.

During a labor dispute between a dairy and its drivers, an injunction was issued to restrain all union conduct "violent and peaceful."[63] Widespread violence had been associated with the strikes, including "more than fifty instances of window-smashing," bombs, stench bombs, shootings, and beatings.[64] Given the scope of the injunction, the question before the Court was whether "a state can choose to authorize its courts to enjoin acts of picketing in themselves peaceful when they are enmeshed with contemporaneously violent conduct which is concededly outlawed."[65]

---

[60] *Id.* at 113.
[61] *Id.*
[62] 312 U.S. 287 (1941).
[63] *Id.* at 291.
[64] *Id.* at 292.
[65] *Id.*

While upholding the broad injunction, Justice Frankfurter reaffirmed *Thornhill, Carlson*, and the importance of peaceful picketing, "the workingman's means of communication."[66] Frankfurter also underscores the importance of properly scrutinizing infringements on constitutional freedoms so that they are not "defeated by insubstantial findings of fact screening reality."[67]

Nevertheless, scrutinizing the injunction, Frankfurter concludes that the history and possibility of violence justify the broad prohibition on even peaceful picketing. Yet Frankfurter is quick to point out that *Thornhill* and *Carlson* are not being qualified; they are being reaffirmed because "[t]hey involved statutes baldly forbidding all picketing near an employer's place of business."[68] A history of violence was expressly not a factor in those cases, which, because they were statutes, had to be dealt with facially.[69]

Frankfurter also makes a crucial comparison between an injunction and ordinance that will be relevant to the question of abortion-picketing injordinances. Specifically, he comments that "just as a state through its legislature may deal with specific circumstances menacing the peace by an appropriately drawn act, so the law of a state may be fitted to a concrete situation through the authority given by the state to its courts."[70] But injunctions and ordinances are also importantly distinct because "[i]t distorts the meaning of things to generalize the terms of an injunction derived from and directed towards violent misconduct as though it were an abstract prohibition of all picketing wholly unrelated to the violence involved."[71]

In his dissent, Justice Hugo Black has little patience for the distinctions drawn by Frankfurter. "The injunction," writes Black, "like a statute, stands as an overhanging threat of future punishment. The law of Illinois has been declared by its highest court in such manner as to infringe upon constitutional guaranties. . . . It surely cannot be

---

[66] *Id.* at 293.
[67] *Id.*
[68] *Id.* at 297.
[69] *Id.*
[70] *Id.*
[71] *Id.* at 298.

doubted that an act of the Illinois legislature, couched in this sweeping language, would be held invalid on its face."[72]

In *Milk Wagon*, we see many concepts that will be crucial to cases dealing with both abortion-picketing injunctions and abortion-picketing injordinances. Although Justice Frankfurter upheld the injunction, his decision seems to predominantly rest on the history of violence in that specific dispute. A similar injunction issued in a dispute that didn't have the same history of violence would likely have been struck down or greatly narrowed to only enjoin violent and disruptive behavior. Unlike Chief Justice Taft in *American Steel*, Frankfurter seems genuinely concerned that picketing injunctions impinge on major First Amendment values and thus deserve some level of scrutiny.

In Justice Black's dissent, we also see a proto-version of many arguments that would later be raised by Justice Scalia in abortion-picketing cases. Justice Black believes that injunctions and statutes should be seen as essentially identical for First Amendment purposes. He considers there to be an element of viewpoint discrimination in labor-picketing injunctions and believes that something resembling strict scrutiny—although that term was not yet available to him—should govern labor-picketing cases.[73] Because of Justice Black's belief in strictly scrutinizing injunctions, we also see him carefully assessing the facts for a better understanding of the proper scope of injunctions. All of these are similar to Justice Scalia's approach to the abortion-picketing cases, as we will see.

Abortion Injunctions and Abortion Injordinances

After the "heyday" of labor disputes and the early cases on labor picketing discussed above, there wasn't a significant public-picketing problem until the pro-life abortion movement galvanized after *Roe v. Wade*. Like labor-union picketing, what started off as injunctions soon became ordinances—or, again, injordinances.

---

[72] *Id.* at 308 (Black, J., dissenting).

[73] *Id.* at 305 ("[I]t is still nothing more than an attempt to persuade people that they should look with favor upon one side of a public controversy."); *id.* at 316 ("But it is going a long way to say that because of the acts of these few men, six thousand other members of their union can be denied the right to express their opinion to the extent accomplished by the sweeping injunction here sustained.").

In *Madsen v. Women's Health Center,* the Court upheld part of a sweeping injunction against abortion protesters. The petitioners challenged a second, broader injunction issued by a Florida state court. The first injunction, issued in 1992, prohibited petitioners from "blocking or interfering with public access to the clinic, and from physically abusing persons entering or leaving the clinic."[74]

Yet the protesters were largely undeterred. They blocked access to the clinic by congregating on the street and made noise that "varied from singing and chanting to the use of loudspeakers and bullhorns."[75] As a result, the patients "manifested a higher level of anxiety and hypertension," according to the testimony of one doctor.[76] The clinic sought and was granted a second injunction that prohibited, inter alia, "congregating, picketing, patrolling, demonstrating or entering that portion of public right-of-way or private property within [36] feet of the property line of the Clinic" and "singing, chanting, whistling, shouting, yelling, use of bullhorns, auto horns, sound amplification equipment or other sounds or images observable to or within earshot of the patients inside the Clinic."[77]

In an opinion by Chief Justice William Rehnquist, the Court upheld the 36-foot buffer zone around the clinic and certain noise restrictions.[78] The Court struck down, however, broader parts of the injunction, such as a 300-foot buffer zone where the petitioners were forbidden from "physically approaching any person seeking services of the clinic 'unless such person indicates a desire to communicate.'"[79]

The Court also ruled that injunctions would receive a different level of scrutiny because "there are obvious differences . . . between an injunction and a generally applicable ordinance."[80] "Ordinances," wrote Rehnquist, "represent a legislative choice regarding the promotion of particular societal interests. Injunctions, by contrast, are remedies imposed for violations (or threatened violations) of a leg-

---

[74] Madsen v. Women's Health Ctr., 512 U.S. 753, 758 (1994).

[75] *Id.*

[76] *Id.*

[77] *Id.* at 759–60.

[78] 512 U.S. 753 (1994).

[79] *Id.* at 773.

[80] *Id.* at 764.

islative or judicial decree."[81] Injunctions thus carry a greater risk of "censorship and discriminatory application" and therefore should be judged under a stricter standard than mere time, place, and manner analysis.[82] When reviewing injunctions, therefore, courts should ask "whether the challenged provisions of the injunction burden no more speech than necessary to serve a significant government interest."[83]

Justice Scalia's *Madsen* dissent can be said to be the first in a quadrilogy of cases dealing with abortion-picketing injunctions and injordinances. Like Justice Black in *Milk Wagon*, who extensively examined the incidents of violence and how they corresponded to the injunction, Scalia begins by carefully describing a video of the protesters because "[a]nyone who is seriously interested in what this case was about must view that tape."[84] To Scalia, "[w]hat the videotape, the rest of the record, and the trial court's findings do not contain is any suggestion of violence near the clinic, nor do they establish any attempt to prevent entry or exit."[85]

That he spends nearly four pages of his dissent describing a video scene-by-scene illustrates something about Justice Scalia's approach in these cases. He seems to believe that those in the majority are presuming a level of violence, or possibility of violence, that is not supported by the record. Similarly, in *Milk Wagon*, Justice Black included a chart of the incidents of violence in order to argue that the injunction overly burdened peaceful speech. Both justices seem to be trying to get their respective majorities to carefully scrutinize the record for actual incidents of violence rather than presume it to exist.

Scalia argues that the *Madsen* majority constructed an unworkable and illegitimate test to apply to injunctions that burden speech. "[A] restriction upon speech imposed by injunction . . . is at least as deserving of strict scrutiny as a statutory, content-based restriction," writes Scalia.[86] Injunctions are issued by individual judges, and "[t]he

---

[81] *Id.*

[82] *Id.*

[83] *Id.* at 765.

[84] *Id.* at 786 (Scalia, J., dissenting).

[85] *Id.* at 790.

[86] *Id.* at 792.

right to free speech should not be lightly placed within the control of a single man or woman."[87]

At the end of his dissent, Scalia accuses the majority of leaving a "powerful loaded weapon lying about" that is "'ready for the hand of any authority that can bring forward a plausible claim of an urgent need.'"[88] By applying intermediate scrutiny on injunctions, the majority created a situation where "injunctions against speech need not be closely tied to any violation of law, but may simply implement sound social policy," and trial-court conclusions permitting injunctions will be accepted "without considering whether those conclusions are supported by any findings of fact."[89]

Justice Scalia got another chance to vent his spleen at an abortion-picketing injunction three years later in *Schenck v. Pro-Choice Network of Western New York*. The majority, in a decision again by Rehnquist, overturned part of an injunction against abortion protesters.[90] Chief Justice Rehnquist upheld a fixed 15-foot buffer zone around clinics' doorways, entrances, and parking lot entrances. The Court overturned, however, a 15-foot floating buffer zone around persons or vehicles seeking access to the clinic because it burdened more speech than was necessary to serve the government's interest.

Schenck is the last abortion-picketing injunction case before the Court dealt with the injordinances in *Hill v. Colorado*—and then in *McCullen v. Coakley*. Many concepts present in *Hill* and *McCullen* can be found in *Schenck*, in particular the heavily debated "right to be free of unwelcome speech on the public streets while seeking entrance to or exit from abortion clinics," which, according to Scalia, is "tucked away" in the majority's opinion and is at odds with First Amendment jurisprudence.[91]

Content Neutrality?

As mentioned, the First Amendment makes only the occasional appearance in early labor-injunction cases—and, if it appears at all, the justices don't use the language familiar to modern First Amendment

---

[87] *Id.* at 793.

[88] *Id.* at 815 (quoting Korematsu v. United States, 323 U.S. 214, 246 (1944)).

[89] *Id.*

[90] Schenck v. Pro-Choice Network of W. N.Y., 519 U.S. 357 (1997).

[91] *Id.* at 386 (Scalia, J., concurring in part and dissenting in part).

jurisprudence. Indeed, early free-speech cases seem often to be ad hoc and based mostly on the justices' senses of propriety. Concepts like "content neutrality" or "secondary effects" are not articulated.

One of the first cases to focus on content-based or subject-matter restrictions was *Police Department of Chicago v. Mosley*, which dealt with a restriction on picketing within 150 feet of schools.[92] Picketing for labor disputes, however, was expressly exempted from the ordinance. The Court struck down the law as a violation of the Equal Protection Clause more than of the First Amendment, with Justice Thurgood Marshall writing that the "Equal Protection Clause requires that statutes affecting First Amendment interests be narrowly tailored to their legitimate objectives."[93]

Although the *Mosley* Court used the Equal Protection Clause, it was actually employing an early version of the test for content neutrality. An ordinance that discriminates on its face between types of picketing through reference to the speech-content of the picketing is clearly not content-neutral. The Court affirmed that public streets are traditionally open to the public for gathering and that "[s]elective exclusions from a public forum may not be based on content alone, and may not be justified by reference to content alone."[94]

Interestingly, in light of the history of labor violence, Chicago argued that exempting labor picketing was justified because "nonlabor picketing is more prone to produce violence than labor picketing."[95] The Court said this determination could not be made on such a broad level because "[p]redictions about imminent disruption from picketing involve judgments appropriately made on an individualized basis, not by means of broad classifications, especially those based on subject matter."[96] In other words, injunctions might be better for handling specifically violent groups than ordinances.

Three years later, in *Erznoznik v. City of Jacksonville*, the Court added a bit more clarity and predictability to its First Amendment jurisprudence.[97] *Erznoznik* dealt with a challenge to an ordinance preventing

---

[92] 408 U.S. 92 (1972).
[93] *Id.* at 101.
[94] *Id.* at 96.
[95] *Id.* at 100.
[96] *Id.* at 100–01.
[97] 422 U.S. 205 (1975).

the display of nudity at drive-in movie theaters. In striking down the ordinance as eliminating more speech than necessary—it made no distinction between types of nudity "however innocent or even educational"[98]—the Court sketched out "some general principles" that had emerged from previous cases:

> A State or municipality may protect individual privacy by enacting reasonable time, place, and manner regulations applicable to all speech irrespective of content. But when the government, acting as censor, undertakes selectively to shield the public from some kinds of speech on the ground that they are more offensive than others, the First Amendment strictly limits its power.[99]

While it is relatively easy to identify a content-based regulation if the statute explicitly refers to the content of speech, the test has proved difficult to apply in many situations. In *Minneapolis Star*, a case striking down sales taxes that applied only to some publications, the Court said that "[i]llicit legislative intent is not the *sine qua non* of a violation of the First Amendment."[100] Yet even if there is no censorial motive, a law can be content-based if it applies to only certain speakers and if it requires officials to "examine the content of the message that is conveyed."[101] When officials scrutinize the content of "publications as the basis for imposing a tax," it is "entirely incompatible with the First Amendment's guarantee of freedom of the press."[102]

The question of whether a regulation is content-based became less clear, however, when the Court began deciding cases based on the "secondary effects" test. That test first emerged when the Court began reviewing challenges to zoning ordinances that regulated adult theaters and strip clubs. The secondary effects test claims not to regulate the speech itself but only the side effects of that speech. So, for example, in *Young v. American Mini Theaters, Inc.*, a four-justice plurality held that the purpose of a zoning ordinance applied to

[98] *Id.* at 212.

[99] *Id.* at 209 (citations omitted).

[100] Minneapolis Star & Tribune Co. v. Minn. Comm'r of Revenue, 460 U.S. 575, 592 (1983).

[101] Ark. Writers' Project, Inc. v. Ragland, 481 U.S. 221, 228 (1987).

[102] *Id.* at 230.

adult theaters was "justified by the city's interest in preserving the character of its neighborhoods."[103] A decade later, in *City of Renton v. Playtime Theaters, Inc.*, the Court fully embraced the secondary effects doctrine in another case dealing with regulating adult-oriented businesses.[104] Then-Justice Rehnquist held that the "resolution of this case is largely dictated by our decision in *Young*."[105]

The secondary effects doctrine creates problems for the traditional inquiry into whether a law is content-based or content-neutral. When governments can claim that courts should look at the purpose behind regulating speech—that is, that courts should focus on what secondary effects the government was seeking to regulate, then whether a law is deemed content-based becomes a more difficult and less clear inquiry. Cases like *Mosley* looked at the terms of the statute and thus gave clear guidance to the content-based inquiry. Looking at the secondary effects and government purpose, however, is vague enough to fundamentally transform the content-based inquiry into one that is less protective of speech. In fact, that is precisely what happened after *Ward v. Rock Against Racism*, which has become the key case in analyzing whether a law is content-based.

In *Ward*, the Court looked at a content-neutral rule requiring musicians to use city-provided sound equipment while performing in Central Park.[106] In upholding the regulation, the Court focused on the legislative purpose rather than the terms of the regulation. "The principal inquiry in determining content neutrality . . . is whether the government has adopted a regulation of speech because of disagreement with the message it conveys. The government's purpose is the controlling consideration."[107] Citing *Renton*, the Court held that a regulation that "serves purposes unrelated to the content of expression is deemed neutral, even if it has an incidental effect on some speakers or messages but not others."[108]

As a result of this new inquiry into government purpose, laws that may be explicitly content-based can be turned into "content-neutral"

---

[103] 427 U.S. 50, 71 (1976).

[104] 475 U.S. 41 (1986).

[105] *Id.* at 46.

[106] Ward v. Rock Against Racism, 491 U.S. 781 (1989).

[107] *Id.* at 791.

[108] *Id.*

regulations of secondary effects if judged on the government-purpose test. Moreover, they can be changed almost at a judge's or justice's whim, depending on whether she wants to uphold or strike down a law.[109] After all, almost any speech can be said to have secondary effects that were the actual purpose of the government's regulation.

This is precisely what happened in *Hill v. Colorado*. *Ward*'s "government purpose" test was perfectly adaptable to turning an obviously content-based law into a "content-neutral" one if some justices felt that abortion-protesting was a big enough evil to proscribe. Even though the statute at issue in *Hill* explicitly referred to a type of speech—"The general assembly recognizes that . . . the exercise of a person's right *to protest or counsel against certain medical procedures* must be balanced against another person's right to obtain medical counseling and treatment in an unobstructed manner"[110]—the majority decided to overlook it in favor of applying *Ward*'s "government purpose" test.

A truly content-neutral law would apply equally to all types of speech. *Ward*'s rule about using certain sound equipment, for example, applied whether the band was punk or country. But a rule that required the government to examine the music to determine whether and if the sound regulations applied would certainly be content-based.

This was precisely what the supposedly content-neutral law in *Hill* required the government to do: examine the content of the speech. Recall the rule in *Mosley*: "Selective exclusions from a public forum may not be based on content alone, and may not be justified by reference to content alone."[111] Paying attention to the content of the speech is precisely what enforcing the law required. The statute prohibited approaching within eight feet "for the purpose of passing a leaflet or handbill to, displaying a sign to, or engaging in oral protest, education, or counseling," not asking the time or talking about the weather.[112] As Justice Kennedy points out in his dissent,

---

[109] For further discussion see, John Fee, Speech Discrimination, 85 B.U. L. Rev. 1103 (2005).

[110] Colo. Rev. Stat. § 18-9-122(1) (2013) (emphasis added).

[111] Mosley, 408 U.S. at 96.

[112] Colo. Rev. Stat. § 18-9-122(1) (2013).

> When a citizen approaches another on the sidewalk in a
> disfavored-speech zone, an officer of the State must listen
> to what the speaker says. If, in the officer's judgment, the
> speaker's words stray too far toward 'protest, education, or
> counseling'—the boundaries of which are far from clear—the
> officer may decide the speech has moved from the permissible
> to the criminal.[113]

This fact by itself should have kept the law in *Hill* from being upheld. In the words of one critic of the *Hill* decision, "if that is not content based, I just do not know what 'content-based' could possibly mean."[114]

In *McCullen*, although the Court rightly struck down the law, it did so without properly ruling that the law was content-based. More important, it did so without clarifying that the *Ward* government-purpose test is not broad enough or effective enough to properly suss out invidious content-based laws. "Government purpose" is one important inquiry, but it is equally important not to abandon an inquiry into a statute's plain terms, as well as the effect it has on protected speech.

In other contexts, the Court has been very good at realizing that a statute can be content-based without being passed for censorial reasons. In *Holder v. Humanitarian Law Project*, for example, the Court ruled that a law prohibiting providing "'material support or resources to a foreign terrorist organization'. . . regulates speech on the basis of its content. Plaintiffs want to speak to the PKK and the LTTE, and whether they may do so under § 2339B depends on what they say."[115] And in *United States v. Stevens*, the Court had no difficulty saying that a statute prohibiting depictions of animal cruelty "explicitly regulates expression based on content: The statute restricts 'visual [and] auditory depiction[s],' such as photographs, videos, or sound recordings, depending on whether they depict conduct in which a living animal is intentionally harmed. As such, § 48 is 'presumptively invalid,' and the Government bears the burden to rebut that presumption."[116]

So if the Court is easily convinced that a statute is content-based on its face, then why does it have so much trouble with abortion-clinic

---

[113] Hill, 530 U.S. at 766–67 (Kennedy, J., dissenting).

[114] Michael W. McConnell, Response, 28 Pepp. L. Rev. 747, 748 (2000).

[115] Holder v. Humanitarian Law Project, 561 U.S. 1, 27 (2010) (citation omitted).

[116] United States v. Stevens, 559 U.S. 460, 468 (2010) (citations omitted).

buffer zone in jordinances? It is easy to be cynical about this question and to simply say that some of the justices want to silence abortion critics and some don't. Perhaps, however, if we are being properly respectful and charitable, we again should look to whether the laws are properly regulating a secondary effect of the picketing, such as violence and obstruction of entrances.

In trying to achieve some of those valid purposes, the statute in *McCullen* can be said to have been less content-based than the one in *Hill*. Yet, as Justice Scalia points out, the fact that it applies only to abortion clinics, and that it explicitly allows abortion-clinic employees to escort women into the facility, makes the law clearly content-based. As Scalia properly observes, "Is there any serious doubt that *abortion-clinic employees or agents* 'acting within the scope of their employment' near clinic entrances may—indeed, often will—speak in favor of abortion ('You are doing the right thing')? Or speak in opposition to the message of abortion opponents—saying, for example, that 'this is a safe facility' to rebut the statement that it is not?"[117] Of course not.

A proper application of the content-based test would look at both the realistic effects of the statute, *Ward*'s government purpose test, and the terms of the statute. In *McCullen*, the exemption explicitly offered to clinic employees puts the statute clearly into the content-based category. The effect of that exemption, in the memorable words of Justice Scalia, is that it "license[s] one side of a debate to fight free-style, while requiring the other to follow Marquis of Queensberry rules."[118]

Perhaps most surprising, however, is that rather than looking at the employee exemption on its face, the majority opinion decides to look to the record for evidence that employees had spoken in favor of abortion. This is a shocking affront to common sense in the area of our most cherished freedoms. Again, in the memorable words of Justice Scalia: "Here is a brave new First Amendment test: Speech restrictions favoring one viewpoint over another are not content based unless it can be shown that the favored viewpoint has actually been expressed."[119]

---

[117] McCullen, 134 S. Ct. at 2546 (Scalia, J., dissenting) (emphasis in original).

[118] R.A.V. v. St. Paul, 505 U.S. 377, 392 (1992).

[119] McCullen, 134 S. Ct. at 2548 (Scalia, J., dissenting).

Although it is good that the *McCullen* majority struck down the statute, it is unfortunate that it did further harm to First Amendment jurisprudence on content-based regulations of speech. *Ward's* government-purpose test is clearly inadequate for finding all content-based regulations, and the majority should simply have applied the lessons of *Humanitarian Law Project* and *Stevens* and looked at the terms of the statute. That the Court seemingly makes such errors exclusively in abortion-picketing cases makes it difficult to ignore as evidence of Justice Scalia's "ad hoc nullification machine" for laws touching the issue of abortion.[120]

Hill, *McCullen*, **and the Future of Injordinances**

In this article, I have examined the history of the jurisprudence around labor-picketing injunctions, labor-picketing injordinances, abortion-picketing injunctions, and, now, abortion-picketing injordinances. It is interesting that two disparate sets of actors that are often at partisan loggerheads—pro-life activists and pro-union protesters—would find themselves to be precedential bedfellows in the matter of picketing injunctions and injordinances. Yet those who prefer to take their cause to the streets are likely to run afoul of the same legal rules, no matter what their ideology.

This is why the AFL-CIO has been a consistent supporter of pro-life protesters in cases before the Supreme Court.[121] What was once labor's fight has now become the pro-life movement's cross to bear, as it were.

What lessons can we learn from reviewing these cases? I began this article by asking whether and how much the First Amendment adds to common-law principles prohibiting obstruction, intimidation, and interference with business. The answer seems to be "not a lot." Despite developing a more protective and defined First Amendment jurisprudence since the days of *American Steel*, the Supreme Court continued and continues to generally uphold broad labor injunctions (*Milk Wagon*), abortion-picketing injunctions (*Madsen* and *Schenck*), and abortion injordinances (*Hill*).

---

[120] Madsen, 512 U.S. at 785 (Scalia, J., dissenting).

[121] See, e.g., Brief for the Am. Fed. of Labor and Cong. of Indus. Orgs. as Amicus Curiae Supporting Petitioners, Hill v. Colorado, 530 U.S. 703 (2000) (No. 98-1856).

McCullen is partially an aberration in this line of cases, but not entirely so. A careful reading of the majority opinion in *McCullen*, paired with the majority opinion in *Hill*, leads to a conclusion that abortion-clinic buffer zones need to be tailored to fix specific, non-speech-related problems—namely, obstruction of entrances and potential violence. Future litigants will have to focus on those specific harms. Eight-foot buffer zones, such as what was upheld in *Hill*, can arguably help diminish the possibility of violence, and the obstruction of entrances can also be alleviated by narrower means than a 35-foot no-go area.

One of the most interesting parts of *McCullen* is the discussion of alternative means to alleviate the obstruction of entrances. Those alternate means include pre-existing statutes—"No person shall stand, or place any obstruction of any kind, upon any street, sidewalk or crosswalk in such a manner as to obstruct a free passage for travelers thereon"—as well as "generic criminal statutes forbidding assault, breach of the peace, trespass, vandalism, and the like."[122] By invoking these specific rules, it is clear that the Court is taking seriously the necessity for narrow tailoring. Future courts will have to do the same, and more injordinances will likely fall.

Although there are many similarities between labor protesters and abortion protesters, one is perhaps the most important to their shared legal history: a reputation for violence. Labor protesters did their cause no favors by using violence to help make their point, and abortion protesters are in a similar situation. Violence breeds judicial skepticism about purity of motive to the point that even elderly women like Eleanor McCullen can carry its stain. Nevertheless, McCullen won her case and the Court—like it did in *Thornhill* and *Carlson*—struck down an injordinance that was inimical to free speech. Perhaps, in the end, it was just a victory for "counselors" over "protesters."

---

[122] McCullen, 134 S. Ct. at 2538 (quoting Worcester, Mass., Rev. Ordinances of 2008, ch. 12, § 25(b)(2008)).

Harris v. Quinn:
A Win for Freedom of Association

Jacob Huebert*

When can the government force someone to give money to a union to speak on his or her behalf? For several decades, under the precedent set in *Abood v. Detroit Board of Education*, the Supreme Court has maintained that the government can require its employees who don't want to join a union to pay the union an "agency fee" to cover its ostensible costs of representing them.[1]

But what about someone who merely receives a state subsidy for something he or she does? Can the state make that person turn over a portion of that payment to a union? That's the question the Court considered in *Harris v. Quinn*, which challenged an Illinois scheme that unionized "personal assistants" who receive a Medicaid subsidy to provide home care to a disabled person (in many cases, a family member).[2]

The Court concluded that the First Amendment prohibits forcing those people, who are not "full-fledged" government employees, to support a union because it constitutes coerced speech and association that was not justified by any compelling governmental interest. But it also did more: it tore apart the Court's reasoning in *Abood*, suggesting that, in an appropriate case, the Court may put an end to compulsory union payments for all government employees. The decision was therefore a great blow to unions' efforts to coerce support for their political activities and a triumph for First Amendment rights—and it opens the door for a much greater triumph in the future.

---

*Senior attorney, Liberty Justice Center, Illinois Policy Institute.
[1] 431 U.S. 209 (1977).
[2] 134 S. Ct. 2618 (2014).

Illinois and SEIU's Schemes to Unionize Subsidy Recipients

In March 2003, Illinois Governor Rod Blagojevich issued an executive order authorizing the state to recognize an exclusive representative for "personal assistants" in a state-administered Medicaid program, commonly called the "Rehabilitation Program," who provide home care to individuals who are not able to care for themselves.[3] Until then, the personal assistants had not been considered state employees. In fact, the Illinois State Labor Board rejected a 1985 attempt by the Service Employees International Union (SEIU) to unionize personal assistants in Chicago and parts of Cook County, Illinois, for that very reason: "There is no typical employment arrangement here, public or otherwise," the board ruled; "rather, there simply exists an arrangement whereby the state of Illinois pays individuals (the service providers) to work under the direction and control of private third parties (the service recipients)."[4] The person receiving care through the program, as the "customer," has sole discretion over hiring, supervising, and terminating his or her personal assistant. The state's only role is to establish basic requirements for personal assistants and to pay them.

Blagojevich's order acknowledged all of this, including the 1985 Labor Board ruling, which it intended to overrule. The order stated that the "personal assistants are not State employees for purposes of eligibility to receive statutorily mandated benefits because the State does not hire, supervise or terminate" them and that the order would "not in any way alter the 'unique' employment arrangement of personal assistants and recipients, nor [would] it in any way diminish the recipients' control over the hiring, in-home supervision, and termination of personal assistants."[5] In other words, the personal assistants would still not be state employees—except for purposes of collective bargaining. The order's stated purpose was to allow personal assistants to "effectively voice their concerns about the organization of the . . . program, their role in the program, or

---

[3] See *id.* at 2623–26; Ill. Exec. Order 2003-08 [hereinafter "EO 2003-08"], available at http://www.illinois.gov/Government/ExecOrders/Pages/2003_8.aspx.

[4] SEIU/Illinois Dep't of Cent. Mgmt. Servs. and Dep't of Rehab. Servs., 2 PERI ¶2007 (IL LRB-SP 1985).

[5] EO 2003-08.

the terms and conditions of their employment," so the state could "receive feedback from [them] in order to effectively and efficiently deliver home services."[6]

In July 2003, Blagojevich codified his order by signing legislation amending the state's Disabled Persons Rehabilitation Act to declare that personal assistants would be considered public employees "[s]olely for purposes of coverage under the Illinois Public Labor Relations Act."[7] To be even clearer, the amendment declared that the state would not be considered the personal assistants' employer for any other purposes, "including but not limited to, purposes of vicarious liability in tort and purposes of statutory retirement or insurance benefits."[8]

The state and the SEIU hadn't waited for the General Assembly to pass legislation to begin unionizing personal assistants. In the same month that Blagojevich issued his executive order, the state recognized an SEIU local as the personal assistants' exclusive representative. This happened even though the personal assistants never actually had an opportunity to vote on whether to join a union. Instead, the state recognized the union upon determining that a majority of providers wanted to be represented by SEIU based on the number of providers who, according to payroll records, were already SEIU members and the number of signed membership cards SEIU submitted.[9]

The state and SEIU soon entered a collective-bargaining agreement for personal assistants, which included an agency-fee provision requiring assistants who did not join the union to nonetheless pay fees to the union for the assistant's pro rata share of collective-bargaining expenses, as state law allows for all public-sector union contracts.[10]

After Blagojevich was removed from office in 2009, his successor, Governor Pat Quinn, attempted to unionize personal assistants in the

---

[6] *Id.*

[7] 20 Ill. Comp. Stat. 2405/3(f) (2012).

[8] *Id.*

[9] Letter from Benno Weisberg, Illinois Dep't of Cent. Mgmt. Servs., to Justin Hegy, Illinois Policy Institute (Nov. 21, 2013), available at http://illinoispolicy.org/wp-content/uploads/2013/11/WeisbergLetter.pdf. *Harris* incorrectly states that a vote was held. 134 S. Ct. at 2626, 2641.

[10] *Harris*, 134 S. Ct. at 2626; 5 Ill. Comp. Stat. 315/6(e) (2003) (authorizing agency-fee provision in collective-bargaining agreements).

state's "Disabilities Program," another state-administered Medicaid program that provides subsidies to people who care for disabled individuals—again, often for a family member—in their homes.[11] The Disabilities Program is identical to the Rehabilitation Program in all relevant details. Disabilities Program personal assistants are hired, fired, and supervised by the individuals for whom they care, not by the state. As with the Rehabilitation Program providers, the state's only role is to set basic requirements and pay the assistants.

In June 2009, Quinn issued an executive order, substantially similar to Blagojevich's 2003 order, authorizing the state to recognize an exclusive representative for personal assistants in the Disabilities Program. Like Blagojevich, Quinn acknowledged that his order would not change the relationship between the assistants and the people they care for.[12] As discussed below, Quinn's attempt to unionize Disabilities Program assistants failed because of the efforts of Pamela Harris, the lead plaintiff in *Harris v. Quinn*.

Blagojevich's and Quinn's efforts were part of a nationwide strategy by public-sector unions, particularly SEIU, and their allies in government to boost diminishing union membership[13] by unionizing people who receive a government subsidy for providing services to a private third party.[14] SEIU's first victory in this campaign came in 1999, when it unionized some 74,000 home-care providers

---

[11] See 405 Ill. Comp. Stat. 80/2-1 et seq. (1989); Ill. Admin. Code tit. 59, §§ 117.100 et seq. (2008).

[12] Ill. Exec. Order 2009-15, available at http://www.illinois.gov/Government/ExecOrders/Pages/2009_15.aspx.

[13] Union membership peaked in 1954, when 28.3 percent of Americans belonged to a union; by 2013, only 11.3 percent of American workers—and just 6.7 percent of private-sector workers—belonged to a union. Yoonsoo Lee & Beth Mowry, Union Membership, Federal Reserve Bank of Cleveland (Nov. 9, 2007), http://www.clevelandfed.org/research/trends/2007/1107/04ecoact.cfm (historical rates); Union Membership (Annual) News Release, Bureau of Labor Statistics (Jan. 24, 2014), available at http://www.bls.gov/news.release/union2.htm (current rates).

[14] See Brief for Mackinac Center for Public Policy as Amicus Curiae in Support of Petitioners at 3–16, Harris v. Quinn, 134 S. Ct. 2618 (2014) (No. 11-681), available at http://www.mackinac.org/archives/2013/NR11-681tsac.pdf; Linda Delp & Katie Quan, Homecare Worker Organizing in California: An Analysis of a Successful Strategy, 27 Lab. Studs. J. 1 (2002); Patrice M. Mareschal, Innovation and Adaptation: Contrasting Efforts to Organize Home Care Workers in Four States, 31 Lab. Studs. J. 25 (2006); Peggie R. Smith, The Publicization of Home-Based Care Work in State Labor Law, 92 Minn. L. Rev. 1390 (2008).

in Los Angeles County, California.[15] Unions then successfully campaigned for recognition of an exclusive representative on behalf of home-care providers in Oregon (2000), Washington (2001), Illinois (2003), Michigan (2004), Wisconsin (2005), Iowa (2005), Massachusetts (2006), Missouri (2008), Ohio (2009), Pennsylvania (2010), Connecticut (2011), Maryland (2011), Minnesota (2013), and Vermont (2013).[16] (Four of those states, however—Ohio, Pennsylvania, Wisconsin, and Michigan—later effectively reversed the authorization to recognize a union for the providers.)[17] In addition, before the Court decided *Harris*, 11 states authorized compulsory union fees for home childcare providers, such as people who operate a day care out of their homes and accept children who receive state child-care subsidies, and people who receive subsidies to take care of relatives' children in their own homes.[18] And two states, Washington and Oregon, have authorized exclusive representatives for adult foster-care providers.[19]

[15] Smith, *supra* note 14, at 1405–06; Cal. Welf. & Inst. Code § 12302.25(a) (1999).

[16] See Conn. Gen. Stat. § 17b-706a(e)(1); Iowa Exec. Order No. 43 (July 4,); 20 Ill. Comp. Stat. 2405/3(f); Md. Code Ann., Health-Gen. §§ 15-901 et seq.; Mass. Gen. Laws ch. 118E, § 73(b); Interlocal Agreement Between Mich. Dep't of Cmty. Health & Tri-County Aging Consortium (Apr. 24), available at http://goo.gl/lhZrho; Mo. Rev. Stat. § 208.853; Ohio House Bill 1 §§ 741.01-06 (expired); Or. Const. art. XV, § 11; Or. Rev. Stat. § 410.612; Pa. Exec. Order 2010-04 (Sept. 14) (rescinded); Vt. Stat. Ann. tit. 21, §§ 1631-44; Wash. Rev. Code § 74.39A.270); Wis. Stat §§ 111.81 (repealed).

[17] The Ohio provision expired as scheduled when the term of the then-current governor, Ted Strickland, ended; the Pennsylvania executive order was rescinded; and the Wisconsin statute was repealed. Michigan's scheme dissolved after repeated attempts by the legislature to redefine "public employee" to exclude home-care providers, an SEIU lawsuit challenging the legislature's changes, and a failed attempt by SEIU to amend the state's constitution through a ballot initiative. The government entity that "employed" the providers finally announced its own dissolution after voters rejected the ballot measure. See Brief of Amicus Curiae Mackinac Center, *supra* note 14, at 28–32.

[18] See Conn. Gen. Stat. §§ 17b-705 et seq. (2012); 5 Ill. Comp. Stat. 315/3, 315/7; Md. Code. Ann. Fam. Law § 5-595 et seq.; Mass. Gen. Laws ch. 15D, § 17; Minn. Stat. § 179A.52; N.M. Stat. Ann. § 50-4-33; N.Y. Lab. Law § 695-a et seq.; Or. Rev. Stat. § 329A.430; R.I. Gen. Laws § 40-6.6-4; Wash. Rev. Code § 41.56.028. Compulsory union fees were also previously permitted in Michigan, Ohio, and Wisconsin.

[19] Or. Rev. Stat. § 443.733; Wash. Rev. Code § 41.56.029.

Pamela Harris Takes Action

Pamela Harris is a mother in northern Illinois whose son, Joshua, requires constant care because of a rare genetic syndrome that causes severe developmental and intellectual disabilities. Harris receives a subsidy through the Disabilities Program so she can take care of her son at home rather than see him institutionalized.[20]

Harris learned of Quinn's executive order one Sunday morning in 2009 when some union representatives showed up unannounced at her door and urged her to join. She declined their offer because she wanted the money from her checks to go toward her son's care, not toward a union's agenda, and she was concerned that a union might intrude upon her home or attempt to interfere with her relationship with her son.

So she took action. With her own money and small contributions from other families that participate in the Disabilities Program, she sent notices to other personal assistants warning them of what she believed was a threat to their finances and their independence. And she succeeded: the Disabilities Program personal assistants voted against joining a union.

Harris then asked Quinn to respect the personal assistants' wishes and rescind his executive order, but he refused. She knew the unions' deep pockets would allow them to continue their unionization efforts and she couldn't afford to keep fighting them forever, so she looked for help. She got it from the National Right to Work Legal Defense Foundation, which brought a class-action lawsuit on behalf of personal assistants in the Rehabilitation and Disabilities Programs in the U.S. District Court for the Northern District of Illinois challenging the assistants' forced payment of agency fees as a violation of their First Amendment rights.

---

[20] For these and other background details on Pamela Harris, see Sean Higgins, Forced Unionization Turned Illinois Homemaker into Supreme Court Plaintiff in *Harris v. Quinn* Case, Wash. Examiner (May 1, 2014), http://washingtonexaminer. com/forced-unionization-turned-illinois-homemaker-into-supreme-court-plaintiff-in-harris-v.-quinn-case/article/2547312; Ben Yount, US Supreme Court to Hear Illinois Union Strong-Arm Case, Illinois Watchdog (Oct. 4, 2013), http://watchdog. org/109220/us-supreme-court-to-hear-illinois-union-strong-arm-case/; Video: *Harris v. Quinn*: A Mother's Fight for Justice (Illinois Policy Institute Dec. 5, 2013), available at https://www.youtube.com/watch?v=kOM6gPbBzsg.

The First Amendment and Forced Support for Unions

On its face, forcing personal assistants to pay an organization to speak on their behalf would strike many people as a clear violation of the rights to free speech and free association that the First Amendment is supposed to protect. But the federal district court dismissed the *Harris* plaintiffs' suit for failing to state a First Amendment claim, and the U.S. Court of Appeals for the Seventh Circuit affirmed. To understand why—and to understand the importance of the Supreme Court's decision—one must review not only First Amendment principles but also the history of Supreme Court case law on compulsory unionism.

First Amendment fundamentals

The Supreme Court has held that the First and Fourteenth Amendments do indeed protect a right to freedom of association. In the Court's words: "It is beyond debate that freedom to engage in association for the advancement of beliefs and ideas is an inseparable aspect of the 'liberty' assured by the Due Process Clause of the Fourteenth Amendment, which embraces free speech," regardless of "whether the beliefs sought to be advanced by association pertain to political, economic, religious or cultural matters."[21] The Court has recognized that freedom of association, "like free speech, lies at the foundation of a free society."[22] The Court has also made clear that the freedom of association "plainly presupposes a freedom *not* to associate."[23]

Similarly, the Court has held that the First Amendment "may prevent the government from . . . compelling certain individuals to pay subsidies for speech to which they object," and it has recognized that "First Amendment values are at serious risk if the government can compel a particular citizen, or a discrete group of citizens, to pay special subsidies for speech on the side that it favors."[24] The Court has approvingly cited Thomas Jefferson's statement that "[t]o compel a man to furnish contributions of money for the propagation of

[21] NAACP v. Alabama, 357 U.S. 449, 460 (1958).

[22] Buckley v. Valeo, 424 U.S. 1, 25 (1976) (internal marks and citations omitted).

[23] Roberts v. U.S. Jaycees, 468 U.S. 609, 623 (1984) (emphasis added).

[24] United States v. United Foods, Inc., 533 U.S. 405, 410–11 (2010) (internal citations omitted).

opinions which he disbelieves, is sinful and tyrannical."[25] The Court has held that First Amendment rights are impinged regardless of how little money is taken, or for how little time the individual is deprived of his or her money, if it is used to support political or ideological causes he or she opposes.[26] Applying these principles, the Court has held, for example, that "patronage" practices that require government employees to support a particular political party to keep their jobs violate the First Amendment.[27]

First Amendment scrutiny and Abood

Given those principles, how could the lower federal courts in *Harris* uphold Illinois's unionization scheme? Because the Constitution's guarantees of individual rights aren't as absolute as they appear to be: the Supreme Court allows the government to violate constitutional rights when it offers a good enough reason—with the government's burden ranging from heavy to negligible, depending on which constitutional right is at stake. The Court has said that infringements on freedom of association "may be justified by regulations adopted to serve compelling state interests, unrelated to suppression of ideas, that cannot be achieved through means significantly less restrictive of associational freedoms."[28]

That would appear to mean that, to infringe on personal assistants' right not to associate with a union, the government must at least prove that (1) making personal assistants pay union fees serves a compelling governmental interest that is unrelated to controlling people's speech, and (2) there is no other way the government could serve that interest while interfering substantially less with First Amendment rights.

[25] Abood, 431 U.S. at 235 n.31 (quoting Irving Brant, James Madison: The Nationalist 354 (1948)).

[26] See Chicago Teachers Union v. Hudson, 475 U.S. 292, 305 (1986) (dissenters' funds may not be used for union political purposes even temporarily and "[t]he amount at stake for each individual dissenter does not diminish this concern"); cf. Elrod v. Burns, 427 U.S. 347, 360 n.13 (1976) (plurality opinion) ("[T]he inducement afforded by [government] placing conditions on a benefit need not be particularly great in order to find that rights have been violated. Rights are infringed both where the government fines a person a penny for being a Republican and where it withholds the grant of a penny for the same reason.").

[27] See Elrod, 427 U.S. at 355–71.

[28] Roberts, 468 U.S. at 623.

But the lower courts in *Harris* didn't really require the government to make that showing. Indeed, the Supreme Court has never really required the government to make that showing to justify forcing actual government employees to pay union agency fees.

In *Abood*, the Court held for the first time that the government could require public employees who did not want to join a union to pay agency fees to cover their share of collective-bargaining costs. Any infringement this caused to employees' speech and association rights was justified because it prevented "free riders" from taking advantage of the union's representation services and because it served the interests of "labor peace"—that is, it would allow the government to avoid "the confusion and conflict that could arise if rival . . . unions, holding quite different views . . . each sought to obtain the employer's agreement."[29]

Are the prevention of free riding and the preservation of labor peace compelling governmental interests? Is there no way to serve those interests that would better respect dissenting employees' First Amendment rights? *Abood* never really examined those questions. Instead, the Court simply pointed to two other decisions that it believed stood for the proposition that the government could force people to pay union fees in the interest of labor peace: *Railway Employees' Dep't v. Hanson* and *International Association of Machinists v. Street*.[30]

But *Hanson* and *Street* didn't actually address those questions, either.

Hanson considered a provision of the federal Railway Labor Act (1926) that authorized private railway companies to enter into "union shop" agreements that would require all employees to pay union fees, regardless of any state "right-to-work" laws.[31] The Court held that the act was within Congress's Commerce Clause power "to regulate labor relations in interstate industries" and noted that collective bargaining may serve the "legitimate objective" of "[i]ndustrial peace along the arteries of commerce."[32] In response to the argument that

[29] Abood, 431 U.S. at 224.

[30] See *id.* at 217–32 (discussing Hanson, 351 U.S. 225 (1956) and Street, 367 U.S. 740 (1961)).

[31] *Id.* at 227–28.

[32] *Id.* at 233.

a union-shop agreement violates workers' freedom of association, the Court stated that "[o]n *the present record*," there was no evidence of any First Amendment violation.[33] In other words, in the absence of actual evidence of anyone being compelled to support speech with which he or she disagreed—of which there was none, because the Nebraska courts had enjoined the act—the law did not violate the First Amendment. As the Court later noted in *Street*, *Hanson* left open the question of whether evidence of compelled support for union political speech could establish a First Amendment violation.[34]

The closest *Hanson* came to endorsing compulsory support for a union was a statement that the record presented "no more an infringement or impairment of First Amendment rights than there would be in the case of a lawyer who by state law is required to be a member of an integrated bar."[35] That was an odd thing to say because the Court had never considered whether the First Amendment allows a state to force lawyers to support an integrated bar—and when it did consider that issue five years later in *Lathrop v. Donahue*,[36] it hardly treated the question as uncontroversial or settled. The Court did uphold such fees with a plurality opinion, but Justice William O. Douglas, the author of *Hanson*, dissented, writing:

> Once we approve this measure, we sanction a device where men and women in almost any profession or calling can be at least partially regimented behind causes which they oppose. I look on the *Hanson* case as a narrow exception to be closely confined. Unless we so treat it, we practically give carte blanche to any legislature to put at least professional people into goose-stepping brigades. Those brigades are not compatible with the First Amendment.[37]

As for *Street*, it considered a collective-bargaining agreement between a railroad company and a union that required nonmembers to support campaigns for political candidates they opposed and ideas

---

[33] *Id.* at 238 (emphasis added).

[34] See Street, 367 U.S. at 747–49.

[35] Abood, 431 U.S. at 238. An "integrated bar" is an association to which attorney must pay dues as a condition of practicing law in a state. Keller v. State Bar of Cal., 496 U.S. 1, 4–5 (1990).

[36] 367 U.S. 820 (1961).

[37] *Id.* at 884 (Douglas, J., dissenting) (footnote omitted).

with which they disagreed.[38] The Court acknowledged that the case raised "constitutional questions . . . of the utmost gravity," but then avoided those questions by determining that the Railway Labor Act did not authorize the forced payments.[39]

As Justice Lewis Powell observed in his *Abood* opinion concurring in the judgment, *Street* left open several important questions: (1) whether withholding financial support for union political activities is protected "speech"; (2) whether Congress could "go further in approving private arrangements that would interfere with [First Amendment] interests than it could in commanding such arrangements"; and (3) whether any First Amendment violation that results from the mandatory payment of union fees "could be justified by the governmental interest asserted on its behalf."[40]

In sum, *Hanson* and *Street* never engaged in any analysis of whether government-coerced union support infringes First Amendment rights or, if so, whether that infringement could be justified by some compelling governmental interest. That is, the two decisions left open *precisely* the essential First Amendment questions the Court needed to answer in *Abood*. Yet the Court in *Abood* acted as though *Hanson* and *Street* had resolved them.

Compelled union support is compelled political speech

One of *Abood*'s fatal flaws is its failure to consider the difference between compelled support for private-sector unions and compelled support for public-sector unions. When unions represent government employees—or subsidy recipients—all of their speech is inherently "political," and forced support for that speech would seem to be precisely what the Supreme Court's First Amendment case law generally prohibits. The Court has noted that, even in traditional public employment, a union inevitably "takes many positions during collective bargaining that have powerful political and civic consequences."[41] The government is not like a private employer because its decisions regarding employee (or subsidy recipient) pay and benefits directly affect public policy and implicate issues on

---

[38] Street, 367 U.S. at 742–45.

[39] *Id.* at 749, 768–69.

[40] Abood, 431 U.S. at 248–49 (Powell, J., concurring).

[41] Knox, 132 S. Ct. at 2289.

which members of the public—taxpayers, for example—may have opinions. A plurality opinion of the Court therefore acknowledged that "[t]he dual roles of government as employer and policymaker . . . make the analogy between lobbying and collective bargaining in the public sector a close one."[42]

This is especially obvious in the case of personal assistants. If a union negotiates on their behalf, it can do little more than argue that the state should give them more money and benefits—making the union much like anyone else who lobbies for more or less spending on a Medicaid program, except that the union can legally force people to pay for its advocacy.

Abood held that the government could compel nonmembers to support a union's activities related to collective bargaining, but it also held that nonmembers had a First Amendment right to opt out of paying for a union's political and ideological activities that are not "germane" to collective bargaining on their behalf.[43]

That distinction doesn't make sense because both kinds of speech are actually political, particularly in the public-sector context—and both could be equally objectionable to a dissenter—but in any event, opting out hardly guarantees that a nonmember won't still be forced to pay for union political speech on matters that aren't related to collective bargaining. As the Supreme Court recently observed in *Knox v. SEIU*, a union's auditors typically do not question the union's determinations of which expenses are and aren't "chargeable" to nonmembers—so if a union says political expenditures are chargeable, its auditors will take the union's word for it and classify them as chargeable.[44] And although nonmembers may contest any chargeability determination, "the onus is on [them] to come up with the resources to mount a legal challenge in a timely fashion," which, the Court has noted, is "a significant burden . . . to bear simply to avoid having their money taken for speech with which they disagree."[45]

Indeed, it's difficult to imagine a personal assistant who provides constant care to a severely disabled family member spending whatever free time he or she can find making sure that the union isn't

---

[42] Lehnert v. Ferris Faculty Ass'n, 500 U.S. 507, 520 (1991) (plurality opinion).

[43] See Abood, 431 U.S. at 235–36.

[44] 132 S. Ct. at 2294.

[45] *Id.* (internal footnote and citations omitted).

spending nonmembers' fees on political activity. That would require the individual to review the union's report of its many expenditures, determine whether each was proper, and then, if he or she believed certain expenditures were improper, to take the steps required to challenge them. In Illinois, that could include filing an unfair-labor-practice charge, participating in a hearing on the charge, and if necessary, pursuing appeals before an administrative law judge and then a court—all to challenge a fraction of his or her fees.[46] Even for someone who highly values First Amendment rights, the effort would make little economic sense.

If a personal assistant in the Illinois Rehabilitation Program did take time to review the LM-2 form that the providers' SEIU local filed with the U.S. Department of Labor for 2012, he or she would find that the union's expenditures for purported representation expenses included numerous contributions to groups that appear to engage primarily or exclusively in political activities unrelated to collective bargaining.[47] They include contributions to Action Now, Home Care First, Inc., and Missourians Organizing for Reform and Empowerment—groups whose activities have respectively consisted of running "issue campaigns,"[48] funding a 2012 Michigan ballot initiative campaign,[49] and waging campaigns against "an economic system that prioritizes corporations above all else."[50] Perhaps the union could provide an innocuous explanation for those expenditures; the problem is that it is unlikely that anyone will ever find out because the costs of challenging them are prohibitively high.

Compelled union support distorts the marketplace of political ideas

The First Amendment harm from coerced union support doesn't just infringe the rights of people forced to pay; it also distorts the

[46] See Ill. Admin. Code tit. 80, §§ 1200.135, 1220.10 et seq.

[47] U.S. Dep't of Labor Form LM-2 for Service Employees Healthcare IL IN, schedule 15 (2012), available at http://illinoispolicy.org/wp-content/uploads/2013/11/SEIUHII2012LM2.pdf.

[48] Action Now Campaigns, http://www.actionnow.org/campaigns.

[49] Tim Martin, Proposal 4: SEIU Union Pumps Money into Michigan's Home Health Ballot Measure, MLive.com (Oct. 26, 2012), http://www.mlive.com/politics/index.ssf/2012/10/proposal_4_seiu_union_pumps_mo.html.

[50] Our Work—Missourians Organizing for Reform and Empowerment (MORE), http://www.organizemo.org/our_work.

marketplace of political ideas in the union's favor, which may affect everyone else's relative ability to influence public policy. The Supreme Court has stated that "[t]he First Amendment creates a forum in which all may seek, without hindrance *or aid* from the state, to move public opinion and achieve their political goals."[51] That "forum" cannot exist if the government is coercing one group of people to support another group with opposing views. It gives the union an unfair advantage not only over dissenting personal assistants but also over all other groups in society, such as taxpayers, for whom the costs of organizing to oppose the union's views may be prohibitively high.

If *Abood* were expanded to cover government subsidy recipients, there is no reason to believe that this distortion would be limited to relatively narrow issues affecting home care providers or other subsidy recipients the state chooses to unionize, though that's bad enough. By forcing subsidy recipients to pay fees to a union, the state also gives the union more funds to achieve its broader political goals, which may include reelecting the state officials who facilitated the unionization and supporting their policies. In light of the burden placed on unionized workers to opt out of political funding and unions' tendency to take a broad view of what constitutes representation expenses, there's little doubt that people who opt out of supporting the union's political advocacy will nonetheless be made to pay for some of it. And by appointing representatives for various groups of subsidy recipients, incumbent officials may place themselves in a position to "tip[] the electoral process in [their] favor" and undermine the "competition in ideas and governmental policies" that the First Amendment is supposed to protect.[52]

Illinois's efforts to unionize personal assistants suggest that government officials are well aware of the political opportunities this tool offers them. The *Harris* plaintiffs alleged that Governors Blagojevich and Quinn issued their executive orders in exchange for SEIU's political support and campaign contributions.[53] Regardless of whether there was actually a quid pro quo agreement, it is certain

[51] Knox, 132 S. Ct. at 2295 (emphasis added).

[52] Elrod, 427 U.S. at 357 (internal marks omitted).

[53] Complaint at ¶¶ 19, 30, Harris v. Quinn, 2010 WL 4736500 (N.D. Ill. Nov. 12, 2010) (No. 10-cv-02477).

that the executive orders benefited a top political supporter of both governors. SEIU was the second-largest contributor to Blagojevich's 2002 campaign, giving $821,294, or 3.3 percent of all contributions.[54] Less than two months after Blagojevich took office, he issued his executive order, and the state recognized SEIU as the Rehabilitation Program providers' exclusive representative. In the 2006 election for governor, SEIU was the top contributor to Blagojevich's reelection campaign by a wide margin, giving $908,382, or nearly 5 percent of the total.[55]After Quinn issued his 2009 executive order, SEIU-affiliated groups together became the largest contributor to Quinn's narrowly successful 2010 election campaign, by far, giving a total of at least $4.3 million, about 18 percent of all contributions—much more than he received from, for example, all Democratic Party committees combined. [56]

If the governors issued their executive orders in exchange for SEIU's contributions as the *Harris* plaintiffs alleged, SEIU's investment paid off. From 2009 through 2013, Rehabilitation Program providers have given SEIU an average of about $10.4 million per year in representation fees, plus about $298,285 per year in fees for SEIU's political action committee.[57] Illinois's experience illustrates how the power to compel union support could facilitate a cycle in which a union gives money to political officials; the officials force subsidy recipients to give money to the union; and the union, with the benefit of the additional funds, makes more contributions to public officials with the expectation that they will deliver more new dues payers.

Knox v. SEIU

Despite its dubious foundations and disturbing implications, *Abood* has held on. Later decisions related to mandatory union fees have considered issues related to what activities are "chargeable"

---

[54] Contributions to Rod Blagojevich for 2002 Election, Nat'l Inst. on Money in State Politics, http://www.followthemoney.org/database/StateGlance/candidate.phtml?c=3756.

[55] Contributions to Rod Blagojevich for 2006 Election, Nat'l Inst. on Money in State Politics, http://www.followthemoney.org/database/StateGlance/candidate.phtml?c=79667.

[56] Contributions to Pat Quinn for 2010 Election, Nat'l Inst. on Money in State Politics, http://www.followthemoney.org/database/StateGlance/candidate.phtml?c=116445.

[57] E-mail from Agostino Lorenzini, Illinois Dep't of Human Servs., to Justin Hegy, Illinois Policy Institute (Oct. 9, 2013), available at http://illinoispolicy.org/wp-content/uploads/2013/11/LorenziniEmail2.pdf.

to nonmembers[58] and what procedural protections are necessary to ensure that nonmembers aren't forced to pay for non-"germane" political activity[59]—but *Abood*'s conclusion that nonmember employees can be forced to pay union fees has remained untouched. In 2012, however, a five-justice "conservative" majority of the Court, led by Justice Samuel Alito, suggested in *Knox v. SEIU* that it recognizes *Abood*'s flaws and might be willing to reconsider *Abood* in an appropriate case.

Knox concerned whether a union could require nonmembers to pay a temporary fee increase for political purposes without giving them notice and an opportunity to opt out.[60] Seven justices agreed that the First Amendment did not allow the union to do so.

Although the issue in *Knox* was relatively narrow, Justice Alito's majority opinion took the occasion to review—and question—the Court's decisions on mandatory union fees. Alito noted that "free-rider" arguments, such as the one the Court relied on in *Abood*, "are generally insufficient to overcome First Amendment objections."[61] For example, citizens might "free ride" off the clean-up efforts of a community organization, or doctors who are not members of a medical lobbying group might benefit from that group's efforts—but few would argue that those "free riders" could be compelled to give money to those groups.[62] Therefore, Alito wrote, "[a]cceptance of the free-rider argument as a justification for compelling nonmembers to pay a portion of union dues represents something of an anomaly—

[58] See Locke v. Karass, 555 U.S. 207, 210 (2009) (nonmembers can be charged for national union organization's litigation expenses under some circumstances); Lehnert v. Ferris Faculty Ass'n, 500 U.S. 507 (1991) (nonmembers can be charged for pro rata share of state and local union affiliates' activities and for expenses of preparing for a strike that would have been illegal, cannot be charged for union lobbying); Ellis v. Bhd. of Ry., Airline & S.S. Clerks, 466 U.S. 435, 455–57 (1984) (nonmembers can be charged for union social activities, publications, conventions).

[59] See Knox, 132 S. Ct. at 2284–86 (nonmembers must be given notice and an opportunity to opt out of temporary fee to be used for political purposes); Hudson, 475 U.S. at 310–11 (nonmembers must be given adequate explanation of basis for fee, opportunity to challenge amount before impartial decisionmaker, and escrow for amounts reasonably in dispute).

[60] See Knox, 132 S. Ct. at 2284–86.

[61] *Id.* at 2289.

[62] See *id.* at 2289–90 (quoting Clyde Summers, Book Review: Sheldon Leader, Freedom of Association: A Study in Labor Law and Political Theory, 16 Comparative Lab. L.J. 262, 268 (1995)).

one that [the Court has] found to be justified by the interest in furthering 'labor peace.' But it is an anomaly nevertheless."[63]

Knox also expressed concern about the burden placed on nonmembers to ensure that their funds weren't used for political activity. Alito observed that requiring employees who don't want to pay for political activity to opt out—rather than requiring those who do want to pay for it to opt in—"represents a remarkable boon for unions" and asked rhetorically what justification could exist for forcing employees to take action simply to protect themselves against coerced speech.[64] "An opt-out system creates a risk that the fees paid by nonmembers will be used to further political and ideological ends with which they do not agree," which constitutes a "substantial impingement on First Amendment rights."[65] And he noted the problem, discussed above, that even those who opt out bear a "significant burden" if they want to ensure that their funds really aren't being used for impermissible political purposes.[66]

Knox declined to "revisit . . . whether the Court's former cases have given adequate recognition to the critical First Amendment rights at stake."[67] But it gave hope to those who would like to see *Abood* overturned, including the plaintiffs in *Harris v. Quinn*.

Harris v. Quinn

In *Harris*, the Seventh Circuit concluded that *Abood* controlled the outcome because, in the court's view, the Rehabilitation Program personal assistants were state employees and therefore could be made to pay union fees. It had "no difficulty" concluding that an employer-employee relationship existed between the assistants and the state based on the state's setting of qualifications, ability to refuse payments to personal assistants who do not meet its standards, approval of a mandatory "service plan" for each personal assistant, and control over "all of the economic aspects of employment," including the setting of salaries and work hours, payment for worker

---

[63] *Id.* at 2290 (internal citation omitted).

[64] *Id.*

[65] *Id.*

[66] Knox, 132 S. Ct. at 2294.

[67] Knox, 132 S. Ct. at 2289.

training, and payment of wages.[68] The court summarily rejected the assistants' argument that they were actually employed by the people they cared for because of the care recipients' exclusive ability to hire, fire, and supervise them, ruling that it was enough that the state was their "joint employer."[69]

The court also rejected the plaintiffs' argument that forcing them to support the union did not serve the interests of "labor peace" as the coerced contributions in *Abood* supposedly did. It interpreted "labor peace" broadly to include anything that would "'stabilize[] labor-management relations,' which are at issue in any employer-employee relationship, regardless of whether the employees share the same workplace."[70] Because the court considered the state and personal assistants to have an employer-employee relationship, stabilizing that relationship through coerced union support would serve the interests of labor peace.[71]

As for the personal assistants in the Disabilities Program, the court held that they lacked standing. The Disabilities Program plaintiffs argued that the existence of Quinn's executive order authorizing their unionization "ma[de] it significantly more likely that they [would] be forced to financially support [a] union's speech," creating a "reasonable probability of future harm to the plaintiffs' constitutional interests, which the plaintiffs [felt] they should not have to spend resources to defeat."[72] But the court concluded that this was a mere "hypothetical future violation" of the Disabilities Program plaintiffs' rights and therefore was not ripe.[73]

The plaintiffs then asked the Supreme Court to reverse the Seventh Circuit, not only on the basis that it had incorrectly applied *Abood*, but also on the basis that *Abood* was wrongly decided in the first place.

In a 5-4 decision, the Supreme Court reversed the Seventh Circuit's ruling on the Rehabilitation Program plaintiffs' First Amendment claims, ruling that *Abood* did not apply to the Rehabilitation

[68] Harris v. Quinn, 656 F.3d 692, 698 (7th Cir. 2011).
[69] *Id.*
[70] *Id.* at 699.
[71] *Id.*
[72] *Id.* at 700.
[73] *Id.* at 700–01.

Program plaintiffs because they were not "full-fledged" government employees. (The Court agreed with the Seventh Circuit that the Disabilities Program plaintiffs lacked standing.)[74] The Court did not overrule *Abood*, but it did take the opportunity to disparage *Abood* and cast more doubt on its long-term prospects for survival.

Writing for the same five-justice majority he had in *Knox*, Justice Alito reviewed the *Hanson* and *Street* decisions' lack of support for the Court's decision in *Abood*, as discussed above, concluding that "[t]he *Abood* Court seriously erred in treating *Hanson* and *Street* as having all but decided the constitutionality of compulsory payments to a public-sector union" because "*Street* was not a constitutional decision at all, and *Hanson* disposed of the critical question in a single, unsupported sentence that its author essentially abandoned a few years later."[75] The Court added that "[t]he *Abood* Court fundamentally misunderstood the holding in *Hanson*, which was really quite narrow. As the Court made clear in *Street*, 'all that was held in *Hanson* was that [the Railway Labor Act] was constitutional in its bare authorization of union-shop contracts requiring workers to give 'financial support' to unions legally authorized to act as their collective bargaining agents.'"[76] In *Abood*, in contrast, the government "actually imposed that fee," which "presented a very different question."[77]

The Court further criticized *Abood* for failing to distinguish between the unionization of public-sector and private-sector workers, noting that "[i]n the public sector, core issues such as wages, pensions, and benefits are important political issues, but that is generally not so in the private sector."[78] *Abood* also did not foresee the problems that would arise in attempting to separate "chargeable" and "nonchargeable" union expenditures, a "substantial judgment call" the Court has been forced to make in a number of cases since *Abood*.[79] *Abood* also "did not foresee the practical problems that

---

[74] 134 S. Ct. at 2644 n.30.

[75] *Harris*, 134 S. Ct. at 2627–32.

[76] *Id.* at 2632 (quoting Street, 367 U.S. at 749)).

[77] *Id.*

[78] *Id.*

[79] *Id.* at 2633 (citing Ellis, 466 U.S. 435; Hudson, 475 U.S. 292; Lehnert, 500 U.S. 507; Locke, 555 U.S. 207).

would face objecting nonmembers," who "must bear a heavy burden if they wish to challenge the union's actions."[80]

"Finally," the Court added, "a critical pillar of the *Abood* Court's analysis rests on an unsupported empirical assumption, namely, that the principle of exclusive representation in the public sector is dependent on a union or agency shop."[81] It was not evident that the union would be unable to represent providers without compelling nonmembers' support; after all, other successful advocacy groups rely on voluntary contributions.[82]

Despite its thorough trashing of *Abood*, the Court nonetheless declined to overrule it, because it did not have to. "Because of *Abood*'s questionable foundations," however, and also "because the personal assistants are quite different from full-fledged public employees," it refused to extend *Abood* to allow compelling Rehabilitation Program providers to support a union.

To distinguish *Harris* from *Abood*, the Court emphasized the differences between personal assistants and ordinary government employees. For true employees, the state establishes all of each person's duties, vets applicants and chooses which ones to hire, provides or arranges training, supervises and evaluates each employee's job performance, "imposes corrective measures," and may discharge the employee "in accordance with whatever procedures are required by law."[83] In contrast, personal assistants' job duties are specified in service plans approved by the customer and the customer's physician; the customer has complete discretion to hire (and fire) anyone who meets the state's basic requirements; customers supervise the personal assistants; the state has no right to enter the home to check on the assistant's job performance; the state-mandated annual review of each assistant and the assistant's work are both controlled by the customer.[84] The Court also listed the many state laws that provide benefits to state employees but not to personal assistants, including the State Employee Vacation Time Act, the State Employee Health Savings Account Law, the State Employee Job Sharing Act, the State

---

[80] Harris, 134 S. Ct. at 2633.

[81] *Id.*

[82] *Id.* at 1240–41.

[83] *Id.* at 2634.

[84] *Id.*

Employee Indemnification Act, the Sick Leave Bank Act, and the Illinois Whistleblower Act.[85] The Court also noted many other state employee benefits apparently unavailable to personal assistants, including "a deferred compensation program, full worker's compensation privileges, behavioral health programs, a program that allows state employees to retain health insurance for a time after leaving state employment, a commuter savings program, dental and vision programs, and a flexible spending program."[86] And the Court noted the state's explicit disclaimer of vicarious liability in tort, "[s]o if a personal assistant steals from a customer, neglects a customer, or abuses a customer, the state washes its hands."[87] The Court also contrasted the many things subject to collective bargaining for ordinary employees under federal law—such as "the days of the week and the hours of the day during which an employee must work, lunch breaks, holidays, vacations, termination of employment, and changes in job duties"—with the limited scope of bargaining that unions could do on personal assistants' behalf. [88]

The Court concluded that the free-rider justification, whatever its merits for ordinary government employees, "has little force" for personal assistants. "What justifies the agency fee [for ordinary government employees], the argument goes, is the fact that the state compels the union to promote and protect the interests of nonmembers."[89] That means the union cannot simply seek to benefit its members—for example, it can't seek higher wages for members only—but must seek equal benefits for all employees, and must also provide equal and effective representation to all in grievance proceedings.[90] That concern does not exist for personal assistants because Illinois law requires them all to be paid the same; "therefore the union cannot be in the position of having to sacrifice higher pay for its members in order to represent nonmembers whom it is obligated to represent."[91] As for grievances, "the union has no authority with respect to any

---

[85] *Id.* at 2635.

[86] *Id.* (footnotes omitted).

[87] *Id.*

[88] *Id.* (footnotes omitted).

[89] *Id.* at 2636 (citing Lehnert, 500 U.S. at 556 (opinion of Scalia, J.)).

[90] Harris, 134 S. Ct. at 2637 (citing 5 Ill. Comp. Stat. 315/6, 315/8).

[91] *Id.*

grievances that a personal assistant may have with a customer, and the customer has virtually complete control over a personal assistant's work."[92]

Because of those differences and *"Abood*'s questionable foundations," the Court "refuse[d] to extend *Abood*" to cover "partial-public employees, quasi-public employees, or simply private employees."[93] At least *Abood* has a relatively clear boundary: it applies to government employees. If it applied to others who receive government money, "it would be hard to see just where to draw the line," and "a host of workers who receive payments from a governmental entity would be candidates for inclusion within *Abood*'s reach."[94]

Having determined that *Abood* was not controlling, the Court performed the sort of First Amendment analysis that it should have done in *Abood* in the first place but did not. Citing *Knox*, the Court noted that forcing anyone to pay agency fees to a union "imposes 'a significant impingement on First Amendment rights'" and therefore "cannot be tolerated unless it passes 'exacting First Amendment scrutiny.'"[95] The Court then easily concluded that the agency-fee provision at issue could not survive exacting scrutiny because it "does not serve a compelling governmental interest that cannot be achieved through means significantly less restrictive of associational freedoms."[96]

"Labor peace," whatever its merits as a justification in *Abood*, was not a compelling governmental interest in this context. If personal assistants were not forced to pay agency fees, the government would not have to contend with conflicting claims by rival unions because the assistants did not seek to create a rival union; "all they [sought was] the right not to be forced to contribute to the union, with which they broadly disagree."[97] And in any event, there was no need to actually maintain "peace" in a workplace "because the personal assistants do not work together in a common state facility but instead spend all their time in private homes, either the customers' or their

---

[92] *Id.*

[93] *Id.* at 2638.

[94] *Id.*

[95] *Id.* at 2639 (quoting Knox, 132 S. Ct. at 2289).

[96] Harris, 134 S. Ct. at 2639 (internal marks omitted).

[97] *Id.* at 2640.

own."[98] The "specter of conflicting demands by personal assistants" was also lessened by the union's ability to bargain for little more than greater pay and benefits—"[a]nd, of course, state officials must deal on a daily basis with conflicting pleas for funding in many contexts."[99]

The Court also rejected the purported benefits provided to personal assistants as a justification for making them pay fees. A fatal problem with that argument was the lack of evidence that the union could not achieve the same results by relying on voluntary funding. After all, the state in this context "is not like the closed-fisted employer that is bent on minimizing employee wages and benefits and that yields only grudgingly under intense union pressure"[100] —its stated purpose for unionizing personal assistants was to get "feedback" about their needs. There is no reason to think that the dues paid by personal assistants who are willing to pay them would not be enough for the union to provide "feedback" to its apparently eager audience in government.[101]

The Court rejected an argument that it should apply a "balancing test" derived from *Pickering v. Board of Education*, under which government employees' speech is not protected if it does not pertain to matters of public concern, and their speech on matters of public concern may be restricted "only if 'the interest of the state, as an employer, in promoting the efficiency of the public services it performs through its employees' outweighs 'the interests of the [employee], as a citizen, in commenting upon matters of public concern.'"[102] In the view of the U.S. government (as amicus) and the dissent, the union speech at issue did not pertain to matters of public concern.[103] The Court cited evidence to the contrary regarding the impact of Medicaid expenditures on state budgets.[104]

The Court also rejected an argument that its ruling would undermine the Court's decisions approving integrated bar fees and

[98] *Id.*

[99] *Id.*

[100] *Id.* at 2641.

[101] *Id.*

[102] *Id.* at 2642 (quoting Pickering, 391 U.S. 563, 568 (1968)).

[103] Harris, 134 S. Ct. at 2642; *id.* at 2655 (Kagan, J., dissenting).

[104] *Id.* at 2642.

student-activity fees.[105] Bar fees used in connection with "proposing ethical codes and disciplining bar members" served the government's interests in regulating the legal profession and having members of the bar, rather than the public, bear the costs of keeping lawyers ethical.[106] Student fees were "viewpoint neutral" and helped promote expression by a "broad array of student groups."[107] Neither of those cases, the Court implied, required individuals to pay funds specifically to support lobbying activity from a particular perspective as mandatory union fees do.

Is *Abood* Doomed?

Justice Elena Kagan's dissenting opinion in *Harris*, joined by the other three "liberal" justices, argues primarily that it doesn't make sense to treat personal assistants any differently from ordinary government employees for First Amendment purposes simply because the government has chosen to give the "customer" authority over some aspects of their relationship.[108] In the dissent's view, the majority creates a "perverse result" by essentially punishing the state for administering its program in a decentralized manner that "respect[s] the dignity and independence of program beneficiaries."[109]

Kagan has a point. Should a person's First Amendment right to not support a union turn on whether his or her relationship with the state crosses some arbitrary line into "employment"? And if Illinois and other states restructure their benefit programs to make caregivers more like employees—if they start making people like Pam Harris contribute to state pension funds and convert some of their subsidy money into state-employee "benefits" they never asked for—would that make forcing them to pay union fees any more just? The results—greater government control over personal assistants and the people they care for *and* coerced union fees—could indeed be "perverse."

---

[105] *Id.* at 2643–44 (citing Keller v. State Bar of Ca., 496 U.S. 1 (1990); Bd. of Regents of Univ. of Wis. Sys. v. Southworth, 529 U.S. 217 (2000)).

[106] Harris, 134 S. Ct. at 2543–44 (citing Keller, 496 U.S. at 14).

[107] Harris, 134 S. Ct. at 2544.

[108] *Id.* at 2645–51 (Kagan, J., dissenting).

[109] *Id.* at 2651 (Kagan, J., dissenting).

So arguably *Harris* does introduce some (more) arbitrariness into the law. But that's not a reason why the Court should have upheld Illinois's infringements on personal assistants' First Amendment rights; it's a reason why the Court should have gone all the way and overruled *Abood*.

The majority's evisceration of *Abood* strongly suggests that the five justices in the majority are ready to overrule it in a case that forces the issue. *Stare decisis* seems unlikely to restrain them. In *Citizens United*, the majority opinion joined by these same justices stated that the Court "has not hesitated to overrule decisions offensive to the First Amendment" and overruled a 20-year-old precedent.[110] *Citizens United* identified several factors that the Court considers in deciding whether to overturn precedent: "the antiquity of the precedent, the reliance interests at stake, . . . whether the decision was well reasoned, . . . [and] whether experience has pointed up the precedent's shortcomings."[111] The *Harris* majority certainly considers *Abood* to be poorly reasoned, and its decision discusses "practical administrative problems" regarding classification of union expenditures and "practical problems [facing] objecting nonmembers" that *Abood* "did not foresee," which suggests that the justices believe that experience has exposed *Abood*'s shortcomings. As for the other two factors, *Knox*'s concern for the injustice that mandatory fees inevitably cause to dissenting union members suggests that the justices would not give much weight to the unions' "reliance" interest in preserving the flow of funds from dissenters (and taxpayers) to their coffers, even if they have been getting away with it for a long time. Of course, the Court's composition could change by the time the next challenge to *Abood* arrives—and the liberal wing has made clear that it is committed to *Abood* both on its merits and as a matter of *stare decisis*.[112]

In any event, *Harris* is a victory for First Amendment rights that will benefit thousands of Americans. Illinois personal assistants will no longer be forced to pay for union speech they disagree with. Neither will other subsidy recipients in similar programs. Illinois

---

[110] Citizens United v. FEC, 558 U.S. 310, 363 (2010) (quoting FEC v. Wis. Right to Life, 551 U.S. 449, 500 (2007) (opinion of Scalia, J.)).

[111] Citizens United, 558 U.S. at 363 (internal marks omitted). See also Ilya Shapiro & Nicholas Mosvick, *Stare Decisis* After *Citizens United*: When Should Courts Overturn Precedent, 16 Nexus: Chapman's J. L. & Pol'y 121 (2011).

[112] Harris, 134 S. Ct. at 2651–53 (Kagan, J., dissenting).

day care providers, for example, have already taken advantage of *Harris* to escape the forced unionization that Governor Blagojevich imposed on them in 2005. After the Supreme Court issued *Harris*, my colleagues and I at the Liberty Justice Center and the Illinois Policy Institute helped one of those day care providers, Laura Baston, petition Governor Quinn to stop taking union fees from day care providers in light of the Supreme Court's decision. We didn't think the state and SEIU would give that money up without a fight—we were ready to file a lawsuit—but they backed down. In a letter responding to Baston, the state said that, in light of *Harris*, it and SEIU had decided to immediately stop taking union fees from any day care provider who had not signed a union card.[113] At this writing, Connecticut has suspended the collection of agency fees from personal assistants,[114] and other states are likely to follow. If any state doesn't comply, the National Right to Work Legal Defense Foundation and others will no doubt be ready to go to court to make sure they do[115]—until no one is forced to give money to a union simply because he or she receives a government subsidy.

Meanwhile, *Harris* has forced public-sector unions to try a new "experiment": persuading people to give them money voluntarily to advance their ideas, just like the rest of us have to.[116]

---

[113] Press Release, Illinois Policy Institute, Unionized Illinois Daycare Providers No Longer Forced to Pay $10 Million to SEIU (July 31, 2014), available at http://www.illinoispolicy.org/press_releases/unionized-illinois-daycare-providers-no-longer-forced-to-pay-10-million-to-seiu/.

[114] Hugh McQuaid, State Delays Collection of Union Fees, CTNewsJunkie (July 21, 2014), http://www.ctnewsjunkie.com/archives/entry/state_delays_collection_of_union_dues/.

[115] Less than one month after the Court's decision in *Harris*, the National Right to Work Legal Defense Foundation sued to enjoin the forced unionization of home-care providers in Minnesota. See Press Release, National Right to Work Legal Defense Foundation, Minnesota Homecare Providers File Federal Lawsuit Challenging Forced Unionization Scheme (July 28, 2014), available at http://www.nrtw.org/en/press/2014/07/minnesota-homecare-providers-file-federal-suit-07282014.

[116] David Moberg, Has AFSCME Found the Cure to *Harris v. Quinn?*, In These Times (July 16, 2014), http://inthesetimes.com/working/entry/16963/has_afscme_found_the_cure_to_harris.

NLRB v. Noel Canning: The Separation-of-Powers Dialogue Continues

*Bryan J. Leitch**

I. Introduction

In *National Labor Relations Board v. Noel Canning*, the Supreme Court unanimously invalidated President Obama's 2012 recess appointments to the National Labor Relations Board (NLRB).[1] Under the Recess Appointments Clause, the president has authority to "fill up all vacancies that may happen during the Recess of the Senate, by granting Commissions which shall expire at the End of their next Session."[2] Writing for a five-justice majority, Justice Stephen Breyer concluded that the president's authority under that clause was constrained by, among other things, the Senate's "authority . . . to determine how and when to conduct its business."[3] If the Senate is in session—or its break in business is not sufficiently long—the president has no constitutional authority to make recess appointments. Thus, because the president's 2012 recess appointments were made during an "[in]substantial" break in Senate business, all nine justices agreed that "the President lacked the power to make the recess appointments here at issue."[4]

* Associate, Jones Day, and part of the litigation team in *NLRB v. Noel Canning*. The views set forth herein are the personal views of the author and do not necessarily reflect those of the law firm with which he is associated. The author wishes to thank Noel Francisco and James Burnham for the opportunity to write this article and valuable edits, Richard Re for extraordinarily helpful criticism and feedback on an earlier draft, and Jordan L. Von Bokern for preliminary research assistance.

[1] NLRB v. Noel Canning, 134 S. Ct. 2550 (2014).

[2] U.S. Const. art. I, § 2, cl. 3.

[3] Noel Canning, 134 S. Ct. at 2574.

[4] *Id.* at 2557; see also *id.* at 2591–92 (Scalia, J., concurring in the judgment).

Broadly stated, *Noel Canning* involved a structural tension between the executive branch—which operates continuously—and the legislative branch—which operates periodically in sessions separated by recesses. On one hand, the Appointments Clause grants the Senate authority to participate in the appointment of executive officers—and to prevent such appointments by withholding its advice and consent.[5] On the other side of the ledger, however, the Recess Appointments Clause permits the president to appoint executive officers unilaterally for limited periods when the Senate is in recess.[6]

In *Noel Canning*, the Court unanimously reaffirmed the structural relationship between the Appointments and Recess Appointments Clauses. As Alexander Hamilton made clear in Federalist 67, while the latter serves as a narrow, "auxiliary method of appointment," the former's requirement of advice and consent remains "the general mode of appointing officers of the United States."[7] On the basis of that structural logic, the Court concluded that the president could not utilize the recess-appointments power in a way that circumvented the Senate's power of advice and consent. Otherwise, the recess-appointments exception would swallow the advice-and-consent rule.

Despite the unanimity of the Court's holding, however, the majority and concurring opinions differed greatly in their respective methodologies. For Justice Breyer and those members of the Court joining his opinion, the Recess Appointments Clause was to be read broadly in light of its functional purposes of ensuring convenient executive administration. For Justice Antonin Scalia and the three justices joining his concurrence, the clause's text was dispositive and its purposes largely irrelevant. Like other structural features of the Constitution, Justice Scalia argued, the Recess Appointments Clause was not a generic "good government" provision; it was instead one component of a carefully calibrated division of authority designed to ensure the liberty of citizens—not the efficiency of government.

This article discusses the origins of the *Noel Canning* litigation and evaluates the significance of the Court's decision. In analyzing the majority and concurring opinions, the article shows not only that

---

[5] U.S. Const. art. I, § 2, cl. 2.

[6] U.S. Const. art. I, § 2, cl. 3.

[7] The Federalist No. 67 (Alexander Hamilton).

the debate between Justices Breyer and Scalia continues long-standing jurisprudential conversations regarding separation-of-powers principles, but also that both opinions highlight important, under-examined features of that dialogue. Indeed, just as Howard Bashman predicted in the pages of this journal last year, *Noel Canning* provides a "noteworthy opportunity for comparing and contrasting the justices' varied approaches to constitutional construction."[8]

Part II lays out the origins of the *Noel Canning* litigation and the relevant legal background. Part III provides an overview of the Court's decisions, describing the analyses and conclusions of the majority and concurring opinions. Part IV analyzes the key constitutional themes in the *Noel Canning* opinions, situating them within broader conversations about the division of federal power and the role of text and history in constitutional law. Finally, Part V discusses the implications of the *Noel Canning* decision. Ultimately, this article argues that the Court reached the correct result in *Noel Canning* and that the case provides unique insight into the Constitution's separation of powers.

II. Background

A. Factual Background

The events underlying *Noel Canning* began on January 4, 2012, when President Obama made three recess appointments to the National Labor Relations Board.[9] Like many others in the modern era, each of those appointments filled a vacancy that arose during a session of the Senate rather than "during the Recess." But, unlike any other recess appointment in American history, these occurred during a three-day period falling between so-called "pro forma" sessions of the Senate.

The Senate convened pro forma sessions on January 3 and 6, 2012, pursuant to its formal adjournment order entered in December 2011. Under that order, the Senate agreed to meet every three days between December 17, 2011, and January, 20, 2012, in pro forma sessions in

---

[8] See Howard J. Bashman, Looking Ahead: October Term 2013, 2012–2013 Cato Sup. Ct. Rev. 393, 394–95 (2013).

[9] The president also recess-appointed Richard Cordray to the Consumer Financial Protection Bureau on January 4, 2012. See, e.g., Nat'l Bank of Big Spring v. Lew, 958 F. Supp. 2d 127 (D.D.C. 2013).

which "no business" would be conducted.[10] But although it agreed to avoid official action at these pro forma sessions, the Senate remained fully capable of performing its duties under its rules of procedure. Not only did the Senate's rules permit legislative business during these pro forma sessions,[11] but the Senate in fact passed tax-related legislation during its pro forma session on December 23, 2011.[12]

The Senate's pro forma sessions, moreover, not only possess the functional characteristics of "normal" sessions, but also have historical pedigree and constitutional justification. As a functional matter, the Senate regularly passes legislation and confirms nominees through the same procedures available during pro forma sessions. Because the Senate possesses a presumptive quorum at all times—regardless of a session's length—many of its legislative acts occur via unanimous consent.[13] Historically, while such meetings have been more prevalent in recent years, the Senate has employed pro forma sessions since at least the "Renovation of the Hall" in 1854, when it met every three days without conducting business so that renovations to the Senate Chamber could be completed.[14] Pro forma sessions also serve an important constitutional function as well. Because the Constitution's Adjournments Clause prohibits one chamber of Congress from adjourning for more than three days without the consent of the other,[15] the Senate has often used pro forma sessions to keep its breaks in business under three days.[16] And, as the Senate did in January 2012, it has occasionally utilized pro forma sessions in order to satisfy its obligations under the Twentieth Amendment—which requires Congress to meet every year at noon on January 3 to mark

---

[10] 157 Cong. Rec. S8783–84 (daily ed. Dec. 13, 2011).

[11] See Floyd M. Riddick, Riddick's Senate Procedure 1038 (Alan S. Frumin ed., 1992).

[12] See The Temporary Payroll Tax Cut Continuation Act of 2011, Pub. L. No. 112-78, 125 Stat. 1281 (2011).

[13] See, e.g., Elizabeth Rybicki, Cong. Research Serv., Senate Consideration of Presidential Nominations: Committee and Floor Procedure 9 (2013) ("Most nominations are brought up by unanimous consent and approved without objection . . . .").

[14] See, e.g., Cong. Globe, 33d Cong., 1st Sess. 1347 (1854).

[15] U.S. Const. art. I, § 5, cl. 4.

[16] Indeed, this was the very reason for the Senate's 1854 pro forma sessions. The House would not consent to an adjournment exceeding three days in order to complete renovations and therefore the Senate met in pro forma sessions in order to ensure the constitutionality of its processes. See, e.g., Cong. Globe, 33d Cong., 1st Sess. 1347 (1854).

the beginning of a new session, "unless they shall by law appoint a different day."[17]

But despite the Senate's presumptive availability between December 17, 2011, and January 20, 2012, the administration concluded that it was not "bound by the Chamber's own understanding of [its] pro forma sessions."[18] Rather, in the administration's view, the president had discretion to determine the nature of the Senate's operations and to determine whether the Senate was in session or in recess for purposes of the recess-appointments power. Deeming the Senate's pro forma sessions illegitimate, and accordingly deciding for itself that the Senate was in recess, the administration went forward with its recess appointments on January 4, 2012.

The unprecedented nature of the administration's action, however, drew widespread objection. Many questioned not only the political legitimacy of the president's recess appointments, but also their constitutionality. As Richard Epstein wrote in January 2012, "it *is for the Senate and not for the President to determine whether the Senate is in session,*" and therefore the Senate's pro forma sessions precluded the existence of a Senate recess and rendered the president's appointments unconstitutional.[19] The administration and its supporters, however, remained steadfast in their view that the appointments were fully consistent with "the text of the Constitution and precedent and practice thereunder."[20]

As that controversy persisted, the newly recess-appointed NLRB members began hearing and deciding cases within days of receiving their commissions. One of the earliest cases they decided involved the Noel Canning Corporation of Yakima, Washington ("Noel Canning"). Although the recess-appointee NLRB did not oversee Noel Canning's September 2011 hearing, that incarnation of the board did issue a formal order against Noel Canning, finding it guilty of

---

[17] U.S. Const. amend. XX, § 2.

[18] Lawfulness of Recess Appointments during a Recess of the Senate Notwithstanding Periodic Pro Forma Sessions, Op. O.L.C. 1, 20 (2012) ("OLC Memo").

[19] Richard Epstein, The Constitution Is Clear on Recess Appointments, Ricochet (Jan. 5, 2012), http://ricochet.com/archives/the-constitution-is-clear-on-recess-appointments/ (last visited July 30, 2014).

[20] OLC Memo at 23; see also Laurence H. Tribe, Games and Gimmicks in the Senate, N.Y. Times, Jan. 5, 2012, at A25.

alleged unfair labor practices.[21] Shortly thereafter, Noel Canning appealed the NLRB's decision to the U.S. Court of Appeals for the D.C. Circuit.

B. Procedural Background

1. Noel Canning *in the D.C. Circuit*

On appeal to the D.C. Circuit, Noel Canning argued that the president's NLRB appointments violated the Recess Appointments Clause, and accordingly the NLRB lacked jurisdiction to issue a binding order against Noel Canning. Under the Supreme Court's 2010 decision in *New Process Steel*, the NLRB must have a lawful, three-member quorum in order to exercise jurisdiction.[22] But because these recess appointments were not made "during the Recess of the Senate," and because the vacancies at issue had not "happen[ed] during the Recess," the board issuing the order against Noel Canning comprised only *one* lawfully appointed member. As a result, Noel Canning argued that the unconstitutionality of the January 4, 2012, recess appointments divested the NLRB of jurisdiction and thus the board's order was *ultra vires* and unenforceable.[23]

The D.C. Circuit unanimously agreed with Noel Canning's originalist construction of the recess-appointments power.[24] As the court explained, "the Recess of the Senate" referred to the formal recess that takes place between formal sessions. It did not include informal, intra-session breaks in Senate business, even if those periods qualified as recesses in a colloquial sense. Moreover, the clause requires that the relevant vacancy must "happen during the Recess," which meant that it must arise during the same inter-session recess in which it is filled. In sum, because the Senate had been in an intra-session recess on January 4, 2012, and because the vacancies predated that recess, the president was without authority to make these unilateral appointments. The panel thus unanimously invalidated the NLRB appointments, and accordingly determined that the board

---

[21] See Noel Canning, 358 NLRB No. 4 (Feb. 8, 2012).

[22] See New Process Steel L.P. v. NLRB, 130. S. Ct. 2635 (2010).

[23] Joint Brief of Petitioner, Noel Canning v. NLRB., 705 F.3d 490 (D.C. Cir. 2012) (No. 12-1115).

[24] Noel Canning v. NLRB, 705 F.3d 490 (D.C. Cir. 2013).

lacked a jurisdictionally necessary quorum when issuing its order against Noel Canning.

The D.C. Circuit's analysis of the Recess Appointments Clause, however, differed from that of its sister circuits in earlier cases. Beginning with the Second Circuit's decision in *United States v. Allocco* in 1962, federal appellate courts had largely deferred to presidents on their use of the recess-appointments power, holding in essence that the text of the clause must yield to executive practices and "the orderly functioning of the government."[25] In *Evans v. Stephens*, the Eleventh Circuit sitting en banc went so far as to accord a presumption of constitutionality to all presidential uses of the recess-appointments power.[26]

But things changed following the D.C. Circuit's opinion in *Noel Canning*. In a series of related cases, a number of courts—including the Third and Fourth Circuits—held the president's January 4 recess appointments unconstitutional.[27] And while other circuits either avoided the constitutional issue or were constrained by precedent to decide the matter differently, it was clear that the tide shifted in the wake of the D.C. Circuit's decision. [28] As a result of these mounting challenges, the government sought a writ of certiorari from the Supreme Court in *Noel Canning*.

2. Noel Canning *in the Supreme Court*

Certiorari Stage. In its certiorari petition, the government initially sought review of only two questions: whether the recess-appointment power must be exercised during an inter-session recess, and whether the vacancy in question must arise during the same recess

---

[25] See United States v. Allocco, 305 F.2d 704, 710–11 (2d Cir. 1962); see also Evans v. Stephens, 387 F.3d 1220 (11th Cir. 2004) (en banc); United States v. Woodley, 751 F.2d 1008 (9th Cir. 1985) (en banc); Mackie v. Clinton, 827 F. Supp. 56, 57 (D.D.C. 1993); Staebler v. Carter, 464 F. Supp. 585 (D.D.C. 1979).

[26] See Evans, 387 F.3d at 1222.

[27] See, e.g., NLRB v. Enter. Leasing Co. Se., LLC, 722 F.3d 609 (4th Cir. 2013); NLRB v. New Vista Nursing & Rehab., 719 F.3d 203 (3d Cir. 2013).

[28] See, e.g., D.R. Horton, Inc. v. NLRB, 737 F.3d 344, 350–51 (5th Cir. 2013); Kreisberg v. HealthBridge Mgmt., LLC, 732 F.3d 131, 137 (2d Cir. 2013); Ambassador Servs., Inc. v. NLRB, 544 F. App'x 846, 847 (11th Cir. 2013) (per curiam).

in which it is filled.[29] Noel Canning did not oppose the government's request for certiorari, but it did ask the Court to consider a third question: "Whether the President's recess-appointment power may be exercised when the Senate is convening every three days in pro forma sessions."[30]

Although the D.C. Circuit had not addressed that issue, it provided an independent basis for affirmance. If the Senate's periodic pro forma sessions counted as constitutionally legitimate "sessions" of the Senate, then the January 4 appointments were unconstitutional regardless of the Court's resolution of the other issues. Even if the recess-appointments power extended to pre-recess vacancies, and even if it extended to both inter- and intra-session recesses, a three-day break in Senate business did not count as a "Recess of the Senate" within the meaning of the clause.

Ultimately, the Court granted certiorari on June 24, 2013. Rejecting the government's request to ignore Noel Canning's question regarding pro forma sessions, the Court asked the parties to address three issues: (1) whether the president's recess-appointment power may be exercised during a recess that occurs within a session of the Senate, or is instead limited to recesses that occur between sessions of the Senate; (2) whether the president's recess-appointment power may be exercised to fill vacancies that exist during a recess, or is instead limited to vacancies that first arose during that recess; and (3) whether the president's recess-appointment power may be exercised when the Senate is convening every three days in pro forma sessions.[31]

Merits Briefing. On the first question, the government argued that the "the term 'recess' . . . applie[d] to both inter- and intrasession recesses," based on its "plain meaning," the "central purposes" of the Recess Appointments Clause, and what it viewed as a robust history of executive practices and the "long-settled equilibrium between the political Branches."[32] On the second question presented, the govern-

[29] Petition for Certiorari at I, NLRB v. Noel Canning, 134 S. Ct. 2550 (2014) (No. 12-1281).

[30] Brief of Respondent on Petition for Certiorari at i, 9, NLRB v. Noel Canning, 134 S. Ct. 2550 (2014) (No. 12-1281).

[31] See NLRB v. Noel Canning, 133 S. Ct. 2861, 2861–23 (2013).

[32] Brief for the Petitioner at 7–8, NLRB v. Noel Canning, 134 S. Ct. 2550 (2014) (No. 12-1281).

ment contended that "the Clause's reference to 'Vacancies that may happen during the Recess of the Senate'" was "ambiguous," and thus the Court should construe it broadly to include vacancies that arise during the recess in which they are filled, as well as vacancies that arise before a recess while the Senate is still in session.[33] According to the government, the broader reading was not only consistent "with long-settled practice," but also "best served" the "Clause's purposes" by "ensur[ing] a genuine opportunity at all times for vacancies to be filled, even if only temporarily."[34] On the final question, the government contended that the Senate's pro forma sessions could not "extinguish the President's express constitutional authority to make recess appointments."[35] Rather, in the government's view, "[w]hen the Senate is absent in fact but present only by virtue of a legal fiction," the president may make unilateral appointments "when the Senate is unavailable to provide its advice and consent and there are vacancies that the public interest requires to be filled, even if only on a *temporary basis.*"[36]

Noel Canning and its amici, by contrast, contended that the government's position would "eradicate all meaningful limits on the President's recess-appointments power."[37] It would do so by permitting unilateral appointments "(1) *whenever* the President deems appropriate, so long as he believes there has been a 'cessation' in the Senate Session (or, perhaps, a cessation exceeding three days); (2) to fill *whatever* office the President chooses, no matter how long vacant; and (3) *regardless* of whether the Senate is convening regularly."[38] On the first question, Noel Canning argued that, by linking "the Recess" and "the Session," "the Clause makes clear that the President may make unilateral appointments only during 'the Recess' between enumerated Senate 'Sessions.'"[39] On the second question, Noel Canning contended that "the text means what it says: The vacancy must 'happen during'—*i.e.*, arise during—the Recess." The

33 *Id.*

34 *Id.* at 8.

35 *Id.* at 9.

36 *Id.* at 11.

37 Brief for Respondent at 1–2, NLRB v. Noel Canning, 134 S. Ct. 2550 (2014) (No. 12-1281).

38 *Id.* (emphasis in original).

39 *Id.* at 6.

government's contrary reading "erases 'may happen during' from the Clause, while contravening the uniform understanding of the framers."[40] Finally, the Senate's pro forma sessions were not, as the government suggested, "constitutional nullities." They were instead official meetings "at which the Senate could and did conduct official business," and therefore the three-day break between the pro forma sessions was—as the government conceded—insufficient to "'trigger the President's recess-appointment authority.'"[41]

Oral Argument. On January 13, 2014, the Court held argument in *Noel Canning.* During oral argument, several themes emerged that would feature prominently in the Court's ultimate decision. The first involved competing characterizations of the clause's purpose as well as the substantive aims of the Constitution's tripartite structure.[42] The government argued, as it had in its briefs, that the recess-appointments power was a "safety valve" designed to "protect the Executive against encroachment by the legislature."[43] On that view of the clause's purpose and functional properties, Solicitor General Donald Verrilli argued that Noel Canning's interpretation "would diminish presidential authority in a way that is flatly at odds with the constitutional structure the Framers established."[44]

Justice Breyer, however, appeared skeptical of the government's safety-valve characterization. "I can't find anything," he exclaimed, "that says the purpose of this clause [h]as anything at all to do with political fights between Congress and the President."[45] "To the contrary," Justice Breyer went on, "Hamilton says that the way we're going to appoint people in this country is Congress and the President have to agree."[46] But reaching "that agreement" is "a political problem, not a constitutional problem."[47] The pace of the subsequent

[40] *Id.* at 6–7.

[41] *Id.* at 7 (quoting the Govt's Brief at 18).

[42] See, e.g., Transcript of Oral Argument at 3, 21–24, 31–34, 48–49, 64–65, 71–72, NLRB v. Noel Canning, 134 S. Ct. 2550 (2014) (No. 12-1281). Justice Breyer, for one, was particularly concerned with the "purpose" of the clause and the "practicalities" of the parties' interpretations. See *id.* at 49.

[43] *Id.* at 21, 22.

[44] *Id.* at 3.

[45] *Id.* at 31.

[46] *Id.*

[47] *Id.*

questioning prevented the solicitor general from fully answering these issues. But the message was clear: Justice Breyer harbored serious doubts that the clause was a safety valve designed "to allow the President to try to overcome political disagreement."[48]

Picking up on Justice Breyer's line of questioning, Noel Canning's counsel, Noel Francisco of Jones Day, characterized the clause as an auxiliary method of appointment and disputed the notion that the clause's purpose was to permit the president to fill vacancies any time the Senate was unavailable. Rather, Francisco argued, the "full purpose of the clause" was "to ensure that the President could not easily do an end-run around advice and consent."[49] After all, the clause embodies a "contingent power that arises only when the Senate triggers it"[50]—and thus, "the one thing that the President may not do is force the Senate to act against its will."[51] Regardless of the practical inefficiencies of the advice-and-consent rule, Francisco argued, the Court should "enforc[e] the strictures of the Constitution"[52] and reject the government's attempt to "creat[e] a unilateral appointments power available for every vacancy at virtually any time with advice and consent to be used only when convenient to the President."[53]

The second theme pervading the *Noel Canning* argument involved the proper approach to interpreting the Constitution when the document's text conflicts with purportedly entrenched government practices. Early in the argument, for example, Justice Scalia pointedly asked the solicitor general: "What do you do when there is a practice that . . . flatly contradicts a clear text of the Constitution? Which . . . of the two prevails?"[54] The underlying premise of Justice Scalia's question, which he made explicit moments later, was that it simply cannot be the case that "if you ignore the Constitution . . . often enough, its meaning changes."[55]

---

48 *Id.* at 32.
49 *Id.* at 60.
50 *Id.* at 54; see also *id.* at 52, 60.
51 *Id.* at 42.
52 *Id.* at 65–67.
53 *Id.* at 41.
54 *Id.* at 6.
55 See, e.g., *id.*

In response, Verrilli offered a nuanced, if somewhat evasive, answer. Initially, he responded that "the practice has to prevail."[56] But after additional questioning from the bench he attempted to clarify his answer. He argued that, "in this situation, the meaning of the clause . . . has been a matter of contention since the first days of the Republic," and thus this is not a case in which clear constitutional text is pitted against a contrary historical practice.[57] But even if the text were clear, the solicitor general further clarified, "the practice should govern" when, as here, "the practice go[es] back to the founding of the Republic."[58]

By contrast, Noel Canning's counsel offered a dramatically different answer to a variant of the same question. When asked by Justice Samuel Alito what the Court should do if "a 200-year-old consistent practice" contradicted clear constitutional text, Francisco responded "that the language has to govern."[59] And when pushed further by Justice Elena Kagan, he made clear the structural and normative premises for privileging the text over the practice. "The political branches of the government," he argued, "have no authority to give or take away the structural protections of the Constitution."[60] Rather than "exist[ing] to protect the Senate from the President or the President from the Senate," the Constitution's structural edicts are "liberty-protecting provisions that protect the people from the government as a whole."[61] Therefore, Francisco contended, "if the Constitution is quite clear as to what those structural protections are, but the political branches . . . have conspired to deplete them, that is illegitimate, and it should be rejected by this Court."[62]

While these were not the only noteworthy colloquies that occurred at oral argument in *Noel Canning*,[63] they are important to understanding the decision the Court ultimately rendered. In the justices'

---

[56] *Id.*

[57] *Id.* at 6–8.

[58] *Id.* at 8.

[59] *Id.* at 42–43.

[60] *Id.* at 44.

[61] *Id.*

[62] *Id.* at 44–45.

[63] Another critically important discussion surrounded the issue of the Senate's institutional autonomy. See *id.* at 22, 25–28, 38–39, 42, 57, 67–70. That issue is discussed more fully in Part V.A.1.

questions and the advocates' answers, one can see that the fulcrum of the dispute in *Noel Canning* was an overlapping series of tensions between text and formalism, on the one hand, and historical practice and functionalism on the other.

III. The Court's Decision in *Noel Canning*: An Overview

On the next-to-last day of the October 2013 term, the Supreme Court issued its decision in *Noel Canning*, unanimously holding that the president's January 4, 2012, recess appointments were unconstitutional.[64] The case produced two opinions. Justice Breyer wrote for a five-justice majority, which included Justices Anthony Kennedy, Ruth Bader Ginsburg, Sonia Sotomayor, and Elena Kagan. Justice Scalia, however, wrote an opinion concurring only in the judgment, which was joined in full by Chief Justice John Roberts as well as Justices Clarence Thomas and Samuel Alito.

In the majority's view, the president exceeded the bounds of his authority under the Recess Appointments Clause, because the January 4 recess appointments were not made during "the Recess" of the Senate. Because the Senate's pro forma sessions on January 3 and January 6 were legitimate meetings of that legislative body, and because three days is simply too short a period to count as a "Recess" for purposes of the clause, the president had no authority on January 4 to appoint executive officers without the advice and consent of the Senate. In so holding, the Court adopted Noel Canning's position on the third question presented—the same question Noel Canning had requested the Court to address in seeking certiorari.

Justice Scalia, however, took a different approach to reaching the same ultimate conclusion. Although he did not squarely address Noel Canning's position on pro forma Senate sessions, Scalia reasoned that the January 4 appointments were unconstitutional first and foremost because they were inconsistent with the "key textual limitations" in the Recess Appointments Clause.[65] A close examination of the text, he contended, revealed that the president's power to make unilateral appointments exists only when the Senate is in a formal, inter-session recess and the vacancy filled arose *during* that same recess. In *Noel Canning*, Justice Scalia concluded that neither

[64] NLRB v. Noel Canning, 134 S. Ct. 2550 (2014).

[65] *Id.* at 2591–92 (Scalia, J., concurring in the judgment).

precondition of the recess-appointments power was satisfied. First, the Senate was not in the midst of an inter-session recess on January 4, 2012, because the break in business between January 3 and 6 did not fall between formal enumerated sessions of the Senate. Second, as a factual matter, neither side could dispute that the NLRB vacancies at issue arose long *before* the Senate's informal break between January 3 and 6, 2012. Although Scalia responded to the majority's arguments grounded in custom and historical practices, his opinion found the text of the clause conclusive.

IV. Constitutional Themes in *Noel Canning*

The justices' resolution of the critical interpretive questions in *Noel Canning* reveals a great deal about constitutional interpretation in general and separation-of-powers jurisprudence in particular. This part outlines two overarching themes that pervade the majority and concurring opinions in *Noel Canning*. First, the opinions vivify and complicate the tension between functionalist and formalist approaches to deciding separation-of-powers issues. Second, the opinions highlight the role of written and unwritten sources of law in constitutional adjudication.

A. Separation of Powers: Functionalism and Formalism

As a matter of doctrine and theory, questions about the Constitution's separation of powers are generally approached from either a *functionalist* or a *formalist* perspective.[66] Although the terminology varies, functionalist approaches typically decide separation-of-powers questions by evaluating the purposes of the power at issue and the relative competencies of the competing branches. By contrast, a formalist approach decides such disputes principally according to the literal terms of the Constitution, drawing structural inferences where appropriate but generally limiting itself to textual considerations.

Both on and off the bench, Justices Scalia and Breyer have been important participants in this debate. A self-identified pragmatic–purposivist, Justice Breyer has long adhered to the functionalist

---

[66] See, e.g., John F. Manning, Separation of Powers as Ordinary Interpretation, 124 Harv. L. Rev. 1939, 1942 (2011).

program in deciding separation-of-powers cases.[67] Whether concurring, dissenting, or writing for a majority of the Court, Justice Breyer's approach to such questions can best be described as flexible, embodying a general reluctance to articulate strict rules when differentiating among the federal branches.[68] Only when governmental action "embodies risks of the very sort that our Constitution's 'separation-of-powers' prohibition seeks to avoid," Justice Breyer has written, should the Court hold such action unconstitutional—and even then only if there are no "offsetting . . . safeguards" to "minimize those risks."[69]

Justice Scalia, on the other hand, is the Court's most ardent separation-of-powers formalist.[70] In a series of forceful and influential opinions, Justice Scalia has articulated a vision of the Constitution's structure as embodying bright-line prophylactic rules that demand rigorous and consistent judicial enforcement.[71] In contrast to the pragmatism of Justice Breyer, Justice Scalia has stressed that "the separation of powers doctrine is a structural safeguard rather than a remedy to be applied only when specific harm, or risk of specific harm, can be identified."[72] Although practical considerations "may be appropriate at the margins, where the outline of the framework itself is not clear," courts must not "treat the Constitution as though it were no more than a generalized prescription that the functions of the Branches should not be commingled too much."[73]

---

[67] See, e.g., Stephen Breyer, Making Our Democracy Work: A Judge's View 73–75, 81–82 (2010); Stephen Breyer, Active Liberty: Interpreting Our Democratic Constitution 128 (2007).

[68] See, e.g., Free Enter. Fund v. Pub. Co. Accounting Oversight Bd., 561 U.S. 477 (2010) (Breyer, J., dissenting).

[69] See, e.g., Plaut v. Spendthrift Farm, Inc., 514 U.S. 211, 245–46 (1995) (Breyer, J., concurring in the judgment).

[70] See Antonin Scalia, Common-Law Courts in a Civil-Law System: The Role of United States Federal Courts in Interpreting the Constitution and Law, in A Matter of Interpretation: Federal Courts and the Law 3, 25 (Amy Gutmann, ed. 1997) ("Of all the criticisms leveled against textualism, the most mindless is that it is 'formalistic.' The answer to that is, *of course it's formalistic!* The rule of law is *about* form. . . . Long live formalism. It is what makes a government a government of law and not of men.") (emphasis in original).

[71] See, e.g., Plaut, 514 U.S. at 239–40 (maj. op.); Morrison v. Olson, 487 U.S. 654, 711, 733 (1988) (Scalia, J., dissenting).

[72] Plaut, 514 U.S. at 239.

[73] Mistretta v. United States, 488 U.S. 361, 426–27 (1989) (Scalia, J., dissenting).

In *Noel Canning*, the contrast between the justices' jurisprudential approaches stood out in bold relief. As Section 1 explains, in many respects, the majority and concurring opinions in *Noel Canning* illuminate the distinction between functionalism and formalism. But as Section 2 demonstrates, the opinions also show that the distinction between functionalism and formalism represents more of a spectrum than a dichotomy.

1. Exposing the Functionalism–Formalism Distinction

Although Justices Breyer and Scalia ultimately reached the same conclusion in *Noel Canning*, their opinions illuminate the sometimes sharp rhetorical and substantive divide between functionalist and formalist approaches to separation-of-powers issues. Take, for example, the opinions' varied approaches to construing the key phrases of the Recess Appointments Clause. As noted, the first question before the Court involved the meaning of the clause's term "Recess." The government contended that "the Recess" included any substantial break in Senate business, regardless of whether the break fell between formal sessions. Noel Canning, on the other hand, construed the term according to its plain text, arguing that "the Recess" included only the formal break between enumerated sessions of the Senate.

Adopting a functionalist approach, Justice Breyer disagreed with the D.C. Circuit and Noel Canning's interpretation of the clause. Instead, he found the phrase linguistically ambiguous and concluded that the clause's underlying purposes called for a "broader," more "functional" interpretation. Characterizing the recess-appointments power as "ensur[ing] the continued functioning of the Federal Government when the Senate is away," Justice Breyer reasoned that the term "Recess" "should be practically construed to mean a time when the Senate is unavailable to participate in the appointments process."[74] After all, he wrote, the Senate "is equally away during both an inter-session and an intra-session recess," and its "capacity to participate in the appointments process has nothing to do with the words it uses to signal its departure."[75] Rejecting "the formalistic approach that Justice Scalia endorsed," Justice Breyer interpreted the

[74] Noel Canning, 134 S. Ct. at 2561, 2563–64, 2566 (2014) (maj. op.).
[75] *Id.* at 2561, 2563.

recess-appointments power to include both inter-session recesses as well as those intra-session recesses having "substantial length."[76]

Justice Scalia, however, rejected what he described as the majority's "vague, unadministrable limits."[77] For him, the text of the clause unambiguously limited the president's power to inter-session recesses. As Noel Canning had argued in its briefs, the Recess Appointments Clause "uses the term 'Recess' in contradistinction to the term 'Session,'" thus conveying that these are "mutually exclusive, alternating states."[78] The key flaw of the majority's construction, Justice Scalia wrote, was that it read the Constitution's structural provisions "on the narrow-minded assumption that their only purpose is to make the government run as efficiently as possible."[79] Indeed, in contrast to Justice Breyer's functionalist emphasis on workable government, Justice Scalia stressed that the text of the Recess Appointments Clause must be construed in light of the Constitution's central reason for separating federal powers—which in Justice Scalia's view was individual liberty and not governmental "[c]onvenience and efficiency."[80]

A similar dispute arose over the meaning of the clause's language specifying when the vacancies must "happen." As noted, the clause authorizes the president to fill "vacancies that *may happen during* the Recess." A key question in *Noel Canning* was whether that language extended only to vacancies that arose *during* a recess, or whether it also included those that arose *before* but *persisted during* a recess.

In answering that question, Justice Breyer again relied on functional considerations. Given the clause's purpose of ensuring executive efficiency in the absence of the Senate, Justice Breyer concluded that pre-recess vacancies should fall within the ambit of the clause. Otherwise, he wrote, a critically important executive office would remain empty—and thus "paralyze a whole line of action"—simply because it became vacant "too soon before the recess . . . for the President to appoint a replacement."[81] Although Justice Breyer candidly

---

[76] *Id.* at 2561, 2563–64.

[77] *Id.* at 2595 (Scalia, J., concurring in the judgment).

[78] *Id.* at 2596.

[79] *Id.* at 2597.

[80] *Id.* (internal quotation marks and citation omitted).

[81] See *id.* at 2568 (internal quotation marks omitted).

acknowledged that this broader interpretation threatened to nullify the Senate's power of advice and consent, he nevertheless found that reading "most accordant with the Constitution's reason and spirit."[82]

In Justice Scalia's view, however, the "original understanding of the Clause" refuted Justice Breyer's construction.[83] According to Founding-era sources, Justice Scalia argued, "vacancies *happen during* the Recess of the Senate" when they *"arise during* the recess in which they are filled."[84] While it is possible for the word "happen" to have different meanings in different contexts, a "vacancy" is "a state of affairs that comes into existence at a particular moment in time."[85] Therefore, it does not "happen" in the same way that an "ongoing activity or event" "happens" "for as long as it continues."[86]

The majority's contrary construction, he concluded, was not only "inconsistent with the Constitution's text and structure," but also disturbed "the balance the Framers struck between Presidential and Senatorial power."[87] That strictly delineated division of authority—giving the Senate control over the president's appointments and recess-appointments powers—was "not a bug to be fixed by this Court" but rather "a calculated feature of the constitutional framework."[88] Even if "clumsy" and "inefficient," the majority's failure to enforce that framework "undermin[ed] respect for the separation of powers."[89]

2. Complicating the Functionalism–Formalism Distinction

The *Noel Canning* opinions, however, were not in all respects paradigmatically functionalist or formalist decisions. Justice Breyer's majority opinion, for instance, at times challenged the distinction between formalism and functionalism in drawing on the "purpose of the Clause" while also expressly constraining that "function[al]"analysis to the text of the Constitution's structural

---

[82] See *id.* at 2568–69 (internal quotation marks omitted).

[83] *Id.* at 2607 (Scalia, J., concurring in the judgment).

[84] *Id.* at 2598, 2606 (emphasis added).

[85] *Id.* at 2606 & n.8.

[86] *Id.*

[87] *Id.* at 2606.

[88] *Id.* at 2598, 2606.

[89] *Id.* at 2598, 2607, 2618.

provisions.[90] The majority's resolution of the pro forma sessions issue exemplifies this blending of methodologies.

As discussed, Noel Canning asked the Court at the certiorari stage to address the question of whether the Senate's pro forma sessions on January 3 and 6, 2012, constituted legitimate sessions of the Senate, such that the president could not make recess appointments during the three-day period between the sessions. The issue ultimately proved dispositive for the following reasons. In order for the Court to decide whether the break in Senate business between January 3 and January 6 counted as a "Recess" within the meaning of the clause, it had to determine the significance of the Senate's pro forma sessions held on those days. If those meetings were legitimate "sessions" of the Senate, the "period between January 3 and January 6 was a 3-day recess, which is too short to trigger the President's recess-appointment power."[91] But if those meetings were *not* legitimate sessions, "then the 3-day period was part of a much longer recess during which the President *did* have the power to make recess appointments."[92]

The Court adopted the former position, advocated by Noel Canning.[93] Rejecting the government's "functional" argument to the contrary, the majority reasoned that pro forma sessions "count as sessions" when "the Senate sa[ys] it was in session," regardless of "what the Senate actually does (or here, *did*) during its *pro forma* sessions."[94] More specifically, Justice Breyer held that, "for purposes of the Recess Appointments Clause, the Senate is in session when it says it is, provided that, under its own rules, it retains the capacity to transact Senate business."[95]

In one sense, Justice Breyer's logic tracks his pragmatic, functionalist philosophy. Indeed, for mostly purposive reasons, Justice Breyer stopped short of endorsing the position that the Senate is in session *any* time it says it is. Instead, he concluded that, although

[90] *See id.* at 2573–77 (majority op.).

[91] *Id.* at 2574.

[92] *Id.* at 2574 (emphasis added).

[93] Justice Scalia did not squarely address the legitimacy of pro forma sessions. See *id.* at 2617 (Scalia, J., concurring in the judgment).

[94] *Id.* at 2574–76 (majority op.) (emphasis in original).

[95] *Id.* at 2574.

the Constitution formally delegated broad "authority to the Senate to determine how and when to conduct its business," the Senate "is not in session" when it "is without the *capacity* to act under its own rules"—even if the Senate itself declares otherwise.[96] Between December 2011 and January 2012, Justice Breyer observed, not only was the Senate perfectly *capable* of conducting business, but it also in fact *did* conduct official business during its pro forma sessions—passing a bill at one meeting and receiving messages from the president at another. Hence, because the Senate was functionally capable of acting, it was in session for purposes of the Recess Appointments Clause.

But in important respects, Justice Breyer's resolution of the pro forma sessions issue was deeply formalistic. For one thing, Justice Breyer's standard for determining when the Senate is in session was derived from—even if not compelled by—constitutional text and structure, as well as original understandings of parliamentary autonomy. Regardless of the Constitution's purposes, the majority suggested, the document's text and structure have always been understood to provide the Senate "wide latitude" to determine its own rules of procedure.[97] In analyzing those provisions, Justice Breyer expressed comparatively less concern over the deeper purposes of the Constitution's division of federal power, and comparatively greater interest in simply determining how the Constitution's *text* divided that power among the branches.

Similarly formalistic was the majority's indifference toward the potential consequences of its decision. In the majority's view, even if the Constitution did not give the president tools of his own for waging inter-branch conflict—which it does[98]—"serious institutional friction" and its accompanying civic costs were not concerns to be addressed through the recess-appointments power.[99] Instead, as he had indicated at oral argument, Justice Breyer viewed "friction between the branches [as] an inevitable consequence of our

---

[96] *Id.* at 2575.

[97] *Id.*

[98] See, e.g., U.S. Const. art. 11, § 3 (providing that, when the House and Senate disagree "with Respect to the Time of Adjournment, [the President] may adjourn them to such Time as he shall think proper").

[99] Noel Canning, 134 S. Ct. at 2577.

constitutional structure."[100] Therefore, when "judicial interpretation and compromise among the branches" fail to resolve political differences, the "constitutional balance" is not preserved by rewriting the Constitution but by channeling the resolution of such disputes to "the ballet box."[101] This line of formalistic, "damn the torpedoes"[102] analysis stands in sharp contrast to other portions of Justice Breyer's decision in which the majority relied expressly on consequentialist reasoning.[103]

Even more to the point was the substantial deference Justice Breyer's opinion accorded to the Senate's institutional prerogatives. As Frederick Schauer theorized, formalism's preoccupation with rules necessarily involves deference to rule makers.[104] Regardless of how the *applier* of the rule might view matters, a formalist approach to decisionmaking suppresses contrary impulses and defers to the judgment inscribed in the terms of the rule.

In *Noel Canning*, Justice Breyer echoed these formalist concerns when he reasoned that, because the Constitution "broad[ly] delegat[ed]" authority to the Senate to determine whether and when to have its sessions, it was institutionally unjustifiable for the Court to "engage in a more realistic appraisal of what the Senate actually did" during its pro forma sessions.[105] Not only do judges lack the epistemic resources to "easily determine such matters," he wrote, but close, ongoing scrutiny of the Senate's procedures would also "risk undue judicial interference with the functioning of the Legislative Branch."[106] Thus, by finding that the Constitution allocated to the Senate the authority to decide the validity of its own sessions, Justice Breyer's opinion exhibited formalism's tendency to "screen [ ] off" potentially relevant countervailing information.[107]

---

[100] *Id.*

[101] *Id.*

[102] Martin Shapiro, The Supreme Court and Constitutional Adjudication: Of Politics and Neutral Principles, 31 Geo. Wash. L. Rev. 587, 602 (1963).

[103] Noel Canning, 134 S. Ct. at 2577 (disagreeing with Justice Scalia's analysis because it "would render illegitimate thousands of recess appointments reaching all the way back to the founding era").

[104] See Frederick Schauer, Formalism, 97 Yale L.J. 509, 543–44 (1988).

[105] Noel Canning, 134 S. Ct. at 2576–77.

[106] *Id.* at 2575, 2577.

[107] See, e.g., Schauer, Formalism, *supra* note 104, at 510.

In seamlessly blending these functionalist and formalist rationales, Justice Breyer's opinion challenges the integrity of the distinction between formalism and functionalism. And inasmuch as functionalist interpretation involves an "all things considered" judgment of the best possible outcome in a particular case, there is nothing inconsistent about functionalist judges relying on formalist considerations. Indeed, if a strict, horizontal division of federal authority appears salient to a functional analysis of the relevant constitutional issues, then a rigid distinction between formalism and functionalism seems substantially less plausible in practice.

Similar observations could be made with regard to the formalist model as well. As Professor Martin Redish has written, "It is not necessarily anomalous . . . to incorporate elements of common sense into an otherwise rigid formalist approach."[108] Indeed, although formalist separation-of-powers jurisprudence generally eschews functionalist concerns regarding flexibility, purposes, and consequences,[109] the formalist mode is nonetheless suffused with precisely those same considerations.[110]

In *Noel Canning*, Justice Scalia's dissection of the majority opinion illustrates at least two ways in which formalist separation-of-powers jurisprudence integrates functionalist logic. First, Justice Scalia argued that the vagueness of the majority's decision failed to constrain official behavior in predictable ways. For example, Justice Scalia reasoned that, even if his construction of the clause risked aggrandizing the president's power by allowing recess appointments "during very short inter-session breaks," his approach was functionally superior to the majority's in that it at least provided a definitional, rule-like principle for determining when the clause applies.[111] Under Justice Scalia's interpretation, there must "actually *be* a recess" "no

---

[108] Martin H. Redish, Separation of Powers, Judicial Authority, and the Scope of Article III: The Troubling Cases of Morrison and Mistretta, 39 DePaul L. Rev. 299, 315 (1990).

[109] See, e.g., Plaut v. Spendthrift Farm, Inc., 514 U.S. 211, 237 (1995) ("It is no indication whatever of the invalidity of [a] constitutional rule . . . that it produces unhappy consequences.").

[110] See *id.* at 240 (rejecting a "delphic alternative" standard because it would "prolong[] doubt and multipl[y] confrontation" among the political branches); see also Morrison v. Olson, 487 U.S. 654, 727 (1988) (Scalia, J., dissenting) (contending that "[t]he purpose of the separation and equilibrium of powers" is preserving individual liberty).

[111] Noel Canning, 134 S. Ct. at 2599 n.4 (Scalia, J., concurring in the judgment).

matter how short" before the recess-appointments power may be exercised.[112] By contrast, the majority's standard that a recess simply "be *long enough*," was, in Justice Scalia's view, too "indetermina[te]" to apprise relevant officials of the propriety of their conduct. As a result, he argued, the majority's standard was bound to produce unnecessary governmental instability and confusion.[113]

Second, Justice Scalia expressed concern over the long-term effects of the majority's decision on the equilibrium between the political branches. In criticizing what he called the majority's "adverse possession" theory of executive power—by which the executive branch could expand its power through a persistent pattern of constitutional violations—Justice Scalia worried that the majority had conferred on the executive an insuperable institutional advantage vis-à-vis the legislature.[114] Not only will the majority's decision, he wrote, "place on the Legislative Branch" an overly "excessive burden" in future "contests with the Executive over the separation of powers," but it also "all but guarantee[d] the continuing aggrandizement of the Executive Branch" by deferring too heavily to contested executive practice.[115]

On these points, Justice Scalia's critique of the majority decision in *Noel Canning* highlights formalism's pragmatic streak. Because formalism must contend with the inevitable imperfections of language and law, its focus on rules can never in practice be unyielding. And because formalism takes as a given that the Constitution separates powers to preserve liberty, its focus on text and structure necessarily involves a concern with the Constitution's purposes and the potential consequences of the Court's decisions. Justice Scalia's *Noel Canning* concurrence, therefore, illustrates that—in practice, if not in theory—the formalist decisionmaking model is appropriately inbued with certain pragmatic, functionalist concerns.

3. Reconciling the Functionalism–Formalism Distinction

The *Noel Canning* opinions thus highlight the blurry edges that separate functionalism and formalism in separation-of-powers

[112] *Id.* (emphasis in original).
[113] *Id.*
[114] Noel Canning, 134 S. Ct. at 2614–15.
[115] *Id.*

cases. On one hand, they illuminate clear differences between the two approaches, with Justice Breyer construing the Recess Appointments Clause in light of its "purposes" and "the actual practice of Government,"[116] and Justice Scalia by contrast interpreting the clause as part of "a system of 'carefully crafted restraints' designed to 'protect the people from the improvident exercise of power.'"[117] On the other hand, both opinions suggested that functionalism and formalism are not just two sides of the same coin but, in many ways, the *same* side of the same coin. Just as Justice Breyer's majority opinion integrated formalist logic into its otherwise functionalist methodology, so too did Justice Scalia rely on implicit functional reasoning in adhering closely to the Constitution's text and structure. In these ways, *Noel Canning* substantiates Professor William Eskridge's observation that "formalism cannot avoid functional inquires, any more than functionalism can avoid formalist lines."[118]

B. Text and Practice

Just as at oral argument, the *Noel Canning* opinions highlight a similarly complicated debate involving reliance on interpretive sources outside the text of the Constitution.[119] In one sense, there is overwhelming consensus in the legal community that extra-textual sources are legitimate bases for giving meaning to constitutional text. Judicial precedent and the *Federalist Papers* come to mind as uncontroversial examples. But beyond a limited range of canonical sources, the legitimacy of extra-textual materials and unwritten practices remains deeply contested insofar as they purport to be dispositive sources of law.

---

[116] Noel Canning, 134 S. Ct. at 2566 (maj. op.).

[117] See *id.* at 2610 (Scalia, J., concurring in the judgment) (quoting INS v. Chadha, 462 U.S. 919, 957, 959 (1983)).

[118] See William N. Eskridge, Jr., Relationships between Formalism and Functionalism in Separation of Powers Cases, 22 Harv. J.L. & Pub. Pol'y 21, 25 (1999).

[119] The literature on this issue is vast and diverse. See, e.g., Akhil Reed Amar, America's Unwritten Constitution: The Precedents & Principles We Live By (2012); see also Richard H. Fallon, Implementing the Constitution 111–26 (2001); Thomas C. Grey, Do We Have an Unwritten Constitution?, 27 Stan. L. Rev. 703 (1975); Stephen E. Sachs, The "Unwritten Constitution" and Unwritten Law, 2013 Ill. L. Rev. 1797 (2013).

Because there is no "Separation of Powers Clause,"[120] the debate over the written and unwritten Constitution is particularly acute in cases involving the appropriate division of federal authority.[121] While courts often resolve such questions by drawing structural inferences from the Constitution's text, they also rely in part on extra-textual or unwritten sources, like "historical understanding and practice,"[122] as well as "the 'settled and well understood construction of the Constitution.'"[123] Indeed, as Professor Ernest Young has observed, separation-of-powers disputes are not simply "a contrast between formalism and functionalism"—they also reflect "a contrast between exclusive reliance on the canonical Constitution and broader attention to other constitutive sources."[124]

In *Noel Canning*, the opinions of Justices Breyer and Scalia provided real-world insight on these issues. Section 1 discusses the ways in which the justices differed in their approach to extra-textual sources of interpretation. Section 2 analyzes a deeper connection and distinction between the opinions, showing that the justices did not simply rely on extra-textual information to resolve linguistic ambiguities—they also relied on such information to determine the existence or nonexistence of such ambiguity.

1. Text and Practice in Resolving Ambiguity

In his opinion for the majority, Justice Breyer made clear that un-written "historical practice" would be given "significant weight" in "interpreting the [Recess Appointments] Clause."[125] In Justice Breyer's view, because the case "concern[ed] the allocation of power between two elected branches of Government," there was a greater, rather than lesser, need to rely on such extra-textual sources.[126] Indeed, "even when the nature or longevity of [an unwritten historical]

---

[120] See, e.g., Richard A. Epstein, The Classical Liberal Constitution: The Uncertain Quest for Limited Government 86–87 (2013).

[121] See generally Curtis Bradley & Trevor Morrison, Historical Gloss & the Separation of Powers, 126 Harv. L. Rev. 411 (2012).

[122] Printz v. United States, 521 U.S. 898, 905 (1997).

[123] Free Enter. Fund v. Pub. Co. Accounting Oversight Bd., 130 S. Ct. 3138, 3152 (2010).

[124] See Ernest A. Young, The Constitution Outside the Constitution, 117 Yale L.J. 408, 442 (2007).

[125] Noel Canning, 134 S. Ct. at 2559 (maj. op.) (emphasis omitted).

[126] Id. (emphasis omitted).

practice is subject to dispute, and even when that practice began after the founding era," he wrote, such practices are "an important interpretive factor," and one that should "inform [the Court's] determination of 'what the law is.'"[127]

Justice Scalia, by contrast, took a more circumspect view of judicial reliance on unwritten custom and practice. In keeping with his past decisions, Justice Scalia saw nothing per se illegitimate about an unwritten practice "guid[ing]" the Court's interpretation of the Constitution—so long as the relevant constitutional provision was "deeply ambiguous" and the practice at issue "has been open, widespread, and unchallenged since the early days of the Republic."[128] But "when the Constitution is clear," he stressed, the "historical practice of the political branches is irrelevant."[129] Because "the political branches cannot by agreement alter the constitutional structure," a "self-aggrandizing practice adopted by one branch well after the founding, often challenged, and never before blessed by this Court," cannot supplant the Constitution's "text, structure, and original understanding."[130]

These differing approaches played out in the resolution of the textual issues in *Noel Canning*. Take, for example, the way in which Justice Breyer construed the temporal meaning of "the Recess."[131] Because the text of the Constitution did not specify "how long a recess must be in order to fall within the Clause," Justice Breyer looked to, among other sources, extra-textual information regarding historical executive practices.[132] That history showed, in the majority's view, that presidents have generally not utilized the recess-appointments power during intra-session recesses lasting fewer than 10 days. Accordingly, the majority concluded, the Recess Appointments Clause presumptively applied only to inter-session recesses and intra-session recesses of 10 days or more. Put more succinctly, the majority read the meaning of the words in the Constitution to embody a presumptive time limit drawn in significant part from unwritten sources of customary practice.

---

[127] *Id.* at 2560.

[128] Noel Canning, 134 S. Ct. at 2594 & n.4 (Scalia, J., concurring in the judgment).

[129] *Id.* at 2600 (citing, inter alia, Alden v. Maine, 527 U.S. 706, 743–44 (1999)).

[130] *Id.* at 2600.

[131] *Id.* at 2565–66 (maj. op.).

[132] *Id.* at 2566–67.

Justice Scalia, however, disputed the majority's reliance on extra-textual sources. In his view, the majority's construction of the phrase "the Recess" amounted to "judicial adventurism."[133] Because there was "no textual basis whatsoever for limiting the length of 'the Recess'" in the way the majority did, Justice Scalia contended that the Court's reliance on unwritten "executive practice" was without constitutional basis.[134] After all, Justice Scalia asked rhetorically, if the Court was correct that "the Constitution's text empowers the President to make appointments during any break in the Senate's proceedings, by what right does the majority subject the President's exercise of that power to vague, court-crafted limitations with no textual basis?"[135] Regardless of the historical record, therefore, Justice Scalia concluded that the majority was not justified in diminishing the authority of future presidents based on nothing more than the voluntary self-restraint of their predecessors.[136]

Despite their methodological differences, however, Justice Breyer's and Justice Scalia's opinions share a common interpretive premise: when the text is clear, the text governs. For Justice Breyer, the text was not clear in *Noel Canning*—and therefore, supplemental materials were needed. For Justice Scalia, just the opposite was true. But that difference of opinion does not detract from the depth of the justices' agreement on first principles. Indeed, even the majority opinion, which Justice Scalia criticized for disregarding the Constitution's text, nevertheless invalidated the January 2012 appointments because the Senate was not in "Recess" (with a capital R) when they were made—a clear textual requirement of the clause. The majority never intimated that the appointments failed constitutional scrutiny simply because they departed from customary practices. In this way, *Noel Canning* suggests that—although textual reasoning is but one mode of constitutional analysis—it nevertheless remains first among equals.

2. *Text and Practice in Ascertaining Ambiguity*

The *Noel Canning* opinions also reveal a deeper respect in which extra-textual or unwritten sources of law influence constitutional

---

[133] *Id.* at 2600 (Scalia, J., concurring in the judgment).
[134] *Id.* at 2598, 2600.
[135] *Id.*
[136] *Id.*

interpretation. As Professors Curtis Bradley and Neil Siegel have recently argued, "the perceived clarity" of constitutional text is not simply "a product of traditional 'plain meaning' considerations."[137] Rather, just as the resolution of ambiguous constitutional language often relies on extra-textual sources, so too does the threshold determination of ambiguity depend on "a variety of other considerations," including those found beyond the document's text—for example, customary practice and historical development.[138]

Certain aspects of the opinions in *Noel Canning* lend credence to Bradley and Siegel's account of constitutional construction. For instance, in outlining the "background considerations" upon which he relied, Justice Breyer indicated that "historical practice" played a "significant" role in applying relevant norms and purposes, and not just in abstractly determining the proper allocation of power among the federal political branches.[139] Rather, Justice Breyer and the majority employed unwritten "historical practice" "in *interpreting* the Clause"—that is, ascertaining whether its "true construction" was evident from its "literal terms."[140]

To illustrate this point, consider also Justice Breyer's construction of the phrase "the Recess." In finding that language ambiguous, the majority looked beyond the Constitution's plain language, relying upon various Founding-era sources as well as the unwritten practices of the political branches throughout the 19th and 20th centuries.[141] Noting that, in its view, the modern-era executive branch had generally endorsed a capacious reading of the phrase, the Court deemed the "constitutional text . . . ambiguous" and consequently sought to resolve that ambiguity by further recourse to extra-textual materials.[142]

What is more, while Justice Scalia's interpretation of "the Recess" differed greatly from the majority's, he too relied on interpretive sources outside the text in finding that the clause was *not*

---

[137] See Curtis A. Bradley & Neil S. Siegel, Constructed Constraint and the Constitutional Text at 4, 64 Duke L.J. (forthcoming 2014).

[138] See *id.*

[139] Noel Canning, 134 S. Ct. at 2559 (maj. op.).

[140] *Id.* (emphasis altered) (internal quotation marks omitted).

[141] *Id.* at 2561 (internal quotation marks omitted).

[142] *Id.* at 2561, 2563.

ambiguous. But unlike the majority, Justice Scalia's reliance on extra-textual sources reflected his long-standing commitment to original-ism. Whereas Justice Breyer relied substantially on contemporary unwritten practices, Justice Scalia looked primarily to pre-ratifica-tion materials or early post-ratification statements from knowledge-able authorities.[143] But while the *Federalist Papers* and the actions of the First Congress are virtually canonical, neither is embodied in the Constitution's text, and thus even Justice Scalia's careful, textualist opinion in *Noel Canning* ascertained the clarity of the text by looking beyond the four corners of the document.

Both opinions in *Noel Canning*, therefore, reflect an important truth about constitutional interpretation: on its own, the text is neither self-interpreting nor self-clarifying. Indeed, even for originalists, this is a commonplace.[144] In the same way that the text alone cannot estab-lish its status as supreme law, neither can it independently establish the conditions of its own ambiguity. Such interpretive constraints *instead arise from the context, shared meanings,* and "norms of a highly specialized argumentative and adjudicative practice."[145] In this way, the practice and discipline of constitutional interpretation are themselves "a *structure* of constraints," in which "[i]nterpreters are constrained by their tacit awareness of what is possible and not possible to do," and "what will and will not be heard as evidence."[146]

V. *Noel Canning*'s Implications

The implications of any Supreme Court decision are notoriously difficult to predict. Nowhere is this more true than in separation-of-powers cases.[147] Nonetheless, *Noel Canning* might carry important implications for separation-of-powers jurisprudence and the ongo-ing institutional dynamic between the president and the Senate.

---

[143] See *id.* at 2608 (Scalia, J., concurring in the judgment).

[144] See, e.g., Antonin Scalia, Is There an Unwritten Constitution?, 12 Harv. J.L. & Pub. Pol'y 1 (1989).

[145] Fallon, *supra* note 119, at 118.

[146] See Stanley Fish, Doing What Comes Naturally: Changes, Rhetoric, and the Practice of Theory in Literary and Legal Studies 98 (1989).

[147] See, e.g., Louis Fisher, The Legislative Veto: Invalidated, It Survives, 56 L. & Contemp. Probs. 273 (1993) (reporting that, even after *Chadha*, the "legislative veto continue[d] to thrive," and that over "two hundred new legislative vetoes ha[d] been enacted").

Section A synthesizes the separation-of-powers narrative in *Noel Canning*. Section B examines how that story may or may not affect related aspects of American law and whether the political branches will succeed in formulating new strategies to sustain or resolve their differences.

A. What Is the Take-Away from Noel Canning?

Although it is too early to tell, history may end up viewing *Noel Canning* as merely a story about presidential usurpation. On that account, the case will add little to the separation-of-powers repertoire. Cases like *Bowsher v. Synar, INS v. Chadha, Plaut v. Spendthrift Farm*, among others, already make clear that one branch of the federal government may not "arrogat[e] power to itself" or "impair another in the performance of its constitutional duties."[148]

But in important respects, *Noel Canning* was not such a run-of-the-mill separation-of-powers case. Consider the nature of the president's 2012 recess appointments. While the Court was quite correct in holding those appointments unconstitutional, the president's action was not *simply* a case of the executive branch seeking to usurp authority entrusted to another branch. No one questioned whether the recess-appointments power was a presidential power, and few would question the president's responsibility to interpret the Constitution (even if wrongly). Rather, the distinguishing constitutional infirmity in *Noel Canning* was the president's independent appraisal—and unilateral disregard—of the legitimacy of the Senate's pro forma sessions.

In deciding that it had authority to independently evaluate and disregard the Senate's official actions, the administration violated the Constitution's separation of powers not necessarily by exercising another branch's powers but by impinging another branch's *right of self-definition*. Because that basic right is inexorably tied to the exercise of each branch's constitutional authority, any infringement of the right necessarily involves an infringement of the Constitution's structure. As the Court recognized long ago, the same separation-of-powers "principle that makes one master in his own house" also

---

[148] See Free Enter. Fund v. Pub. Co. Accounting Oversight Bd., 130 S. Ct. 3138, 3156 (2010) (internal quotation marks omitted).

"precludes him from imposing his control in the house of another who is master there."[149]

The *Noel Canning* Court saw these issues clearly from the start. As several members of the Court noted at oral argument, not only has the Senate "an absolute right not to confirm nominees that the President submits,"[150] but there is "a long tradition of Congress defining what th[e] session is."[151] When dealing with the "considered judgment by both houses of the Legislative Branch as to" its own operations,[152] several justices indicated their view that "the question of how to define a recess really does belong to the Senate."[153]

Justice Breyer's majority opinion translated these concerns into law. On the unstated premise that no branch "should be dependent upon either of the other two in the exercise of ancillary powers and privileges logically related to its separate constitutional responsibilities,"[154] Justice Breyer held that "the Senate's own determination of when it is and when it is not in session" is entitled to "great weight."[155] Indeed, in "giv[ing] the Senate wide latitude to determine . . . *how* to conduct [its] session[s]," Justice Breyer correctly recognized that the constitutional structure requires each branch to respect the internal procedures of its "coequal and independent departments."[156]

Justice Breyer's concern, then, in *Noel Canning* was not simply with achieving a workable government or ensuring that each branch was able to perform its essential functions successfully. It was also about the authority of each branch to define its own institutional identity. In order for the Senate to remain the Senate—rather than an executive subordinate—it must be able to define authoritatively the terms of its own operation and the nature of its own collective judgments. Put differently, the president's authority and obligation to interpret

---

[149] Humphrey's Ex'r v. United States, 295 U.S. 602, 630 (1935).

[150] Tr. of Oral Arg., *supra* note 42, at 22 (question of Chief Justice Roberts).

[151] *Id.* at 27 (question of Justice Kennedy).

[152] *Id.* at 28 (question of Justice Kennedy).

[153] *Id.* at 39 (question of Justice Kagan).

[154] William W. VanAlstyne, The Role of Congress in Determining Incidental Powers of the President and of the Federal Courts: A Comment on the Horizontal Effect of the Sweeping Clause, 40 L. & Contemp. Probs. 102, 108 (1976).

[155] Noel Canning, 134 S. Ct. at 2574 (maj. op.).

[156] *Id.* (emphasis added).

the Constitution do not extend to matters that diminish the institutional autonomy of coordinate branches.

A simple counterfactual illustrates the point. Were the president able to trump the Senate's own determination of when it is or is not in recess, there is no principled reason for prohibiting the president from independently deciding, for example, whether the Senate has given its advice and consent under the Appointments Clause. Rather, if the executive branch may determine when the Senate is in recess, it could also decide—based on the passage of time, prolonged deliberation, or simple intransigence—that the Senate has impliedly consented to a particular nominee, and thus issue that individual an authoritative commission.[157] In either case, the president would be interpreting a structural provision that conditions presidential power on Senate action of some sort. And in either case, the president's judgment would marginalize the Senate's internal operation as a chamber of Congress and its collective judgments as a public law-making body.

Thus, *Noel Canning* can be read to stand for the proposition that, as a matter of separation of powers, each branch's constitutional authority is defined as much by *what* it does, as it is by its right to determine *when* and *how* it does what it does. On that reading, *Noel Canning* represents an important and unique addition to the separation-of-powers *corpus juris*.

B. What Is the Potential Impact of Noel Canning?

1. Noel Canning's Potential Impact on Past Agency Decisions

An obvious place to start in estimating *Noel Canning*'s institutional impact is with its effect on the past decisions of federal agencies in general and the NLRB in particular. As Roger King and I have written, the potential impact of the Court's decision in *Noel Canning* could be substantial—particularly for the NLRB.[158] Between January 2012 and August 2013, the NLRB "recess" appointees issued roughly

---

[157] At least one academic has advanced a qualified version of this argument. See Matthew C. Stephenson, Can the President Appoint Principal Executive Officers without a Senate Confirmation Vote?, 122 Yale L.J. 940 (2013).

[158] See, e.g., G. Roger King & Bryan J. Leitch, The Impact of the Supreme Court's *Noel Canning* Decision—Years of Litigation Challenges on the Horizon for the NLRB, Bloomberg BNA (June 26, 2014), www.bna.com/impact-supreme-courts-n17179891624.

700 reported and unreported decisions while sitting on quorum-less boards. Each of those decisions is arguably invalid and may have to be reconsidered by the NLRB. Additionally, a number of NLRB regional directors whose appointments were approved by the quorum-less 2012–2013 board may find their enforcement actions subject to collateral challenge. These are but a few of the potential consequences for the NLRB, independent of any peripheral effects on cognate federal agencies.

But the ominous prospect of the NLRB rehearing hundreds upon hundreds of past cases is not a foregone eventuality. For one thing, many past decisions that might warrant reconsideration will be mooted through settlement or the subsequent insolvency of the employer or union. And even for those cases that are still live, the NLRB can at least partly deflect *Noel Canning*'s impact by employing certain administrative practices and judicial doctrines.

First, the NLRB may attempt to retroactively authorize, or "ratify," its past decisions. Under Supreme Court doctrine, agencies may ratify unlawful past actions so long as they possessed authority to perform the ratified act both "at the time the act was done" and "at the time the ratification was made."[159] Although the NLRB has avoided this strategy in the past, its aversion to wholesale ratification may prove too costly in the wake of *Noel Canning*.[160]

Second, as Justice Scalia and the solicitor general noted at oral argument in *Noel Canning*,[161] the de facto officer doctrine may provide an important palliative. As the Court has explained it, the de facto officer doctrine "confer[s] validity upon acts performed by a person acting under the color of official title even though it is later discovered that the legality of that person's appointment or election to office is deficient."[162] The doctrine "springs from the fear of the chaos that would result from multiple and repetitious suits challenging every action taken by every official whose claim to office could be open to question."[163] Accordingly, the de facto officer doctrine "seeks

---

[159] See FEC v. NRA Political Victory Fund, 513 U.S. 88, 98–100 (1994).

[160] See Paulsen v. All Am. Sch. Bus Corp., No. 13-CV-3762, 2013 WL 5744483, at *3–5 (E.D.N.Y. Oct. 23, 2013).

[161] Tr. of Oral Arg., *supra* note 42 at 5.

[162] Ryder v. United States, 515 U.S. 177, 180 (1995).

[163] *Id.*

to protect the public by insuring the orderly functioning of the government despite technical defects in title to office."[164]

What is more, the Court has already applied the de facto officer doctrine to insulate a recess appointment from collateral challenge, albeit more than a century ago.[165] In *Ex parte Ward*, an inmate challenged the legality of his detention by attacking the constitutionality of his sentencing judge's recess appointment. The Supreme Court rejected the inmate's suit. Under the de facto officer doctrine, the Court held that, although the vacancy filled by the judge did not "happen during" the Senate's recess, a judge is "an officer de facto" when the "*court* has jurisdiction" and "the proceedings are otherwise regular."[166] In such circumstances, "the validity of [the judge's] title" and "his right to exercise the judicial functions" may not be collaterally attacked.[167] Following *Ex parte Ward*, therefore, federal courts might reject collateral challenges to NLRB decisions so long as the agency itself had jurisdiction over the subject matter of the case and the proceedings were otherwise regular. Thus, although the NLRB likely has its work cut out for it following *Noel Canning*, the prediction that it will be paralyzed by a flood of litigants seeking reconsideration appears to be quite overstated.

2. *Noel Canning*'s Potential Impact on Senate Authority

To the extent *Noel Canning* emboldened presidential recess-appointment power, even if only symbolically, the Senate could push back in several ways. First and most obvious, Congress and the Senate could prevent the Recess Appointments Clause from ever being triggered by staying in session year-round or employing periodic pro forma sessions, as it did in January 2012. Such a course may be politically or practically infeasible in the long run, but as *Noel Canning* makes clear, nothing in the Constitution precludes the Senate from acting in this manner.

---

[164] *Id.*

[165] See Ex parte Ward, 173 U.S. 452, 452–54 (1899).

[166] *Id.* (emphasis added).

[167] *Id.;* see also Ryder, 515 U.S. at 181–83 (reaffirming *Ward*); Roell v. Withrow, 538 U.S. 580, 598–99 (2003) (Thomas, J., dissenting) (citing *Ex parte Ward* for the proposition that "defect[ive]" or "improper[]" recess appointments are precisely the kinds of "technicalities" to which the de facto officer doctrine applies).

Second, Congress overall has at its disposal innumerable formal devices for influencing executive action—and specifically for discouraging excessive use of the recess-appointments power.[168] Congress, for example, might utilize targeted appropriations riders to defund those agencies heavily staffed with recess appointees. Congress could also impose burdensome reporting and certification requirements on such agencies, requiring them to submit costly, time-intensive reports detailing their budgetary and operational activities. By increasing the transaction costs for agencies run by recess-appointed officers, Congress could eliminate most of the perceived advantages of recess appointments.

Third, the Senate itself also has informal methods of discouraging recess appointments.[169] The Senate could, for instance, issue official resolutions denouncing certain recess appointments or otherwise undermine the public legitimacy of such officials through negative publicity campaigns. The Senate could also make life difficult for such officials and their agencies through repeated committee hearings or intrusive information requests. And while each of these formal options occurs *ex post*—that is, after the recess appointments are made—they nevertheless may generate enough *ex ante* disincentives that presidents would avoid excessive reliance on the recess-appointments power.

Fourth, the Senate also presumably has authority to *end* those recess appointments with which it disagrees. After all, the commissions granted to recess appointees "expire at the End of [the Senate's] next Session."[170] Following a recess in which the president unilaterally appointed a disfavored nominee, therefore, the Senate could immediately divest that official of authority by adjourning *sine die*— thereby ending its session. In this way, the Senate possesses both the front-end power to trigger the Recess Appointments Clause, as well as the back-end power to terminate the authority of recess appointees. Although the Court in *Noel Canning* did not broach this issue specifically, the logic of the majority opinion suggests that the Senate's "wide latitude to determine whether and when to have a

[168] See generally Jack M. Beermann, Congressional Administration, 43 San Diego L. Rev. 61, 69–138 (2006).

[169] See *id.* at 70, 121–22; see also Jacob E. Gersen & Eric A. Posner, Soft Law: Lessons from Congressional Practice, 61 Stan. L. Rev. 573, 577–78 (2009).

[170] U.S. Const. art. II, § 2, cl. 3.

session" would include the authority to determine when its "next Session" has "End[ed]."[171] And so long as the Senate kept its break in business sufficiently brief, its adjournment would not require the consent of the House and would not permit the president to make new recess appointments.

3. *Noel Canning*'s Potential Impact on Presidential Authority

As the previous discussion makes clear, Congress in general and the Senate in particular enjoy a substantial degree of power over the practices of the executive branch. Although the president has statutory avenues for filling important offices that fall vacant at inopportune times, I explore below a few constitutionally based workarounds that the president might employ to balance the scales of power. Ultimately, however, I conclude that none is independently adequate as a constitutional or political matter to thwart senatorial intransigence.

First, the president could seek to defeat political resistance over executive appointments by reconvening the Senate during its recess in order to goad a recalcitrant majority into confirming potential nominees. Under Article II, Section 3, the Constitution authorizes the president "on extraordinary Occasions" to convene both houses of Congress—"or *either* of them"—in what have been termed "special sessions."[172] Exercising this authority, a future president could reallocate the burden of inertia by forcing the Senate to consider and approve appointments.

The drawbacks of this approach, however, are three-fold. First, the president's actions would be highly public and thus potentially subject to derisive political criticism. Second, if the Senate is meeting in periodic pro forma sessions—and therefore is in session as it was in January 2012—it is not clear the president has authority to convene a "special session." After all, if the Senate is in session, it is arguably already "convene[d]," and thus the president's convention authority may be inapposite. Third, and more important, even if called back into special session, the Senate nevertheless retains an absolute right to reject the president's nominees. A special session, therefore,

---

[171] NLRB v. Noel Canning, 134 S. Ct. 2550, 2574–75 (2014).
[172] U.S. Const. art. II, § 3, cl. 2 (emphasis added).

would entail substantial political risks with no countervailing guarantee of a practical benefit.

Next, under imaginable conditions, the president could manufacture the preconditions of the recess-appointments power by adjourning both chambers of Congress for a sufficient period of time. Article II, Section 3, of the Constitution empowers the president to adjourn Congress "to such Time as he shall think proper" when the chambers themselves cannot agree "with Respect to the Time of Adjournment."[173] If the president's party controlled the House, but the Senate was controlled by an oppositional party that refused to confirm the president's nominees, the House could, at the president's behest, seek an unexpected or inconvenient adjournment in order to create a disagreement between the chambers. And, once the chambers disagreed as to the date of adjournment, the president could exercise his or her authority to adjourn both houses unilaterally. At that point, any preexisting vacancies could be filled under the Court's construction of the Recess Appointments Clause in *Noel Canning*.

This second strategy, however, has at least two potential infirmities. First, it is worth questioning whether such maneuvering would comport with the institutional dignity and character of the presidency. Simply because the Constitution ostensibly contemplates such action does not mean it lives up to the highest and best aspirations for the executive branch as a constitutional functionary. Second, aside from the institutional implications, the president's adjournment power presumably depends on the Senate's understanding of its dispute with the House. If the Senate, for example, characterized the chambers' dispute as pertaining to some other matter—such as the substance of proposed legislation rather than the timing of adjournment—the president's power to adjourn the Senate may not arise. The Senate, in other words, could thwart this maneuver through some sort of official resolution proclaiming its institutional understanding of the chambers' disagreement. Thus, because there is no guarantee that the two chambers will agree about the subject of their disagreement, and because it is not clear whether the president would have authority independently to determine the subject of that

---

[173] U.S. Const. art. II, § 3, cl. 3.

disagreement, this second option may also fail to circumvent Senate intransigence.

Finally, as Tom Goldstein has suggested, a member of the Senate who is sympathetic to the president's agenda might be able to "wipe away the fiction" of a pro forma session simply "by making a quorum call."[174] Under its rules, the Senate operates on the presumption of a quorum unless, among other things, a senator makes a "quorum call," and thereby initiates a roll call of the Senate to determine how many of its members are present.[175] If made during a pro forma session, a quorum call would likely reveal the absence of a quorum, in which case the Senate's own rules would forbid it from taking further legislative action.[176] Therefore, by rendering the Senate unable to act, a quorum call would render the Senate unable to provide its advice and consent. And without "the ability to provide its 'advice and consent,'" the Senate would be "without the *capacity* to act" in the relevant sense and would therefore not be "in session" according to the Court's decision in *Noel Canning.*[177] Assuming that the absence of a "session" means that the Senate is in recess, the president might then have authority to make unilateral executive appointments.

Although this "pierce-the-veil" strategy appears quite promising, it too has limitations. First, as a practical matter, it seems unlikely that any senator would be willing to make such a quorum call and thereby risk alienating his or her colleagues. Second, because the Senate would be unable to act only until a quorum was reestablished,[178] there would be only a narrow window of time in which to make any subsequent recess appointments—and even then such appointments may be short-lived. Given the speed of modern travel, the Senate could reconvene a quorum within a matter of hours, and thereby end any manufactured recess. Moreover, even

---

[174] Tom Goldstein, Can a President (with a Little Help from One Senator of His Party) Circumvent Most of the Court's Limitation on the Recess Appointments Power?, SCOTUSblog (Jun. 27, 2014), http://www.scotusblog.com/2014/06/can-a-president-with-a-little-help-from-one-senator-of-his-party-circumvent-most-of-the-courts-limitation-on-the-recess-appointments-power.

[175] See Floyd M. Riddick, Riddick's Senate Procedure 1038–39 (Alan S. Frumin ed., 1992).

[176] *Id.*

[177] See NLRB v. Noel Canning, 134 S. Ct. 2550, 2575 (2014) (emphasis in original).

[178] See Riddick, *supra* note 175, at 1038–39.

if recess appointments had been made during that brief intervening period, the Senate might—as already discussed—be able to terminate such appointments by immediately adjourning *sine die* and thus "End[ing]" its "next Session."[179]

In the end, therefore, presidents may have to rely upon what Professor Keith Whittington has referred to as the executive's "intrinsic advantages over the Senate" in the appointments process.[180] As Whittington notes, despite the Senate's apparent superiority, presidents actually enjoy an important advantage regarding executive appointments because, unlike "a collective body such as the Senate," "the unitary and hierarchical executive" can choose a course of action without "bear[ing] the organizational costs of mobilizing" and "sustaining" "a majority of their colleagues."[181] In the wake of the Court's decision in *Noel Canning*, it could very well be that such inherent institutional advantages are the president's strongest—and *only*—weapons against Senate intransigence.

VI. Conclusion

NLRB v. Noel Canning counts as a rare and remarkable case. At its core, the case clarified the Constitution's structure—specifically, its tripartite division of federal powers. At its core, the case clarified certain aspects of the Constitution's tripartite division of federal power—specifically, the general metes and bounds of the president's authority to make unilateral executive appointments under the Recess Appointments Clause. Going beyond the propriety of one presidential action, *Noel Canning* highlighted important jurisprudential debates and brought to the fore the intricate institutional relationships among the federal branches—illustrating the ways in which the Constitution advantages and disadvantages each in the performance of its essential functions. Indeed, while the Court's judgment is final as to the propriety of the president's 2012 recess appointments, the overarching themes implicated here will surely arise again as the Court continues to articulate the proper division of authority among the federal political branches.

---

[179] Noel Canning, 134 S. Ct. at 2574–75.
[180] See Keith E. Whittington, Presidents, Senates, and Failed Supreme Court Nominations, 2006 Sup. Ct. Rev. 401, 406 (2007).
[181] *Id.* at 407.

"Reverse *Carolene Products*," the End of the Second Reconstruction, and Other Thoughts on *Schuette v. Coalition to Defend Affirmative Action*

*David E. Bernstein**

In 2003, the Supreme Court upheld the constitutionality of affirmative-action preferences in public university admissions in *Grutter v. Bollinger*.[1] Michigan activists opposed to these preferences responded by successfully pursuing a state constitutional amendment via a referendum question known as the Michigan Civil Rights Initiative or Proposition 2.[2] Proposition 2 banned the use of race- and sex-based preferences by state entities, including universities.

A group of plaintiffs successfully challenged Proposition 2 in federal court. The U.S. Court of Appeals for the Sixth Circuit, sitting en banc, held in an 8–7 ruling that it violated the Fourteenth Amendment's Equal Protection Clause by selectively altering the political process in ways that disfavored members of minority groups, a transgression of the "political process doctrine."[3] The Supreme Court agreed to hear an appeal.

The case was styled *Schuette v. Coalition to Defend Affirmative Action*, and informed observers expected the Court to overrule the Sixth Circuit.[4] A majority of the justices have barely tolerated affirmative

---

* GMU Foundation Professor, George Mason University School of Law. The author thanks Ilya Somin for his helpful comments on a draft of this article.

[1] 539 U.S. 306, 325 (2003).

[2] See Barbara A. Perry, The Michigan Affirmative Action Cases 166–70 (2007).

[3] Coal. to Defend Affirmative Action v. Regents of Univ. of Mich., 701 F.3d 466 (6th Cir. 2012) (en banc).

[4] See, e.g., David E. Bernstein, *Schuette v. Coalition to Defend Affirmative Action* and the Failed Attempt to Square a Circle, 8 NYU J.L. & Lib. 210 (2013); Stuart Benjamin, Litigation Strategy and Coalition to Defend Affirmative Action v. Regents, The Volokh Conspiracy (Nov. 15, 2012), http://www.volokh.com/2012/11/15/litigation-strategy-

action preferences by government entities and only in narrow circumstances.[5] It seemed unlikely that the Court would ban a state from forbidding what the Court only very grudgingly permitted.[6] The Court's conservative majority, moreover, would almost certainly agree that holding that a state constitutional amendment banning government race-based classifications violates the federal Equal Protection Clause "would be to torture the English language to the point where constitutional text is absolutely meaningless."[7]

Nevertheless, Court watchers were held in suspense. Would the Court distinguish this case from other political process doctrine cases, thus leaving the underlying doctrine intact, or would it dispense with the doctrine entirely? As expected, the Court overruled the Sixth Circuit. The political process doctrine, however, managed to survive, albeit in diminished form.

Justice Anthony Kennedy, joined by Chief Justice John Roberts and Justice Samuel Alito, wrote a narrow plurality opinion retaining the doctrine but rejecting its application to Proposition 2. Justice Antonin Scalia, concurring for himself and Justice Clarence Thomas, would have eliminated the doctrine. Justice Stephen Breyer, in a lone concurrence, argued that the political process precedents were inapplicable in *Schuette*. Unlike those precedents, *Schuette* only involved transferring political authority from the state university bureaucracy to a referendum, not transferring authority from ordinary legislation to a referendum. Justice Sonia Sotomayor, joined by Justice Ruth Bader Ginsburg, wrote a lengthy and heartfelt dissent defending not just the political process doctrine but racial preferences more broadly. Justice Elena Kagan was recused.

---

and-coalition-to-defend-affirmative-action-v-regents/ ("I will bet anyone . . . that the Supreme Court will reverse the Sixth Circuit in Coalition to Defend Affirmative Action v. Regents."); Melissa Hart, *Schuette* Symposium: Keep it Simple, SCOTUSblog (Sept. 16, 2013), http://www.scotusblog.com/?p=169437 ("[T]he Supreme Court is not going to affirm the Sixth Circuit's decision.").

[5] See Bernstein, *supra* note 4, at 215–16.

[6] *Id.*

[7] Ilya Shapiro, It's Constitutional for Voters to Stop Their Government from Discriminating Based on Race, Cato at Liberty (Apr. 22, 2014), http://www.cato.org/blog/its-constitutional-voters-stop-their-government-discriminating-based-race.

The Plurality Opinion

Justice Kennedy's plurality opinion tries gamely to make some sense out of the rather incoherent political process doctrine. Kennedy begins with a discussion of *Reitman v. Mulkey*. *Mulkey* involved a California fair housing act that was overturned by a referendum that created a state constitutional amendment banning such laws. The Supreme Court, in a 5–4 decision, held that the referendum was an unconstitutional violation of the Fourteenth Amendment's Equal Protection Clause because its "design and intent" were to "establish a purported constitutional right to privately discriminate." The result was to "significantly encourage and involve the State in private racial discriminations."[8]

Justice Kennedy summarized *Mulkey* without further comment and then proceeded to discuss *Hunter v. Erickson*,[9] a case "central to the arguments" in *Schuette*.[10] *Hunter* invalidated a referendum that amended the Akron, Ohio, city charter to overturn a fair housing law and require that any new such law be approved by referendum. *Hunter* held that, by singling out a category of antidiscrimination laws as requiring a special form of approval, the referendum illicitly "places special burdens on racial minorities within the governmental process."[11]

According to Justice Kennedy, "*Hunter* rests on the unremarkable principle that the state may not alter the procedures of government to target racial minorities. The facts in *Hunter* established that invidious discrimination would be the necessary result of the procedural restructuring. Thus, in *Mulkey* and *Hunter*, there was a demonstrated injury "on the basis of race that, by reasons of state encouragement of participation, became more aggravated."[12]

Justice Kennedy hints at, but ultimately shies away from, an entirely plausible rationale for *Mulkey* and *Hunter*. It seems undeniable in retrospect that support for repeal of the fair housing laws in question—though it may have had some basis in libertarian attitudes and purely pragmatic concerns about property values—also had

---

[8] Reitman v. Mulkey, 387 U.S. 369, 374, 381 (1967).

[9] 393 U.S. 385 (1969).

[10] Schuette v. Coalition to Defend Affirmative Action, 134 S. Ct. 1623, 1631 (2014).

[11] Hunter, 393 U.S at 391.

[12] Schuette, 134 S. Ct. at 1632.

a substantial racist component. The Supreme Court in those cases could have but did not explicitly state that the referenda in question were both motivated by discriminatory intent and had discriminatory effects. This combination was later established as unconstitutional, even when applied to a decades-old state constitutional amendment that had mixed motives but included a significant element of racial bias.[13] If such a constitutional amendment was illicit, surely the amendments at issue in *Mulkey* and *Hunter* were vulnerable to the same reasoning.

This theory would have saved Justice Kennedy from the quagmire of endorsing the implicit rationale in *Mulkey* and *Hunter* that private discrimination, and its toleration by state governments, is a *constitutionally* significant injury. Instead, he endorsed the view that private housing discrimination created "a demonstrated injury on the basis of race" that was aggravated by "procedural restructuring" involved in repealing fair housing legislation via referendum and constitutional amendment.[14]

If private housing discrimination creates constitutionally significant injury to racial minorities, it's hard to explain why the mere failure to pass fair housing legislation wouldn't also be a constitutional violation. While Kennedy undoubtedly wouldn't go that far, his implicit endorsement of the notion that basic protections against discrimination are the proper "baseline" for judging referenda that take away such protections is not surprising, because he seemed to endorse just such a notion in *Romer v. Evans*.[15] More surprising is

---

[13] In *Hunter v. Underwood*, the Supreme Court invalidated an almost century-old provision of the Mississippi Constitution that banned certain classes of felons from voting after concluding that the provision in question "would not have been adopted by the convention or ratified by the electorate in the absence of the racially discriminatory motivation." 471 U.S. 222, 231 (1985)

[14] Schuette, 134 S. Ct. at 1632.

[15] 517 U.S. 620, 631 (1996) ("Homosexuals are forbidden the safeguards that others enjoy or may seek without constraint. They can obtain specific protection against discrimination only by enlisting the citizenry of Colorado to amend the state constitution or perhaps, on the State's view, by trying to pass helpful laws of general applicability. This is so no matter how local or discrete the harm, no matter how public and widespread the injury. We find nothing special in the protections Amendment 2 withholds. These are protections taken for granted by most people either because they already have them or do not need them; these are protections against exclusion from an almost limitless number of transactions and endeavors that constitute ordinary civic life in a free society."). Admittedly, like much else in *Romer*, this isn't 100 percent clear.

that Chief Justice Roberts and Justice Alito went along in *Schuette*. Perhaps this was the price for pulling together a narrow three-vote plurality opinion that satisfied Roberts's strong preference for narrowing rather than overturning dubious precedents.

In any event, the plurality endorsed a relatively limited version of the political process doctrine: that a state's alteration of political processes is unconstitutional when it will lead to government encouragement of or participation in "a demonstrated injury on the basis of race." The problem is that the Court had previously endorsed a much broader version of the doctrine in the next case Kennedy takes up, *Washington v. Seattle School District No. 1*.[16]

In *Seattle School District*, the Seattle school board had adopted a busing program to encourage racial integration of Seattle schools. Opponents passed a state initiative that barred the use of busing for desegregation. The Supreme Court, picking up on language from Justice John Marshall Harlan II's concurring opinion in *Hunter*, held that the initiative was unconstitutional based on very broad (and dubious) reasoning. The Court held that any time (1) a government policy "inures primarily for the benefit of the minority;" (2) minorities consider the policy to be "in their interest;" and (3) the state changes where "effective decision-making authority over that policy is placed," then the change must be reviewed under strict scrutiny. Thus, any government action with a "racial focus" that makes it more difficult for racial minorities and for other groups to "achieve legislation that is in their interest" is presumptively unconstitutional.[17]

Despite Justice Sotomayor's valiant attempt to rescue this line of reasoning in her dissent, it is entirely incoherent and unworkable in practice, as both Justice Kennedy and Justice Scalia, concurring in *Schuette*, point out. How does a court determine whether facially neutral legislation has a "racial focus"? Almost any significant piece of legislation will have a disparate negative or positive impact on racial minority groups and thus could be cast in racial terms. As

---

Does Justice Kennedy adopt that baseline because of how important such laws are, or because "everyone else" has them already, but if no one had them it wouldn't be a big deal? Is he referring only to the fact that the amendment in *Romer* barred government from banning state-action discrimination against gays, or is he also referring to private discrimination? His opinion in *Schuette* supports the broader interpretations.

16 458 U.S. 457 (1982).

17 *Id.* at 470–74.

Kennedy elaborates, "tax policy, housing subsidies, wage regulations, and even the naming of public schools, highways, and monuments are just a few examples of what could become a list of subjects that some organizations could insist should be beyond the power of voters to decide, or beyond the power of the legislature to decide when enacting limits on the power of local authorities or other governmental entities to address certain subjects."[18]

Other problems with the *Seattle School District* formulation abound. What does it mean to say that minorities consider a policy to be in their interest? An overwhelming consensus of members of all minority groups? Some smaller majority of all minority groups? Does "minority groups" mean all groups that have been deemed eligible for protection as racial minorities under the Equal Protection Clause, or is it limited only to "people of color," or only to so-called underrepresented minorities? Even if those issues could be resolved, what if there are disagreements among different minority groups? Do we expect African Americans and Hispanics to always perceive their interests the same way? How about Arabs and Jews, who have been recognized as "races" for the purposes of the 1866 Civil Rights Act and likely also receive protection as "racial" minorities under the Fourteenth Amendment?[19] What if there is disagreement within a minority group? What if most Cuban Americans think a law is not in their interest, but most Mexican Americans think it is? Will the Hmong, who have quite poor socioeconomic indicators, have the same interests as much wealthier and better-educated Japanese Americans? As Justice Kennedy notes, the Supreme Court since *Seattle School District* has consistently (and properly) rejected the assumption that "members of the same racial group . . . . [t]hink alike, share the same political interest, and will prefer the same candidate at the polls."[20]

The only plausible answer to these questions is that the views of members of the minority groups themselves must be largely irrelevant to the inquiry. Instead, a five-justice majority of the Supreme Court itself gets to decide what minority groups do (or at least *should*)

[18] Schuette, 134 S. Ct. at 1635.

[19] Saint Francis Coll. v. Al-Khazraji, 481 U.S. 604 (1987); Shaare Tefila Congregation v. Cobb, 481 U.S. 615 (1987).

[20] Schuette, 134 S. Ct. at 1634 (quoting Shaw v. Reno, 509 U.S. 630, 647 (1983)).

think is in their interest. As Justice Kennedy concludes, if the Court were to attempt this inquiry, it would inevitably rely on demeaning stereotypes, classifications of questionable constitutionality on their own terms.[21]

Indeed, obvious difficulties with such a venture are revealed in *Schuette* itself. Justice Sotomayor argues that affirmative-action preferences are clearly in the interest of the minority groups that receive preferences,[22] while Justices Scalia (joined by the Court's only African American justice) and Chief Justice Roberts take a strong opposing view.[23]

Instead, Justice Kennedy cautions that *Seattle School District* must be "understood as a case in which the state actions in question . . . have the serious risk, if not purpose of causing specific injuries on account of race." *Seattle School District*, he says, "rests on the unremarkable principle that the state may not alter the procedures of government to target racial minorities. The facts in *Seattle* established that invidious discrimination would be the necessary result of the procedural restructuring." [24]

Kennedy's narrower rationale would indeed explain the *Seattle School District* result. However, as both Justices Scalia and Sotomayor object, the *Seattle School District* opinion betrays no indication that the Court saw the case as involving the narrow issue of targeting minorities through political restructuring, rather than as involving the invalidation of legislation that inures to the benefit of minorities via political restructuring. Kennedy should have therefore overturned *Seattle School District*, while retaining *Mulkey* and *Hunter*.

Instead, he reinterprets *Seattle School District* in two significant ways. First, in an extremely dubious bit of revisionism, he suggests that while there was no finding of de jure segregation in Seattle, "it appears as though school segregation in the district in the 1940's and 1950's may have been the partial result of school board policies."[25] Oddly enough, he cites Justice Breyer's dissenting opinion in the

---

[21] *Id.* at 1635.

[22] *Id.* at 1660 (Sotomayor, J., dissenting).

[23] *Id.* at 1638–39 (Roberts, C.J., concurring); *id.* at 1644 n.6 (Scalia, J., concurring).

[24] *Id.* at 1633.

[25] *Id.* at 1634.

Parents Involved case for that proposition.[26] That's odd both because Justice Kennedy and the other justices in the *Schuette* plurality were in the majority in that case, and because if there in fact had been significant evidence of de jure segregation in Seattle, the majority opinion should have addressed it.

Kennedy could have more plausibly simply suggested that the Court decided the case in 1982 with the background knowledge that segregation patterns in public schools in any major city in the United States were unlikely to be as yet largely free from the implicit influence of state action that encouraged residential and therefore school segregation nationwide. Such government action included federal mortgage policies that "redlined" black neighborhoods, the siting of roads and highways to separate black and white neighborhoods, zoning policies, and so on.

He then could have raised his second reinterpretation of *Seattle School District,* one that rests on firmer ground. Kennedy notes that both sides in *Seattle School District* accepted the notion, since called into question by *Parents Involved,* that race-conscious student assignments for the purpose of achieving integration were legally permissible, even in the absence of a finding of prior segregation by law. In other words, *Seattle School District* could be seen as the Supreme Court's rejecting a state's attempt to skew the political process to prevent a subdivision from addressing "the very racial injury in which the State was complicit"—that is, school segregation that resulted from housing segregation created by a combination of state and private action.[27]

One might accuse the *Schuette* plurality of hypocrisy, as arguably the Court's ruling in *Parents Involved* also prevented Seattle from addressing the continuing pattern of housing segregation that led to school segregation, but by order of the Supreme Court rather than via referendum. Kennedy himself, however, recognized in his concurrence in *Parents Involved* that long-standing patterns of segregation could be overcome through affirmative government action intended to destabilize those patterns, so long as the government didn't

---

[26] *Id.* at 1633 (citing Parents Involved in Cmty. Schools v. Seattle School Dist. No. 1, 551 U.S. 701, 807–08 (2007) (Breyer, J., dissenting)).

[27] *Id.* at 1633.

classify individuals by race.[28] That would distinguish, for example, a school system that lawfully created a magnet school to encourage integration from one that unlawfully assigned students by race. That doesn't quite explain Roberts's and Alito's willingness to join Kennedy's reasoning in *Schuette*. Perhaps it means that they agree with his concurrence in *Parents Involved* even though they did join it; perhaps it means that they believe that by 2007 school segregation patterns could no longer be fairly traced to discriminatory government policies abandoned decades earlier; or perhaps they have no good rationale to explain the possible discrepancy in their opinions.

In any event, given the reasoning noted above, the outcome of *Schuette* was dependent on whether the denial of affirmative action preferences in Michigan universities amounted to the "infliction of a specific injury of the kind at issue in *Mulkey* and *Hunter* and in the history of the Seattle schools."[29] Kennedy concluded that "there is no precedent for extending these cases to restrict the right of Michigan voters to determine that race-based preferences granted by Michigan governmental entities should be ended."[30] Later in the opinion, he added that, unlike *Mulkey* and *Hunter,* the political restriction at issue in *Schuette* was not "designed to be used, or is likely to be used, to encourage infliction of injury by reason of race."[31]

This leaves Justice Kennedy's opinion vulnerable to the following criticism: it makes little sense to hold that (1) a referendum invalidating a ban on *private* housing discrimination as in *Mulkey* and *Hunter* inflicts a constitutionally cognizable injury on minorities even though private action is not covered by the Equal Protection Clause, but (2) when a referendum invalidates a policy that allowed *state* universities to adopt admissions policies that mitigate the vast "underrepresentation" of black and Hispanic students in *public* colleges, no constitutionally cognizable injury can be recognized.

Justice Kennedy counters that racially neutral admissions standards that happen to disfavor minority applicants do not inflict a racial injury as housing discrimination does but simply fail to grant

---

[28] Parents Involved, 551 U.S. at 788–89 (Kennedy, J., concurring).

[29] Schuette, 134 S. Ct. at 1636.

[30] *Id.*

[31] *Id.* at 1638.

"favored status to persons in some racial categories and not others."[32] This characterization, however, is exactly what's disputed by many advocates of affirmative-action preferences in admissions. They see preferences as partially leveling a tilted playing field. So it turns out that a case that was not supposed to be about the constitutionality or desirability of affirmative action, but was only supposed to be about the "political process doctrine," turned on the justices' attitudes regarding affirmative action after all.[33]

Alternative Paths Not Taken by the Plurality

All of this makes one wonder why Justice Kennedy didn't take one of several easier and more defensible "outs." First, as noted previously, the plurality could have simply overruled *Seattle School District* while leaving *Mulkey* and *Hunter* in place. That would have limited the political process doctrine to situations in which a referendum creates a constitutional amendment invalidating an antidiscrimination law.

Second, Kennedy could have distinguished *Mulkey*, *Hunter*, and *Seattle School District* from *Schuette*. Each of the former three cases involved legislation—fair housing laws and busing for racial integration—that was intended to redress societal discrimination. By contrast, under existing Supreme Court precedent, government affirmative action preferences, in universities and elsewhere, are *illegal* if undertaken to redress societal discrimination.[34] Moreover, *Bakke* and *Grutter*, the cases allowing for affirmative action preferences in higher education, deferred not to affirmative-action legislation but to the educational judgment of university officials who concluded that ethnic diversity in their universities was essential for the educational process. *Mulkey*, *Hunter*, and *Seattle School District* are therefore distinguishable from *Schuette* on the theory that overturning a hard-won political victory for minority rights via a referendum is a "racial

---

[32] *Id.*

[33] Richard Lempert, The *Schuette* Decision: The Supreme Court Rules on Affirmative Action, FixGov, April 25, 2014, http://www.brookings.edu/blogs/fixgov/posts/2014/04/25-schuette-affirmative-action-supreme-court-comment-lempert ("The dirty secret of the jurisprudence of race is, as *Schuette* suggests, that it is not so much a principled jurisprudence as it is an arena where most judges feel free to enact their personal values into law.")

[34] City of Richmond v. J.A. Croson Co., 488 U.S. 469, 499 (1989).

injury," while merely overturning what educational bureaucrats see as sound racial policy is not.

Justice Sotomayor's Dissent

In her dissent, Justice Sotomayor argues that even if university preferences are constitutionally permitted only for diversity purposes, minority students are the primary beneficiaries of such policies. Therefore, making it more difficult for them to pursue preferences creates a racial injury. Yet the Supreme Court's diversity rationale arguably suggests that the main benefit of achieving a critical mass of minority students through affirmative action preferences is that it improves the education of the non-minority students.[35] If white students benefit from "diversity"-based preferences at least as much as minority students, then there is no particular group being disadvantaged by Proposition 2's ban on such preferences. In other words, Proposition 2 can't be unconstitutional because it makes it more difficult for minority students to lobby for benefits for themselves, given that, as Justice Scalia points out, if a public university defended a racial preference policy "on the ground that it was *designed* to benefit primarily minorities . . . *we would hold the policy unconstitutional*."[36]

Nor is Sotomayor's claim persuasive that Proposition 2 is unconstitutional because it allows white alumni to lobby for alumni preferences through the normal legislative process but prohibits minority students from doing so. The obvious doctrinal objection is that racial classifications are subject to strict scrutiny, but alumni classifications,

---

[35] Justice Sandra Day O'Connor's opinion in *Grutter* hedges a bit but ultimately rests her opinion on the fact that a "critical mass of underrepresented minorities is necessary to further its compelling interest in securing the educational benefits of a diverse student body." Grutter v. Bollinger, 539 U.S. 306, 333 (2003). Not surprisingly, the diversity rationale has come under attack from those who advocate affirmative action preferences for "social justice" reasons. See, e.g., Richard T. Ford, Racial Culture 59, 64 (2005); Derrick Bell, Diversity's Distractions, 103 Colum. L. Rev. 1622, 1622 (2003); Richard Delgado, Affirmative Action as a Majoritarian Device: Or, Do You Really Want to Be a Role Model?, 89 Mich. L. Rev. 1222, 1224–25 (1991); Osamudia R. James, White Like Me: The Negative Impact of the Diversity Rationale on White Identity Formation, 89 N.Y.U. L. Rev. 425 (2014); Charles R. Lawrence III, Two Views of the River: A Critique of the Liberal Defense of Affirmative Action, 101 Colum. L. Rev. 928, 953 (2001).

[36] Schuette, 134 S. Ct. at 1640 (emphasis in original).

like the vast majority of classifications, are not.[37] Additionally, states can create policies that do not involve classifying individuals by race but encourage more "minority" admissions, such as admitting all students in the top X percent of their high school class.[38]

Sotomayor also seems to mangle equal protection doctrine. Contrary to Justice Scalia's claim that the political process doctrine runs counter to the accepted notion that the right not to be discriminated against is a personal, not a group right, Sotomayor writes that "there can be no equal protection violation unless the injured individual is a member of a protected group or a class of individuals." Conceptually, there is no reason that an equal protection violation can't involve a class of one. In fact, the Supreme Court has held several times that individuals not associated with a class can sue for equal protection violations.[39]

Perhaps the most notable thing about Sotomayor's opinion, however, is that, as Walter Olson puts it, she "gerrymanders the word race itself in a way convenient to her purposes, using it to include Hispanics (who, as official forms remind us, 'can be of any race'), while breathing not one word about Asian-Americans."[40] She treats it as self-evident that there are two and only two "racial minority" groups in the United States, African

---

[37] See Roger Pilon, Reflections on Schuette v. Coalition to Defend Affirmative Action, Cato at Liberty, Apr. 23, 2014, http://www.cato.org/blog/reflections-schuette-v-coalition-defend-affirmative-action. I explain why even "benign" racial classifications may warrant stricter scrutiny than non-racial classifications in Bernstein, *supra* note 4.

[38] Some argue that such policies are themselves unconstitutional violations of the Equal Protection Clause. I disagree, but even if they are, it's not because they involve classifying individuals by race, but because they have discriminatory intent and discriminatory effects.

[39] Sioux City Bridge Co. v. Dakota Cnty., 260 U.S. 441 (1923); Allegheny Pittsburgh Coal Co. v. Comm. of Webster Cty., 488 U.S. 336 (1989); Village of Willowbrook v. Olech, 528 U.S. 562 (2000). In fairness, this part of her opinion is not exactly a model of clarity, and Sotomayor may have meant that there can be no equal protection violation based on race classification unless the individual discriminated against is a member of a classified group.

[40] Walter Olson, Further Thoughts on Schuette v. Coalition, Cato at Liberty, Apr. 24, 2014, http://www.cato.org/blog/further-thoughts-schuette-v-coalition; see also Ilya Somin, Asian-Americans, Affirmative Action, and the "Political Restructuring" Doctrine: Does the Doctrine Work When There Are Minority Groups on Both Sides of the Issue?, Volokh Conspiracy, Apr. 22, 2014, http://www.washingtonpost.com/news/volokh-conspiracy/wp/2014/04/22/asian-americans-affirmative-action-and-the-political-restructuring-doctrine-does-the-doctrine-work-when-there-are-minority-groups-on-both-sides-of-the-issue.

Americans and Hispanics. It's bizarre to treat Hispanics but not Asians as a racial group. Hispanic Americans (like Americans in general) can be descended from Europeans, indigenous people, Africans, Asians, or any combination of those. The idea that a white American whose father is of German descent and whose mother is a Chilean immigrant of Italian ancestry is in the same "racial" category as a Peruvian immigrant of pure Incan descent and an Afro-Costa Rican immigrant should offend the common sense of anyone who takes a moment to think about it. Moreover, 36 percent of Hispanics consider themselves to be white, and only about a quarter choose to identify themselves as "Hispanics" or "Latinos," preferring instead an identity based on their country of origin.[41] While there are many white Hispanics—not just Hispanics with only partial Hispanic ancestry, but descendants of Spanish and Portuguese immigrants, descendants of Europeans who settled in Latin America, Sephardic Jews, and so on—there are by definition no "white Asians."

Justice Sotomayor's opinion nevertheless ignores Asian Americans *entirely for the obvious reason that their success in winning admission* to universities undermines the statistics she cites that show a sharp decline in "minority" (not including Asian) enrollment in states that ban racial preferences.[42] Indeed, racial preferences in elite university admissions typically operate to the detriment of applicants of Asian descent[43] because they are "overrepresented" at selective universities. So, Asian Americans might well want to lobby for a state constitutional amendment like Proposition 2; indeed, Democratic Asian-American

[41] Paul Taylor et al., When Labels Don't Fit: Hispanics and Their Views of Identity, Pew Research Ctr., Jun. 16, 2014, http://www.pewhispanic.org/2012/04/04/when-labels-dont-fit-hispanics-and-their-views-of-identity.

[42] Schuette, 134 S. Ct. at 1678–80 (Sotomayor, J., dissenting).

[43] Thomas J. Espenshade & Alexandria Walton Radford, Evaluative Judgments vs. Bias in College Admissions, Forbes.com, Aug. 12 2010, http://www.forbes.com/2010/08/01/college-admissions-race-politics-opinions-best-colleges-10-espenshade-radford.html; Thomas J. Espenshade & Chang Y. Chung, The Opportunity Cost of Admission Preferences at Elite Universities, 86 Soc. Sci. Q. 293, 293–99 (2005); David R. Colburn et. al., Admissions and Public Higher Education in California, Texas, and Florida: The Post-Affirmative Action Era, 4 InterActions: UCLA J. Educ. & Info. Stud. 4 (2008), available at http://escholarship.org/uc/item/35n755gf; Daniel E. Slotnick, Do Asian-Americans Face Bias in Admissions at Elite Colleges?, N.Y. Times The Choice Blog, Feb. 8, 2012, http://thechoice.blogs.nytimes.com/2012/02/08/do-asian-americans-face-bias-in-admissions-at-elite-colleges/?_r=0 (citing a study showing that holding other variables equal, Asian American applicants need SAT scores 140 points higher than whites to be admitted to elite colleges).

legislators in California, facing pressure from Chinese-American constituents, recently stifled an attempt to overturn California's state constitutional ban on affirmative action preferences.[44]

If Justice Sotomayor's opinion had been the majority, those who oppose alumni preferences would be allowed to pass a constitutional amendment by referendum banning such preferences, but Asian Americans would be prohibited from seeking a constitutional amendment banning preferences that they oppose. That means that by Sotomayor's own reasoning, if her opinion had attracted five votes it would have deprived Asian Americans of their constitutional rights under political process theory.

Justice Sotomayor's implicit view of race in *Schuette*—that it includes a group with a common linguistic but not racial heritage (Hispanics) but not Asians—also undermines the following widely-quoted language from her dissent:

> And race matters for reasons that really are only skin deep, that cannot be discussed any other way, and that cannot be wished away. Race matters to a young man's view of society when he spends his teenage years watching others tense up as he passes, no matter the neighborhood where he grew up. Race matters to a young woman's sense of self when she states her hometown, and then is pressed, "No, where are you really from?", regardless of how many generations her family has been in the country. Race matters to a young person addressed by a stranger in a foreign language, which he does not understand because only English was spoken at home. Race matters because of the slights, the snickers, the silent judgments that reinforce that most crippling of thoughts: "I do not belong here."[45]

"Race matters" is an odd rallying cry from a justice who for all intents and purposes treats Asian Americans as indistinct from whites. Nor does she provide a rationale for limiting the scope of her concerns for minority groups to African Americans and Hispanics. Are Hispanics and African Americans more likely to be asked where they are from or spoken to in a foreign language than are Asians? Do they

---

[44] Frank Stoltze, Friction Lingers among Asian-Americans over Affirmative Action Debate, KPCC, Apr. 17, 2014, http://www.scpr.org/blogs/politics/2014/04/17/16398/friction-lingers-among-asian-americans-over-affirm.

[45] Schuette, 134 S. Ct. at 1676.

suffer more slights, snickers, and silent judgments than Indian Sikhs wearing traditional headdresses, or, for that matter, Hasidic Jewish men with side-curls and fur hats, Mennonites, and Amish in traditional dress, or Arab women in hijabs? Unlike fair-skinned Hispanics who blend in with the general "white" population, Hasidim, Mennonites, and Arab Muslims are not eligible for affirmative action preferences—nor, in university admissions, are Sikhs or other Asians.[46]

In fact, judging from her opinion, the breadth of Justice Sotomayor's "race matters" concern is not some discernibly logical or empirical theory about for whom "race" or, for that matter, "different appearance from the mainstream" matters. Rather, being a "racial minority" is implicitly defined by an arbitrary combination of artificial census categories, university affirmative action admissions policies, and a sense of which minority groups, broadly construed, are not "making it." The "making it" factor is itself highly problematic, given that some subgroups of the Asian category, not to mention some whites (as in Appalachia), have much worse socioeconomic indicators than some subgroups of Hispanics.

Justice Scalia's Concurrence

Justice Scalia, concurring for himself and Justice Thomas, would have dispensed with the political process doctrine entirely as "[p]atently atextual, unadministrable, and contrary to our traditional equal-protection jurisprudence."[47] According to Scalia, an equal-protection challenge to a facially neutral law can succeed only if the plaintiff proves "[discriminatory] intent and causation."[48] *Hunter* should be overruled because the "Court neither found [that the referendum had targeted minorities] nor considered it relevant, bypassing the question of intent entirely, satisfied that its newly minted political-process theory sufficed to invalidate the charter

---

[46] While Asians are most likely to suffer discrimination in university admissions, the "geographic preferences" of elite universities also serve to ensure that universities don't have "too many" Jews, Jews being concentrated in a few major metropolitan areas. Not that long ago, an acquaintance who is a bigwig in a very respected university's alumni association was shocked when the admissions director told him that they were cutting down on admissions of Jews from the New York area because they had "too many" of them.

[47] Schuette, 134 S. Ct. at 1643.

[48] *Id.*

amendment."[49] *Seattle School District*, Scalia argues, suffers from the same flaw, strongly rejecting Kennedy's claim that the Court's opinion was based on an implicit finding that school segregation in *Seattle School District* was in part a product of state action.

Justice Scalia lost on the broad issue, of course, so the political question doctrine remains viable but diminished. But is the doctrine defensible? In addition to the problems with the doctrine mentioned previously, minority advocates of fair housing policy, busing, and affirmative action have the same access to the referendum process to constitutionally require these policies as their opponents have to ban them, making "identification of a 'neutral' political structure . . . an artifact of the level of generality at which the equality principle was applied."[50]

A Limited Defense of the Political Process Doctrine: Reverse *Carolene Products* and the Second Reconstruction

One possible defense is that the doctrine serves as a sort-of reverse *Carolene Products*. Famous Footnote Four of that 1938 case suggested that the Court should engage in strict review of legislation that is the product of "prejudice against discrete and insular minorities . . . which tends seriously to curtail the operation of those political processes ordinarily to be relied upon to protect minorities, and which may call for a correspondingly more searching judicial inquiry."[51] *Carolene Products*'s focus on judicial protection of minorities from legislation was quite logical in 1938, when African Americans were largely concentrated in the American South and were largely disenfranchised there, Asian immigrants were not permitted to become citizens, and other groups faced persistent gerrymandering to limit their political influence.

Carolene Products lost some of its salience as the African American population spread beyond the South, and even more so once the 1965 Voting Rights Act guaranteed minority voting rights. But African Americans still faced significant political disadvantages because they were largely isolated from the rest of the country via housing and school segregation, low rates of intermarriage, and the like. A

---

[49] *Id.* at 1642.

[50] Girardeau Spann, Racial Supremacy, SCOTUSblog, Sept. 11, 2013, http://www.scotusblog.com/2013/09/schuette-symposium-racial-supremacy/.

[51] United States v. Carolene Products Co., 304 U.S. 144, 152 n.4 (1938).

majority—even a non-prejudiced majority—will not take an isolated minority's interests fully into account in the legislative process. Out of sight, as they say, is out of mind.

That disadvantage, however, is balanced out by the fact that an isolated minority group has significant advantages in organizing around issues of special interest to that group. Modern public-choice theory teaches us that, so long as they are able to participate fully in the political process, "discrete and insular minorities" often have a significant political advantage compared to a dispersed and disorganized majority, especially when it comes to issues of particular interest to the minority group. Once granted the right to vote in an electoral system that rewards concentrated interest groups, African Americans—like other organized interest groups from the Sugar Lobby to AIPAC to military veterans to realtors—could then use those advantages to secure legislation in their interest.

That theory perhaps explains the advent of the political process doctrine in *Hunter* in 1968: the Court was supplementing *Carolene Products*, which provided judicial protection from discriminatory legislation, with reverse *Carolene Products,* which protected the important right of African Americans to use their political muscle as other interest groups do, thereby to some degree balancing out their remaining disadvantages in the political system. African Americans and their political allies used their political muscle to achieve a fair housing law in Akron. The referendum invalidating this victory and making it more difficult to achieve future victories deprived them of the fruit of their electoral heft.

One could have argued that this is simply the way the political ball bounces—if dispersed majorities commonly passed referenda overturning ordinary legislation supported by concentrated interest groups. But such referenda were (and are) in fact quite rare. It's therefore not terribly surprising that the Supreme Court saw the Akron referendum as imposing a racial injury. It denied African Americans not only the opportunity to procure favorable legislation but also denied the ability to counter-balance the disadvantages they faced from prejudice or indifference in the political sphere with the advantages of being an organizable minority group with distinct interests and priorities.[52]

[52] For conflicting views of the extent to which referenda trample on minority rights, see Barbara S. Gamble, Putting Civil Rights to a Popular Vote, 41 Am. J. Pol. Sci. 245

"Reverse *Carolene Products*" would also explain why *Seattle School District* came out the way it did, invalidating a busing policy implemented by elected officials, while in the same term the Court upheld a California referendum that overturned the use of busing as a judicially ordered remedy for desegregation.[53] The Court in the latter case did not feel the need to protect a policy that was not the product of the legislative process, but of judicial fiat.

Of course, as noted previously, the *Mulkey* and *Hunter* Courts could have simply ruled that the referenda in question had discriminatory intent and discriminatory effects. From approximately 1948 to 1972, however, and to some extent through 1982, the Supreme Court openly allied with the civil rights movement but tried to do so without either overtly accusing anti-civil rights forces of racism or massively disrupting the federal-state balance.

Even in its much-celebrated and path-breaking *Brown v. Board of Education* opinion, the Court took a conciliatory and subtle path, suggesting not that school segregation was a product of racism, but rather that it resulted from a lack of understanding of the negative effects of segregation on black students.[54] Relatedly, it's widely recognized that the Court's sudden willingness to incorporate the criminal procedure amendments via the Fourteenth Amendment was less a constitutional epiphany and more an attempt to provide procedural tools to help prevent predominately poor, black defendants from being railroaded. What the Court did not do was declare the entire criminal justice system racist and therefore explicitly raise its level of scrutiny for convictions of African Americans suspects, even in cases that arose in jurisdictions widely known for their racism.[55]

Other examples of the Court's manipulating doctrine to aid the cause of civil rights while not stepping on too many toes abound. In *Shelley v. Kraemer*, the Court could have announced that state courts could not be relied upon to fairly apply the rule against restrictions on alienability, and that the Court could not overlook the fact that

---

(1997) (a lot); Zoltan L. Hajnal et al., Minorities and Direct Legislation: Evidence from California Ballot Proposition Elections, 64 J. Pol. 154 (2002) (not that much).

[53] Crawford v. Bd. of Educ., 458 U.S. 527 (1982).

[54] Brown v. Bd. of Educ., 347 U.S. 483 (1954).

[55] The late William Stuntz criticized the Court for not confronting racism in the criminal justice system more directly. William J. Stuntz, The Collapse of American Criminal Justice (2011).

restrictive covenants were part of a broader system of apartheid widely participated in by American governments.[56] After hinting at those rationales, the Court instead concluded that somehow the mere enforcement of a restrictive covenant was discriminatory state action, a view of discriminatory state action it has refused to adopt in any other context.

Similarly, the Court responded to Mississippi's persecution of civil rights leaders not with a blanket refusal to uphold prosecutions emanating from Mississippi, but with the expressive association doctrine that provided a "neutral" (nonracial) means to prevent successful prosecutions.[57] When Mississippi went after national media outlets reporting on the civil rights movement via common-law tort lawsuits, the Court, rather than calling Mississippi out on its racism, instead created the most liberal libel law in the common-law world in *New York Times v. Sullivan*.[58] And when Virginia tried to shut down civil rights litigation by passing a statute codifying common-law bans on barratry, champerty, and maintenance, the Supreme Court didn't hold that the statute was racially discriminatory. Instead, it held that those practices are protected by the First Amendment, at least when engaged in by "public interest" attorneys seeking to change government policy.[59]

In 1982, the same year as *Seattle School District*, the Court expanded the scope of the First Amendment to protect NAACP Mississippi field director Charles Evers from a civil lawsuit arising from a boycott of white-owned businesses he organized in 1968 (the wheels of justice in Mississippi apparently turn very slowly). The Court held that peaceful activity related to the boycott was protected from civil lawsuit by the First Amendment. The Court also came to the counterintuitive conclusion that "peaceful conduct " included the following threat by Evers: "If we catch any of you going into these racist stores, we're going to break your damn neck."[60]

The Court also held that the 1868 Civil Rights Act, in providing "all persons with the same right to make and enforce contracts as

---

[56] 334 U.S. 1 (1948).

[57] NAACP v. Alabama, 357 U.S. 449 (1958).

[58] 376 U.S. 254 (1964).

[59] NAACP v. Button, 371 U.S. 415 (1963).

[60] NAACP v. Claiborne Hardware Co., 458 U.S. 886, 902 (1982).

white persons," actually provided a private right of action against private discrimination.[61] This nontextual interpretation of the act had escaped lawyers and civil rights activists for a century, including during debates over the 1964 Civil Rights Act.

More examples could be provided from cases involving the scope of federal jurisdiction, the availability of private rights of action against the government, and other issues. For approximately 34 years, the Supreme Court saw as part of its mission an alliance with the civil rights movement in general—and more specifically with the aspirations of African Americans for full and equal citizenship. But the Court did so not with fiery denunciations of southern or general American racism and by threatening to upend the entire system to combat that racism, but by inventing novel doctrines that allowed the movement to succeed incrementally. The advent of the political process doctrine should be understood in that context.

Whether and to what extent the Court's tinkering with doctrine to serve civil rights goals was justified, and whether, for that matter, it didn't go far enough and continue for a long enough time, as Justice Sotomayor seems to believe, are valuable questions beyond the scope of this article. For current purposes, (1) it's perfectly understandable that the Court did what it did given that justice and history were clearly on the side of the civil rights movement, and that a more direct confrontation with racist state and local governments could have led to a much greater political backlash against the Court; and (2) any notion that the Court should revive its policy to help eliminate vestiges of America's racist past would be far more defensible if the scope of concern were limited to American descendants of slaves and American Indians who live on reservations. These two groups have suffered the most persecution by and isolation from the American mainstream. Unlike groups dominated by post-1965 immigrants and their descendants, descendants of slaves and Indians on reservations have faced both wide-scale discrimination by government and private entities largely unmitigated by civil rights laws. Modern equal-protection doctrine, however, suggests an absolute symmetry among all "racial" groups under the Equal Protection Clause, and

[61] See Runyon v. McCrary, 427 U.S. 160 (1976); Jones v. Alfred H. Mayer Co., 392 U. S. 409 (1968).

any attempt to create a rule applicable only to one or two groups would be swimming upstream against waves of precedent.

In any event, for several decades, the Court has been controlled by a majority that implicitly believes that the so-called Second Reconstruction ended with the passage of broad-based civil rights legislation and the increased acceptance and assimilation of minority groups. This majority has not been inclined to tinker with doctrine to favor minority groups, and indeed has, to the chagrin of its liberal critics, stood largely in opposition to the policies favored by most organized civil rights groups.

But the Rehnquist and Roberts Courts, whether from inertia or otherwise, have mostly retained the doctrines modified and invented by the Court in alliance with the civil rights movement, even when the underlying racial context has receded. *New York Times v. Sullivan* seems secure, as does the incorporation of the criminal procedure amendments and *NAACP v. Button*. *NAACP v. Claiburne Hardware* seems secure as well, though it arguably gives excessive protection to threatening speech. A broad version of the Court's expansion of the 1868 Civil Rights Act was endorsed and codified by Congress in the 1991 Civil Rights Act.[62] The expressive association doctrine has held up for over 50 years, though it's in danger now that it's being used primarily to provide constitutional protection for private discrimination against homosexuals, and is therefore unpopular among liberals. *Shelley v. Kraemer* has held up perhaps the least well, as it's virtually a dead letter outside the defunct sphere of restrictive covenants.

The Future of the Political Process Doctrine

The political process doctrine made a certain amount of prudential sense when created in the late 1960s for the reasons discussed previously: the Court no doubt correctly believed that the repeal of fair housing legislation was motivated in substantial part by racism—though in keeping with its general modus operandi, it preferred to create new doctrine rather than take the more confrontational path of overtly condemning Akron's electorate for intentional racism. Moreover, although the Court didn't articulate it, the justices likely thought that the constitutional-amendment-by-referendum process

---

[62] Civil Rights Act of 1991, 42 U.S.C. § 1981.

was grossly unfair to blacks for "reverse *Carolene Products*" reasons, preventing them from counteracting the political disadvantages of an isolated and unpopular minority with the advantages of a concentrated interest group.

The political process doctrine became entirely unstable once the issue of "what's good for African Americans" and "what's motivated by racism" became less clear. This had occurred both because of a huge decline since the 1960s in racist attitudes by whites and because the issues have changed from rectifying overt racial discrimination to more complex social policies. For example, in *Seattle School District*, the Court seemed convinced that busing for the purpose of racial integration was obviously in African Americans' interest. A substantial minority of blacks opposed busing, however, and the resulting white flight and turn of many white Democrats against urban liberalism[63] likely left African Americans worse off than if busing had never been implemented.

Other policies, like school vouchers, tend to be opposed by black political elites while being embraced by a majority of black voters. Even with regard to affirmative action, not only is there debate over whether it serves African-American interests, but there are those, black and otherwise (including Justice Clarence Thomas), who oppose it precisely because they think it does grave harm.[64] And with African Americans far less isolated in American life than they were in 1968 or even 1982 (consider, for example, rising rates of intermarriage[65]), the reverse *Carolene Products* rationale is less compelling now.

If the political process doctrine is unstable with regard to African Americans, for reasons discussed previously it becomes positively

---

[63] See Jonathan Reider, Canarsie: The Jews and Italians of Brooklyn against Liberalism (1985).

[64] See Richard H. Sander & Stuart Taylor, Jr., Mismatch: How Affirmative Action Hurts Students It's Intended to Help, & Why Universities Won't Admit It (2012).

[65] Since 1980, the percentage of African-American newlyweds marrying someone of a different race has more than tripled, to 17 percent. Carol Morrello, Intermarriage rates soar as stereotypes fall, Wash. Post, Feb. 16, 2012, http://www.washingtonpost.com/local/intermarriage-rates-soar-as-stereotypes-fall/2012/02/15/gIQAvyByGR_story.html. 87 percent of Americans now approve of black-white marriage, compared with 4 percent (not a misprint) in 1958. Frank Newport, In U.S., 87% Approve of Black-White Marriage, vs. 4% in 1958, Gallup, July 25, 2013, http://www.gallup.com/poll/163697/approve-marriage-blacks-whites.aspx.

incoherent and unworkable once one considers the diversity both among and within other "minority" groups.

So the Supreme Court is left with four options when it confronts the political process doctrine in the future. Option one is to either overrule *Seattle School District* or ignore it as an anomaly. Instead, the Court would limit the political process doctrine to the facts analogous to those of *Hunter*: a minority group and its allies manage to get a law or law passed protecting them from discrimination, but the majority overturns those laws via a constitutional amendment that changes the political process to their disadvantage. "Reverse *Carolene Products*" would be a plausible justification for this rule, though this rationale has become more problematic as racial isolation diminishes. This justification for *Hunter* would suit Justice Kennedy in particular because it provides a rationale for his notoriously opaque opinion in *Romer v. Evans*[66] and would allow the political process doctrine to be applied to "emerging" minority groups like homosexuals.

The second option is to strictly limit *Hunter* and *Seattle School District* to their facts, as interpreted by Justice Kennedy in *Schuette*. The doctrine would apply only when voters overturn government policy meant to mitigate an unambiguous "racial injury" identified by the Court. This category is likely to be vanishingly small, at best. Indeed, this version of the political process doctrine may put the political process doctrine in the *Shelley v. Kraemer* category of doctrines that briefly served to advance civil rights objectives but now are in essence defunct.

Third, if a liberal majority retakes the Court, it could follow Justice Sotomayor's lead and adopt *Seattle School District* wholeheartedly (though Justice Breyer's *Schuette* concurrence suggests that she needs at least two more votes). The Court could try to limit the doctrine to African Americans to make it more workable, but that wouldn't really solve the underlying problems with the doctrine. In any event, it's hard to see the Court's self-described "wise Latina" leading

---

[66] It's true that gays, unlike African Americans, are not a "suspect class" for constitutional purposes. Justice Kennedy, however, clearly would like to undermine a strict dividing line between suspect and nonsuspect classes in modern equal-protection doctrine. See Calvin Massey, The New Formalism: Requiem for Tiered Scrutiny?, 6 U. Pa. J. Const. L. 945, 948 (2004); Ernest A. Young & Erin C. Blondel, Federalism, Liberty, & Equality in *United States v. Windsor*, 2012–13 Cato Sup. Ct. Rev. 117, 139–40 (2013).

the charge to exclude "Hispanics," the largest recognized minority group. By necessity, then, the political process doctrine would be used very selectively to overturn referenda that especially offend liberal sensibilities, as with affirmative action. This offense would be phrased in terms of "racial injury."

Finally, the Court could follow Justice Scalia's lead and reverse *Seattle School District* and *Hunter*. This path would have the virtue of forthrightness and clarity, but that goes against the grain of the Supreme Court's jurisprudence on race, which has long preferred opacity and complication. Even more important, Justice Scalia is shy three votes for this reversal. Given Justice Kennedy's need to protect *Romer* and Chief Justice Roberts's penchant for narrow opinions (unconstrained, as we saw in *NFIB v. Sebelius*, by any reasonable canons of interpretation[67]), he's unlikely to get them any time soon. And so the political process doctrine, problematic though it may be, seems likely to survive for quite some time.

---

[67] See, e.g., Ilya Shapiro, Like Eastwood Talking to a Chair: The Good, the Bad, and the Ugly of the Obamacare Ruling, 17 Tex. Rev. L. & Pol. 1 (2013).

Bond v. United States: Concurring in the Judgment

*Nicholas Quinn Rosenkranz**

Introduction

When Mr. Bond first impregnated Mrs. Bond's best friend, the international Chemical Weapons Convention was probably the furthest thing from his mind.[1] But when Mrs. Bond found out, her thoughts ran right to potassium dichromate and 10-chloro-10H-phenoxarsine.

Mrs. Bond promptly decided to spread these chemicals on the pregnant paramour's doorknob and mailbox.[2] And even though the "best friend" was scarcely harmed (because the chemicals were farcically easy to spot), Mrs. Bond found herself charged with violation of the Chemical Weapons Convention Implementation Act.[3] Improbably enough, this lurid local drama, which played out entirely in Norristown, Pennsylvania, would present momentous constitutional questions about the foreign relations law of the United States.

Now, the Chemical Weapons Convention was quite obviously inspired by a more fearsome set of concerns—paradigmatically, state use of chemical weapons in wartime and/or terrorist use of chemical weapons against civilian populations. No one suggests that the treaty-makers had jilted wives like Mrs. Bond in mind.[4] And the federal statute was expressly enacted to implement this treaty. But, nevertheless, the statute seemed to reach Mrs. Bond's conduct, and

---

* Professor of law, Georgetown University Law Center; senior fellow in constitutional studies, Cato Institute. Thanks to Stacey L. Bennett and Nita A. Farahany. And thanks, also, to Stephanie Freudenberg and the Georgetown Law Library, for first-rate research assistance.

[1] Bond v. United States, 134 S. Ct. 2077 (2014).

[2] *Id.* at 2085.

[3] *Id.*

[4] *Id.* at 2088.

an ambitious assistant United States attorney decided to make it a federal case.

Mrs. Bond entered a conditional guilty plea, reserving the right to appeal. The government, bizarrely, started by contending that Mrs. Bond lacked standing to make a Tenth Amendment/enumerated powers argument, even though her liberty was on the line; and the U.S. Court of Appeals for the Third Circuit, oddly, agreed.[5] Then, though, the government reversed course and confessed error: of course a criminal defendant has standing to argue that Congress lacked power to enact the statute at issue.[6] And in 2011, the Supreme Court reversed 9-0.[7]

This term, the case was back at the Supreme Court on the merits. Mrs. Bond argued, first, that the statute did not reach her conduct—a statutory interpretation argument that turned out to have surprising traction.

Second, in the alternative, Mrs. Bond argued that if the statute does reach her conduct, then Congress had no constitutional power to enact it and it could not be applied to her. Congress's legislative powers are enumerated, primarily in Article I, Section 8. So, as a general matter, for every federal statute, one ought to be able to find a corresponding power over the subject matter in the enumerated list. Mrs. Bond took a look at the list and argued that she found no enumerated power over purely local chemical assault.

The government, oddly, largely conceded this point, waiving any argument that this statute was a regulation of interstate commerce.[8] Instead, the government made the following remarkable assertion. It argued that because the United States had entered into a treaty concerning chemical weapons, Congress automatically has the power to enact a statute on this subject, even if it would have lacked this power otherwise. It argued, in other words, that *a treaty can increase the legislative power of Congress.*

And indeed, in 1920, the Supreme Court seemed to say exactly that. Justice Oliver Wendell Holmes wrote for the Court: "If the treaty is valid there can be no dispute about the validity of the [implementing]

---

[5] United States v. Bond, 581 F.3d 128, 137 (3d Cir. 2009).

[6] Bond, 134 S. Ct. at 2086.

[7] Bond v. United States, 131 S. Ct. 2355, 2359 (2011).

[8] United States v. Bond, 681 F.3d 149, 151 n.1 (3d Cir. 2012).

statute under Article I, § 8, as a necessary and proper means to execute the powers of the government."[9]

This was the proposition that caught the interest of the Cato Institute. In 2005, in the *Harvard Law Review*, I argued that this sentence is fundamentally inconsistent with constitutional text and structure, and that it should be overruled.[10] If a treaty could increase the legislative powers of Congress, then enumerating those powers in the first place was a fool's errand; the president and Senate, with the concurrence of, say, Zimbabwe, could easily circumvent the enumeration and vest Congress with plenary legislative power. Cato agreed (as did the Center for Constitutional Jurisprudence and the Atlantic Legal Foundation), and so we filed an amicus brief to that effect,[11] based on my article.[12] We argued that *Missouri v. Holland* was wrong: a treaty cannot increase the legislative power of Congress.

In what must be a new record for a criminal defendant, the Supreme Court again ruled for Mrs. Bond, and again the vote was 9-0.[13] (Meanwhile, for the Obama administration, this is one of at least a dozen unanimous losses in the last three terms,[14] which may also be some sort of record.) Mrs. Bond's conviction was overturned.

But although all nine justices agreed about the result, there were substantial disagreements about the reasoning. Unfortunately, Chief Justice John Roberts, writing for the Court, managed to sidestep the constitutional issue, expressing no view on the important constitutional question of whether a treaty can increase the legislative power of Congress. But the Court's opinion is nevertheless worth studying, if only as an object lesson in dodgy statutory interpretation. Meanwhile, Justices Antonin Scalia, Clarence Thomas, and Samuel Alito rightly did reach the important constitutional question, each writing

---

[9] Missouri v. Holland, 252 U.S. 416, 432 (1920).

[10] Nicholas Quinn Rosenkranz, Executing the Treaty Power, 118 Harv. L. Rev. 1867 (2005).

[11] Brief of Amici Curiae Cato Institute, Center for Constitutional Jurisprudence, and Atlantic Legal Foundation in Support of Petitioner at 2, Bond v. United States, 134 S. Ct. 2077 (2014) (No. 12-158) [hereinafter Cato Brief].

[12] Rosenkranz, *supra* note 10.

[13] Bond v. United States, 134 S. Ct. 2077, 2082 (2014).

[14] See Ilya Shapiro, No, Mr. President, You Can't Do Whatever You Want, Forbes, June 27, 2014, http://www.forbes.com/sites/ilyashapiro/2014/06/27/no-mr-president-you-cant-do-whatever-you-want.

a separate concurrence in the judgment. Collectively, these three opinions grapple with the intertwined issues of (1) the scope of the treaty power and (2) the scope of Congress's power to legislate pursuant to treaty. Because these issues have rarely arisen, these concurrences stand as some of the most scholarly and thoughtful treaty opinions ever to emanate from the Supreme Court.

I. Was Mrs. Bond's Conduct Covered by the Statute?

The Court began with the statutory interpretation question: *Did the statute reach Mrs. Bond's conduct?* This is standard practice. The Court does and should avoid difficult constitutional questions when it fairly can,[15] and if Mrs. Bond's conduct was not covered by the statute, then that is the end of the case. It is undisputed that Mrs. Bond possessed and used a chemical to harm her neighbor. But did this constitute possession and use of a "chemical weapon" under the Chemical Weapons Convention Implementation Act?

The statute provides that no person may knowingly "develop, produce, otherwise acquire, transfer directly or indirectly, receive, stockpile, retain, own, possess, or use, or threaten to use, any *chemical weapon*."[16] At first glance, the key term is ambiguous. Mrs. Bond clearly possessed and used *something*, but was it a "chemical weapon"? Under normal circumstances, this might pose an interpretive riddle, but in this case, Congress itself has expressly defined the term. The statute defines the phrase "chemical weapon" to mean "[a] *toxic chemical* and its precursors, except where intended for a *purpose not prohibited* under this chapter as long as the type and quantity is consistent with such a purpose."[17] Now, this definition itself may appear to be ambiguous. A "chemical weapon" is a "toxic chemical," but this just begs the question: did Mrs. Bond possess and use a "toxic chemical"? And even if so, was her "purpose not prohibited"? Happily, Congress expressly defined both of these terms too. A "toxic chemical" is defined very broadly as *"any chemical* which through its chemical action on life processes can cause death, temporary incapacitation or

---

[15] Escambia County v. McMillan, 466 U.S. 48, 51 (1984) (per curiam); see also Ashwander v. TVA, 297 U.S. 288, 347 (1936) (Brandeis, J., concurring).

[16] 18 U. S.C. § 229(a)(1) (2012) (emphasis added).

[17] 18 U.S.C. § 229F(1)(A) (2012) (emphasis added).

permanent harm to humans or animals."[18] To remove all doubt, the definition goes on to specify that "[t]he term includes *all such chemicals*, regardless of their origin or of their method of production, and regardless of whether they are produced in facilities, in munitions or elsewhere."[19] And a "purpose not prohibited" is "[a]ny *peaceful* purpose related to an industrial, agricultural, research, medical, or pharmaceutical activity or other activity."[20]

In short, the Chemical Weapons Convention Implementation Act is a model of legislative drafting in one important sense. Several of its key terms may be ambiguous at first glance, *but Congress has expressly defined these terms*. Each time a term seems to pose an interpretive puzzle, there is a definitional provision that solves the puzzle.

Working bottom to top through these interlocking definitions takes some doing, but there is nothing ambiguous about the process or the result. Definitional provisions are like algebraic substitutions: where one sees X, one should read Y. Here is Justice Scalia, demonstrating, in one paragraph, how this is done:

> [1] Bond possessed and used "chemical[s] which through [their] chemical action on life processes can cause death, temporary incapacitation or permanent harm." [2] Thus, she possessed "toxic chemicals." [3] And, because they were not possessed or used only for a "purpose not prohibited," §229F(1)(A), they were "chemical weapons." Ergo, Bond violated the Act. End of statutory analysis, I would have thought.[21]

Alas, this inexorable logic garnered only three votes at the Supreme Court. "The Court does not think the interpretive exercise so simple. But that is only because its result-driven antitextualism befogs what is evident."[22]

The Court's basic objection to Justice Scalia's analysis "is that it would 'dramatically intrude[] upon traditional state criminal jurisdiction,' and we avoid reading statutes to have such reach in the

---

[18] 18 U.S.C. § 229F(8)(A) (emphasis added).

[19] *Id*. (emphasis added).

[20] 18 U.S.C. § 229F(7)(A) (emphasis added).

[21] Bond v. United States, 134 S. Ct. 2077, 2094 (2014) (Scalia, J., concurring in the judgment).

[22] *Id*. at 2095.

absence of a clear indication that they do."[23] This, the Court suggests, is a fundamental principle of federal statutory interpretation: "it is appropriate to refer to basic principles of federalism embodied in the Constitution to resolve ambiguity in a federal statute."[24]

Fair enough, and this solicitude for federalism is to be applauded, but the key word here is "ambiguity." As the Court acknowledges, this principle does not come into play if the statute is clear. And, again, at the end of the chain of statutory definitions in this case is a provision that could not be clearer: the statute applies to chemicals that "can cause death, temporary incapacitation or permanent harm." It is undisputed that Mrs. Bond's chosen chemicals can cause such harm. In order to bring its federalism canon into play, the Court must struggle mightily to find ambiguity in a carefully defined term. The effort is unpersuasive.

The Court gets off on the wrong foot with the first sentence of analysis: "Section 229 exists to implement the Convention, so we begin with that international agreement."[25] In a question of statutory interpretation, one should always begin not with why a statute purportedly exists but with what it actually says.[26] Here, the Court begins, not with the text of the statute, or even the text of the treaty, but rather with the Court's own guess as to the intention of the treaty makers. "There is no reason to think the sovereign nations that ratified the Convention were interested in anything like Bond's common law assault."[27] Probably true, but surely beside the point. Mrs. Bond was charged with violating a United States statute, duly passed by the House of Representatives, passed by the Senate, and signed by the president. The private intentions of, say, Vladimir Putin, should have nothing to do with its interpretation.

In any case, after positing the private intentions of foreign sovereigns, the Court then turns to the statute itself, ostensibly to divine the meaning of "chemical weapon." But here again, the Court starts off on the wrong foot: "To begin, as a matter of natural meaning, an educated user of English would not describe Bond's crime as

[23] *Id.* at 2088 (majority opinion) (quoting United States v. Bass, 404 U.S. 336, 350 (1971)).

[24] *Id.* at 2090.

[25] *Id.* at 2087.

[26] See, e.g., U.S. v. Alvarez, 511 U.S. 350, 356 (1994) ("When interpreting a statute, we look first and foremost to its text.").

[27] Bond, 134 S. Ct. at 2087.

involving a 'chemical weapon.'"[28] True, but irrelevant. There is no call to speculate about the "natural meaning" of "chemical weapon," because *Congress has defined the term.*

> To understand how statutory definitions work, it is useful first to consider how statutes work without them. If Congress uses a vague phrase . . . without defining it, then courts must give the phrase content by bringing various tools of statutory interpretation to bear on the ambiguity . . . . Courts might look the words up in a dictionary. They might look to other uses of the phrase in the same statute or perhaps in other statutes and compare contexts. They might look to committee reports and other forms of legislative history. They might try to discern the purpose of the act . . . . Conversely, when Congress inserts a definitional section, courts resort not to their usual grab bags of interpretive tools, but to the statutory definition alone. Congress in effect replaces a complicated and fuzzy algorithm with a simple cut-and-paste function: "Where one sees X, one shall read Y." No guesswork is necessary . . . . Cut and paste.[29]

The entire point of a statutory definition is to obviate an unstructured judicial inquiry into "natural meaning." When Congress fails to define a term, the Court may try to discern its "natural meaning," and this judicially derived definition will win the day. But when Congress does define a term, the congressional definition must trump any judicial divination of "natural meaning" in exactly the same way, and for the same reason, that statutes trump common law.[30] This is so even if—one might say especially if—the legislative

---

[28] *Id.* at 2090.

[29] Nicholas Quinn Rosenkranz, Federal Rules of Statutory Interpretation, 115 Harv. L. Rev. 2085, 2103–04 (2002).

[30] *Id.* at 2107; see also *id.* at 2119 ("The 'interpretive indicia' of a text depend entirely on the interpretive methodology applied to it. That is why it is essential, when asking whether Congress may pass a general prospective interpretive rule, to ask first: *what is the constitutional status of the rule that Congress would displace?* To claim, as [Laurence] Tribe does, that all 'rules of construction contained in the United States Code' may be trumped by 'other interpretive indicia' is in effect to claim that all the interpretive tools currently used by the courts—even mere syntactical canons—are constitutionally required. Since it is implausible that the Constitution requires a completely specified interpretive methodology, this view amounts to an untenable endorsement of imperial judging at the expense of democratic legislation."(footnotes omitted) (emphasis in original)).

definition differs substantially from common usage. As Justice Scalia writes:

> There is no opinion of ours, and none written by any court or put forward by any commentator since Aristotle, which says, or even suggests, that "dissonance" between ordinary meaning and the unambiguous words of a definition is to be resolved in favor of ordinary meaning. If that were the case, there would hardly be any use in providing a definition.[31]

To see the point most simply, consider the use of dictionaries. The judicial search for "natural meaning" will often begin with a turn to dictionaries. But an immediate problem presents itself. To which dictionary should courts turn? In this case, the Court chooses *Webster's Third New International Dictionary* and *The American Heritage Dictionary*.[32] But how can it be sure that Congress didn't have the *Oxford English Dictionary* in mind instead?[33]

Rather than leaving potential ambiguities to the vagaries of "natural meaning" or dictionary roulette, Congress may choose to define key terms itself. In effect, Congress declares that, for certain specified terms, the U.S. Code itself is the official and exclusive dictionary.[34] When Congress does so, its definition should be the final word on the matter. The Court has generally been perfectly clear about this point: "When a statute includes an explicit definition, we must follow that definition, even if it varies from that term's ordinary meaning."[35]

But in *Bond*, the Court turns this principle on its head. In Part III-B, the heart of the Court's opinion, it quotes both *Webster's Third New International Dictionary* and *The American Heritage Dictionary*. Yet not once in this section does it quote, let alone parse, the definition that Congress itself provided in the U.S. Code. Only by overlooking Congress's definition altogether does the Court find the ambiguity that it seeks. In an act of interpretive perversity, the Court (1) posits a "natural meaning" of "chemical weapons," (2) declares that "natural

---

[31] Bond, 134 S. Ct. at 2096 (Scalia, J., concurring in the judgment).

[32] *Id.* at 2090 (majority opinion).

[33] See generally Rosenkranz, *supra* note 29, at 2147.

[34] See *id.* at 2103–06.

[35] Stenberg v. Carhart, 530 U.S. 914, 942 (2000) (emphasis added).

meaning" to be ambiguous, and then (3) holds that this ambiguous "natural meaning" trumps Congress's own clear definition.

Here is the Court, explaining the source of the supposed ambiguity:

> [A]mbiguity derives from the improbably broad reach of the key statutory definition given the term—"chemical weapon"—being defined; the deeply serious consequences of adopting such a boundless reading; and the lack of any apparent need to do so in light of the context from which the statute arose—a treaty about chemical warfare and terrorism. We conclude that, in this curious case, we can insist on a clear indication that Congress meant to reach purely local crimes, before interpreting the statute's expansive language in a way that intrudes on the police power of the States.[36]

And here is Justice Scalia's devastating reply: "Imagine what future courts can do with that judge-empowering principle: Whatever has improbably broad, deeply serious, and apparently unnecessary consequences . . . is ambiguous!"[37]

Oddly, the Court seems to have overlooked the strongest precedent for its position. In *Will v. Mich. Dep't of State Police*, the Court seemed to allow "common usage" to trump the Dictionary Act, holding that a general definition at the beginning of the U.S. Code was not a clear enough statement to overcome a particular federalism presumption of statutory interpretation.[38] This holding is much closer to the Court's approach than any of the other cases on which it relies.

In any event, though, *Will* is distinguishable and Justice Scalia would still have the better of the argument. The Dictionary Act is generally applicable throughout the U.S. Code, and perhaps federalism canons are "constitutional default rule[s] required by the Tenth Amendment,"[39] which cannot be reversed *wholesale* by a global interpretive rule. But in this case, the definitional provision is not *generally applicable*; it is *statute-specific*. When a statute specifies that X shall mean Y *for purposes of that particular statute*, that definition should constitute a clear enough statement to overcome any such presumption.[40]

---

[36] Bond, 134 S. Ct. at 2090.

[37] *Id.* at 2096 (Scalia, J., concurring in the judgment).

[38] 491 U.S. 58, 69–70 (1989).

[39] See Rosenkranz, *supra* note 29, at 2122.

[40] See *id.* at 2121–23.

The silver lining of the Court's statutory sleight-of-hand is that it may be limited to these facts. At each key point in its analysis, the Court is at pains to emphasize that this is an "unusual case."[41] One senses that the Court—or at least the chief justice—was a bit unnerved by Justice Scalia's prediction that the majority's "interpretive principles never before imagined . . . will bedevil our jurisprudence (and proliferate litigation) for years to come."[42]

Not so, coos the Court, for this is a "curious case."[43]

> This case is unusual, and our analysis is appropriately limited. Our disagreement with our colleagues reduces to whether section 229 is "utterly clear." Post, at 5 (SCALIA, J., concurring in judgment). We think it is not, given that the definition of "chemical weapon" in a particular case can reach beyond any normal notion of such a weapon, that the context from which the statute arose demonstrates a much more limited prohibition was intended, and that the most sweeping reading of the statute would fundamentally upset the Constitution's balance between national and local power. *This exceptional convergence of factors* gives us serious reason to doubt the Government's expansive reading of section 229, and calls for us to interpret the statute more narrowly.[44]

Happily, this sounds almost like the infamous *Bush v. Gore* one-train-only disclaimer: "Our consideration is limited to the present circumstances."[45] It is to be hoped that "[t]his exceptional convergence of factors" will never converge again, and the Court will return to its prior practice of honoring statutory definitions provided by Congress.

In any event, the Court concluded, by dubious statutory interpretation, that the statute did not reach Mrs. Bond's conduct. Thus, her conviction must be overturned—the right result, but for the wrong reason. For the majority, that was the end of the case.

---

[41] *Id.* at 2092.

[42] *Id.* at 2102.

[43] Bond v. United States, 134 S. Ct. 2077, 2090 (2014).

[44] *Id.* at 2093 (emphasis added).

[45] Bush v. Gore, 531 U.S. 98, 109 (2000).

II. Can a Treaty Increase the Legislative Power of Congress?[46]

But for Justices Scalia, Thomas, and Alito, the statute is crystal clear, and it clearly covers Mrs. Bond's conduct. So they are obliged to answer a momentous constitutional question: *did Congress have power to enact the statute in the first place?*

As to this point, the government argued that, because the United States has entered into a treaty about chemical weapons, Congress automatically has the power to enact a statute on this subject, even if it would have lacked this power otherwise. It argued, in other words, that *a treaty can increase the legislative power of Congress.* For this proposition, it relied on a single sentence from *Missouri v. Holland*: "If the treaty is valid there can be no dispute about the validity of the [implementing] statute under Article I, § 8, as a necessary and proper means to execute the powers of the government."[47]

Cato filed a brief as amicus, based on my *Harvard Law Review* article, arguing that *Missouri v. Holland* is wrong on this point and should be overruled.[48] Justice Scalia, joined by Justice Thomas, agreed with us, adopting not just our conclusion but our reasoning as well. Cato's record at the Court is remarkably good,[49] but it is rare that an opinion ends up tracking our brief so closely.

A. Text

The two relevant clauses of the Constitution are the Necessary and Proper Clause and the Treaty Clause, though you would never know it from Justice Holmes's cryptic opinion in *Missouri v. Holland*. "Justice Holmes did not quote either the Treaty Clause or the Necessary and Proper Clause, let alone discuss how they fit together grammatically. Indeed, it is striking to find that the phrase 'necessary and proper' and the phrase 'to make treaties' *never* appear in

---

[46] This part is largely derived from Nicholas Quinn Rosenkranz, Justice Scalia's Masterful Concurrence in Bond v. United States, Volokh Conspiracy (June 3, 2014), http://www.washingtonpost.com/news/volokh-conspiracy/wp/2014/06/03/justice-scalias-masterful-concurrence-in-bond-v-united-states.

[47] Missouri v. Holland, 252 U.S. 416, 432 (1920).

[48] Cato Brief, *supra* note 11, at 2; Rosenkranz, *supra* note 10, at 1867.

[49] See, e.g., Ilya Shapiro, Cato Went 10-1 at Supreme Court This Term, Cato at Liberty (Jul. 2, 2014), http://www.cato.org/blog/cato-went-10-1-supreme-court-term.

the same sentence in the *United States Reports*."[50] But now, at last, they shall. Justice Scalia quotes both clauses and carefully conjoins them: "Read together, the two Clauses empower Congress to pass laws 'necessary and proper for carrying into Execution . . . [the] Power . . . to make Treaties.'"[51]

Once the clauses are properly conjoined, it becomes clear that they do not give Congress the power that the government claimed in this case. Per Justice Scalia: "It is obvious what the Clauses, read together, do *not* say. They do not authorize Congress to enact laws for carrying into execution 'Treaties.'"[52] The key phrase is the infinitive "to make": "The Congress shall have Power . . . To make all Laws which shall be necessary and proper for carrying into Execution . . . [the] Power . . . *to make* Treaties."

As Justice Scalia explains: "the power of the President and the Senate 'to make' a Treaty cannot possibly mean to 'enter into a compact with a foreign nation and then give that compact domestic legal effect.'"[53] The distinction between "making" a treaty and giving it domestic legal effect goes back at least as far as Blackstone.[54] As Justice Scalia writes: "Upon the President's agreement and the Senate's ratification, a treaty . . . has been *made* and is not susceptible of any more making."[55]

In short, as Justice Scalia explains:

> [A] power to help the President *make* treaties is not a power to *implement* treaties already made. See generally Rosenkranz, Executing the Treaty Power, 118 Harv. L. Rev. 1867 (2005).

[50] Rosenkranz, *supra* note 10, at 1882 (emphasis in original).

[51] Bond v. United States, 134 S. Ct. 2077, 2098 (2014) (Scalia, J., concurring in the judgment).

[52] *Id.* at 2098 (emphasis in original); see also Rosenkranz, *supra* note 10, at 1882 ("The Power granted to Congress is emphatically not the power to make laws for carrying into execution 'the treaty power,' let alone the power to make laws for carrying into execution 'all treaties.'").

[53] Bond, 134 S. Ct. at 2099 (Scalia, J., concurring in the judgment); see also Rosenkranz, *supra* note 10, at 1884 ("Nor will it do to say that the phrase 'make Treaties' is a term of art meaning 'conclude treaties with foreign nations and then give them domestic legal effect.'").

[54] Rosenkranz, *supra* note 10, at 1867.

[55] Bond, 134 S. Ct. at 2098 (Scalia, J., concurring in the judgment); see also Rosenkranz, *supra* note 10, at 1884 ("The 'Power . . . to make Treaties' is exhausted once a treaty is ratified; implementation is something else altogether.") (emphasis in original).

> Once a treaty has been made, Congress's power to do what is "necessary and proper" to assist the making of treaties drops out of the picture. To legislate compliance with the United States' treaty obligations, Congress must rely upon its independent (though quite robust) Article I, § 8, powers.[56]

In this case, Congress could not rely on any other Article I, Section 8, power (oddly, the government waived reliance on the Commerce Clause), and so the statute should have fallen.

B. Structure

The textual point coheres perfectly with constitutional structure. Justice Scalia begins with the constitutional axiom that Congress has limited and enumerated powers, and then explains how the government's argument would constitute a "loophole" to that fundamental principle.[57] If the government is right, "then the possibilities of what the Federal Government may accomplish, with the right treaty in hand, are endless and hardly farfetched . . . . It could begin, as some scholars have suggested, with abrogation of this Court's constitutional rulings."[58] But this is, as Justice Scalia says, "the least of the problem."[59] The government's position "places Congress only one treaty away from acquiring a general police power."[60] This is an unthinkable result: countless canonical opinions insist that Congress can have no such power.

To see the point another way, consider that, under *Reid v. Covert*, a treaty cannot empower Congress to violate the Bill of Rights.[61] But under *Missouri v. Holland*, the Tenth Amendment is treated differently: a treaty *can* empower Congress to exceed its enumerated powers and violate the Tenth Amendment. This distinction is untenable. "The distinction between provisions protecting individual liberty, on the one hand, and 'structural' provisions, on the other, cannot be the explanation, since structure in general—and especially the

---

[56] Bond, 134 S. Ct. at 2099 (Scalia, J., concurring in the judgment) (emphasis in original).

[57] *Id.*

[58] *Id.* at 2100.

[59] *Id.*

[60] *Id.* at 2101.

[61] Reid v. Covert, 354 U.S. 1, 16 (1957) (plurality).

structure of limited federal powers—is *designed* to protect individual liberty."[62] *Reid* and *Holland* cannot be reconciled; *Reid* is right and *Holland* is wrong.

This leaves one last quirk. If a self-executing treaty can reach matters other than those in Article I, Section 8, isn't it odd to say that a non-self-executing treaty followed by an implementing statute cannot? At first glance, this may seem anomalous, but it actually makes perfect structural sense. Justice Scalia explains:

> Suppose, for example, that the self-aggrandizing Federal Government wishes to take over the law of intestacy. If the President and the Senate find some foreign state as a ready accomplice, they have two options. First, they can enter into a treaty with "stipulations" specific enough that they "require no legislation to make them operative," *Whitney* v. *Robertson*, 124 U. S. 190, 194 (1888), which would mean in this example something like a comprehensive probate code. But for that to succeed, the President and a supermajority of the Senate would need to reach agreement on all the details—which, when once embodied in the treaty, could not be altered or superseded by ordinary legislation. The second option—far the better one—is for Congress to gain lasting and flexible control over the law of intestacy by means of a non-self-executing treaty. "[Implementing] legislation is as much subject to modification and repeal by Congress as legislation upon any other subject." *Ibid.* And to make such a treaty, the President and Senate would need to agree only that they desire power over the law of intestacy.[63]

One could say the same thing about family law:

> [A]ssume that the federal government desires power that it would otherwise lack over some subject matter—say, for example, family law. One option would be to make a self-executing treaty with the prolixity of a family law code, which would, of its own force, constitute the family law of the United States. This option is unlikely to be very tempting, however, because it would require that the President and two-thirds of the Senate agree on a particular family law code, to be frozen into the treaty (and arguably beyond the

---

[62] Bond, 134 S. Ct. at 2101 (Scalia, J., concurring in the judgment) (emphasis in original); see also Cato Brief, *supra* note 11, at 21.

[63] Bond, 134 S. Ct. at 2101–02 (Scalia, J., concurring in the judgment).

power of Congress to amend or supersede). But if Justice Holmes were correct, there would be a second option: the United States could enter into a *non-self-executing* treaty that simply promised (to attempt) to regulate family law in the United States "in a manner that best protects the institution of the family." This treaty would be far more tempting to the treatymakers on the American side, because it would require the President and two-thirds of the Senate to agree on only one thing: *that they want power over family law.*[64]

The ultimate point here is that "the Constitution should not be construed to create this doubly perverse incentive—an incentive to enter 'entangling alliances' merely to attain the desired side effect of increased domestic legislative power."[65] This deep structural problem can be solved only by repudiating *Missouri v. Holland* and holding that a treaty cannot increase the legislative power of Congress.

III. Are There Subject-Matter Limitations on the Scope of the Treaty Power?

A. Justice Thomas's Concurrence

The discussion above has an unspoken premise: Justice Scalia assumed that the treaty itself was a valid treaty. It is this assumption that sets up the question of whether the treaty can increase the legislative power of Congress. Justice Scalia made that assumption because the parties did too. Mrs. Bond did not argue that the president lacked the power to enter into the treaty, and she did not contend that the treaty itself was invalid.

Nevertheless, Justice Thomas wrote a separate concurrence about the scope of the treaty power, which Justices Scalia and Alito joined. The Constitution provides that "The President . . . shall have Power, by and with the Advice and Consent of the Senate, to make Treaties, provided two thirds of the Senators present concur."[66] As Justice Thomas points out, though: "The Constitution does not . . . comprehensively define the proper bounds of the Treaty Power, and this Court has not yet had occasion to do so."[67] In other words, the

---

[64] Rosenkranz, *supra* note 10, at 1930 (emphasis in original).

[65] *Id.* at 1932.

[66] U.S. Const. art. II, § 2, cl. 2.

[67] Bond, 134 S. Ct. at 2103 (Thomas, J., concurring in the judgment).

Constitution spells out the procedure for making treaties, but it does not expressly define the word "Treaties" or specify what are proper treaties under the clause. "As a result," explains Justice Thomas, "some have suggested that the Treaty Power is boundless—that it can reach any subject matter, even those that are of strictly domestic concern."[68]

This is a startling suggestion, especially when combined with the *Missouri v. Holland* point discussed above.[69] Again, *Missouri v. Holland* seemed to say that Congress automatically has power to make a law implementing a treaty, even if it would have lacked the power to make that same law absent the treaty. It seemed to say, in other words, that a treaty can increase the legislative powers of Congress. If this is so, and if it is correct that a treaty "can reach any subject matter, even those that are of strictly domestic concern,"[70] then "the legislative powers are not merely somewhat expandable by treaty; they are expandable virtually without limit."[71]

Justice Thomas emphatically rejects that possibility. First, he joins Justice Scalia's concurrence, concluding that *Missouri v. Holland* is wrong: a treaty cannot increase the legislative power of Congress. Second, he "write[s] separately to suggest that the Treaty Power is itself a limited federal power."[72]

The balance of his concurrence is a thorough and scholarly historical exploration of what those limits might be. His opinion is a model of originalism—parsing early treatises, Founding-era dictionaries, pre-constitutional practice, constitutional ratification debates, the Jay Treaty debates, and any other source that might shed light on the original meaning of the word "Treaties." And while he does not reach a final conclusion—again, Mrs. Bond did not challenge the validity of the treaty in this case—Justice Thomas does find powerful historical evidence "suggesting that *the Treaty Power can be used to*

---

[68] *Id.* at 2100 (citing Restatement (Third) of Foreign Relations Law of the United States § 302, cmt. c (1986)).

[69] See *supra* Part II.

[70] See *supra* note 61 and accompanying text.

[71] Rosenkranz, *supra* note 10, at 1893.

[72] Bond, 134 S. Ct. at 2103 (Thomas, J., concurring in the judgment).

arrange intercourse with other nations, but not to regulate purely domestic affairs."[73]

This distinction is quite plausible. It makes good structural sense, and Justice Thomas's historical evidence is compelling. In practice, however, it might prove to be a very difficult line to draw. Justice Thomas recognizes this problem, but he insists that the Court should not be daunted:

> In an appropriate case, I would draw a line that respects the original understanding of the Treaty Power. I acknowledge that the distinction between matters of international intercourse and matters of purely domestic regulation may not be obvious in all cases. But this Court has long recognized that the Treaty Power is limited, and hypothetical difficulties in line-drawing are no reason to ignore a constitutional limit on federal power.[74]

B. Justice Alito's Concurrence

Justice Alito's opinion is, in some ways, the most intriguing of them all. But to understand its significance, it is crucial to recall where he stands on the other three opinions.

Again, the majority opinion held that the Chemical Weapons Convention Implementation Act did not reach Mrs. Bond's conduct. For those six justices, that conclusion is enough to decide the case: her conviction must be overturned. But Justice Alito did not sign on to the majority opinion; instead, he signed onto the statutory interpretation section of Justice Scalia's opinion, concluding that the statute clearly *does* reach her conduct. This conclusion cannot end the case, because Mrs. Bond's constitutional arguments remain.

Justice Scalia's opinion concludes that *Missouri v. Holland* is wrong: a treaty cannot increase the legislative power of Congress. Since the treaty could not sustain the statute, the statute could not constitutionally be applied to Mrs. Bond. For Justice Scalia, joined by Justice Thomas, that conclusion resolves the case: Mrs. Bond's conviction must be overturned. So those two opinions suffice to resolve the case

---

[73] *Id.* (emphasis added).
[74] *Id.* at 2110.

for eight of the justices. But Justice Alito did not join that part of Justice Scalia's opinion.

Justice Thomas's opinion "suggest[s]"[75] a possible limit on the president's power to make treaties, and Justice Alito does join that opinion. But nowhere in that opinion does Justice Thomas suggest that anything is wrong with this particular treaty. Again, Mrs. Bond conceded the validity of the treaty, and so Justice Thomas had no occasion to second-guess it or to apply his proposed "international intercourse" test to the present case. His disposition of the case was already determined by Justice Scalia's opinion, which he joined.

So, as a matter of logic, Justice Alito's votes on the prior three opinions do not suffice to decide the case. Absent an opinion of his own, there would not be enough information to determine why he votes to reverse. With that context in mind, it is interesting to parse his one-page concurrence in the judgment. Here is the constitutional analysis in full:

> For the reasons set out in Parts I–III of JUSTICE THOMAS' concurring opinion, which I join, I believe that the treaty power is limited to agreements that address matters of legitimate international concern. The treaty pursuant to which §229 was enacted, the Chemical Weapons Convention, is not self-executing, and thus the Convention itself does not have domestic effect without congressional action. The control of true chemical weapons, as that term is customarily understood, is a matter of great international concern, and therefore the heart of the Convention clearly represents a valid exercise of the treaty power. But insofar as the Convention may be read to obligate the United States to enact domestic legislation criminalizing conduct of the sort at issue in this case, which typically is the sort of conduct regulated by the States, the Convention exceeds the scope of the treaty power. Section 229 cannot be regarded as necessary and proper to carry into execution the treaty power, and accordingly it lies outside Congress' reach unless supported by some other power enumerated in the Constitution. The Government has presented no such justification for this statute.[76]

---

[75] *Id.* at 2103, 2105, 2109.

[76] *Id.* at 2111 (Alito, J., concurring in the judgment).

This is a rich and dense paragraph, but it seems perhaps a bit too quick. Justice Alito may well be right that "the treaty power is limited to agreements that address matters of legitimate international concern." But simply adverting to Justice Thomas's opinion may not suffice to make the point. After all, by its own terms, Justice Thomas's opinion merely "suggests"[77] such a limit; remember, Justice Thomas joined Justice Scalia's opinion, so for him, any limits on the treaty power were not necessary to decide the case. And, in any event, Justice Thomas's opinion "suggest[ed]" that the treaty power was limited to "matters of international intercourse,"[78] whereas Justice Alito adopts a subtly different formulation: "matters of legitimate international concern."[79] One can imagine that these two different formulations might have substantially different consequences.

The heart of Justice Alito's opinion is this passage:

> But insofar as the Convention may be read to obligate the United States to enact domestic legislation criminalizing conduct of the sort at issue in this case, which typically is the sort of conduct regulated by the States, the Convention exceeds the scope of the treaty power. Section 229 cannot be regarded as necessary and proper to carry into execution the treaty power, and accordingly it lies outside Congress' reach.[80]

The key word here is "insofar." Did the convention in fact oblige the United States to enact Section 229? The word "insofar" is a neat hedge, but the opinion is rather striking either way. Consider both possibilities.

First, assume that the answer is yes. If so, then Justice Alito concludes that the treaty "exceeds the scope of the treaty power." In 225 years, the Court has never declared a treaty unconstitutional.[81] Even Justice Thomas, who wrote separately to suggest limits on the treaty power, did not endeavor to apply his suggested limits to this

---

[77] See *supra* note 75 and accompanying text.

[78] Bond, 134 S. Ct. at 2104 (Thomas, J., concurring in the judgment).

[79] *Id.* at 2111 (Alito, J., concurring in the judgment).

[80] *Id.*

[81] See Cong. Research Serv., The Constitution of the United States of America: Analysis and Interpretation, S. Doc. No. 112-9, at 508 (Centennial ed. 2014) ("It does not appear that the Court has ever held a treaty unconstitutional.").

particular treaty, let alone declare it unconstitutional. Moreover, Mrs. Bond herself did not argue that this treaty is unconstitutional. If, in fact, Justice Alito meant to declare this treaty unconstitutional *sua sponte*, that would be a dramatic and important conclusion, worthy of a more comprehensive opinion.

Alternatively, assume that the answer is no: the word "insofar" also leaves open the possibility that the convention is *not* best read to obligate the United States to enact the statute at issue in this case. If not, then the treaty is presumably valid and constitutional. But then, consider Justice Alito's next sentence: "Section 229 cannot be regarded as necessary and proper to carry into execution the treaty power, and accordingly it lies outside Congress' reach." The logic here seems to be that if a treaty does *not* "obligate" the United States to enact a particular statute (as we are assuming in this paragraph), then it cannot empower Congress to enact that statute.

Now, Cato certainly agrees with that proposition; it is *a fortiori* from our brief, from my article, and from Justice Scalia's concurrence. We would say that a treaty cannot empower Congress to enact a statute even if the treaty *does* purport to obligate Congress to do so, let alone if it does not. But again, Justice Alito did not sign on to that part of Justice Scalia's concurrence. So, for him, this is a new proposition of law. The logical summary of this position is as follows: a valid treaty that *does* obligate Congress "to enact domestic legislation criminalizing . . . the sort of conduct [typically] regulated by the States" *might* empower Congress to enact such legislation (*Holland* says yes; Scalia and Cato and I say no; Justice Alito does not say); but a valid treaty that does *not* obligate (but perhaps cajoles?) Congress to pass such legislation *cannot* empower Congress to do so. This might be right, but it is new and important, and it is in tension with at least a few cases (which seem to suggest that implementing legislation need only be *rationally related* to a treaty).[82] Again, if this

---

[82] See Missouri v. Holland, 252 U.S. 416, 432 (1920); United States v. Lue, 134 F.3d 79, 84 (2d Cir. 1998); United States v. Eramdjian, 155 F. Supp. 914, 920 (S.D. Cal. 1957) ("Although no mention of marihuana is made in the treaties, marihuana is definitely related to the drug problem and the evils that flow from the use of drugs. A statute which has its impact on both the drugs named in the treaty and on marihuana, related as it is to the drug addiction problem, would seem to us a valid statute to implement a valid treaty." (footnote omitted)); see also Rosenkranz, *supra* note 10, at 1931.

is the true gravamen of Justice Alito's concurrence, then it is a very important point, worthy of a more detailed opinion.

In short, Justice Alito clearly has subtle intuitions about the scope of the treaty power and about the scope of Congress's power to legislate pursuant to treaty. Unfortunately, there are only hints of these intuitions in his rich but cryptic concurrence. At any rate, Justice Alito correctly concludes that the statute "lies outside Congress' reach" and so cannot constitutionally be applied to Mrs. Bond.[83]

Conclusion

Bond v. United States was, in a way, a disappointment; many had hoped that the Court would at last disavow Justice Holmes's pernicious suggestion that a treaty can increase the legislative power of Congress. Instead, a majority of the Court avoided this important issue, but only by an implausible stretch of statutory interpretation.

The Court should generally be commended for avoiding difficult constitutional questions when it is fairly possible to do so. But the Roberts Court seems to take this principle too far. When the statute is clear and the constitutional issue is squarely presented, there is no "judicial restraint" in rewriting the statute to dodge the constitutional question. As Justice Scalia says:

> We have here a supposedly "narrow" opinion which, in order to be "narrow," sets forth interpretive principles never before imagined that will bedevil our jurisprudence (and proliferate litigation) for years to come. The immediate product of these interpretive novelties is a statute that should be the envy of every lawmaker bent on trapping the unwary with vague and uncertain criminal prohibitions. All this to leave in place an ill-considered *ipse dixit* that enables the fundamental constitutional principle of limited federal powers to be set aside by the President and Senate's exercise of the treaty power. We should not have shirked our duty and distorted the law to preserve that assertion; we should have welcomed and eagerly grasped the opportunity—nay, the obligation—to consider and repudiate it.[84]

[83] Bond, 134 S. Ct. at 2111 (Alito, J., concurring in the judgment).
[84] *Id.* at 2102 (Scalia, J., concurring in the judgment).

Happily, though, three justices did grasp this opportunity. Justice Thomas, joined by Justices Scalia and Alito, wrote an originalist tour de force suggesting "that the Treaty Power can be used to arrange intercourse with other nations, but not to regulate purely domestic affairs."[85]

And Justice Scalia, joined by Justice Thomas, produced a textual and structural masterpiece, concluding that the Necessary and Proper Clause does not empower Congress to implement treaties. "To legislate compliance with the United States' treaty obligations, Congress must rely on its independent (though quite robust) Article I, § 8, powers."[86]

As for *Missouri v. Holland*, Justices Scalia, Thomas, and Alito all agree that it "upheld a statute implementing [a] treaty based on an improperly broad view of the Necessary and Proper Clause."[87] Two of them—Scalia and Thomas—went further and made clear that a treaty cannot increase the legislative power of Congress; *Missouri v. Holland's* single "unreasoned and citation-less sentence"[88] to the contrary was an "ill-considered *ipse dixit*"[89] that should be "repudiate[d]."[90]

Unfortunately, these were concurrences, not majorities. However, it is important to remember that the other six justices expressed no view about whether a treaty can increase the legislative power of Congress. These powerful concurrences went unanswered, and they may well provide a roadmap in a future case. *Missouri v. Holland* remains the law of the land, but in a proper case, it may yet be overruled.

---

[85] *Id.* at 2103 (Thomas, J., concurring in the judgment).

[86] *Id.* at 2099 (Scalia, J., concurring in the judgment).

[87] *Id.* at 2109 (Thomas, J., concurring in the judgment).

[88] *Id.* at 2098 (Scalia, J., concurring in the judgment).

[89] *Id.* at 2102; see also Rosenkranz, *supra* note 10, at 1932.

[90] Bond, 134 S. Ct. at 2102 (Scalia, J., concurring in the judgment).

Evolving Technology and the Fourth Amendment: The Implications of *Riley v. California*

Andrew Pincus*

How should constitutional principles take account of changes in technology?

The Supreme Court has faced this question in a variety of contexts: under the First Amendment, as technology advanced from pamphlets and printing presses to broadcast television (with its limited number of channels),[1] to cable systems (with myriad channels),[2] and to the internet;[3] under the Second Amendment, with the Court explaining that although long guns were the self-defense weapon of choice when the amendment was adopted, today "the handgun [is] the quintessential self-defense weapon" and "a complete prohibition of their use is invalid";[4] and under the Commerce Clause, applying the critical phrase "Commerce . . . among the several States" to new forms of transportation and business.[5]

This term's decision in *Riley v. California*[6] charts the course for applying the Fourth Amendment's protection against unreasonable

---

* Partner, Mayer Brown LLP; counsel of record for briefs submitted for the Center for Democracy and Technology, the Electronic Frontier Foundation, and other parties in *United States v. Jones*; *Riley v. California* and *United States v. Wurie*; and *City of Ontario v. Quon*.

[1] Red Lion Broad. Co. v. FCC, 395 U.S. 367 (1969).

[2] Turner Broad. Sys., Inc. v. FCC, 512 U.S. 622 (1994).

[3] Reno v. ACLU, 521 U.S. 844 (1997).

[4] District of Columbia v. Heller, 554 U.S. 570, 629 (2008).

[5] See, e.g., Gonzales v. Raich, 545 U.S. 1, 16 (2005) (observing that "in response to rapid industrial development and an increasingly interdependent national economy, Congress 'ushered in a new era of federal regulation under the commerce power,'" and that the Court's "understanding of the reach of the Commerce Clause . . . has evolved over time").

[6] 134 S. Ct. 2473 (2014).

government searches and seizures in the context of new technologies. The particular question here was whether the general rule that government agents do not need a warrant or any individualized suspicion to examine documents and other objects found on an individual placed under arrest—which courts have applied to things such as wallets, papers, purses, and cigarette packs—permits the government to examine all of the digitally stored information contained in a cell phone found on an arrestee.

Building upon several prior rulings, the Court refused simply to extend to this new technology the exception to the Fourth Amendment's general requirement of a warrant based on probable cause that had been developed in a pre-digital era. It instead examined the practical, real-world intrusion on long-standing legitimate privacy expectations that would result from taking that step and, finding a significant intrusion, held that the warrant requirement, rather than the less-protective standard developed for the pre-digital environment, should apply.

Riley's analytic framework is likely to be applied in a variety of different contexts, as new technologies collect and preserve personal information previously inaccessible to government agents. It will go a long way toward maintaining the Fourth Amendment's vitality as a bulwark for protecting individuals' privacy against the threat of unjustified government intrusion.

I. Fourth Amendment Background

The Fourth Amendment states:

> The right of the people to be secure in their persons, houses, papers, and effects, against unreasonable searches and seizures, shall not be violated, and no Warrants shall issue, but upon probable cause, supported by Oath or affirmation, and particularly describing the place to be searched, and the persons or things to be seized.

The amendment's origins lie in one of the principal grievances of the Founding generation: "the reviled 'general warrants' and 'writs of assistance' . . ., which allowed British officers to rummage through homes in an unrestrained search for evidence of criminal activity."[7]

---

[7] *Id.* at 2494.

General warrants were "not grounded upon a sworn oath of a specific infraction by a particular individual, and thus not limited in scope and application"—they permitted officers of the Crown to search anywhere and anyone they wished.[8]

Although a 1763 court ruling held general warrants unlawful in England,[9] Parliament expressly authorized their continued use in the colonies and "[g]eneral warrants and affiliated methods were still central to colonial search and seizure in 1776."[10] Opposition to these searches

> was in fact one of the driving forces behind the Revolution itself. In 1761, the patriot James Otis delivered a speech in Boston denouncing the use of writs of assistance. A young John Adams was there, and he would later write that "[e]very man of a crowded audience appeared to me to go away, as I did, ready to take arms against writs of assistance." According to Adams, Otis's speech was "the first scene of the first act of opposition to the arbitrary claims of Great Britain. Then and there the child Independence was born."[11]

Many of the states included prohibitions of general warrants in their constitutions, but there was concern following the Constitutional Convention that the new federal government was not subject to such a constraint. "Antifederalists sarcastically predicted that the general, suspicionless warrant would be among the Constitution's 'blessings.' . . . Patrick Henry warned that the new Federal Constitution would expose the citizenry to searches and seizures 'in the most arbitrary manner, without any evidence or reason.'"[12]

The Fourth Amendment "answered these charges" by adding to the Constitution a specific protection against the abuse represented

---

[8] Maryland v. King, 133 S. Ct. 1958, 1980 (2013) (Scalia, J., dissenting).

[9] Wilkes v. Wood, 98 Eng. Rep. 489, 499 (1763).

[10] William Cuddihy, The Fourth Amendment: Origins and Original Meaning 538 (2009). See generally Brief of Constitutional Accountability Center as Amicus Curiae Supporting Petitioner Riley and Respondent Wurie, Riley v. California, 134 S. Ct. 2473 (2014) (No. 13-132) (detailed discussion of Fourth Amendment's historical origin).

[11] Riley v. California, 134 S. Ct. at 2494.

[12] Maryland v. King, 133 S. Ct. at 1981 (Scalia, J., dissenting).

by general warrants. The amendment "protects individual privacy against certain kinds of governmental intrusion."[13]

The general principle established by the amendment is that government agents may not conduct a search without first obtaining a warrant, issued by a neutral magistrate based on a showing of probable cause to believe that the search will uncover evidence of crime and particularly delineating the scope of the search. But that general rule is subject to a raft of exceptions:

- Some government collections of information or things do not constitute a "search" and therefore do not trigger the amendment's protections,[14]
- Some categories of searches are permissible without any showing of a particularized justification for searching the individual or place, without a warrant, or without both;[15]
- Still other categories of searches may be undertaken on a showing of particularized justification less demanding than probable cause, such as "reasonable suspicion."[16]

This common-law elaboration of the Fourth Amendment's basic protection has been justified by the Supreme Court on the ground that"[t]he touchstone of the Fourth Amendment is reasonableness, and the reasonableness of a search is determined 'by assessing, on the one hand, the degree to which it intrudes upon an individual's privacy and, on the other, the degree to which it is needed for the promotion of legitimate governmental interests.'"[17] Faced with a particular factual setting, the Court considers the "totality of the

[13] Katz v. United States, 389 U.S. 347, 350 (1967).

[14] See, e.g., Illinois v. Caballes, 543 U.S. 405 (2005) (dog sniff); Maryland v. Macon, 472 U.S. 463 (1985) (items in plain view).

[15] See, e.g., Arizona v. Johnson, 555 U.S. 323 (2009) (pat-down of car occupants during a traffic stop permissible without suspicion of criminal activity); Skinner v. R. Labor Exec. Ass'n, 489 U.S. 602 (1989) (drug test of railroad workers following accidents); Payton v. New York, 445 U.S. 573 (1980) (warrant not required in exigent circumstances).

[16] See, e.g., New Jersey v. T.L.O., 469 U.S. 325 (1985) (search in the school context); Terry v. Ohio, 392 U.S. 1 (1968).

[17] United States v. Knights, 534 U.S. 112, 118-19 (2001) (quoting Wyoming v. Houghton, 526 U.S. 295, 300 (1999)).

circumstances" in determining whether the general Fourth Amendment standard, or some modified version, should apply.[18]

Changes in technology can have a significant impact on the "circumstances" that the Court considers in striking the appropriate balance under the Fourth Amendment. For example, the intrusion on individual privacy may be expanded if government agents use technology not contemplated at the time the Supreme Court determined that a particular factual setting should not be subject to the general warrant-supported-by-probable-cause standard. On the other hand, what is "needed for the promotion of legitimate government interests" can be affected by changes in technology that make it easier for wrongdoers to conceal their criminal activity.

The Court has grappled with these issues in a series of recent decisions, reflecting the dramatic advances in technology that are producing rapid, fundamental changes in every aspect of our lives—our ability to communicate, our work environment, our homes, our leisure. These rulings culminated in this term's decision in *Riley*, which emphatically reaffirmed the Court's determination to preserve the Fourth Amendment's core guarantee: protection against unreasonable government intrusion on individuals' privacy.

II. First Steps in Addressing New Technologies: *Kyllo, Jones*, and *King*

The impact of the Court's unanimous ruling in *Riley* cannot be understood without examining the Court's efforts to grapple with the intersection of new technology and the Fourth Amendment in three prior decisions, *Kyllo v. United States*,[19] *United States v. Jones*,[20] and *Maryland v. King*.[21]

A. Kyllo

Growing marijuana indoors generally requires high-intensity lights, which emit substantial amounts of heat. Agent William Elliott

---

[18] Ohio v. Robinette, 519 U.S. 33, 39 (1996) ("We have long held that the 'touchstone of the Fourth Amendment is reasonableness.' Reasonableness, in turn, is measured in objective terms by examining the totality of the circumstances.").

[19] 533 U.S. 27 (2001).

[20] 132 S. Ct. 945 (2012).

[21] 133 S. Ct. 1958 (2013).

of the U.S. Department of the Interior suspected that Danny Kyllo was growing marijuana in his apartment on Rhododendron Drive in Florence, Oregon. Agent Elliott, sitting in a car across the street from the apartment, scanned the exterior of Kyllo's apartment using a thermal imager, which detects infrared radiation invisible to the naked eye, converting the radiation "into images based on relative warmth—black is cool, white is hot, shades of gray connote relative differences; in that respect, it operates somewhat like a video camera showing heat images."[22] The scan indicated that the roof and wall of Kyllo's apartment were warmer than those of the neighboring apartments; Elliott obtained a search warrant based on that information and found 100 marijuana plants in Kyllo's apartment.

Did the thermal scan—undertaken without a warrant and without probable cause—constitute a search in violation of the Fourth Amendment?

Supreme Court precedent stated that the Fourth Amendment does not "require law enforcement officers to shield their eyes when passing by a home on public thoroughfares. Nor does the mere fact that an individual has taken measures to restrict some views of his activities preclude an officer's observations from a public vantage point where he has a right to be and which renders the activities clearly visible."[23] And that was true even when the "public vantage point" was an aircraft flying 1,000 feet or more over the defendant's property—whether the observation was made by naked eye[24] or a camera.[25]

As in those cases, Agent Elliott neither entered Kyllo's house nor used technology that physically intruded into the house, and four justices found that fact dispositive. Because "[a]ll that the infrared camera did in this case was passively measure heat emitted from the exterior surfaces of [Kyllo's] home," and that "information [was] exposed to the general public from the outside of petitioner's home," the "outside observation" principle could be applied to permit the use of this new technology.[26]

---

[22] Kyllo v. United States, 533 U.S. at 29–30.

[23] California v. Ciraolo, 476 U.S. 207, 213 (1986).

[24] Id. at 213–14.

[25] Dow Chem. Co. v. United States, 476 U.S. 227 (1986).

[26] Kyllo v. United States, 533 U.S. at 42–43 (Stevens, J., dissenting).

The majority, in an opinion by Justice Antonin Scalia, disagreed. Recognizing that it "would be foolish to contend that the degree of privacy secured to citizens by the Fourth Amendment has been entirely unaffected by the advance of technology," the Court framed the question before it as whether there are "limits . . . upon this power of technology to shrink the realm of guaranteed privacy."[27]

With respect to the home, which the Court characterized as the "prototypical" private area that the Fourth Amendment was intended to protect, the Court held that there is a limit: "[w]here, as here, the Government uses a device that is not in general public use, to explore details of the home that would previously have been unknowable without physical intrusion, the surveillance is a 'search' and is presumptively unreasonable without a warrant."[28]

Key to this conclusion was the Court's recognition that technology will continue to advance. It pointed out that a "powerful directional microphone" could detect conversations inside a home, and "[t]he ability to 'see' through walls and other opaque barriers is a clear, and scientifically feasible, goal of law enforcement research and development."[29] The dissent's approach "would leave the homeowner at the mercy of advancing technology—including imaging technology that could discern all human activity in the home."[30]

Finally, the Court rejected the government's fallback suggestion of an "intimate details" test: thermal imaging would violate the Fourth Amendment only if personal information was revealed. In the home, the Court emphasized, "*all* details are intimate details, because the entire area is held safe from prying government eyes."[31]

More significantly, an "intimate details" test would not provide law enforcement officers with a "workable" standard. The Court "would have to develop a jurisprudence specifying which home activities are 'intimate' and which are not"; and in any event a government

---

[27] *Id.* at 33–34 (majority op.).

[28] *Id.* at 40; see also *id.* at 34 (observing that this test "assures preservation of that degree of privacy against government that existed when the Fourth Amendment was adopted").

[29] *Id.* at 35 & 36 n.3.

[30] *Id.* at 35–36.

[31] *Id.* at 37 (emphasis in original).

agent could not know in advance whether his surveillance would pick up impermissible "intimate" details.[32]

Three elements of *Kyllo*'s analysis set the course for the Court's subsequent Fourth Amendment rulings addressing new technology. First, the refusal to apply mechanically to new technology a Fourth Amendment rule developed before the advent of that technology. The Court squarely rejected the government's attempt to shoehorn thermal imaging under the legal standard for unaided visual observation based on the "no physical intrusion" standard that justified the pre-technology rule.

Second, the importance of examining the practical effect on individuals' privacy interests of the new technology, and of future advances in the area, both in general and in terms of the reduction in the protection of privacy interests that would result from mechanically applying the pre-technology legal standard in this new context. Critical to the Court's decision was its determination regarding the range of previously unavailable information that government agents would be able to obtain through thermal imaging—and other similar technologies, both in existence and under development—if the "no physical intrusion" standard were applied.

Third, the refusal to adopt a Fourth Amendment standard turning on the type of information uncovered by the government search, because that approach would be difficult for law enforcement officers to apply and would have as its practical consequence a significant diminution in the scope of Fourth Amendment protection. The government's "intimate details" test would have opened the door to widespread use of thermal imaging, with its consequent diminution of individuals' ability to maintain a private sphere free from government intrusion. The government simply would have been precluded from utilizing evidence gained from such intrusions on the basis of an after-the-fact "intimacy" analysis.

B. Jones

Following suspects—in the hope that they will take actions that reveal their culpability, or lead police to evidence of crime or to co-conspirators—has long been a staple of law enforcement. Under the principle that "[w]hat a person knowingly exposes to the public . . .

---

[32] *Id.* at 38–39.

is not a subject of Fourth Amendment protection,"[33] tailing suspects on foot could not implicate the Fourth Amendment's protections.[34]

But what if the government agent's ability to monitor a suspect is augmented by technology? The Supreme Court first addressed that issue in 1983 in the context of a "beeper."[35]

Tristan Armstrong had been purchasing large amounts of chloroform, and police believed he was using the substance to manufacture illegal drugs. They accordingly placed a beeper in a drum of chloroform—with the permission of the seller—and the drum was sold to Armstrong. Following the drum's progress through visual surveillance combined with monitoring the electronic signal emitted by the beeper (including use of a helicopter to find the beeper signal after it was lost), the police traced the drum to a cabin owned by Leroy Knotts. Obtaining a search warrant based in part on the presence of the drum, they found equipment and chemicals sufficient to produce large quantities of amphetamine.

The Court rejected Knotts's argument that the use of the beeper to track the chloroform to his cabin and confirm that the drum had come to rest on his property constituted a search triggering the Fourth Amendment. The critical question was whether the officers' monitoring of the drum's movements intruded on a reasonable expectation of privacy. Holding that "[a] person traveling in an automobile on public thoroughfares has no reasonable expectation of privacy in his movements from one place to another," the Court stated that traveling over public streets "voluntarily conveyed to anyone who wanted to look the fact that [the driver] was traveling over particular roads in a particular direction, the fact of whatever stops he made, and the fact of his final destination when he exited from public roads onto private property."[36]

The use of the beeper did not warrant a different result, because the Fourth Amendment did not "prohibit[] the police from augmenting the sensory faculties bestowed upon them at birth with

---

[33] Katz v. United States, 389 U.S. at 351.

[34] See United States v. Lee, 274 U.S. 559, 563 (1927) (use of searchlight or binoculars to enhance officer's visual observation does not constitute a search under the Fourth Amendment).

[35] United States v. Knotts, 460 U.S. 276 (1983).

[36] *Id.* at 281–82.

such enhancement as science and technology afforded them in this case."[37] The defendant argued that a ruling in favor of the government would mean "that 'twenty-four hour surveillance of any citizen of this country will be possible, without judicial knowledge or supervision,'" but the Court declined to base its decision on that mere possibility.[38] "[I]f such dragnet-type law enforcement practices as respondent envisions should eventually occur, there will be time enough then to determine whether different constitutional principles may be applicable."[39]

The Court's ruling in *Knotts* was influenced by the limited impact of the technology—although the beeper enhanced the ability of the police to track the drum, it was far from foolproof: the signal had been lost for approximately one hour. Indeed, the Court compared the beeper to a police officer's use of a searchlight or binoculars. And although the Court wrote broadly in some parts of the opinion, it was careful to limit its ruling to the "enhancement [that] science and technology afforded . . . *in this case*" and to leave open the possibility that "dragnet-type law enforcement practices" could produce a different result.[40]

That circumstance was presented for decision in 2012, when the Court—in *United States v. Jones*—addressed a Fourth Amendment challenge to the use by government agents of a Global Positioning System (GPS) tracking device to monitor with precision the movements of a vehicle over a four-week period.

The principal opinion in *Jones* did not turn on the nature of GPS tracking technology. Instead, the Court held that the physical intrusion on private property resulting from the government's installation of the GPS device on the car constituted a "search" triggering the Fourth Amendment's warrant requirement.

But four justices rejected that rationale, concluding instead that it was the characteristics of GPS technology, as applied in this case, that led to an outcome opposite from *Knotts*. And Justice Sonia Sotomayor agreed with that conclusion as well as the physical-intrusion rationale.

---

[37] *Id*. at 282.
[38] *Id*. at 283.
[39] *Id*. at 284.
[40] *Id*. at 282 (emphasis added).

As she explained, GPS surveillance is "unique" because it "generates a precise, comprehensive, record of a person's public movements that reflects a wealth of detail about her familial, political, professional, religious, and sexual associations. The Government can store such records and efficiently mine them for information years into the future."[41] Moreover, "GPS monitoring is cheap in comparison to conventional surveillance techniques and, by design, proceeds surreptitiously."[42]

Justice Samuel Alito, in his concurring opinion for himself and Justices Ruth Bader Ginsburg, Stephen Breyer, and Elena Kagan, framed the issue more broadly:

> In the pre-computer age, the greatest protections of privacy were neither constitutional nor statutory, but practical. Traditional surveillance for any extended period of time was difficult and costly and therefore rarely undertaken. The surveillance at issue in this case—constant monitoring of the location of a vehicle for four weeks—would have required a large team of agents, multiple vehicles, and perhaps aerial assistance.[43]

For these justices, the critical question was whether—notwithstanding *Knotts*'s conclusion that an individual had no legitimate expectation of privacy in his movements on public roads—the gathering of precise, detailed information about a person's movements, not possible in the pre-computer age, did intrude on such a legitimate expectation. They concluded that it did: "society's expectation has been that law enforcement agents and others would not—and indeed, in the main, simply could not—secretly monitor and catalogue every

---

[41] United States v. Jones, 132 S. Ct. at 955–56. Amicus briefs explained that the precise, detailed records produced by GPS tracking, which can be produced around the clock for long periods of time, can be combined with information regarding the businesses at locations visited by the vehicle being tracked, to identify intimate details of a person's life. For example, the fact that a tracked car suddenly began stopping at an oncologist's office several times a month could reveal that a member of the family had cancer. The buildings that a person regularly visits could reveal his or her religious or political affiliations. See, e.g., amicus briefs filed by the Center for Democracy and Technology; ACLU; and Yale Law School Information Society Project Scholars.

[42] United States v. Jones, 132 S. Ct. at 956.

[43] *Id.* at 963.

single movement of an individual's car for a very long period"—and four weeks exceeded the permissible period.[44]

The analysis employed by these justices, and by Justice Sotomayor, paralleled the Court's approach in *Kyllo*. They refused the government's invitation simply to extend *Knotts* to this new and very different technology and instead reviewed the characteristics of GPS technology and assessed the impact of the government's use of that technology on individuals' privacy expectations pre-dating the development of the new technology. In view of the significant intrusion on those expectations, they concluded that the use of the technology constituted a search.

Indeed, the difference in result between *Jones* and *Knotts* rests principally on the different real-world impact of the two technologies. Justice Alito's opinion in *Jones* expressly recognizes that the detailed, long-term surveillance that GPS makes "easy and cheap" would "have been exceptionally demanding" to accomplish using a beeper.[45] For example, "[t]he signal had a limited range and could be lost if the police did not stay close enough"—limitations inapplicable to GPS.[46]

The Court's next decision involving new technology and the Fourth Amendment, *Maryland v. King*, confirms this conclusion. The Court followed the course charted in *Kyllo* and the *Jones* concurring opinions, but the government side prevailed because the Court's assessment of the real-world impact of the new technology found little or no erosion of legitimate, pre-existing privacy interests.

C. King

DNA technology plays an important role in identifying those responsible—and not responsible—for crime. The Supreme Court has acknowledged its "unparalleled ability both to exonerate the wrongly convicted and to identify the guilty. It has the potential to

---

[44] *Id.* at 964. See also *id.* at 956 (Sotomayor, J., concurring) ("I would take these attributes of GPS monitoring into account when considering the existence of a reasonable societal expectation of privacy in the sum of one's public movements. I would ask whether people reasonably expect that their movements will be recorded and aggregated in a manner that enables the Government to ascertain, more or less at will, their political and religious beliefs, sexual habits, and so on").

[45] *Id.* at 964 & 963 n.10.

[46] *Id.* at 963 n.10.

significantly improve both the criminal justice system and police investigative practices."[47]

To help realize these benefits, the federal government has sponsored creation of a nationwide database of DNA profiles provided by local, state, and national laboratories based on samples collected from convicted offenders and, in some circumstances, from arrestees. The question in *Maryland v. King* was whether the Fourth Amendment permits the collection and analysis of DNA samples from arrestees in the absence of a warrant based on individualized probable cause.

The Court divided 5-4 on the issue, with Justice Scalia writing an emphatic dissent on behalf of himself and Justices Ginsburg, Sotomayor, and Kagan. The majority, applying the general standard of reasonableness—"weigh[ing] 'the promotion of legitimate governmental interests' against 'the degree to which [the search] intrudes upon an individual's privacy'"[48]—concluded that a warrant is not required and that collecting and analyzing arrestees' DNA does not violate the Fourth Amendment.

On the government interest side of the ledger, the Court cited the "need for law enforcement officers in a safe and accurate way to process and identify the persons and possessions they must take into custody."[49] And "a suspect's criminal history is a critical part of his identity that officers should know when processing him for detention," which is why fingerprints are routinely obtained and compared with databases of known criminals and unsolved crimes.[50] "[T]he only difference between DNA analysis and the accepted use of fingerprint databases is the unparalleled accuracy DNA provides."[51]

By comparison, "the intrusion of a cheek swab to obtain a DNA sample is a minimal one" and "[t]he expectations of privacy of an individual taken into police custody 'necessarily [are] of a diminished scope.'"[52] Moreover, the processing of the DNA sample was structured to prevent disclosure of the arrestee's genetic traits, and

---

[47] Dist. Attorney's Office v. Osborne, 557 U.S. 52, 55 (2009).

[48] Maryland v. King, 133 S. Ct. at 1970 (quoting Wyoming v. Houghton, 526 U.S. 295, 300 (1999)).

[49] *Id.*

[50] *Id.* at 1971.

[51] *Id.* at 1972.

[52] *Id.* at 1977, 1978.

statutory protections barred use of a sample for purposes other than identifying individuals. The Court specifically observed that use of samples "to determine an arrestee's predisposition for a particular disease or other hereditary factors not relevant to identity" would "present additional privacy concerns not present here."[53]

In these circumstances, the Court concluded, obtaining the DNA sample from an arrestee "is, like fingerprinting and photographing, a legitimate police booking procedure that is reasonable under the Fourth Amendment."[54]

The difference in outcome between this case and *Kyllo* and *Jones* stems directly from the Court's analysis of the nature of the information gained through DNA analysis. Because the new technology was simply a more accurate means of ascertaining the arrestee's identity and prior criminal history—and did not reveal other types of personal information—the Court concluded that additional Fourth Amendment protection was not warranted.

III. *Riley* Reaffirms the Fourth Amendment's Vitality

The Supreme Court has long held that the Fourth Amendment permits government agents to search individuals placed under arrest without first obtaining a warrant and without probable cause to believe that the search would uncover evidence of crime. This "search incident to arrest" exception has been applied by courts to permit a search of the arrestee's person and of the area within the arrestee's immediate control.[55]

That is, if documents or other objects are discovered on the arrestee's person or within his or her control, the police are permitted to examine them. As the Supreme Court explained in upholding the search of a cigarette pack found in the course of a search incident to arrest, "[h]aving in the course of a lawful search come upon the crumpled package of cigarettes, [the officer] was entitled to inspect it."[56]

---

[53] *Id.* at 1979.

[54] *Id.* at 1980.

[55] Riley v. California, 134 S. Ct. at 2483–84. See also Arizona v. Gant, 556 U.S. 332, 343 (2009); United States v. Robinson, 414 U.S. 218, 235–36 (1973); Chimel v. California, 395 U.S. 752, 762–63 (1969).

[56] United States v. Robinson, 414 U.S. at 236.

But what if the object discovered on the arrestee's person is not a wallet or a cigarette pack, but instead a smartphone or a tablet or a thumbdrive? May the government "inspect" all of the digitally stored information, without obtaining a warrant, by invoking the search-incident-to-arrest exception? That is the question that the Court addressed this term in *Riley*. And the answer is a resounding "no."

The Court granted review in two cases presenting the same question regarding cell phone searches. David Riley was arrested on a firearms offense; an officer searched him incident to the arrest and found a cell phone in his pocket. Accessing the phone's digital memory, the officer found words that he believed stood for a criminal gang. During a subsequent examination of the phone at the police station, a detective found photographs of Riley standing in front of a car that had been involved in a shooting.

Riley was charged under California law in connection with the shooting and the charge included an enhancement based on his alleged involvement with a criminal street gang. He moved to suppress the evidence obtained in the searches of his phone, but the motion was denied on the ground that the warrantless search was permissible under the search-incident-to-arrest exception. The California appellate court affirmed that determination on the basis of a California Supreme Court decision holding that the digital content of a cell phone could be examined as part of a search incident to arrest.[57]

Brima Wurie, the defendant in the second case, was arrested on a drug charge, and the police seized two cell phones. One of the phones received calls from a source that the phone's screen identified as "my house." The officers opened the phone, accessed its call log, identified the phone number associated with "my house," and—using an online directory—ascertained its location. Upon arriving at the building, they saw through a window a woman who resembled someone in a photograph on Wurie's phone. Based on this information, the police obtained a warrant authorizing a search of the apartment; they seized illegal drugs, firearms, and drug paraphernalia.

Wurie was charged with drug and firearms violations and moved to suppress the evidence obtained in the search of the apartment on

[57] People v. Riley, No. D059840, 2013 WL 475242 (Cal. App. 4th Dist. Feb. 8, 2013).

the ground that it was the product of an unconstitutional search of his cell phone. The trial court denied the motion, but the U.S. Court of Appeals for the First Circuit reversed, holding that the search of a cell phone could not be justified under the search-incident-to-arrest exception.

The Supreme Court began its analysis by observing that a "mechanical application" of the search-incident-to-arrest principle could justify the searches in these cases. But, the Court said, "neither of its rationales has much force with respect to digital content on cell phones."[58]

Searches incident to arrest are justified by the interest in police safety, but "[d]igital data stored on a cell phone cannot itself be used as a weapon to harm an arresting officer. . . . Once an officer has secured a phone and eliminated any potential physical threats, . . . data on the phone can endanger no one."[59]

The second interest justifying the exception is preventing destruction of evidence. Again, however, "[o]nce law enforcement officers have secured a cell phone, there is no longer any risk that the arrestee himself will be able to delete incriminating data from the phone."[60]

The Court observed, however, that the search-incident-to-arrest exception also rests on "an arrestee's reduced privacy interests upon being taken into police custody. . . . [A] patdown of [the arrestee's] clothing and an inspection of the cigarette pack found in his pocket constituted only minor additional intrusions compared to

---

[58] Riley v. California, 134 S. Ct. at 2484.

[59] *Id.* at 2485.

[60] *Id.* at 2486. California and the United States argued strenuously that the threat of remote wiping—receipt by the phone of a signal erasing the stored data—justified an immediate search to prevent destruction of evidence. But the Court pointed out that this argument was distinct from the concern expressed in prior cases, because it did not relate to the potential acts of the arrestee but rather "turns on the actions of third parties who are not present at the scene of arrest." *Id.* Moreover, there was no evidence that the problem is prevalent; it was not clear that permitting searches at the time of arrest would address the problem, because officers preoccupied with securing the arrestee and the scene would be delayed in turning their attention to the contents of a cell phone; and a phone could be turned off or isolated from radio waves (through placement in a "Faraday bag"—a simple aluminum bag or wrapping named for the scientist William Faraday). *Id.* at 2486–87.

the substantial government authority exercised in taking [him] into custody."[61]

That diminished privacy interest did not mean that "the Fourth Amendment falls out of the picture entirely."[62] The Court had previously held that an arrest does not permit a warrantless search of the arrestee's home, because it could not "join in characterizing the invasion of privacy that results from a top-to-bottom search of a man's house as 'minor.'"[63]

The government argued that a search of the data stored on a cell phone was "materially indistinguishable" from the search of a wallet, address book, or purse when the latter are found on an arrestee. But the Court squarely rejected that mechanistic approach:

> Modern cell phones, as a category, implicate privacy concerns far beyond those implicated by the search of a cigarette pack, a wallet, or a purse. A conclusion that inspecting the contents of an arrestee's pockets works no substantial additional intrusion on privacy beyond the arrest itself may make sense as applied to physical items, but any extension of that reasoning to digital data has to rest on its own bottom.[64]

The Court then turned to the inquiry that was dispositive in *Kyllo* and in the *Jones* concurrences: whether extending an existing legal rule (here, the search-incident-to-arrest exception) to encompass a new technology would undermine previously existing, legitimate privacy expectations. It surveyed the characteristics of digital information stored on cell phones—based in large part on discussions in amicus briefs submitted by organizations with expertise in technology and privacy.[65]

The Court focused principally on cell phones' "immense storage capacity."[66] Before the development of digital storage technology, "a search of a person was limited by physical realities and tended as

---

[61] *Id.* at 2488.

[62] *Id.*

[63] Chimel v. California, 395 U.S. at 766–67 n.12.

[64] Riley v. California, 134 S. Ct. at 2488–89.

[65] See, e.g., amicus curiae briefs filed by the Center for Democracy and Technology and Electronic Frontier Foundation; the Electronic Privacy Information Center, et al.; the National Association of Criminal Defense Lawyers et al.; and the ACLU et al.

[66] Riley v. California, 134 S. Ct. at 2489.

a general matter to constitute only a narrow intrusion on privacy. Most people cannot lug around every piece of mail they have received for the past several months, every picture they have taken, or every book or article they have read."[67]

Digital storage means that "the possible intrusion on privacy is not [so] physically limited."[68] Cell phones have the capacity to store "millions of pages of text, thousands of pictures, or hundreds of videos"; moreover, the types of information preserved can include "photographs, picture messages, text messages, Internet browsing history, a calendar, a thousand-entry phone book, and so on."[69]

The Court found that these capabilities had "several interrelated consequences for privacy":

- "[A] cell phone collects in one place many distinct types of information—an address, a note, a prescription, a bank statement, a video—that reveal more in combination than any isolated record" and a large volume of even one type of information will "convey more than previously possible" about the individual;

- The information "can date back to purchase of the phone, or even earlier"—"[a] person might carry in his pocket a slip of paper reminding him to call Mr. Jones; he would not carry a record of all his communications with Mr. Jones for the past several months, as would routinely be kept on a phone";

- Digitally stored information has "an element of pervasiveness" that does not characterize physical records, because "[p]rior to the digital age, people did not typically carry a cache of sensitive information with them as they went about their day. Now it is the person who is not carrying a cell phone, with all that it contains, who is the exception";

- Some types of data stored on phones are "qualitatively different" from physical records: internet browsing history, which can "reveal an individual's private interests or concerns—perhaps a search for certain symptoms of disease"; GPS-generated location data, which "can reconstruct someone's specific movements down to the minute, not only around town but also within a

[67] Id.
[68] Id.
[69] Id.

particular building"; and mobile applications, which "together can form a revealing montage of the user's life."[70]

"Allowing the police to scrutinize such records on a routine basis," the Court said, "is quite different from allowing them to search a personal item or two in the occasional case."[71] Indeed, the Court pointed out that its search-incident-to-arrest precedent distinguished between an impermissible warrantless search of the arrestee's house and a permissible warrantless search of what might be found in the arrestee's pockets, because of the significantly reduced intrusion on privacy in the latter situation. But if "the arrestee's pockets contain a cell phone, that is no longer true."[72] The Court explained that

> a cell phone search would typically expose to the government far *more* than the most exhaustive search of a house: A phone not only contains in digital form many sensitive records previously found in the home; it also contains a broad array of private information never found in a home in any form—unless the phone is.[73]

In light of this very substantial difference in the impact on legitimate privacy expectations, compared with the effect of the search-incident-to-arrest exception as applied to physical records, the Court held—unanimously—that the exception does not apply to digitally stored information contained in a device seized in the course of an arrest, and that government agents must obtain a warrant to conduct such a search.

The Court distinguished its prior decision in *King* by pointing to the recognition in that case that "when 'privacy-related concerns are

---

[70] *Id.* at 2488–89. The Court pointed out another attribute of cell phones: a cell phone user may not know whether information being accessed through the phone is stored on the device or on a remote server. Thus, although the government conceded that the search-incident-to-arrest doctrine could not be used to search files stored remotely, "officers searching a phone's data would not typically know whether the information they are viewing was stored locally at the time of arrest or has been pulled from" a remote server. *Id.* at 2491. It concluded that "[t]he possibility that a search might extend well beyond papers and effects in the physical proximity of an arrestee is yet another reason that the privacy interests here dwarf those" in prior cases. *Id.*

[71] *Id.* at 2490.

[72] *Id.* at 2491.

[73] *Id.* (emphasis in original).

weighty enough' a 'search may require a warrant notwithstanding the diminished expectations of privacy of the arrestee.'"[74] The vast quantity and numerous different types of personal information revealed by searching the digital contents of a cell phone were dramatically different from the one kind of information—identity—revealed by the DNA sample.

The Court rejected a number of arguments advanced by the federal government and the State of California, reaffirming the conclusion that the substantial and varied information contained in cell phones (and other devices with digital storage capability) renders inapplicable legal standards developed in other contexts.

For example, the federal government urged the Court to import into the cell phone context a Fourth Amendment rule governing searches of automobiles, which permits officers to search an automobile incident to an arrest if it is "'reasonable to believe evidence relevant to the crime of arrest might be found in the vehicle.'"[75] That rule, however, was expressly tied to "circumstances unique to the vehicle context"—in particular "'a reduced expectation of privacy' and 'heightened law enforcement needs' when it comes to motor vehicles," due to their mobility.[76]

Not only do "cell phone searches bear neither of these characteristics," but such a rule would provide "no practical limit at all when it comes to cell phone searches" because of the comprehensive nature of the data stored on them, compared with the relatively limited material likely to be found in a car.[77] It therefore "would in effect give 'police officers unbridled discretion to rummage at will among a person's private effects.'"[78]

California argued that officers should be permitted to search cell phone data when they would have been able to examine a physical counterpart: because an address book found on the arrestee could be searched, the theory went, the police should be able to search a digital phone book. But that argument ignored the comprehensive nature of digitally stored data: "the fact that a search in the pre-digital

---

[74] *Id.* at 2488.
[75] Arizona v. Gant, 556 U.S. at 343.
[76] Riley v. California, 134 S. Ct. at 2492.
[77] *Id.*
[78] *Id.*

era could have turned up a photograph or two in a wallet does not justify a search of thousands of photos in a digital gallery."[79] Moreover, such a standard would lead to difficult line-drawing by police and judges: "Is an e-mail equivalent to a letter? Is a voicemail equivalent to a phone message slip?"[80]

The Court recognized its ruling would hamper to some degree government's ability to fight crime. But "[p]rivacy comes at a cost."[81]

Of course the Court's decision did not ban searches of digitally stored information, but only required government agents to obtain a warrant. Advances in technology have made that process easier for the police, with requests sent via email and processed electronically by judges.

Finally, other exceptions to the warrant requirement—such as the rule that police may proceed without a warrant when confronting particular "exigent circumstances"—will enable government agents to search a cell phone if necessary to "prevent the imminent destruction of evidence in individual cases, to pursue a fleeing suspect, and to assist persons who are seriously injured or are threatened with imminent injury."[82] Critically, however, the police will have to establish that "an emergency justified a warrantless search in each particular case"[83]—a significant difference from the across-the-board exemption that would have resulted from extension of the search-incident-to-arrest rule to digitally stored information.

The Court ended its opinion with a flourish, revisiting the Fourth Amendment's origins; in particular, the general warrants that outraged the Founding generation. Modern cell phones, the Court said, "hold for many Americans 'the privacies of life,'" and permitting government agents to search them without a warrant would allow government to exercise the very arbitrary authority that the amendment was intended to prevent.[84] "The fact that technology now allows an individual to carry such information in his hand does not

---

[79] *Id.* at 2493.

[80] *Id.*

[81] *Id.*

[82] *Id.* at 2494.

[83] *Id.*

[84] *Id.* at 2494–95.

make the information any less worthy of the protection for which the Founders fought."[85]

Riley establishes a clear paradigm for application of the Fourth Amendment to new technology:

- Courts should not mechanically extend exemptions from the warrant requirement recognized in the pre-digital era to encompass information resulting from new technology.
- Instead, a court must (1) determine whether the rationale justifying the rule developed with respect to physical information makes sense in the context of the new technology; and (2) examine the real-world effect on individuals' privacy expectations of extending the rule to the new technology.
- If the rationale makes no sense or the impact on privacy expectations would be substantial, then the exemption should not be extended and government agents should be required to obtain a warrant.
- New exclusions from the warrant requirement that lack significant constraints on officer discretion, and would give government agents access to significant amounts of personal information previously protected by the warrant requirement, should not be recognized.

By refusing to accept the very substantial erosion of protection against government power that would have resulted from turning a blind eye to the real-world impact of reflexively combining old legal rules with new technologies, the Court's decision lays an excellent foundation for ensuring that the Fourth Amendment's protections remain real and vital in our age of advancing technology.

IV. What's Next?

Riley addressed digitally stored information on a cell phone, but it is difficult to see how a different result could possibly apply to searches incident to arrest of the contents of tablets, laptops, or thumb

---

[85] *Id.* at 2495.

drives. All share the characteristics relied on by the *Riley* Court, and a warrant therefore should be required to conduct such searches.[86]

Moreover, we will not have to wait long to see how *Riley*'s approach will be applied outside the search-incident-to-arrest context. Federal and state governments have argued in a variety of other contexts that other exemptions from the warrant requirement should be applied to permit searches of digital information. Most of those arguments are likely to suffer the same fate as they did in *Riley*, as lower courts follow the Supreme Court's lead and focus broadly on practical realities and not simply on legal tests developed in the pre-digital era. Three examples demonstrate *Riley*'s impact.

A. Email Messages

Americans conduct personal business using email accounts provided by a third party: an employer; a school; or an email service provider, such as Gmail, Hotmail, or Yahoo. All of these third parties reserve the right to access the content of emails sent by their users. Does that mean that the government may obtain any email messages that it wishes, without obtaining a warrant?

The answer depends on the scope of a Fourth Amendment principle known as the "third-party doctrine," which holds that "'[w]hat a person knowingly exposes to the public . . . is not a subject of Fourth Amendment protection.'" The Supreme Court in 1976 applied this principle to conclude that an individual has no legitimate expectation of privacy with respect to checks, account statements, and other financial information in the possession of his banks, because it was "information voluntarily conveyed to the banks and exposed to their employees in the ordinary course of business. . . . The [customer] takes the risk, in revealing his affairs to another, that the information will be conveyed by that person to the Government."[87]

---

[86] Information-collecting sensors—one example is the increasingly ubiquitous "Fitbit" device that monitors an individual's movements and could, for example, record data indicating that the wearer was likely involved in a physical altercation—should fall within the same category. Government prosecutors might try to argue that sensors collecting a single category of information should not be encompassed under *Riley*'s rationale, but the comprehensive nature of that information, and the fact that it previously has been unavailable to government agents, fit well within *Riley*, as well as the approach taken by *Kyllo* and the *Jones* concurrences.

[87] United States v. Miller, 425 U.S. 435, 442–43 (1976).

Three years later, the Court held that the same rationale precluded Fourth Amendment protection for telephone numbers dialed by an individual: "When he used his phone, [the individual] voluntarily conveyed numerical information to the telephone company and 'exposed' that information to its equipment in the ordinary course of business. In so doing, petitioner assumed the risk that the company would reveal to police the numbers he dialed."[88]

Government lawyers have been arguing that this rationale precludes Fourth Amendment protection for the content of email messages because the email provider—whether employer, commercial service, or otherwise—always reserves the right to access messages to detect abuse of the service or other wrongful activity and, sometimes, for other purposes.

Yet the Supreme Court has refused one invitation to extend the third-party doctrine to digital messages. *City of Ontario v. Quon,*[89] decided in 2010, involved a suit under 42 U.S.C. § 1983 alleging that the plaintiffs—police officers employed by the city—suffered a violation of their Fourth Amendment rights when their supervisors read messages sent via a city-provided pager and disciplined the officers for use of the pager for inappropriate personal messages. The court of appeals held that the officers had a reasonable expectation of privacy in the text messages and that the city's review of the messages violated the Fourth Amendment.

The city and the federal government urged the Supreme Court to hold that the Fourth Amendment did not apply at all, because the officers had no legitimate expectation of privacy in the messages on the ground that the city's policy stated that pager messages were not private and could be accessed by city officials. The Court declined to rest its decision on that ground, because "[a] broad holding concerning employees' privacy expectations vis-à-vis employer-provided technological equipment might have implications for future cases that cannot be predicted."[90] It therefore assumed that the employees had a reasonable expectation of privacy, but held that the warrantless search fell within a previously recognized exception to

---

[88] Smith v. Maryland, 442 U.S. 735, 744 (1979).
[89] 560 U.S. 746 (2010).
[90] *Id.* at 760.

the warrant requirement based on the "special needs" of the government workplace.[91]

The Court explained its decision by pointing to "[r]apid changes in the dynamics of communication and information transmission" affecting "what society accepts as proper behavior."[92] For example, "many employers expect or at least tolerate personal use of such equipment by employees because it often increases worker efficiency" and "some States have recently passed statutes requiring employers to notify employees when monitoring their electronic communications."[93] "At present," the Court said, "it is uncertain how workplace norms, and the law's treatment of them, will evolve."[94]

Justice Sotomayor made the same point in her concurring opinion in *Jones*, stating that "it may be necessary to reconsider the premise that an individual has no reasonable expectation of privacy in information voluntarily disclosed to third parties. This approach is ill suited to the digital age, in which people reveal a great deal of information about themselves to third parties in the course of carrying out mundane tasks" such as sending emails or visiting websites.[95]

More fundamentally, inviting friends into my home does not vitiate my expectation of privacy vis-à-vis government agents. They still must obtain a warrant if they wish to search the premises. Why then should sharing my private information with individuals or businesses that I select vitiate my expectation of privacy as against the government? To be sure, those individuals or businesses could choose to provide government with the information voluntarily—my decision to share the information creates that risk (just as an individual invited into my home could choose to describe its contents, or events transpiring there, to government agents). But the decision to share the information should not relieve the government of the need to obtain a warrant if neither I nor the individuals I have taken into my confidence are willing to provide it to the government voluntarily.

One court of appeals addressed this issue—pre-*Riley*—in the email message context, and concluded that a warrant is required to permit

---

[91] *Id.*

[92] *Id.* at 759.

[93] *Id.*

[94] *Id.*

[95] United States v. Jones, 132 S. Ct. at 957.

the government to access the content of email messages. The Sixth Circuit's analysis in *United States v. Warshak*[96] largely anticipated the Supreme Court's approach in *Riley*.

The court of appeals first observed that—in the absense of consent or some other generally applicable exception—the government is obliged to obtain a warrant in order to access the content of old-technology private communications, in the form of telephone conversations and letters. Failing to extend the warrant requirement to email communications would mean that "the Fourth Amendment would prove an ineffective guardian of private communications, an essential purpose it has long been recognized to serve. As some forms of communication begin to diminish, the Fourth Amendment must recognize and protect nascent ones."[97] In the terms used by the Supreme Court in *Riley*, failing to recognize a reasonable expectation of privacy would significantly erode the privacy protection previously provided by the Fourth Amendment, in light of the then-existing technology.

The Sixth Circuit went on to reject the government's reliance on the third-party doctrine—which was based on the internet service provider's right to access the email messages. It held that a right of access is insufficient to eliminate a reasonable expectation of privacy, pointing out that tenants have a privacy expectation in their apartments notwithstanding the landlord's reservation of a right of access. And the bank records case was distinguishable in that the information was "conveyed to the bank so that the bank could put [it] to use 'in the ordinary course of business,'" while the internet service provider was "an *intermediary*, not the intended recipient of the emails."[98]

As in *Riley*, the court of appeals rejected a mechanical application of the pre-existing standard, focusing instead on whether the rationale underlying the third-party principle applied in this very different context. Concluding that it did not, and that applying the third-party principle would significantly intrude on legitimate expectations of privacy, the court instead concluded that the general requirement of a warrant should govern.

---

[96] 631 F.3d 266 (6th Cir. 2010).

[97] *Id.* at 286.

[98] *Id.* at 288 (emphasis in original).

Warshak's analysis seems likely to be accepted, not simply for email service providers, but also for personal information in email accounts provided by employers, schools, and others—at least in the absence of an extraordinarily clear warning by the account provider that the email account may not be used for personal purposes. And it is also likely to apply to other categories of information stored by increasingly ubiquitous cloud service providers; for example, calendars, documents, and photographs.

B. Cell Phone Location Information

Cell phone service providers maintain "cell site location information"—a record of calls made by the customer and of the particular cell tower that carried the call to or from the customer. Because the cell tower used will normally be the one closest to the customer, and the location information often includes the customer's location vis-à-vis the tower, it is possible to use this information to identify the customer's movements over a long period of time.

Several courts of appeals have addressed whether the government must obtain a warrant in order to access this information, reaching conflicting results.[99] All of these decisions pre-date *Riley*, however.

Under a *Riley* analysis, the threshold question is whether an individual has a legitimate expectation of privacy in information regarding his location. The concurring opinions in *Jones* indicate that the answer to that question is likely "yes." Although the cell tower information is not as accurate as GPS tracking, it nonetheless provides a highly detailed picture of an individual's movements—the very information that the concurring justices found protected in *Jones*.

In the cell tower context, however, the government argues that this location information has been "shared" with the cell phone service provider—indeed, it is embodied exclusively in the service provider's records—and that the third-party doctrine therefore precludes protection under the Fourth Amendment. But the overwhelming majority of customers are unaware that these data are collected and maintained by cell companies; a customer therefore "has not voluntarily

---

[99] See United States v. Davis, 754 F.3d 1205 (11th Cir. 2014); In re Application of the United States, 724 F.3d 600, 615 (5th Cir. 2013); In re Application of the United States, 620 F.3d 304 (3d Cir. 2010).

disclosed his cell site location information to the provider in such a fashion as to lose his reasonable expectation of privacy."[100]

Given the ubiquity of cell phones, a contrary result would give government agents an easy way to obtain comprehensive location information regarding virtually any American—something that government agents could not do before the advent of this technology. In the terms used in *Riley*, failing to recognize a legitimate expectation of privacy would produce a very substantial diminution of the privacy protection that Americans previously enjoyed.

As Professor Orin Kerr has pointed out, however, recognizing a protectable Fourth Amendment interest in this information collected by a private party is not compelled by any existing Supreme Court decision.[101] Here, however, the customer plays an essential role in enabling collection of the information (the customer's phone sends the signal to the tower)—and that involvement should supply the essential link.

One final issue: a federal statute (the Stored Communications Act) requires the government to obtain an order from a magistrate based upon a showing of reasonable grounds to believe that the information is relevant and material to an ongoing criminal investigation.[102] Although this standard is less demanding than probable cause, it does impose a limit on law enforcement officers.

Justice Alito in both *Jones* and *Riley* expressed the view that determinations by Congress and state legislatures regarding the appropriate standards for reconciling privacy interests and law enforcement needs would be more appropriate than leaving those questions "primarily to federal courts using the blunt instrument of the Fourth Amendment."[103]

---

[100] United States v. Davis, 754 F.3d at 1215–16.

[101] O. Kerr, DoJ Petitions for Rehearing in Eleventh Circuit Cell-Site Case, The Volokh Conspiracy (Aug. 1, 2014), http://www.washingtonpost.com/news/volokh-conspiracy/wp/2014/08/01/doj-petitions-for-rehearing-in-eleventh-circuit-cell-site-case.

[102] 18 U.S.C. § 2703(d) (2011).

[103] Riley v. California, 134 S. Ct. at 2497; see also United States v. Jones, 132 S. Ct. at 963–64.

C. Border Searches of Digitally Stored Information

Another area of Fourth Amendment controversy involving digitally stored information involves searches at the border. As a general matter, the federal government has extremely broad authority to conduct searches of people and things entering the United States:

> Since the founding of our Republic, Congress has granted the Executive plenary authority to conduct routine searches and seizures at the border, without probable cause or a warrant, in order to regulate the collection of duties and to prevent the introduction of contraband into this country. [The Supreme] Court has long recognized Congress' power to police entrants at the border. . . . "'Import restrictions and searches of persons or packages at the national border rest on different considerations and different rules of constitutional law from domestic regulations. The Constitution gives Congress broad comprehensive powers "[t]o regulate Commerce with foreign Nations." Historically, such broad powers have been necessary to prevent smuggling and to prevent prohibited articles from entry.'"[104]

Does that mean that a customs officer may search all of the digitally stored data on the cell phone, tablet, or laptop computer of an individual entering the country without a warrant and without any individualized suspicion?

The U.S. Court of Appeals for the Ninth Circuit addressed that question in *United States v. Cotterman* and rejected the government's argument that no individualized suspicion was required to justify such a search at the border.[105] It held, however, that the Fourth Amendment requires only a showing of "reasonable suspicion," as opposed to the probable cause generally needed to justify a search.

The Supreme Court has applied a reasonable suspicion requirement in the context of the extended detention *of an individual*.[106] It has not been receptive to limits on the government's authority with respect to property, rejecting the argument that a reasonable suspicion showing was necessary to permit the government to remove a car's gas tank.[107]

---

[104] United States v. Montoya de Hernandez, 473 U.S. 531, 537–38 (1985).

[105] 709 F.3d 952 (9th Cir. 2013) (en banc).

[106] United States v. Montoya de Hernandez, 473 U.S. at 540–41.

[107] See, e.g., United States v. Flores-Montano, 541 U.S. 149 (2004).

For these reasons, it is not clear whether the significant impact on privacy interests recognized in *Riley* will be sufficient to require a showing of individualized suspicion for border searches of digitally stored information.

* * *

Evolving technology is certain to provide courts with a steady diet of questions regarding the appropriate scope of Fourth Amendment rules developed in earlier eras. With its decision in *Riley*, the Supreme Court has charted a course for addressing these questions that promises to ensure that this vital protection remains meaningful, continuing to safeguard Americans' privacy against arbitrary invasion through abuse of government power.

Looking Ahead: October Term 2014

Miguel A. Estrada* and Ashley S. Boizelle**

The Supreme Court's October 2014 term will follow a term marked by both unanimity and a spate of 5-4 decisions spanning topics that include the limits of executive power in making recess appointments, cell phone searches and the Fourth Amendment, the First Amendment rights of abortion protestors and home health care providers, and the religious rights of closely held corporations. Although pundits and the public are still digesting the implications of the Court's decisions, the polarizing nature of much of the Court's jurisprudence shows no sign of abating. Indeed, only a few weeks after the Court's 5-4 decision striking down the government's contraceptive mandate for closely held corporations that object on religious grounds, congressional Democrats introduced legislation to override it.[1]

As the dust from the previous term settles and new battles begin, the Court's new docket is taking shape and promises to feature its fair share of high-profile cases. As of this writing, the Court has granted review in 39 cases and asked for the view of the solicitor general in 10 others. The 2014 caseload includes important questions such

* Partner in the Washington, D.C. office of Gibson, Dunn & Crutcher and has argued 22 cases before the Supreme Court. Prior to entering private practice, Mr. Estrada served as Assistant to the Solicitor General of the United States and as an Assistant U.S. Attorney and Deputy Chief of the Appellate Section, U.S. Attorney's Office, Southern District of New York. He also served as a law clerk to the Honorable Anthony M. Kennedy in the U.S. Supreme Court in 1988–1989 and to the Honorable Amalya L. Kearse in the U.S. Court of Appeals for the Second Circuit in 1986–1987.

** Associate in the Washington, D.C. office of Gibson, Dunn & Crutcher, where she specializes in appellate and constitutional litigation. Prior to joining Gibson Dunn, she clerked for the Honorable Sandra S. Ikuta in the U.S. Court of Appeals for the Ninth Circuit.

[1] See, e.g., Kristina Peterson, Senate Bill to Nullify Hobby Lobby Decision Fails, Wall St. J., July 16, 2014, available at http://online.wsj.com/articles/senate-bill-against-hobby-lobby-decision-fails-1405537082.

as whether a prison can prohibit a Muslim inmate from growing a beard that he claims is required by his religion, whether Congress can direct the State Department to recognize Jerusalem as part of Israel on the passports of Jerusalem-born U.S. citizens, and whether a person can be prosecuted under the anti-shredding provision of Sarbanes-Oxley for destroying undersized fish. In this article, we discuss these and other significant cases from the upcoming term and offer a few predictions about additional cases that may end up on the Court's calendar come October.

I. Fourth Amendment

After winning widespread acclaim for unanimously bringing the Fourth Amendment into the 21st century in *Riley v. California*,[2] the Court will open the 2014 term with oral argument in *Heien v. North Carolina*, which presents the question whether a police officer's mistake of law can provide the individualized suspicion that the Fourth Amendment requires to justify a traffic stop.[3]

In 2009, Nicholas Heien and a friend were driving through North Carolina and were pulled over by a police officer for a nonfunctioning brake light. The officer performed the traffic stop on the mistaken belief that North Carolina law requires that a vehicle have *two* functioning brake lights, rather than merely "*a* stop lamp," as the relevant statute provides.[4] During the stop, the officer asked for and received permission to search the vehicle, and discovered a plastic bag containing cocaine. Based on that evidence, the state charged Heien with trafficking in cocaine. At trial, Heien moved to suppress it on the ground that the stop was an illegal seizure under the Fourth Amendment. The trial court denied the motion, and Heien was sentenced to two consecutive prison terms of 10 to 12 months. The appeals court unanimously reversed, but the North Carolina Supreme Court agreed with the trial court, holding that "so long as an officer's mistake is reasonable, it may give rise to reasonable suspicion."[5] Relying in part on the Supreme Court's decision in

[2] 134 S.Ct. 2473 (2014).

[3] No. 13-604 (OT 2014).

[4] N.C.G.S. § 20-129(g) (2013) (emphasis added).

[5] State of North Carolina v. Heien, 737 S.E.2d 351, 358 (N.C. 2012).

Michigan v. DeFillippo,[6] the North Carolina Supreme Court reasoned that "requiring an officer to be more than reasonable, mandating that he be perfect, would impose a greater burden than that required under the Fourth Amendment."[7]

DeFillippo is part of a mosaic of decisions in which the Court has strained to protect the truth-finding function of trials from overly technical applications of the exclusionary rule. In that case, the Court recoiled from requiring police officers to second-guess the constitutionality of the laws they are required to enforce, holding that evidence obtained during an arrest under an ordinance that was later declared unconstitutional need not be suppressed under a good-faith exception to the exclusionary rule.[8] The Court has applied the same exception when evidence is obtained in "objectively reasonable reliance" on the basis of binding, but later abrogated, circuit precedent.[9] The Court has not, however, extended this exception to mistakes of *existing* law, nor has it suggested that the good-faith exception goes to the question whether the Fourth Amendment was violated in the first instance, rather than simply to the remedy for a violation.

Nevertheless, the Court has occasionally noted that the text of the Fourth Amendment reflects some tolerance for certain kinds of errors by law enforcement, a question that comes before and stands quite apart from whether the exclusionary rule applies. Indeed, in *Illinois v. Rodriguez*, the Court made clear that "in order to satisfy the 'reasonableness' requirement of the Fourth Amendment, what is generally demanded of the many factual determinations that must regularly be made by agents of the government . . . is not that they always be correct, but that they always be reasonable."[10]

---

[6] 443 U.S. 31 (1979); see also Illinois v. Krull, 480 U.S. 340, 342, 349–50 (1987) (recognizing exception to exclusionary rule when officers act in objectively reasonable reliance on a statute authorizing warrantless administrative searches, but where the statute is ultimately found to violate the Fourth Amendment).

[7] Heien, 737 S.E.2d at 356.

[8] DeFillippo, 134 S. Ct. 2473.

[9] Davis v. United States, 131 S. Ct. 2419 (2011); see also United States v. Leon, 468 U.S. 897 (1984) (permitting admission of evidence obtained on the basis of a facially valid search warrant that is not actually supported by probable cause under a good faith exception to the exclusionary rule).

[10] 497 U.S. 177, 185–86 (1990).

State and federal courts are divided on the question whether a mistake of law, as opposed to fact, violates the Fourth Amendment. The U.S. Court of Appeals for the Eighth Circuit, for example, has held in a case similar to *Heien* that the relevant question is "whether an objectively reasonable police officer could have formed a reasonable suspicion that [the defendant] was committing a code violation."[11] Because the language of the applicable statute was "counterintuitive and confusing," the court determined that the officer had an objectively reasonable basis to believe that he had witnessed a traffic violation and that the stop was permitted under the Fourth Amendment.[12] The Eleventh Circuit, however, has held that "a mistake of law, no matter how reasonable or understandable, . . . cannot provide reasonable suspicion . . . to justify a traffic stop" and has stressed "the fundamental unfairness of holding citizens to 'the traditional rule that ignorance of the law is no excuse,' while allowing those 'entrusted to enforce' the law to be ignorant of it."[13]

Ultimately, *Heien* poses the question whether those charged with enforcing the law should be permitted (if not, encouraged) to acquire a lackadaisical understanding of the law relevant to the execution of their duties. The Court must decide this question in the context of a long-standing rule for criminal defendants that "ignorance of the law is no excuse."[14] The Court appears to have three possible paths. It could hold that mistakes of law (1) do not violate the Fourth Amendment, (2) violate the Fourth Amendment but are not subject to suppression when they are objectively reasonable, or (3) violate the Fourth Amendment and are subject to the exclusionary rule. To be sure, the third option is likely to have a significant deterrent effect, while options 1 and 2 may have the undesirable effect of encouraging willful ignorance of the law by the very people charged with enforcing it. In any event, it would seem an odd bargain indeed for laypersons to be charged with knowledge of criminal law and denied any defense on the basis of mistakes of law—absent certain statutory exceptions—while law enforcement is incentivized to

---

[11] United States v. Martin, 411 F.3d 998, 1001 (8th Cir. 2005).

[12] *Id.* at 1001–02.

[13] United States v. Chanthasouxat, 342 F.3d 1271, 1280 (11th Cir. 2003) (quoting Bryan v. United States, 524 U.S. 184, 196 (1998)).

[14] Bryan, 524 U.S. at 196.

embrace ignorance of the law, even as it purports to enforce those laws on the public's behalf.

II. Criminal Law and Statutory Interpretation

In addition to the Fourth Amendment, the Court's 2014 term will feature several criminal appeals that involve important questions of statutory interpretation.

A. Go Fish

Of the Court's current crop of criminal cases, *Yates v. United States* features the most bizarre fact pattern and the most aggressive application of a federal statute by federal prosecutors.[15] Specifically, the case poses the question whether a commercial fisherman can be convicted under the anti-shredding provision of the Sarbanes-Oxley Act for destroying fish—yes, fish—following receipt of a civil fishing citation from the Florida Fish & Wildlife Commission for harvesting undersized red grouper in the Gulf of Mexico.

To be sure, Sarbanes-Oxley has never been applied in this manner. The statute, which was enacted in 2002 in response to Enron Corporation's systematic destruction of documents and financial records during a federal investigation into the circumstances of its collapse, provides:

> Whoever knowingly alters, destroys, mutilates, conceals, covers up, falsifies, or makes a false entry in any record, document, or tangible object with the intent to impede, obstruct, or influence the investigation of proper administration of any matter within the jurisdiction of any department or agency of the United States . . . shall be fined under this title, imprisoned not more than 20 years, or both.[16]

Based on this provision, federal prosecutors charged Yates with illegally destroying evidence that demonstrated that he had illegally harvested red grouper that were smaller than the minimum 20 inches required under applicable regulations. He was convicted, and the U.S. Court of Appeals for the Eleventh Circuit affirmed.[17]

---

[15] No. 13-7541 (OT 2014).

[16] 18 U.S.C. § 1519 (2014); see also Arthur Andersen v. United States, 544 U.S. 696 (2005).

[17] United States v. Yates, 733 F.3d 1059 (11th Cir. 2013).

The solicitor general submitted a waiver of the United States' right to respond 10 days after the petition for certiorari was filed. Such a waiver is scarcely unusual—the government declines to respond to the vast majority of cert petitions, a practice that can be justified by the plain fact that most petitions require only cursory examination to conclude that the case does not merit further review—but the practice can be troubling when, as in *Yates*, it is apparently used in an attempt to "bury" a petition so that questionable prosecutorial decisions will escape notice. The solicitor general's special standing with the Court, which has earned the office the label "the 10th justice," is not easily compatible with behavior that smacks of abusing procedural rules for narrow tactical advantage. It surely ought to embarrass the solicitor general when his waiver is rejected and certiorari is granted, especially if the judgment is then reversed. His original waiver, after all, implicitly represented to the Court that the issues presented by the petition were not even worth discussing.

That may well be the path that lies ahead for *Yates*. After the Court rejected the solicitor general's waiver and called for a government response, he filed a brief defending the judgment below on the ground that a fish is a "tangible object," and that Yates acted with "obstructive intent."[18] That may be true as far as it goes, but it seems a bit strained in the context of a statute that contemplates that "false entries" might be made on such "tangible object[s]" or that such objects might be "falsified." Sadly, the silly literalism of federal prosecutors in *Yates*, and the solicitor general's willingness to defend the nearly indefensible, appear to be part of a broader pattern of criminal-justice abuse unchecked by any meaningful adult supervision.

Indeed, *Yates* is a fitting sequel to last term's example of the same syndrome, *Bond v. United States*.[19] That case featured a plot straight out of a soap opera—a scorned wife who used chemical irritants on the doorknob, mailbox, and car door handle of her husband's mistress, ultimately causing a minor thumb burn that was easily treated with water. Evidently, federal prosecutors could think of nothing better to do with their time than to prosecute the wronged woman under the Chemical Weapons Convention Implementation Act of 1998, a federal law regulating chemical warfare. The solicitor

---

[18] Brief for the United States in Opposition at 9–10, Yates (No. 13-7451).
[19] 134 S. Ct. 2077 (2014).

general defended that prosecutorial judgment not once, but *twice*, losing *unanimously* each time.[20] To the surprise of no one outside the Department of Justice, the Supreme Court was unwilling to "transform a statute passed to implement the international Convention on Chemical Weapons into one that makes it a federal offense to poison goldfish" or to embrace a reading of the act "that would sweep in everything from the detergent under the kitchen sink to the stain remover in the laundry room."[21]

Despite the Court's obvious antipathy toward the government's creative and capacious interpretation of a federal criminal statute, it appears that federal prosecutors have not been chastened by the experience of *Bond*. Instead, they continue to use their discretion to press the outer bounds of criminal statutes, irrespective of legislative intent and the availability or adequacy of state criminal penalties. And, as in *Bond*, their work is being abetted by the Office of the Solicitor General. This dynamic is understandably disconcerting to criminal defense attorneys and those generally concerned with federal overreach. In *Bond*, the Court responded to this dynamic with a decisive 18 adverse votes. Time will tell whether *Yates* is destined for a similar fate.

B. Aggravated Robbery

Whitfield v. United States is another case in which the Court will determine whether prosecutors and courts have reasonably interpreted and applied a criminal statute.[22] Specifically, 18 U.S.C. § 2113(e) provides a sentence of 10 years to life in prison for anyone who, in the commission of a bank robbery, forces another person "to accompany him without the consent of such person" during the robbery or while in flight.[23]

Larry Whitfield and an accomplice, armed with a handgun and an assault rifle, entered a credit union in North Carolina but were foiled when a metal detector triggered an automatic locking system. They fled the scene by car and were pursued by police, but became stuck on a highway median. After abandoning their vehicle,

[20] *Id.*; see also Bond v. United States, 131 S. Ct. 2355 (2011).
[21] Bond, 134 S. Ct. at 2091.
[22] No. 13-9026 (OT 2014).
[23] 18 U.S.C. § 2113(e) (2014).

they discarded their weapons and separated. Whitfield ended up in the home of Herman and Mary Parnell, where he encountered the 79-year-old Mrs. Parnell and ordered her to accompany him to an interior computer room to avoid detection by police. Whitfield eventually fled the Parnell residence and was apprehended. When Mr. Parnell returned home, he found his wife in the computer room, dead from a heart attack.

Following a jury trial, Whitfield was convicted of attempted bank robbery (Count 1), conspiring to carry a firearm during an attempted bank robbery (Count 2), carrying a firearm during an attempted bank robbery (Count 3), and forcing Mrs. Parnell to accompany him while attempting to avoid apprehension for an attempted bank robbery that resulted in death (Count 4). In accordance with 18 U.S.C. § 2113(e), the district court sentenced Whitfield to life imprisonment on Count 4, although the U.S. Court of Appeals for the Fourth Circuit reversed this portion of the judgment, holding that the indictment alleged only a killing offense and a forced accompaniment offense, rather than a "forced accompaniment resulting in death" offense.[24] The court therefore remanded for resentencing.[25] On remand, the district court sentenced Whitfield to 264 months of imprisonment to be followed by five years of supervised release. The Fourth Circuit affirmed.[26]

Whitfield has challenged his conviction on the ground that compelling Mrs. Parnell to accompany him to an interior room in her home did not constitute "forced accompaniment" within the meaning of Section 2113(e). In granting review, the Supreme Court has agreed to decide whether a conviction under 18 U.S.C. § 2113(e) requires proof of more than *de minimis* movement of the victim.[27] While most courts to consider this issue have held that the amount of movement at issue in this case is sufficient to satisfy the statute,[28] the U.S. Court of Appeals for the Tenth Circuit has held that "more

[24] United States v. Whitfield, 695 F.3d 288 (4th Cir. 2012).

[25] *Id.* at 311.

[26] United States v. Whitfield, 548 F. App'x 70 (4th Cir. 2013).

[27] 134 S. Ct. 2840 (2014).

[28] See, e.g., United States v. Strobehn, 421 F.3d 1017, 1018–20 (9th Cir. 2005); United States v. Turner, 389 F.3d 111, 114, 119–20 (4th Cir. 2004); United States v. Davis, 48 F.3d 277, 278–79 (7th Cir. 1995); United States v. Reed, 26 F.3d 523, 525, 526–28 (5th Cir. 1994); United States v. Bauer, 956 F.2d 239, 241–42 (11th Cir. 1992).

is required than forcing [a bank president] to enter his own house or forcing the [bank president's] family to move from the den to a bedroom."[29]

To be sure, Whitfield is not remotely a sympathetic defendant. And yet, his case presents important questions about statutory structure, fair notice, and lenity. Section 2113(e) defines an *aggravated* form of the bank robbery offense. But relatively minor movements are so commonplace in the context of bank robberies that, under a broad reading of "accompaniment," *every* bank robbery could be charged as an aggravated crime, essentially nullifying the congressional design.[30] On the other hand, the Tenth Circuit's remedy may be worse than the disease, because a *de minimis* exception to this criminal statute would not easily satisfy criminal-law standards of definiteness. It will be interesting to see how the Court ultimately resolves that tension.

C. *First Amendment*

Unlike most recent high-profile First Amendment cases, in *Elonis v. United States*, the Court will address constitutional speech protections in the context of a criminal prosecution.[31] Specifically, 18 U.S.C. § 875(c) makes it a federal crime to "transmit[] in interstate or foreign commerce any communication containing . . . any threat to injure the person of another."[32] Anthony Elonis was indicted for five violations of Section 875(c) after publishing posts on his public Facebook page—frequently in the form of violent rap lyrics—threatening physical harm to various targets, including former coworkers and patrons of an amusement park where he worked, his ex-wife, police officers, a kindergarten class, and an FBI agent. At trial, he insisted that the posts were amateur musical or poetic expressions and requested that the jury be instructed that the government must establish that he possessed a subjective intent to threaten in order to convict him under Section 875(c). The court denied his request, and Elonis was convicted on four of five counts with a sentence of 44 months of imprisonment to be followed by three years of supervised

---

[29] United States v. Marx, 485 F.2d 1179, 1186 (10th Cir. 1973).

[30] See, e.g., United States v. Reed, 26 F.3d 523, 528 (5th Cir. 1994).

[31] No. 13-983 (OT 2014).

[32] 18 U.S.C. § 875(c) (2014).

release. The U.S. Court of Appeals for the Third Circuit affirmed, holding that the district court correctly instructed the jury to apply an objective reasonable-person standard because the First Amendment permits criminal punishment for communications that qualify as "true threat[s]."[33]

In granting Elonis's petition for certiorari, the Supreme Court has agreed to decide (1) whether the First Amendment and *Virginia v. Black*[34] require that a conviction under Section 875(c) be predicated on proof of the defendant's subjective intent to threaten rather than proof that a "reasonable person" would regard the statement as threatening, and (2) whether, as a matter of statutory interpretation, conviction of threatening a person under Section 875(c) requires proof of the defendant's subjective intent to threaten.

As to the first question, *Virginia v. Black* held that a state may ban cross burning carried out with an intent to intimidate, but that a Virginia statute that treated *any* cross burning as prima facie evidence of an intent to intimidate violated the First Amendment.[35] The plurality opinion, authored by Justice Sandra Day O'Connor, concluded that the prima facie evidence provision was facially unconstitutional because it "permit[ted] the Commonwealth to arrest, prosecute, and convict a person based solely on the fact of cross burning itself," when "a burning cross is not always intended to intimidate."[36] Because cross burning could be used to different effects, a statute that criminalized the activity could not ignore "all the contextual factors that are necessary to decide whether a particular cross burning was intended to intimidate."[37]

Although *Black* reflects the Court's concerns about the contours of criminal-threat statutes—with an emphasis on the failure to account for the context in which speech is communicated—the statute at issue expressly incorporated an intent-to-intimidate requirement, and thus the Court was not forced to decide the precise question of whether the First Amendment requires that convictions under such

---

[33] Elonis v. United States, 730 F.3d 321 (3d Cir. 2013); see also Watts v. United States, 394 U.S. 705, 708 (1969) (per curiam).

[34] 538 U.S. 343 (2003).

[35] *Id.* at 365.

[36] *Id.*

[37] *Id.* at 367.

statutes be based on the speaker's subjective intent to threaten the recipient of the speech. Absent clear authority, the majority of federal appellate courts to consider this question have adopted an objective standard, reasoning that the prohibition on true threats "protect[s] individuals from the fear of violence," "from the disruption that fear engenders," and "from the possibility that the threatened violence will occur," rather than simply from the ultimate threatened harm.[38]

The U.S. Court of Appeals for the Ninth Circuit and several state supreme courts have applied a different rule, construing *Black* to require that the subjective test be read into all threat statutes that criminalize pure speech.[39] The Ninth Circuit has reasoned, in part, that the prima facie evidence provision in *Black* could not have offended the First Amendment if intent to intimidate were constitutionally irrelevant.[40]

The Supreme Court must now decide which test is compelled by the First Amendment and whether Section 875(c) itself incorporates an intent-to-threaten element. The Court posed the second question without the parties' request, suggesting that it may believe that there is a basis to link *Elonis* to *Black* after all. Although the relevant provision does not expressly incorporate an intent element, Judge Jeffrey Sutton of the U.S. Court of Appeals for the Sixth Circuit has previously observed that Section 875(c) could be construed to require proof of intent because "[e]very relevant definition of the noun 'threat' or the verb 'threaten,' whether in existence when Congress passed the law (1932) or today, includes an intent component."[41]

Whether the Supreme Court extends the logic of *Black*, adopts Judge Sutton's construction of Section 875(c), or holds that an objective test is permissible, the questions presented in *Elonis* will

---

[38] R.A.V. v. City of St. Paul, 505 U.S. 377, 388 (1992); see also, e.g., United States v. Martinez, 736 F.3d 981, 988 (11th Cir. 2013), petition for cert. filed, (Feb. 21, 2014) No. 13-8837; United States v. Jeffries, 692 F.3d 473, 480 (6th Cir. 2012), cert. denied, 124 S. Ct. 59 (U.S. Oct. 7, 2013)(No. 12-1185); United States v. White, 670 F.3d 498, 508 (4th Cir. 2012); United States v. Mabie, 663 F.3d 322, 330–32 (8th Cir. 2011), cert. denied, 133 S. Ct. 107 (U.S. Oct. 1, 2012)(No. 11-9770); United States v. Stewart, 411 F.3d 825, 828 (7th Cir. 2005); Porter v. Ascension Parish Sch. Bd., 393 F.3d 608, 616 (5th Cir. 2004); United States v. Nishnianidze, 342 F.3d 6, 16 (lst Cir. 2003); United States v. Sovie, 122 F.3d 122, 125 (2d Cir. 1997).

[39] See, e.g., United States v. Bagdasarian, 652 F.3d 1113, 1117 (9th Cir. 2011); accord State v. Miles, 15 A.3d 596, 599 (Vt. 2011); State v. Grayhurst, 852 A.2d 491, 515 (R.I. 2004).

[40] United States v. Cassel, 408 F.3d 622, 633 n.10 (9th Cir. 2005).

[41] Jeffries, 692 F.3d at 483–84 (Sutton, J., concurring).

only become more pressing in the social media age. According to Elonis's petition for certiorari, the Justice Department has brought hundreds of Section 875(c) prosecutions since *Black* was decided,[42] which should come as no surprise given the explosion in available social media outlets and the attendant ease with which individuals across the United States "transmit" messages in "interstate or foreign commerce" that would no doubt qualify as threats of physical harm under an objective standard. Although attempting to predict the outcome in Supreme Court cases is always perilous, the Court's recent First Amendment jurisprudence reflects a robust commitment to free-speech rights and suggests that some portion of the Court is likely to be gravely concerned about any standard that criminalizes amateur rap lyrics, no matter how repugnant, posted to an individual's Facebook page.

III. Freedom of Religion

In addition to its criminal cases, and on the heels of the controversial *Hobby Lobby* ruling, the Supreme Court has agreed to hear another case that addresses the contours of religious freedom, albeit in a prison in lieu of a craft store. Whereas *Hobby Lobby* dealt with the religious views of closely held corporations under the Religious Freedom Restoration Act of 1993 (RFRA), *Holt v. Hobbs* addresses the religious freedom of prisoners under the Religious Land Use and Institutionalized Persons Act (RLUIPA)—a statute enacted to extend to prisoners the same religious protections offered to unincarcerated individuals (and corporations and other legal persons) under RFRA.[43] Whereas *Hobby Lobby* addressed a federal requirement that compelled a corporation to act in a manner inconsistent with its religious practices, *Holt* addresses a prohibition on certain acts that are purportedly required by a prisoner's religious commitments.

Specifically, *Holt* involves the question whether the Arkansas Department of Corrections' no-beard-growing policy violates RLUIPA or the First Amendment, and whether a half-inch beard would satisfy the security goals sought by the policy. The challenge was brought

---

[42] Elonis, 730 F.3d 321 Petition for Certiorari at 33, 134 S.Ct. 2819 (U.S. Feb. 14, 2014) (No. 13-983)(citing U.S. Dep't of Justice, Bureau of Justice Statistics: Federal Criminal Case Processing Statistics, http://www.bjs.gov/fjsrc/tsec.cfm).

[43] No. 13-6827 (OT 2014).

by Gregory H. Holt, who is serving a life sentence for burglary and domestic battery—evidently involving an attempt to slash his girl-friend's throat—and who claims that his Muslim faith requires that he don at least a half-inch beard.

Under RLUIPA, prison officials must demonstrate that policies that burden religious practices serve a compelling penological inter-est through the least restrictive means. The policy that Holt chal-lenges permits mustaches and quarter-inch beards for those with diagnosed dermatologic problems but prohibits all other facial hair on the ground that a ban is needed to promote "health and hygiene," minimize "opportunities for disguise," promote uniformity in in-mate appearance, and help prevent concealment of contraband in inmates' hair and cheeks. In their defense of the Arkansas policy, prison officials insist that "homemade darts and other weapons" and "cellphone SIM cards" can be concealed in half-inch beards and that there are serious practical difficulties in monitoring the lengths of inmates' beards to ensure that they are in compliance with Holt's proposed half-inch limit. The Eighth Circuit held that the justifica-tions offered by the prison officials satisfied the RLUIPA standard, despite evidence that prisons in 41 state corrections systems and the federal system allow prisoners to grow beards for religious reasons.

Solicitor General Donald Verrilli filed an amicus brief in support of Holt's challenge, calling the no-beard policy "religious discrimi-nation" and "a substantial burden on religious exercise."[44] Interest-ingly, this brief was filed only a few months after the government's reply brief in *Hobby Lobby*, which insisted that the requirement that employers provide their employees with no-cost contraceptives did not constitute a substantial burden on the religious beliefs of those employers.[45] In the government's view, prisons can advance their le-gitimate safety objectives in some other way that is more respectful of the inmate's religious beliefs; the federal government, on the other hand, need not be troubled to accommodate the sincere religious be-liefs of business owners.

The federal government's differential treatment of these two cases is odd because RLUIPA was intended to make available to prisoners

[44] Brief for the United States as Amicus Curiae Supporting Petitioner, Holt v. Hobbs, No. 13-6827 (OT 2014).

[45] Reply Brief for Petitioners, Burwell v. Hobby Lobby Stores, Inc., 134 S. Ct. 2751 (2014).

protections that replicate those available to the general citizenry under RFRA. Whatever the relationship between the two statutes, it would be bizarre if those whose liberty is restricted on account of proven antisocial behavior were better protected from the government's incursions on their religion than members of the law-abiding public. Be that as it may, given the Supreme Court's disposition in *Hobby Lobby*, we should not be surprised to see a ruling invalidating the no-beard policy as an unjustified burden on Holt's religion.

IV. Executive Power

As a general rule, no Supreme Court term is complete without a healthy dose of separation-of-powers cases, and the 2014–2015 term has its fair share of them.

A. The Recognition Power

In *Zivotofsky v. Kerry*, for example, the Court will decide whether the Foreign Relations Authorization Act (FRAA)—which directs the secretary of state, on request, to record the birth country of an American citizen born in Jerusalem as "Israel" on a Consular Report of Birth Abroad (CRBA) and on a U.S. passport—"impermissibly infringes on the President's exercise of the recognition power reposing exclusively in him."[46] The case arises out of a dispute over the passport and CRBA of Menachem Zivotofsky, who was born to American parents living in Jerusalem in 2002. Zivotofsky's parents filed a request in accordance with the FRAA but were denied.

The FRAA has been controversial from its inception. Indeed, when President George W. Bush signed it, he issued a statement disclaiming the above statutory requirement as an impermissible interference "with the president's constitutional authority to conduct the nation's foreign affairs."[47] Consistent with this position, the State Department refuses to enforce the law on the ground that it is inconsistent with the government's long-standing neutrality on the status of Jerusalem as part of neither Israel nor Palestine. State

---

[46] No. 13-628 (OT 2014).

[47] George W. Bush, Statement on Signing the Foreign Relations Authorization Act (Sept. 12, 2002), 38 Weekly Comp. Pres. Doc. 40 at 1660 (Oct. 7, 2002), available at http://www.gpo.gov/fdsys/pkg/WCPD-2002-10-07/html/WCPD-2002-10-07-Pg1658-2.htm.

Department policy concerning the birthplace of U.S. citizens born in Jerusalem instead directs that the birthplace on official documents be recorded as "Jerusalem," without any mention of a country.

The case has been before the Court once before, when it reversed the U.S. Court of Appeals for the D.C. Circuit's determination that the case posed a political question that the judiciary should not resolve.[48] Forced to decide the case on the merits, the D.C. Circuit held that the FRAA is unconstitutional because it violates the president's exclusive power to recognize foreign nations. The court explained that while the question of passport authority is not itself in the Constitution, the president's "recognition power" is derived from his or her authority to receive ambassadors and enables the president to speak as the sole representative of the United States in matters of international diplomacy.

Unsurprisingly, members of Congress are displeased with that ruling and have objected, in particular, to the D.C. Circuit's suggestion that the president's recognition power is plenary and exclusive. In an amicus brief in support of certiorari, they argued that the upshot of the court's determination is that "the Executive is given carte blanche to treat as unconstitutional—and to refuse to comply with—any Act of Congress that it determines touches on recognition policy,"[49] thereby interfering with the necessary exercise of *Congress's* powers, including naturalization and immigration.[50]

Ultimately, the case presents a politically and legally contentious question—one made even more controversial by the intensification of hostilities between Israel and Hamas in Gaza and the existing partisan rancor between President Obama and Congress. Whether one believes that Jerusalem is part of Israel, Palestine, or some split authority, it would appear that the president has the constitutional authority to determine when and how to recognize it. The questions the Court must answer are whether that power is exclusive to the executive branch and whether the FRAA unconstitutionally interferes with it.

---

[48] M.B.Z. v. Clinton, 132 S. Ct. 1421 (2012).

[49] Brief for Members of Congress as Amici Curiae in Support of Petitioner at 4, Zivotovsky, No. 13-628 (OT 2014).

[50] *Id.* at 15.

B. The Nondelegation Doctrine

In addition to addressing the scope of the executive's recognition power, the 2014 term will feature the Court's first case in more than 70 years that features the nondelegation doctrine—the idea that one branch of government cannot authorize another entity to exercise its constitutionally authorized powers. Indeed, the Court has not invalidated a federal statute on nondelegation grounds since 1936.[51] In *Department of Transportation v. Association of American Railroads*, the Court will review a decision of the D.C. Circuit holding that Congress violated the nondelegation doctrine when it empowered Amtrak and the Federal Railroad Administration (FRA) to collaborate to develop performance measures to improve enforcement of the statutory priority Amtrak's passenger rail service has over other trains.[52]

As the parties' briefing explains, Congress created Amtrak—an entity with both public and private dimensions—in 1970 to provide intercity passenger rail service and replace railroads that were angling to abandon passenger-rail service.[53] In an attempt to improve Amtrak's profitability and as a condition of releasing railroads from their passenger-service obligations, Congress directed railroads to allow Amtrak to use their tracks and facilities, at rates either agreed to by Amtrak and the host railroads or prescribed by the Surface Transportation Board (STB).[54] To further improve passenger-rail service, Congress also granted Amtrak a general priority over freight transportation in using rail facilities. Most recently, in 2008, Congress passed the Passenger Rail Investment and Improvement Act of 2008 (PRIIA),[55] which provides that the Federal Railroad Administration and Amtrak

> shall jointly, in consultation with the Surface Transportation Board [and others] . . . develop new or improve existing metrics and minimum standards for measuring the performance and service quality of intercity passenger train operations, including cost recovery, on-time performance

[51] Carter v. Carter Coal, 298 U.S. 238, 283–84, 310–12 (1936).

[52] No. 13-1080 (OT 2014).

[53] See Dep't of Transp. v. Ass'n of Am. R.R.'s, 721 F.3d 666 (D.C. Cir. 2013), petition for cert. filed, No. 13-1080 (U.S. Mar. 10, 2014; see also Brief in Opposition, No. 13-1080 (OT 2014)).

[54] 49 U.S.C. § 24308(a)(2014).

[55] Pub. L. No. 110-432, Division B, 122 Stat. 4848, 4907 (codified generally in Title 49).

and minutes of delay, ridership, on-board services, stations, facilities, equipment, and other services.[56]

The statute further provides that any deadlock between Amtrak and the FRA must be resolved via binding arbitration, with an arbitrator appointed by the STB.[57] Amtrak and the FRA published proposed "metrics and standards" in March 2009 and jointly issued their final rule on May 6, 2010.

Shortly thereafter, the Association of American Railroads (AAR) challenged Section 207 of the PRIIA as an unconstitutional delegation of authority to a private actor and a violation of the Due Process Clause. AAR argued that the statute delegated to Amtrak the authority to promulgate the metrics and standards by which its performance, and the performance of other railroads, would be evaluated, and that, in the event of a disagreement between Amtrak and the FRA, the latter would be precluded from implementing its desired standards. The D.C. Circuit agreed.[58]

Although the Supreme Court rarely applies the nondelegation doctrine, it has repeatedly recognized that a statutory scheme may give private entities a rulemaking role provided that they "function subordinately" to the government.[59] Here, it does not appear that Amtrak operates subordinately to the FRA, although whether Section 207 of the PRIIA is an unconstitutional delegation of authority will also turn on whether the Court finds that Amtrak is a private or public entity. The Court has previously held, in *Lebron v. National Railroad Passenger Corp.*, that Amtrak "is part of the Government for purposes of the First Amendment."[60] It has not, however, held that Amtrak should be deemed a governmental entity for all purposes.

Ultimately, the case involves a sui generis delegation of authority that is specific to Amtrak and does not appear elsewhere in federal law. The Court's decision to review it and revisit what many consider a dormant doctrine suggests that it may well take issue with the D.C. Circuit's analysis.

---

[56] 49 U.S.C. § 24101 note (2014).

[57] *Id.*

[58] Ass'n of Am. Railroads v. U.S. Dep't of Transp., 721 F.3d 666 (D.C. Cir. 2013).

[59] Sunshine Anthracite Coal Co. v. Adkins, 310 U.S. 381, 399 (1940).

[60] 513 U.S. 374, 400 (1995).

C. Government Whistleblowers and National Security

Another case that addresses the relationship between Congress and the executive branch is *Department of Homeland Security v. MacLean,* in which the Court will determine whether certain statutory protections in 5 U.S.C. § 2302(b)(8)(A) of the Whistleblower Act of 1989, which are inapplicable when a federal employee makes a disclosure "specifically prohibited by law," can bar a federal agency from taking an enforcement action against an employee who intentionally discloses sensitive security information ("SSI") in violation of an agency regulation.[61]

SSI is defined as sensitive but unclassified information. Disclosure of such information is prohibited by federal regulations.[62] Robert MacLean was employed as an air marshal for the Transportation Security Administration (TSA) but was fired after disclosing to a cable news reporter that the TSA was reducing the number of air marshals that had been put on flights out of Las Vegas after September 11, 2001. MacLean's leak, which was aired anonymously, prompted fierce opposition from Congress, prompting the TSA to abandon the plan. Once the TSA determined that MacLean was the reporter's source, however, he was terminated for violating a TSA regulation barring public disclosure of details concerning how the agency deploys its security staff.

MacLean challenged his termination, arguing that the Whistleblower Act precluded the government from disciplining any federal employee for exposing information that the employee believed would be a "specific danger to public health and safety."[63] Although the statutory protection does not insulate individuals who have disclosed information in violation of federal law, MacLean argued that he had not violated any law because the information he released was covered only by a TSA regulation rather than by a federal statute. The U.S. Court of Appeals for the Federal Circuit unanimously agreed, and the government seeks review of that decision on the ground that the Federal Circuit's decision "effectively permits individual federal

---

[61] No. 13-894 (OT 2014).
[62] 49 C.F.R. § 1520 (2014).
[63] 5 U.S.C. § 2302(b)(8)(A) (2014).

employees to override the TSA's judgments about the dangers of public disclosure."[64]

For those familiar with canons of construction, it is perhaps perplexing that the word "law" is being construed to exclude federal regulations. MacLean insists that the structure and history of the Whistleblower Act make clear that "law" does not include regulations and that it should not be so construed in light of the act's purpose to protect whistleblowers against the agencies that would retaliate against them. Indeed, the conference report accompanying the provision's enactment states that it "does not refer to agency rules and regulations" but instead "to statutory law and counter interpretations of those statutes."[65] The government contends, however, that "agency rules and regulations" cannot be construed to encompass congressionally mandated regulations like those at issue in this case.[66]

In deciding this dispute, the Court is likely to consider the potentially broad implications for the rights of government employee whistleblowers and the need to balance national security interests associated with secrecy and disclosure. Here, MacLean's disclosure was widely lauded by those outside of the executive branch, but one can easily imagine others (such as Edward Snowden imitators) whose disclosures would provoke less sympathy.

D. Agencies and the Administrative Procedure Act

In *Perez v. Mortgage Bankers Association* and *Nickols v. Mortgage Bankers Association*, the Court will again address the limits of executive power in deciding whether a federal agency must engage in notice-and-comment rulemaking pursuant to the Administrative Procedure Act (APA) before it can significantly alter an interpretive rule that sets forth a particular interpretation of an agency regulation.[67]

In these consolidated cases, the plaintiffs challenged a change in the Labor Department's interpretation of the Fair Labor Standards Act (FLSA) to require overtime for mortgage loan officers. The department's 2010 Wage and Hour Division administrative interpretation,

---

[64] Dep't of Homeland Sec. v. MacLean, 714 F.3d 1301 (Fed. Cir. 2013), petition for cert. filed at 11, No. 13-894 (U.S. Jan. 27, 2014).

[65] H.R. Conf. Rep. No. 1717, 95th Cong., 2d. Sess. 130 (1978).

[66] DHS v. MacLean, cert. petition, *supra* n.64, at 15.

[67] Nos. 13-1041, 13-1052 (OT 2014).

which was issued without public comment, reversed an earlier 2006 Bush era administrative opinion letter that concluded that mortgage loan officers were exempt from the FLSA's overtime requirements.

The APA generally requires that agencies promulgating new regulations provide interested parties an opportunity to submit written comments on the proposed regulations.[68] The APA also provides that its notice-and-comment requirement does not apply to interpretative rules unless notice is otherwise required by statute.[69] Under D.C. Circuit case law, however, when an agency has announced a specific and definitive interpretation of a regulation, and then substantially revises that interpretation, the agency has effectively amended its rule, which may not be accomplished without notice-and-comment under the APA.[70] Accordingly, the court ruled that because the department's 2010 administrative interpretation was a "definitive" regulatory interpretation that substantially revised (indeed, reversed) the department's earlier position in its 2006 Opinion Letter, notice-and-comment rulemaking was required under the APA.[71] The D.C. Circuit's interpretation has been adopted by the Fifth Circuit, but the First and Ninth Circuits have held that the APA allows agencies to amend interpretive rules without notice-and-comment.[72]

Although the ultimate question of whether mortgage loan officers are entitled to overtime is not likely to capture the public's imagination, these cases will have important consequences for all federal agencies subject to the APA. Under the existing framework, entities subject to federal regulations have to vigilantly monitor agencies' prevailing interpretive guidance to keep abreast of changes and are often subject to dramatic shifts in regulatory policies under different administrations with different political agendas. A rule affirming the D.C. Circuit would make it more difficult for agencies to change their interpretations without engaging in notice-and-comment,

---

[68] 5 U.S.C. § 553 (2014).

[69] *Id.* at § 553(b).

[70] See Paralyzed Veterans of Am. v. D.C. Arena L.P., 117 F.3d 579 (D.C. Cir. 1997); see also Alaska Prof. Hunters Ass'n v. FAA, 177 F.3d 1030 (D.C. Cir. 1999).

[71] See Mort. Bankers Ass'n v. Harris, 720 F.3d 966, 968 (D.C. Cir. 2013).

[72] See Shell Offshore Inc. v. Babbitt, 238 F.3d 622, 629–30 (5th Cir. 2001); see also Miller v. Cal. Speedway Corp., 536 F.3d 1020, 1033 (9th Cir. 2008); Warder v. Shalala, 149 F.3d 73, 75–79 (1st Cir. 1998).

which generally takes more time and exposes the agency to legal challenge on procedural and substantive grounds under the APA.

V. Anti-Discrimination Laws

The new term will also feature cases involving discrimination claims by a pregnant UPS employee and Democrats and minority voters in Alabama.

A. Pregnancy Discrimination

Accusations of pregnancy discrimination are becoming a pervasive workplace phenomenon, as evidenced by the upsurge in the number of claims filed with the Equal Employment Opportunity Commission (EEOC) annually. In *Young v. United Parcel Service, Inc.*, the Court will wade into that thicket to decide whether an employer can deny pregnant employees accommodations such as light duty that are offered to other workers who are allegedly "similar in their ability or inability to work" under the Pregnancy Discrimination Act (PDA).[73]

The PDA amended Title VII of the Civil Rights Act of 1964. It provides that the prohibition on discrimination "because of sex" or "on the basis of sex" includes but is not limited to discrimination "on the basis of pregnancy, childbirth or related medical conditions," and that "women affected by pregnancy, childbirth or related medical conditions shall be treated the same for all employment-related purposes, including receipt of benefits under fringe benefit programs, as other persons not so affected but similar in their ability or inability to work."[74]

Peggy Young was a driver for UPS when she became pregnant and was directed by her doctor to refrain from lifting heavy objects. She requested a temporary light-duty assignment, but UPS denied her request, contending that light-duty assignments were available only to employees with job-related injuries, those considered permanently disabled under the Americans with Disabilities Act, and injured employees ineligible for their federal driver's certification under the terms of UPS's collective-bargaining agreement. Instead, Young was directed to take unpaid leave.

[73] No. 13-1226 (OT 2014); see also 42 U.S.C. § 2000e(k) (2014).
[74] 42 U.S.C. § 2000e(k) (2014).

Young took this leave but filed a challenge to UPS's policy on the ground that the PDA requires employers to provide accommodations for pregnant employees that are comparable to those received by others with similar "ability or inability to work," regardless of how the person became disabled. Both the district court in Maryland and the U.S. Court of Appeals for the Fourth Circuit ruled against Young, however, holding that UPS's policy was consistent with the PDA because there was no evidence of discriminatory intent, the policy did not exclude only pregnancy, and "where a policy treats pregnant workers and nonpregnant workers alike, the employer has complied with the PDA."[75] The Fourth Circuit's ruling, however, conflicts with a 1996 Sixth Circuit decision that allowed a similar PDA claim to move forward.[76]

Although the solicitor general contended that the Fourth Circuit erred, he recommended that the Court deny the petition for review because of 2008 amendments to the Americans with Disabilities Act that might "lead courts to reconsider their approach to evaluating a pregnant employee's claim that other employees with similar limitations on their ability to work were treated more favorably," and because the EEOC was poised to issue guidance clarifying its interpretation of the PDA.[77] Indeed, the EEOC went on to release that guidance on July 14, 2014.[78] Nevertheless, the Court took the case.

While the EEOC's guidance lacks the force and effect of an act of Congress or a Supreme Court ruling, it reflects the agency's—and presumably the Obama administration's—prevailing interpretation of the PDA. Whether the Court will adopt this interpretation is a separate question altogether. Given the Court's decision to hear *Young* over the solicitor general's opposition, it does not appear to believe

---

[75] Young v. UPS, Inc., 707 F.3d 437, 449 (4th Cir. 2013).

[76] See Ensley-Gaines v. Runyon, 100 F.3d 1220 (6th Cir. 1996).

[77] Brief for the United States as Amicus Curiae at 8, Young v. UPS, Inc., No. 12-1226 (2014).

[78] See EEOC, Enforcement Guidance on Pregnancy Discrimination and Other Issues (July 14, 2014), available at http://www.eeoc.gov/laws/guidance/pregnancy_guidance.cfm. The EEOC's guidance expressly states that a pregnant worker may "establish a violation of the PDA by showing that she was denied light duty or other accommodations that were granted to other employees who are similar in their ability or inability to work." *Id.* at Example 9(b).

that its ultimate interpretation of the PDA requires input from or deference to the EEOC.

B. Voting Rights Act

In a bout of "déjà vu all over again," Alabama is back before the Supreme Court in another Voting Rights Act case. In *Alabama Legislative Black Caucus v. Alabama* and *Alabama Democratic Conference v. Alabama*, the Court will review challenges by Democratic legislators who claim that the Republican-majority Alabama legislature intentionally diluted the voting power of minority voters in violation of Section 2 of the Voting Rights Act and the Fourteenth Amendment by intentionally packing them into a few supermajority districts during recent redistricting undertaken in response to the 2010 census.[79] Separate challenges to that ruling have been filed by the Alabama Democratic Conference and the Alabama Legislative Black Caucus, with both groups seeking a reversal by the Court in time for the general election on November 3, 2014.

The case comes a year after *Shelby County v. Holder*, which also involved the state of Alabama and which struck down Section 4(b) of the Voting Rights Act, thus effectively gutting Section 5, which had required jurisdictions with a history of discrimination to seek permission from federal authorities before changing their voting procedures. Although Alabama is no longer required to obtain preclearance from the Department of Justice, the Voting Rights Act continues to prohibit changes that interfere with voting rights or dilute the electoral power of racial minorities.

Black lawmakers argue that the packing of majority-black districts necessarily increases the political segregation of African Americans and diminishes their ability to influence the outcome of elections throughout Alabama. The state's government contends that it was complying with Section 5 of the Voting Rights Act—which was still valid during the last round of redistricting—by ensuring that the new map did not decrease the number of majority-black districts. Under the Republican plan, 28 of 105 House districts and 8 of 35 Senate districts have a black majority.

A three-judge district court held, by a vote of 2–1, that the district lines approved by the Republican-controlled legislature in 2012 are

[79] Nos. 13-895, 13-1138 (OT 2014).

constitutional.[80] In what Judge Myron H. Thompson, the dissenting judge on the three-judge panel, called a "cruel irony," however, the provision that Alabama had successfully invalidated in *Shelby County* is the very provision that it claims justified the legislative maps.

The ultimate question is whether the redistricting was undertaken to increase Republicans' partisan or racial advantage. Alabama contends that it preserved the number of majority-black districts, which is true. In fact, the number of majority-black districts in the state house increased by one. Nonetheless, Alabama is prohibited from making election changes with the purpose or effect of interfering with minority voting rights. The Court's holding may very well be limited to this question.

VI. Securities Litigation

The Court's 2014 term will also feature at least two securities cases of great importance to the plaintiffs' bar and public companies alike. First, in another case reminiscent of the "subjective intent/objective standard" dichotomy in *Elonis*, the Court has agreed to address a circuit split concerning the scope of liability for so-called "false opinions" under Section 11 of the Securities Act of 1933, in *Omnicare, Inc. v. Laborers District Council Construction Industry Pension Fund*.[81]

Section 11 provides a private remedy for a purchaser of securities issued under a registration statement filed with the Securities and Exchange Commission if the registration statement "contained an untrue statement of material fact or omitted to state a material fact required to be stated therein or necessary to make the statement therein not misleading."[82] The question presented is whether a plaintiff can state a Section 11 claim by pleading that a statement of opinion was "untrue" on the ground that it was objectively wrong, as the Sixth Circuit has held, or whether the plaintiff must also allege that the statement was subjectively false, requiring allegations that the speaker's actual opinion was different from the one expressed, as the Second, Third, and Ninth Circuits have held.

---

[80] Ala. Legislative Black Caucus v. Alabama, 989 F. Supp. 2d 1227 (M.D. Ala. 2013).
[81] No. 13-435 (OT 2014).
[82] 15 U.S.C. § 77k (2014).

Much of the disagreement between the courts of appeals stems from their interpretations of the Supreme Court's decision in *Virginia Bankshares v. Sandberg*, Justice David Souter's first opinion for the Court and a typically impenetrable example of his handiwork.[83] *Virginia Bankshares* held that a claim under Section 14(a) of the Securities Exchange Act, which regulates the solicitation of shareholder votes in proxy statements, must allege that a statement of opinion is both objectively and subjectively false (that it is wrong *and* that the speaker did not actually believe it to be true). The circuit courts that have extended this requirement to Section 11 claims have done so on the theory that a statement of opinion cannot be "false" unless the speaker actually believes that it is untrue.[84]

The Sixth Circuit's test, on the other hand, amounts to a strict liability standard for false opinions.[85] An affirmance by the Supreme Court would effectively relax the pleading standards required of Section 11 plaintiffs and likely would lead to a flurry of Section 11 filings.

Second, the Court has agreed to hear *Public Employees' Retirement System of Mississippi v. IndyMac MBS, Inc.*, in which it will decide whether the filing of a class action tolls the statute of repose under the Securities Act, via operation of *American Pipe* tolling—which the Court first articulated in *American Pipe & Construction Co. v. Utah*—or whether the statute of repose functions as an absolute bar that cannot be tolled.[86]

The statute of limitations for claims under the Securities Act provides that all claims must be brought within one year of the discovery of the violation or within three years from the time the security involved was first offered to the public. Under *American Pipe*, the filing of a securities class action tolls the running of the one-year

---

[83] 501 U.S. 1083 (1991). The first paragraph of Justice Antonin Scalia's concurring opinion attempted to provide a decoder-ring translation—in the spirit of "if the Court is saying that X gives rise to liability but Y does not, I agree." *Id.* at 1108–09 (Scalia, J., concurring).

[84] See Fait v. Regions Fin. Corp., 655 F.3d 105 (2d Cir. 2011); Rubke v. Capital Bancorp Ltd., 551 F.3d 1156 (9th Cir. 2009); In re Donald J. Trump Casino Sec. Litig., 7 F.3d 357, 368–69 (3d Cir. 1993).

[85] Ind. Dist. Council of Laborers v. Omnicare, Inc., 719 F.3d 498 (6th Cir. 2013).

[86] No. 13-640 (OT 2014); see also Am. Pipe & Construction Co. v. Utah, 414 U.S. 538 (1974).

statute of limitations. The question in this case is whether *American Pipe* applies to the three-year statute of repose.

The case is likely to have important implications regardless of how the Court rules. One major consequence of the Court's decision will be its effect on class-action opt-outs and the rigor with which institutional investors must monitor—and potentially intervene in—securities cases to preserve their rights. The Court's ruling will also dictate whether putative securities class members can wait to decide whether to opt out of a class action or must act earlier in order to avoid the running of the statute of repose. Moreover, because the case also implicates the broader question of the difference between statutes of limitation and statutes of repose, it could have effects far beyond the context of securities class actions.

VII. Certiorari Pipeline

As of this writing, the Supreme Court has agreed to hear oral argument in 39 cases, many of which pose important questions with broad implications. In addition to the collection of cases already on the Court's calendar, there are several high-profile cases in the pipeline that could potentially make their way to One First Street when the Court reconvenes after its summer recess. A few of these cases are described below.

1. The Court's decisions in *Hollingsworth v. Perry*[87] and *United States v. Windsor*[88] spawned a litany of state and federal court decisions holding that state same-sex marriage bans—or bans on the recognition of out-of-state same-sex marriages—violate the rights of gays and lesbians who wish to marry. The first post-*Windsor* circuit court to rule that same-sex marriage bans violate the Fourteenth Amendment was the Tenth Circuit, which issued its decision one day before the first anniversary of the *Windsor* ruling.[89] In striking down Utah's same-sex marriage ban, the Tenth Circuit held that marriage is a fundamental right, same-sex marriage bans must be subject to strict scrutiny, and none of the state's arguments, including purported interests in the procreative capacity of opposite-sex couples, satisfied

[87] 133 S. Ct. 2652 (2013).
[88] 570 U.S. 12 (2013).
[89] Kitchen v. Herbert, No. 13-4178, 2011 WL 2868044 (10th Cir. June 25, 2014).

that standard.[90] Utah officials have filed a cert petition, and their calls for Supreme Court review have recently been joined by parties in the Fourth Circuit.[91] Although there is no circuit split at this time, and the Court may wish to avoid deciding these issues, the case presents a question of substantial importance to same-sex couples across the United States. While the Court's last foray into this arena is hardly a model of clarity concerning the appropriate standard of review for these prohibitions, Justice Anthony Kennedy's opinion in *Windsor* suggests that he is sympathetic to the view that same-sex marriage bans violate either a substantive federal right or the equal protection of the laws (or both), which could lead to another divisive 5-4 decision.

2. The Patient Protection and Affordable Care Act (ACA) makes tax credits available to individuals who purchase health insurance through "exchanges" that are "established by the State under section 1311" of the ACA,[92] but the Internal Revenue Service has interpreted that provision to authorize the tax credit also for insurance purchased on a federal exchange.[93] On July 22, 2014, the D.C. Circuit and the Fourth Circuit issued contradictory rulings concerning the government's ability to provide subsidies in the form of tax credits to encourage individuals to purchase health insurance on federally run exchanges.[94]

In a 2–1 vote, the D.C. Circuit ruled that the ACA expressly provides that subsidies are available only for individuals who purchase insurance on exchanges established and run by one of the 50 states or the District of Columbia.[95] The Fourth Circuit, however, unanimously held that the ACA's reference to exchanges "established by the State" was ambiguous and thus that the court should defer to the government's interpretation that subsidies were permitted for its

---

[90] *Id.*

[91] Bostic v. Schaefer, 2014 WL 3702493 (4th Cir. July 28, 2014).

[92] 26 U.S.C. § 36B(c)(2)(A)(i) (2014).

[93] 26 C.F.R. § 1.36B-2(a)(1) (2014).

[94] Halbig v. Burwell, 2014 WL 3579745 (D.C. Cir. July 22, 2014); King v. Burwell, 2014 WL 3582800 (4th Cir. July 22, 2014).

[95] Halbig, 2014 WL 3579745, at *7.

own federal exchanges.[96] The Fourth Circuit plaintiffs have already filed a petition for certiorari, while the government has asked the D.C. Circuit for en banc review. The D.C. Circuit is likely to decide whether to rehear the case before the Supreme Court can act on the cert petition, so if the Court wants to avoid wading into health care again so soon after *NFIB v. Sebelius*, it will probably have that ongoing proceeding (as well as two other cases in Oklahoma and Indiana) as an excuse. It is certainly possible that this issue will miss the Court this term only to resurface in October Term 2015.

3. The Court will almost certainly see a second round in the contraceptive-mandate imbroglio, this time as it pertains to nonprofits with religious objections. The Affordable Care Act's requirement that businesses provide contraceptives to female employees at no cost to the patient is subject to an exception for nonprofit religious institutions, including churches and private universities, which permits them to submit a two-page form to insurance companies stating their religious opposition. Upon receipt of the form, the insurance company must bill the federal government instead of the objecting institution for the cost of providing contraceptives.

In a lawsuit against the Department of Health and Human Services, the University of Notre Dame has argued that even that alternative procedure is unduly burdensome because it forces the university to "trigger" the process of providing contraceptives and to associate with a third party willing to provide the services that Notre Dame finds objectionable—again in violation of RFRA and the First Amendment. The district court and the U.S. Court of Appeals for the Seventh Circuit denied Notre Dame's request for a preliminary injunction, and Notre Dame intends to appeal to the Court. Given the outcry that followed *Hobby Lobby*, any challenge to the ACA brought by churches or private universities is likely to garner considerable attention.

*   *   *

The Supreme Court's 2014 term includes an assortment of important and interesting cases that span a broad swath of topics, many of

---

[96] King, 2014 WL 3582800, at *6.

which are described above. Like recent terms, the Court will have an opportunity to address issues under the Fourth Amendment, the First Amendment, criminal law, separation of powers, and securities laws, among others. To be sure, after a 2013 term that featured several controversial decisions and kept commentators on their toes, all eyes will be on the Court again in October.

Contributors

David E. Bernstein is the George Mason University Foundation Professor at the George Mason University School of Law, where he has been teaching since 1995. Professor Bernstein is a nationally recognized expert on *Daubert v. Merrell Dow Pharmaceuticals* and the admissibility of expert testimony, and he is a past chairperson of the Association of American Law Schools Evidence section. Bernstein is the coauthor of *The New Wigmore: Expert Evidence* (Aspen Law and Business 2004; 2nd edition 2010), and coeditor of *Phantom Risk: Scientific Inference and the Law* (MIT Press 1993). He is also an expert on the *"Lochner* era" of American constitutional jurisprudence. He is the author of *Only One Place of Redress: African-Americans, Labor Regulations, and the Courts from Reconstruction to the New Deal* (Duke University Press 2001), and of *Rehabilitating* Lochner: *Defending Individual Rights against Progressive Reform* (University of Chicago Press 2011). Bernstein is also the author of *You Can't Say That! The Growing Threat to Civil Liberties from Antidiscrimination Laws* (Cato Institute 2003). In addition to his books, Bernstein is the author of dozens of scholarly articles, book chapters, and think tank studies. He is a contributor to the popular Volokh Conspiracy blog. Bernstein earned his B.A. *summa cum laude* from Brandeis University and his J.D. from Yale Law School.

Ashley S. Boizelle is an associate in the Washington, D.C. office of Gibson, Dunn & Crutcher. She practices in the firm's litigation department and is a member of its appellate and constitutional law, administrative and regulatory law, and media, entertainment and technology practice groups. Before joining the firm, Boizelle served as a law clerk to Judge Sandra S. Ikuta of the U.S. Court of Appeals for the Ninth Circuit. Boizelle received her law degree from Yale Law School and graduated with honors from Princeton University's Woodrow Wilson School of Public and International Affairs.

Trevor Burrus is a research fellow at the Cato Institute's Center for Constitutional Studies. His research interests include constitutional law, civil and criminal law, legal and political philosophy, and legal history. His academic work has appeared in journals such as the *Harvard Journal of Law & Public Policy*, the *Albany Government Law Review*, and the *Syracuse Law Review*, and his popular writing has appeared in *Forbes*, *USA Today*, *Huffington Post*, *New York Daily News*, and others. He is the editor of *A Conspiracy Against Obamacare* (Palgrave Macmillan, 2013). He holds a B.A. in Philosophy from the University of Colorado at Boulder and a J.D. from the University of Denver Sturm College of Law.

Allen Dickerson is the legal director for the Center for Competitive Politics in Alexandria, Virginia. He oversees CCP's litigation efforts before state and federal courts. He has represented CCP and outside clients before the U.S. Courts of Appeals for the Fourth, Sixth, and Ninth Circuits and in litigation before the federal district courts for Colorado and the District of Columbia. He was previously an associate with the New York office of Kirkland & Ellis LLP. His writing has appeared in the *Naval Law Review, American University National Security Law Brief,* and a number of general publications, and he has been featured on C-SPAN and NPR, among other media outlets. Dickerson is a graduate of Yale College and New York University School of Law.

Richard A. Epstein is Laurence A. Tisch Professor of Law and director of the Classical Liberal Institute at New York University School of Law. He is also the Peter and Kirsten Bedford Senior Fellow at the Hoover Institution and the James Parker Hall Distinguished Service Professor of Law Emeritus and senior lecturer at the University of Chicago Law School. He is known for his research and writings on a broad range of constitutional, economic, historical, and philosophical subjects. His many books include *Takings: Private Property and the Power of Eminent Domain* (1985), *Simple Rules for a Complex World* (1995), and most recently, *The Classical Liberal Constitution: The Uncertain Quest for Limited Government* (2013). He has taught courses spanning the legal landscape, including on administrative law, antitrust, civil procedure, communications, constitutional law, contracts, criminal law, criminal procedure, environmental law, food and drug law, health law, labor, jurisprudence, land-use planning, patents, property, Roman law, taxation, torts, and water law. Epstein has been a member of the American Academy of Arts and Sciences since 1985. Prior to joining the University of Chicago's faculty in 1972, he taught law at the University of Southern California from 1968 to 1972. Epstein received a B.A. from Columbia College in 1964 *summa cum laude* and Phi Beta Kappa, a B.A. (Juris.) first class from Oxford University in 1966, and his L.L.B. *cum laude* in 1968 from Yale Law School, where he was elected to the Order of the Coif. He has been a member of the California Bar since 1969. He received an honorary degree from the University of Ghent in 2003, was awarded the Bradley Prize in 2011, and received the Norman MacLean Prize for Teaching Excellence from the University of Chicago in 2014.

Miguel A. Estrada is a partner in the Washington, D.C. office of Gibson, Dunn & Crutcher. He has represented clients in federal and state courts throughout the country and in international arbitrations. Estrada has argued 22 cases before the Supreme Court, and briefed many others. He was also part of the team that successfully presented then-Governor Bush's position to the Supreme Court in *Bush v. Gore*. From 1992 until 1997, Estrada served as assistant to the solicitor general of the United States. He previously served as assistant U.S. attorney and deputy chief of the appellate section in the office of the U.S attorney for the Southern District of New York. Before joining the U.S. attorney's office, Estrada practiced corporate law in New York with Wachtell, Lipton, Rosen & Katz. Estrada is a Trustee of the Supreme Court Historical Society and a member of the board of visitors of Harvard Law School. He served as a law clerk to U.S. Supreme Court Justice Anthony M. Kennedy and to Judge Amalya L. Kearse of the U.S. Court of Appeals for the Second Circuit. He received a J.D. *magna cum laude* in 1986 from Harvard Law School, where he was editor of the *Harvard Law Review*. Estrada graduated with an A.B. degree *magna cum laude* and Phi Beta Kappa in 1983 from Columbia College.

Jacob Huebert is senior attorney at the Liberty Justice Center, the Illinois Policy Institute's free-market public-interest litigation center. He litigates cases to protect economic liberty, the First Amendment, and other constitutional rights in federal and state courts in Illinois.

Huebert received his B.A. in economics from Grove City College and his J.D. from the University of Chicago Law School. After law school, he clerked for Judge Deborah L. Cook of the U.S. Court of Appeals for the Sixth Circuit. Huebert then practiced law as a litigator at a large firm in Columbus, Ohio, and then in his own law office, before joining the Liberty Justice Center upon its founding in 2011. He has taught as an adjunct law professor at Chicago-Kent College of Law, Ohio Northern University College of Law, and the Ohio State University Moritz College of Law. Huebert has also spoken to Federalist Society chapters across the country on topics including economic liberty and judicial selection. He is the author of a book, *Libertarianism Today*, and his writing has been published widely in scholarly, professional and popular publications.

Bryan J. Leitch is an associate in the Washington, D.C. office of Jones Day, which he joined in 2013. He holds a J.D. from Duke University Law School, where he served on the *Duke Law Journal*, and a B.M. from Berklee College of Music. After law school, Leitch clerked for Judge Susan H. Black of the U.S. Court of Appeals for the Eleventh Circuit.

Roger Pilon is the founder and director of Cato's Center for Constitutional Studies, which has become an important force in the national debate over constitutional interpretation and judicial philosophy. He is the publisher of the *Cato Supreme Court Review* and is an adjunct professor of government at Georgetown University through The Fund for American Studies. Prior to joining Cato, Pilon held five senior posts in the Reagan administration, including at State and Justice, and was a National Fellow at Stanford's Hoover Institution. In 1989 the Bicentennial Commission presented him with its Benjamin Franklin Award for excellence in writing on the U.S. Constitution. In 2001 Columbia University's School of General Studies awarded him its Alumni Medal of Distinction. Pilon lectures and debates at universities and law schools across the country and testifies often before Congress. His writing has appeared in the *Wall Street Journal, Washington Post, New York Times, L.A. Times, National Law Journal, Harvard Journal of Law & Public Policy, Stanford Law & Policy Review,* and elsewhere. He has appeared on ABC's *Nightline*, CBS's *60 Minutes II*, Fox News Channel, NPR, CNN, MSNBC, CNBC, and other media. Pilon holds a B.A. from Columbia University, an M.A. and a Ph.D. from the University of Chicago, and a J.D. from the George Washington University School of Law.

Andrew Pincus is a partner at Mayer Brown LLP. He focuses his appellate practice on briefing and arguing cases in federal and state appellate courts; developing legal strategy for trial courts; and presenting policy and legal arguments to Congress, state legislatures, and regulatory agencies. Pincus has argued 23 cases in the Supreme Court, including *AT&T Mobility v. Concepcion*. His work in *Concepcion* and successful defense of Chicago Mayor Rahm Emanuel's right to run for office were cited by the *American Lawyer* in its article naming Mayer Brown as one of the top six litigation firms of 2012. His appellate experience has also won him recognition in *The Best Lawyers in America*. A former assistant to the solicitor general in the Justice Department, Pincus co-founded and serves as co-director of Yale Law School's Supreme Court Advocacy Clinic, which provides pro bono representation in 10-15 cases each year. His practice also includes detailed written and oral advocacy before Congress, other legislative bodies, and regulatory agencies. He frequently testifies before Congress on a variety of subjects, including patent reform, the Consumer Financial Protection Bureau, reform of the federal litigation system, and the Supreme Court's decisions in cases involving business law. While serving as general counsel of the U.S. Commerce Department, Pincus had principal responsibility for the Digital Millennium Copyright Act and the Electronic Signatures in Global and National Commerce Act. Before rejoining Mayer Brown, Pincus served as general counsel of Andersen Worldwide S.C. Following law school graduation, Pincus was law clerk to the Judge Harold H. Greene of the U.S. District Court for the District of Columbia. Pincus earned his B.A. *cum laude* from Yale University and his J.D. from Columbia Law School.

Eric Rassbach is deputy general counsel at the Becket Fund, where he has served since 2004. In his practice, he has represented people and institutions from many different faith backgrounds, including Buddhists, Christians, Hindus, Jains, Jews, Muslims, Santeros, and Sikhs, as well as governmental entities. He represents clients in trial and appellate litigation and acts as counselor to religious institutions and governments dealing with church-state issues. He has also been active overseas and has represented clients in appeals to the European Court of Human Rights in Strasbourg, France and in the highest courts of several countries. Rassbach is a well-known commentator on church-state issues and has been quoted in the *New York Times*, the *Washington Post*, the *Times of India*, the *Wall Street Journal*, and many other publications. Before joining the Becket Fund, Rassbach worked at Baker Botts LLP in Houston, where he practiced international project finance, including the Baku-Tbilisi-Ceyhan pipeline project. He also served as a law clerk to U.S. District Judge Lee Rosenthal in Houston. Rassbach graduated from Haverford College with a degree in Comparative Literature, is a member of Fitzwilliam College at Cambridge University, and is a graduate of Harvard Law School.

Nicholas Quinn Rosenkranz is a professor of law at Georgetown, a senior fellow in constitutional studies at the Cato Institute, and co-chair of the board of visitors of the Federalist Society. He is currently developing a new theory of constitutional interpretation and judicial review. The first installment, entitled "The Subjects of the Constitution," was published in the *Stanford Law Review* in 2010, and it is already the single most downloaded article about constitutional interpretation, judicial review, or federal courts in the history of SSRN. The second installment, "The Objects of the Constitution," was published in 2011, also in the *Stanford Law Review*. And the comprehensive version is forthcoming as a book by Oxford University Press. Rosenkranz holds a B.A. and a J.D. from Yale University. He clerked for Judge Frank H. Easterbrook at the U.S. Court of Appeals for the Seventh Circuit and for Justice Anthony M. Kennedy at the U.S. Supreme Court. He served as an attorney-advisor at the Office of Legal Counsel in the U.S. Department of Justice. He often testifies before Congress as a constitutional expert—most recently before the House Judiciary Committee regarding President Obama's failure to "take Care that the Laws be faithfully executed." Rosenkranz has also filed briefs and argued before the U.S. Supreme Court. Most recently, his *Harvard Law Review* article, "Executing The Treaty Power," formed the basis for Cato's amicus brief in *Bond v. United States*, and it was cited by Justice Scalia in his concurrence in the judgment.

David B. Sentelle is senior judge on the U.S. Court of Appeals for the D.C. Circuit. From 1968 to 1970, he was an associate with the firm of Uzzell & Dumont, in Asheville, North Carolina. He served as an assistant U.S. Attorney in Charlotte, North Carolina, from 1970 to 1974. From 1974 to 1977, he was a North Carolina state district judge in Charlotte. In 1977, he became a partner of Tucker, Hicks, Sentelle, Moon & Hodge, where he practiced until 1985. Judge Sentelle taught as an adjunct professor at the law schools of the University of North Carolina, Florida State, and George Mason University, and in the Department of Criminal Justice at the University of North Carolina at Charlotte. In the fall of 1985, he became a U.S. district judge for Western District of North Carolina, where he served until his appointment to the D.C. Circuit. He served as chief judge of the D.C. Circuit from 2008 to 2013, when he assumed senior status. Judge Sentelle served as presiding judge of the Special Division of the Court for the Appointment of Independent Counsels and served as chairman of the U.S. Judicial Conference Committee on Judicial Security. He served on the Judicial Conference Executive Committee from 2008 to 2013, and as chair of that committee from 2010 to 2013. He is also past president of the Edward Bennett Williams Inn of the American Inns of Court. Judge Sentelle was named as the recipient of the 2008 American Inns of Court Professionalism Award in the D.C. Circuit. Judge Sentelle graduated, with honors, from the University of North Carolina Law School.

Ilya Shapiro is a senior fellow in constitutional studies at the Cato Institute and editor-in-chief of the *Cato Supreme Court Review*. Before joining Cato, he was a special assistant/advisor to the Multi-National Force in Iraq on rule of law issues and practiced international, political, commercial, and antitrust litigation at Patton Boggs and Cleary Gottlieb. Shapiro has contributed to a variety of academic, popular, and professional publications, including the *Wall Street Journal*, *Harvard Journal of Law & Public Policy*, *L.A. Times*, *USA Today*, *National Law Journal*, *Weekly Standard*, *New York Times Online*, and *National Review Online*. He also regularly provides commentary for various media outlets, including CNN, Fox News, ABC, CBS, NBC, Univision and Telemundo, *The Colbert Report*, and NPR. Shapiro has testified before Congress and state legislatures and, as coordinator of Cato's amicus brief program, has filed more than 100 "friend of the court" briefs in the Supreme Court. He lectures regularly on behalf of the Federalist Society, is a member of the Legal Studies Institute's board of visitors at The Fund for American Studies, was an inaugural Washington Fellow at the National Review Institute, and has been an adjunct professor at the George Washington University Law School. Before entering private practice, Shapiro clerked for Judge E. Grady Jolly of the U.S. Court of Appeals for the Fifth Circuit, while living in Mississippi and traveling around the Deep South. He holds an A.B. from Princeton, an M.Sc. from the London School of Economics, and a J.D. from the University of Chicago Law School (where he became a Tony Patiño Fellow). Shapiro is a member of the bars of New York, D.C., and the U.S. Supreme Court. He is a native speaker of English and Russian, is fluent in Spanish and French, and is proficient in Italian and Portuguese.

Cato Institute

Founded in 1977, the Cato Institute is a public policy research foundation dedicated to broadening the parameters of policy debate to allow consideration of more options that are consistent with the principles of limited government, individual liberty, and peace. To that end, the Institute strives to achieve greater involvement of the intelligent, concerned lay public in questions of policy and the proper role of government.

The Institute is named for Cato's Letters, libertarian pamphlets that were widely read in the American Colonies in the early 18th century and played a major role in laying the philosophical foundation for the American Revolution.

Despite the achievement of the nation's Founders, today virtually no aspect of life is free from government encroachment. A pervasive intolerance for individual rights is shown by government's arbitrary intrusions into private economic transactions and its disregard for civil liberties. And while freedom around the globe has notably increased in the past several decades, many countries have moved in the opposite direction, and most governments still do not respect or safeguard the wide range of civil and economic liberties.

To address those issues, the Cato Institute undertakes an extensive publications program on the complete spectrum of policy issues. Books, monographs, and shorter studies are commissioned to examine the federal budget, Social Security, regulation, military spending, international trade, and myriad other issues. Major policy conferences are held throughout the year, from which papers are published thrice yearly in the Cato Journal. The Institute also publishes the quarterly magazine Regulation.

In order to maintain its independence, the Cato Institute accepts no government funding. Contributions are received from foundations, corporations, and individuals, and other revenue is generated from the sale of publications. The Institute is a nonprofit, tax-exempt, educational foundation under Section 501(c)3 of the Internal Revenue Code.

CATO INSTITUTE
1000 Massachusetts Ave., N.W.
Washington, D.C. 20001
www.cato.org